TRAINS IN THE SOUTHERN REGION
THE LATE 1960s AND 1970s

DAVID REED

AMBERLEY

To my wife Margaret for her support and encouragement.
May we enjoy many more train trips together.

First published 2022

Amberley Publishing
The Hill, Stroud
Gloucestershire, GL5 4EP

www.amberley-books.com

Copyright © David Reed, 2022

The right of David Reed to be identified as
the Author of this work has been asserted in
accordance with the Copyrights, Designs and
Patents Act 1988.

ISBN 978 1 3981 1015 1 (print)
ISBN 978 1 3981 1016 8 (ebook)

British Library Cataloguing in Publication Data.
A catalogue record for this book is available from
the British Library.

Typesetting by Hurix Digital, India.
Printed in Great Britain.

Introduction

I grew up in Basingstoke, Hampshire, when it was still a small market town and we lived on the outskirts, a short bus ride from the town centre. A pleasant ramble through the fields behind our home would bring my brother, Roger, and me to the Southern Region Waterloo to Bournemouth and Exeter main line at Winklebury, between Worting Junction and Basingstoke station. In our early years many happy hours were spent jotting down steam locomotive names and numbers, and later we graduated to using the Ian Allan *ABC* spotter's books.

In 1967 when I was a teenager studying for my GCE O level exams, steam traction on the Southern Region was ending and I set out to make a personal colour photographic record of the passing of the steam locomotives, as recorded in my first book *Steam Railways: Final Operations in the Southern Region and the Early Preservation Years*. I borrowed a fairly basic Purma Plus camera from my mother and started using my pocket money to buy Kodak Ektachrome 64 ASA colour slide film. I wanted my memories to be in colour, but I had to accept the limitations of relatively slow colour film and a camera with a fixed f6.3 lens aperture and only a couple of rather slow shutter speeds.

After steam had finished in July 1967 I carried on photographing the ever-changing railway scene, non-Southern Region trains being recorded in my second book, *Diesel and Electric Trains: A New Era of Railways*. Locally I also photographed the new rail blue Waterloo to Bournemouth line electric units and the diesel-hauled Waterloo to Exeter trains. However, older pre-Second World War Southern Railway electric stock was still in service, such as the 2BILs, 2HALs, 4SUBs and the famous 4COR 'Nelson' EMUs (electric multiple units). By the 1970s these were gradually disappearing from the scene, so I started to record them as well. The 2BILs and 2HALs on the south coast and the Waterloo to Reading lines gave way to the 4CORs displaced from the Waterloo to Portsmouth and Mid-Sussex line services, which were in turn displaced by more modern VEP and CIG stock. It was a time of considerable change and this is what this book is about: 'in with the new and out with the old.' However I also snapped some diesel and electro-diesel locomotives on the Southern Region, including the Crompton diesel electric locomotives, the Western Region Warship and Hymek diesel-hydraulic locos, and the various Southern Region DEMU (diesel-electric multiple unit) trains. Strictly speaking, one or two of my pictures are off the Southern Region in Western Region territory but I have included them as they do show trains working to or from Southern stations.

On leaving school, over fifty years ago, I joined the Railway Studentship Training Scheme, one of several commercial, operating and engineering training schemes run by British Rail for school leavers. Earning some money, I was able to graduate to a 35 mm single lens reflex camera, albeit a fairly cheap and basic Russian Zenith B, which gave me more flexibility in my photography. I used to meet one or two colleagues at weekends and go roaming the rails. My photography was very much in the amateur category as I had no trackside permit or expensive camera. We always travelled by train, taking pictures from station platforms and other areas accessible to the public. My photographs are basically souvenir pictures to record the journeys, pictures which with the passage of time have turned out to become of historical interest.

It appears to me that when it comes to enthusiast interest over the years, the Southern Electric scene dominated by multiple units has been the poor relation compared with the other regions of British Railways. I hope this book will encourage interest in the Southern scene. The Southern Railway built up a distinctive and modern image. Stations, signal boxes and the trains themselves all had a particularly Southern air about them. The 1930s art deco era had a decided influence on Southern Railway design, and the extensive use of concrete in large and small station designs and other buildings lent itself to modern, streamlined effects. The all-steel 4SUB trains in particular were very modern when introduced in the late 1930s and weathered well the transition into the corporate image era of British Rail blue livery with yellow front ends. In my view they looked even brighter and better in rail blue than the original Southern Region dark green.

As well as introducing a modern image the Southern Railway, under its imaginative and practical general manager Sir Herbert Walker, also developed the concept of regular interval train services in parallel with electrification and modernisation of its routes. This continued in the British Railways Southern Region days and has been adopted by almost all train operators since. The idea of off-peak trains on a particular route operating at the same minutes past each hour with the same station stopping patterns and connections every hour through the day meant that the timetable was easily remembered by passengers as well as staff.

I owe a debt of thanks to my late parents, my father for fostering my interest in railways and my mother for encouraging me to use her old Purma camera. And a big thank you goes to British Rail Southern Region for employing me and enabling me to follow my dreams. Thanks are also due to my friend and colleague of many years, John Dawson, who mapped out the itineraries for many of our trips and who has encouraged me to have the pictorial memories published. He has read through my text and suggested a number of additions and corrections. Any remaining errors or inaccuracies are entirely due to the limitations of my memory over fifty years. I also want to thank my wife, Margaret, for her support and encouragement during the preparation of my books and for reading through my manuscripts.

The photographs in this book have all been taken by me and none have been published previously. They are set out in chronological order as I took them, showing the transition of both designs and liveries from 1967 through to the 1970s.

I hope you will enjoy my photographs of trains in the Southern Region.

Prior to the introduction of new Waterloo to Bournemouth electric services in July 1967, older Southern Region electric stock was used for driver training. Here we see a Bulleid Southern Railway design 2EPB EMU built by British Railways berthed in sidings just outside Basingstoke station.

A trip to Bournemouth on 26 May 1967 to photograph steam locos yielded this picture at Bournemouth of Southern Electric super-power, 4REP No. 3003. The 4REP units had four 400 hp traction motors in each of the two motor coaches giving 3,200 hp in total, virtually as much power available as a Deltic diesel locomotive. On the right, a train comprised of green Bulleid coaching stock awaits departure from the Up platform.

On the same day, I saw No. E6006. This was one of the initial six JA series electro-diesel locos in original green and grey livery, which had arrived with a couple of 4TC sets. The train sitting in the Up platform with the gangway door open is awaiting the arrival and attachment of the portion from Weymouth propelled by a Crompton Type 3 diesel.

Push-pull 4TC unpowered trailer unit No. 403, converted from Mark 1 steam stock, is caught at Poole station on 26 May 1967. It is in original all-over blue livery with small warning panel and is being propelled to Bournemouth by a push-pull fitted Crompton diesel in order to be attached to a 4REP and another 4TC to form a fast service to Southampton and Waterloo.

Also on 26 May 1967, a rather grubby Western Region Hymek diesel-hydraulic on a northbound inter-regional service via Basingstoke and Reading waits for passengers to board at Poole station. This station has since been considerably modernised. The term Hymek derived from its Mekydro Hydraulic transmission.

Brush Type 4 diesel No. D1926 heads one of the last Up 'Bournemouth Belle' Pullman trains east from Basingstoke on 2 July 1967, the day of the Southern Region official 'Last Steam' specials. No. D1926 was one of six Brush Type 4 diesels on loan to the Southern Region towards the end of steam. In the foreground you can see some Bulleid carriages berthed in Long Valley siding.

The other new stock for the Bournemouth electrification of 1967 was the 4VEP units. These were built at York and used on commuter and stopping services to and from Waterloo. 4VEP No. 7708 is seen framed by the iconic semaphore signal gantry at Southampton Central station as it leaves on a stopping service for Bournemouth.

I was fortunate to participate in a British Rail Southern Region course for potential training scheme recruits and the following five pictures were taken on that course. We visited Grove Park EMU sidings, used to berth South Eastern Division electric stock for peak hour workings. On the afternoon of 17 April 1969 we see a blue-and-grey-liveried 4CEP in original condition on the left and a number of BR-built EPB units lurking within the shed.

The evening rush hour is getting under way at London Bridge station on Thursday 17 April 1969, viewed from the old footbridge linking the Central and South Eastern sides of the station. Some EPB units are seen on the South Eastern side in the foreground and in front of the signal box a train of 4CORs approaches the Central Division, or Brighton side, of the station. The enormous steam-age water tower can also be seen.

From the roof of the British Rail Tooley Street offices on 17 April 1969 we see, in front of the water tank and signal box, the two unique 4DD double-deck units Nos 4001 and 4002 arriving at London Bridge en route to Charing Cross. The double-deck experiment was unsuccessful due to ventilation and station delay problems and they last ran on 1 October 1971. Suburban area platforms were extended to accommodate ten-car trains instead.

On the same occasion, with a Kent Coast fast service of CEP stock passing we have a view towards the notorious Borough Market Junction. This is where the South Eastern lines to and from Charing Cross diverged from and crossed those serving Cannon Street. Special category signalmen were employed at Borough Market Junction due to the critical train regulation, and the working floor of the signal box is now preserved at the National Railway Museum, York.

Another photograph from the roof of the Tooley Street offices in April 1969, shows a Hastings DEMU approaching London Bridge station and passing a train of EPB stock on the right. In the background can be seen the perpendicular tower of Southwark Cathedral, and the chimney of Bankside power station, now the Tate Modern gallery, belching smoke into the London sky. The Thameslink project has since transformed this view.

A BR-built 2HAP EMU is seen rising in the Up direction and heading over Battledown Flyover, near Worting Junction east of Basingstoke. The flyover was built in 1897 to provide grade separation of the diverging Bournemouth, Weymouth and Salisbury, Exeter and West of England routes, the junction for which had previously been on the level.

In original blue livery with small yellow warning panel, a 4TC unit leans to the curve as it heads a westbound semi-fast service on the Bournemouth line at Battledown flyover. These were converted from Mark 1 steam stock at the same time significantly more modern Mark 2 stock was being introduced on other regions.

Seen from beside the cab of a BR-built 4EPB unit on a Guildford service, a Bulleid design high-capacity 4SUB EMU on a service from Hampton Court to Waterloo arrives at Surbiton passing the 1930s signal box. These original 4SUB units dated from 1941 and crammed 456 passengers in very narrow compartments.

A train of 4COR (Corridor) stock approaches Woking from Waterloo while a 350 hp diesel shunter idles in the Down sidings. Behind is the 'hutted camp' comprising wooden offices to which some Southern Railway staff evacuated from London during the Second World War.

Powering through Woking station on a fast service from Portsmouth Harbour to Waterloo is an eight-car formation of 4COR stock. Note the large green Southern Railway-style station nameboards on the ends of the platform canopies and the typical 1930s SR concrete footbridge. The bay platform on the extreme right was filled in but in recent years a turn-back arrangement has been provided to accommodate the Waterloo to Woking via Virginia Water and Chertsey service.

The days of the 4COR units on the Portsmouth direct line are numbered as a formation of COR stock heads west from Woking and across the junction for the Portsmouth line. The Portsmouth direct line via Guildford, Petersfield and Havant was electrified in the 1930s as the Southern Railway gradually extended its electrified network. The signal box, on the left, is Grade II listed and is a typical Southern Railway streamlined art deco-style design in brick and concrete.

The 4COR and associated 4BUF (Buffet Car) and 4GRI (Griddle Car) EMUs were built to a Maunsell design especially for the electrification of the London to Portsmouth and Mid-Sussex routes. They differed from their 6PAN (Pantry Car) and 6PUL (Pullman Car) equivalents on the Brighton and Eastbourne lines in that they had end corridor connections allowing passengers to walk the length of the train to find a seat. Comprising only four cars, the COR units were also lighter and consequently fitted with only one motor bogie to each driving coach.

The route indicator to the left of the corridor connection gave rise to the informal name 'Nelsons' after the renowned Royal Navy admiral owing to the one-eyed effect, plus the fact that they served Portsmouth Harbour, home of the Royal Navy.

It was not so many years since steam had passed on the Southern Region and the grey water column is still in place at the country end of the Down slow line platform.

Woking station opened in 1838, then served from Nine Elms prior to the building of Waterloo, and became a junction in 1845 when the line to Guildford was established. Woking Junction, just over 24 miles from Waterloo, where the Portsmouth line diverges from the Bournemouth and Exeter route, is the only remaining flat junction of any importance on the South Western main line and it remains to be seen whether a flyover or fly-under is ever constructed here.

The lines here are paired by direction, Up slow and Up fast lines together and Down fast and Down slow lines together. East of Wimbledon a flyover moves the Up slow line over and across the fast lines so from there to Waterloo the lines are paired by purpose, Up and Down fast lines adjacent and Up and Down slow lines together.

Nose to nose, two 4COR units are caught leaving Woking station and heading west towards the Portsmouth line.

The old and the new, with over thirty years between them, are seen together at Woking station. 4COR EMU No. 3111 in green with a full yellow, insect-bespattered, front leads a headcode 82 semi-fast service from Portsmouth Harbour proceeding non-stop on to Waterloo. On the right a somewhat cleaner 4VEP EMU is heading an Alton to Waterloo headcode 52 stopping service, which will call only at Surbiton on its dash to Waterloo.

Looking surprisingly smart and stylish for its age in corporate rail blue livery and yellow front end, Southern Railway 4SUB EMU No. 4689 arrives at Surbiton station on a headcode 30 Waterloo to Hampton Court service. Surbiton station has received its corporate identity branding with replacement of the individual enamel station name signs by continuous plastic strips with the station name on, and black and white platform number signs.

A photograph taken through the rather grubby 'toplight' in a 4SUB door. The corporate identity has not yet reached Hampton Court, as a superb Southern Railway Hampton Court station run-in sign can be seen on the timber platform spanning the River Mole. The platforms are occupied mostly by green 4SUB EMUs as passengers walk towards the station building.

4SUB No. 4754 poses in its green Southern Region livery at Hampton Court station, ready to depart on a headcode 30 stopping service to Waterloo. Note the whistle mounted vertically to the left side of the driver's window and corresponding absence of air horns on the roof.

The 4SUB and later BR 4EPB units, together with the 1960s 4VEP units, epitomised the Southern Region's enthusiasm for slam-door trains. Slam doors to each compartment enabled speedy boarding and alighting at stations and thus enabled station dwell times to be minimised. 20 seconds were allowed for most station stops, especially during the rush hours when train paths needed to be maximised.

The flat-fronted 4SUBs were introduced by Bulleid from 1946 and were of all-steel construction, compared with the wooden frames and canvas-covered roofs of older stock. They had a mixture of individual compartments and open saloons seating around 400 passengers depending on the internal layout in each unit, and no corridor connections between carriages.

Still incorrectly displaying its 30 headcode stencil on the rear, as well as the obligatory tail lamp, a green 4SUB No. 4692 heads away from Thames Ditton station on the last stage of its journey towards Hampton Court.

With its motor coach leading, denoted by the black triangle, 2HAL No. 2620 forms a Reading General to Waterloo train. The Great Western Railway station building can just be glimpsed on the left above the roof of the train and the canopies.

2BIL unit No. 2104 is seen arriving at Reading General platform 4a. This rather narrow single platform effectively replaced the whole of the old South Eastern Railway Reading South station, which was closed in 1965 and demolished in 1970.

From a 4REP and 8TC train on a Bournemouth line service arriving on the Up main line, we have a panoramic view of the 1922-built terminus at Waterloo. In the middle a train of CIG and BIG stock awaits departure on the Down main line for Guildford and Portsmouth Harbour while a 4SUB unit is leaving on the Down slow line on the right.

Sitting in the sidings at Clapham Junction, rakes of 4COR EMUs wait to form their evening peak services from Waterloo. The footbridge above the trains links all seventeen platforms at what is billed as 'The World's Busiest Station'. It now links the London Overground to Highbury and Willesden, the South Western Reading, Windsor, Weymouth, Salisbury main and suburban lines, the South Central Brighton, Eastbourne and Worthing main and suburban lines and the West London line to Watford Junction.

A view from a train descending the slow line flyover, which moves the Up slow to Waterloo across the fast lines to run adjacent to the Down slow line. It shows the electric traction maintenance sheds at Durnsford Road, Wimbledon. 4SUB, 2HAL units and an E6100 series high-power electro-diesel loco are visible. The grassy area in the foreground was the site of the Southern Railway's Durnsford Road power station with its two prominent chimneys, which had all gone by 1965. This area is now the site of the Wimbledon Traincare Depot.

At Clapham Junction sidings we see a 2HAL unit that has been converted for departmental use. Some were employed as parcels units, while others were used as de-icing or Sandite units to keep the third rails clear of ice and deal with autumn leaves respectively. The unusual staff accommodation can be seen cantilevered out over the sidings on the left.

An 8TC and 4REP formation in the more attractive blue and grey livery approaches Basingstoke under the Reading Road bridge on a semi-fast service to Bournemouth and Weymouth. Contractors are clearing the steam-era sidings and loading dock in the right foreground to provide additional car parking space at what was already becoming a very busy commuter station.

A Warship diesel has arrived at Exeter St David's on a service from Waterloo via Salisbury and the Southern's West of England line. Until the end of locomotive haulage on these trains in the Network SouthEast era, Laira depot at Plymouth on the Western Region was responsible for providing the locomotives and coaching stock for the services between Waterloo and Exeter.

A mixture of locomotive types is portrayed in Basingstoke Up yard. These include a 2,500 hp high-power electro-diesel, and a Birmingham RC&W Co. Crompton Type 3, both in blue, together with a Western Region Hymek diesel-hydraulic still in green with a small yellow warning panel. On the left a classic Bedford flatbed lorry is doing duty with Corralls the coal merchant.

Seen through a line of Southern Railway concrete lamp posts with their white plastic shades, a twelve-car train, with the solitary 8VAB at the rear, heads west from Basingstoke towards Bournemouth. On the right, construction of office buildings is under way on the site of the old Basingstoke locomotive shed.

Sitting in the Down bay platform at Basingstoke with the first of the modern office blocks as a backdrop is Hampshire DEMU No. 1126. Since the 1960s the town has changed dramatically from the small market town it used to be when my family first lived there in the 1950s.

An English Electric Co-Co Type 3 diesel-electric loco in green livery heads through Basingstoke with a train of oil tankers from Fawley refinery. It will branch north towards Reading and a merry-go-round coal hopper wagon is in place as a barrier wagon between the loco and the oil tankers.

At Salisbury we see Hampshire DEMU No. 1131 in the eastbound bay platform awaiting departure for Southampton and Portsmouth. In the middle distance another Hampshire DEMU is ready to head back towards Basingstoke and Reading General. The old Great Western Railway Fisherton Street station is just visible on the right.

Departing from Fratton station is 4VEP No. 7717, still in all-over blue livery but now with full yellow ends, heading for Waterloo on a Portsmouth direct line stopping service. Now preserved, this unit is owned by the Bluebell Railway. It is re-numbered 3417 and named *Gordon Pettitt*, after the well-known and respected former Southern Region General Manager, now President of the Bluebell Railway Preservation Society.

Repair work is in hand at the station, as a formation of 2HAL and 2BIL units heads through Fratton on a South Coast 'Coastway' service towards Portsmouth Harbour. On the right some vans can be seen in Fratton yard.

The same formation of 2BIL and 2HAL units is seen departing from Portsmouth & Southsea High Level station on the final stage of its journey to Portsmouth Harbour. The black triangle indicates the motor coach and luggage van end of the unit. Just behind the train to the right the former Admiralty line used to branch off down an incline to serve the Royal Navy Dockyard.

A BR standard 4EPB No. 5363 heads a Charing Cross to Dartford via Greenwich and the North Kent Line train into Woolwich Arsenal station. The station was built in 1849 to serve the Royal Arsenal ordnance base and rebuilt in 1906. In 2009 it again changed substantially when it was modernised to incorporate a branch of the Docklands Light Railway.

A plethora of SR-style BR-built EPB units is seen from the footbridge at Dartford station during the late afternoon. Dartford was opened by the South Eastern Railway in 1849 as part of its extension from Gravesend westwards towards London. Dartford is a key station on the South Eastern Division, being the meeting point of three busy suburban routes from London, these being the North Kent Line via Greenwich and Woolwich, the Bexleyheath Line and the Dartford Loop via Sidcup. Old and modern signal boxes can be glimpsed in the distance.

This picture shows the driving trailer end of 3R 'Tadpole' DEMU No. 1203, just arrived at Guildford station from Redhill. The South Eastern Railway route from Tonbridge and Redhill via the Surrey Hills to Guildford, and via the Blackwater Valley to Reading, penetrated deeply into the territory of its London Brighton & South Coast and London & South Western Railway competitors.

In this picture unit No. 1203 is heading north from Guildford towards the junction to Ash and the Blackwater Valley line to Wokingham and Reading General. On the right a 4EPB can be seen in the Guildford New Line bay platform ready to form a service to Waterloo via Cobham.

A 4COR unit is waiting at Guildford with a service to Waterloo via Aldershot, Ascot and Staines. It will join at Ascot with another unit from Reading and arrive at Waterloo in the Windsor side platforms. At this time the 4CORs had displaced the 2BIL and 2HAL units from the Waterloo to Reading and Guildford services. In the background, where an EPB unit is berthed, the former steam locomotive coaling sidings were situated.

The old and the new are seen at Guildford. A 4COR unit is berthed in a siding while a CIG and BIG formation arrives from Waterloo. The headcode 84 would appear to indicate that the train has travelled via Cobham and the Guildford New Line rather than the main line via Woking.

Seen through a telephoto lens from the rear carriage, a formation comprising a 4COR from Reading and a 4COR from Guildford, combined at Ascot, winds its way through Staines towards Waterloo. From the other direction a small electro-diesel approaches towards Staines goods yard with a short freight train.

Just over the Southern and Western Region border is Westbury, where on 5 April 1971 we see grubby green-liveried Hymek No. D7016, fitted with miniature snowploughs, on a train of freight vans. The Great Western Railway signal box and bracket signals are worthy of note.

Also on 5 April 1971 but back in the Southern Region, another green-liveried Hymek approaches Warminster station from the Western Region with a passenger service towards Salisbury and Portsmouth.

An unidentified Western Region Warship diesel-hydraulic heads towards Salisbury and Exeter past the derelict site of the old Basingstoke locomotive shed. On the right is the chimney of the erstwhile Percy Fisher's leather works. Beyond the loco are the west signal box and some goods vans in the Down side sidings.

From one of the then new ring road bridges east of Basingstoke we see a Warship-hauled Exeter St David's to Waterloo service heading towards Basing village situated to the right of the line in the distance. The old Basing Hospital is also on the right.

A view from Reading Road bridge just east of Basingstoke sees a smart 8TC formation being propelled by a 4REP heading west towards Basingstoke station on a semi-fast service to Bournemouth and Weymouth. Although the 4TC units were converted from standard Mark 1 steam stock, the 4REP driving power cars were built new and combined with Buffet and Brake First coaches converted from Mark 1 steam stock.

The 'Night Ferry' continental sleeper train arrives in the Eastern side of Victoria station on 11 April 1971. The locomotive is an E5000 series 2,500 hp straight electric locomotive, built in 1958 for the Kent Coast electrification. The Central or Brighton side of Victoria can be seen on the right and this has since been rebuilt with shops and offices. Victoria Eastern signal box, opened in 1920, can be seen squeezed in on the left.

At Ashford in its original livery of blue with small yellow warning panel and white cab window surrounds is seen 1,600 hp JB series small electro-diesel loco No. E6047. Built as one of the second batch by English Electric at the Vulcan Foundry, Newton-le-Willows in the mid-1960s, they served on all three Southern Region divisions hauling passenger and freight trains.

Another 2,500 hp electric locomotive, No. E5005, is heading 'The Man of Kent' rail tour comprised of a single 4TC unit. The train was promoted by the Southern Electric Group on Sunday 11 April 1971 and is seen at Sittingbourne station while we visited the Sittingbourne & Kemsley Light Railway. Prior to the advent of the electro-diesels, these electric locos were fitted with overhead pantograph current collectors for working in freight yards where the third rail would be a danger to shunting staff.

Built by British Railways to a Southern Railway design, 2HAP unit No. 5614 awaits departure on the Sittingbourne–Sheerness shuttle service on 11 April 1971. These units were constructed from 1957 on underframes salvaged in true Southern Railway style from withdrawn stock. The trailer composite vehicles had first and second class seating together with a toilet.

A contrast in styles between a Maunsell-inspired 2BIL No. 2140 on the left and a later Bulleid-inspired 2HAL unit No. 2619 on the right. They are seen at Portsmouth Harbour station on 'Coastway' services towards Brighton. 'Coastway' was the imaginative name given to the Central Division marketing scheme to promote use of the Portsmouth to Brighton and Hastings line, which received grant aid from the government to avoid closure.

The headcodes on the early Southern Electric stock were provided by means of cut-out stencil letters and numbers. This picture of 2BIL No. 2034 shows how the secondman's cab windscreen opened outwards to allow the headcode stencil to be changed by the train crew.

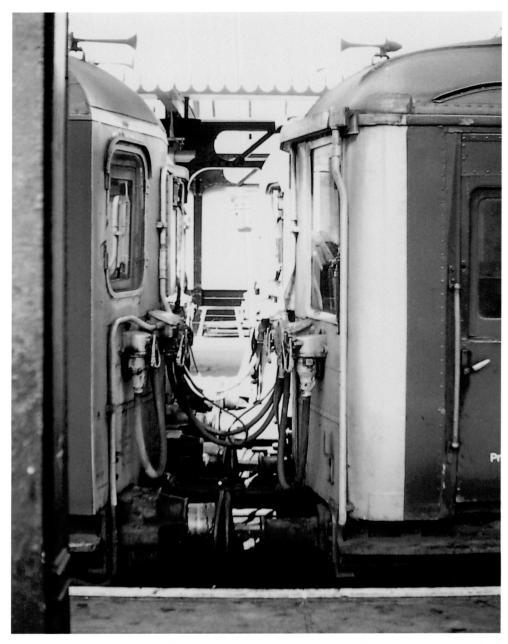

Nose-to-nose at Portsmouth Harbour station we see 2HAL and 2BIL units, the squared-off 2HAL cab contrasting with the rounded front of the 2BIL. The 2BIL units had a toilet and corridor in each coach (BI-Lavatory) and were first introduced for the Eastbourne and Hastings electrification in 1935. Further tranches followed for the electrification to Gillingham and Maidstone and had a toilet and corridor in one coach only (HALf-lavatory) the other coach being basic compartments. I remember the 2HAL interiors were more utilitarian, being painted or rexine-covered rather than varnished woodwork like the 2BILs. The difference in the buffer designs is also worthy of note.

With 2HAL unit No. 2619 at the rear, a four-car train passes over the level crossing as it leaves Chichester station and heads east. Chichester station was rebuilt in 1961 to a typically 1960s modern-image design but the surrounding infrastructure remained decidedly dated.

A formation of two 2BIL units with No. 2074 at the rear has clear signals as it leaves Worthing Central station en route to Brighton. A new station was constructed at Worthing in 1911. The original station building, erected in 1845 when the Portsmouth to Brighton line was built, can be seen on the right and is Grade II listed.

Arriving at Worthing Central is seen 2BIL unit No. 2028. This unit has a pre-war motor coach and a post-war all-steel 2HAL trailer composite similar in style to the 4SUBs. A number of these hybrid units arose out of replacements for wartime losses due to bombing and accident damage.

Judging by the washing on display in the lineside gardens it may have been a Monday! Much of the Coastway route between Brighton and Worthing has hardly any view of the sea, running behind Victorian and Edwardian housing. A westbound 2HAL is reflected in the large corridor windows of an eastbound unit.

Here at 'Hove actually' (as the residents sometimes like to refer to Hove), last station before Brighton, a Victoria service via Haywards Heath is seen heading away towards the junction where the Brighton and the Haywards Heath and London Victoria routes diverge. Hove station has at various times been known as Cliftonville, West Brighton, and Hove & West Brighton and here retains its green Southern signage.

At Brighton station 2BIL No. 2090 has the tail lamp in position ready to leave on another run along the west Coastway route towards Worthing.

Following arrival at Brighton the tail lamp has been removed from 2HAL unit No. 2648 and some parcels have been unloaded. It is seen under the magnificent overall roof of Brighton station. The station was originally built in 1840 but the curved iron and glass overall roof was added in the 1880s.

Both headcode and tail lamp are displayed by 2BIL unit No. 2139 as it heads away from Falmer station towards Lewes. The area on the right has changed significantly with the development of the Sussex and Brighton universities. Brighton & Hove Albion's modern Amex football stadium is also situated here, with fans attending matches being actively encouraged to use the trains to and from Falmer.

The next two pictures show a contrast in rolling stock styles at Lewes, with the cliffs of the South Downs behind. In this picture a 4COR is arriving from the east Coastway line and forking to its left so as to continue towards Brighton.

This picture shows a train consisting of 4CIG and 4BIG units heading away to Eastbourne and Hastings, having arrived on the line coming in from the left from Victoria and Haywards Heath. Lewes signal box controlled the various routes and the electrification substation can also be seen on the right, all more recently brought under the remote control of the Network Rail Operations Centre located at Three Bridges station.

Southern Electric splendour! The magnificent canopies and concourse lantern roof at Eastbourne station dwarf the trains within. The photograph is taken from a train entering from Brighton consisting of 2HAL and 2BIL units, while in the platforms and sidings are 4CIGs and a 4COR. The station was rebuilt in 1886 to replace a smaller one, and is now Grade II listed.

Passengers alight at Hastings station from 2HAL No. 2679 which has just arrived. The current station dates from 1931 when two island platforms were established to allow free passage of trains on the routes to and from Ashford, Brighton, Victoria and Charing Cross.

2BIL No. 2137 and a 2HAL run into Hastings station from Ore. EMU rolling stock sheds were situated adjacent to Ore station, this currently being the extent of the electrification eastwards.

A 600 hp 3D East Sussex area DEMU departs from Hastings towards Rye and Ashford, Kent. Following the success of the 3H Hampshire DEMUs, the 3D units were built in 1962 for service on the Oxted line and other associated routes in Sussex. The 3Ds have a more rounded front end and the jumper cables and brake hoses are recessed in similar fashion to the contemporary 4CIG electric stock.

With bright sunshine slanting across the station, a 6L Hastings line DEMU runs into Hastings station. It subsequently departed on a late afternoon service to Tonbridge and Charing Cross.

I trust the driver's shoulder is visible in the left side driver's window as (hopefully) another member of the train crew gives a wave from the second man's side. The BR-built, Southern Railway-style 2EPB unit has been signalled to take the Chertsey, Addlestone and Weybridge branch at Virginia Water. The main line continuing ahead to Ascot on the left opened in 1856 and the branch to Chertsey in 1866.

Southern Galore! A train of two 4COR units led by No. 3157 call at Virginia Water as they head down towards Ascot, where they split for Guildford and Reading General. A Southern Railway train, signal box, station buildings, signals, lampposts, parcels barrow, and enamel station signs and seats set a vintage Southern Electric scene. Even the gentleman passenger smoking his pipe on the left adds to the distinctive period atmosphere. All was shortly to be swept aside by rebuilding in 1973.

A couple more 4COR units with No. 3137 in the rear depart from Egham station as they head up the Windsor Lines towards Staines and Waterloo. Whoever repainted the rear corridor connection selected a very pretty primrose yellow. Egham station lasted until 1985 before demolition and replacement by a new station building.

With the branch to Windsor & Eton Riverside curving to the right past a stabled 2EPB unit, two 4COR units with No. 3111 at the rear head left from Staines towards Ascot where they will divide for Reading General and Guildford. A 1,600 hp electro-diesel, making good use of its 600 hp diesel engine in the goods yard, waits with a train of bogie bolster wagons carrying steel beams. The yard seems to be astonishingly busy with a continental ferry van, containers, open and bolster wagons evident. The goods yard is now largely overgrown.

Two spick and span 4COR units are seen berthed awaiting their next duty in the Windsor Line sidings on the approaches from Wandsworth Town to Clapham Junction.

In the pouring rain with a clear signal ahead, 3R 'Tadpole' DEMU No. 1203 leaves Reading General platform 4a heading towards Wokingham, the Blackwater Valley, Guildford, the Surrey Hills and Redhill. Meanwhile, a 4COR unit waits on the gradient beyond to enter the platform from the Waterloo direction.

By contrast, on the sunny morning of 2 May 1971, the very clean Warship class diesel-hydraulic No. 831 *Monarch* arrives at Basingstoke from Exeter St David's on the 09.13 service to Woking and Waterloo.

On 2 May 1971, the day of the Historic Commercial Vehicle Club's annual London to Brighton rally, 5BEL units, Nos 3051 and 3053, forming the 'Brighton Belle' are ready to leave Victoria on their dash down to Brighton. Most 'Brighton Belle' cars have been preserved either statically or as part of the Belmond British Pullman. At a considerable cost the 5BEL Trust aims to bring a restored 'Brighton Belle' train back into main line service.

On the left, shiny 4CIG stock is berthed in Lovers Walk sidings, Brighton, as 5BEL set Nos 3053 and 3051 leave for a thrash up the main line to Victoria on 2 May 1971. The 'Brighton Belle' train ran from 1933 until 1972, a year after this picture was taken. The riding of these units was notoriously rough and by journey's end the tablecloths were well stained with tea, coffee or stronger beverage according to taste.

4COR unit No. 3112 arrives at Brighton on the east Coastway route from Lewes on 2 May 1971. Brighton signal box was originally built into the walls of the old Brighton locomotive works, which was situated on the right of the picture. When the works buildings were demolished in 1966 the signal box was left standing alone.

Under the cavernous roof of Brighton's trainshed, post-war 2HAL No. 2698, with 2BIL No. 2090 behind, has its headcode stencil changed ready to depart on a westbound Coastway service towards Worthing. Unit No. 2698 was one of a batch of replacements for war losses built in the late 1940s and had similar accommodation to a pre-war 2HAL but built of steel in the same style as the 4SUBs. They differed slightly in having larger luggage compartments and were used on Victoria to Gatwick Airport services between the late 1950s and 1960s.

By way of a change from standard gauge trains, the 2-foot 8½-inch gauge Volk's Electric Railway runs for about a mile along the Brighton seafront providing a March to October service. It starts at Brighton Aquarium and the nearby Palace Pier, seen in the background. It then calls at Halfway platform, midway along, and terminates at Black Rock near the Brighton Marina.

The Volks Electric Railway was opened in 1883 and is the world's oldest operating electric railway. It is powered from an inset third rail at 110 volts dc. Here is another view on a lovely sunny day of a car, well filled with holidaymakers and trippers, running along its fenced track between Madeira Drive and the beach.

Framed by a Southern Railway enamel live conductor 3rd rail warning notice, 4COR No. 3156 approaches Bishopstone station on the Lewes to Seaford branch on 2 May 1971.

Through some long grass on the same date, a 4COR is seen silhouetted on an embankment near Bishopstone station on the Seaford branch. The nearby Bishopstone Beach Halt was closed in 1942. It served Tide Mills village, the site of a large tide mill and during the First World War the location of a Royal Naval Air Service anti-submarine seaplane base. On closure of the seaplane base in 1919, one of the large metal seaplane hangars was transported to Wimbledon West Goods Yard where it has been in use as an engineering store.

Heading into the setting sun on 2 May 1971, 4COR unit No. 3156 approaches Lewes station with the historic town rising up behind as if to form a backcloth.

4COR No. 3156 leaves Lewes and heads back across the junction towards the Seaford branch on the same date.

Contrasting styles at Waterloo as 4VEPs in both blue and grey and plain blue liveries, with No. 7740 leading, arrive at Waterloo's main line platforms alongside a 4COR leaving the Windsor side platforms. After Southern green, the 4CORs were only painted in all-over blue, never receiving blue and grey livery.

A Southern Railway high-capacity 4SUB in green livery, and with the BR carriage totem on the lower bodysides of the motor coaches, heads out across the pointwork from Waterloo's Windsor side platforms.

While passengers wait to board, a 4TC unit is at the head of a semi-fast Bournemouth and Weymouth service as it crosses from the fast to the slow line and is propelled to platform 1 at Basingstoke.

On the left a Waterloo-bound semi-fast service, with 4REP No. 3011 leading, arrives at Brockenhurst. 4VEP No. 7743 on the right will form the Lymington Pier shuttle service. Brockenhurst station opened in 1847 on the Southampton to Dorchester Railway, which served Dorchester by way of 'Castleman's Corkscrew', the circuitous route via Ringwood and Wimborne Minster. The current direct route via Sway opened in 1888.

Back in the suburbs, and at Hampton Court station the driver of 4SUB No. 4373 has just replaced the headcode stencil through the open cab window ready for the return journey to Waterloo.

A Birmingham RC&W Co Type 3 Crompton diesel-electric loco rushes a special working, or maybe an Exeter to Waterloo service with an incorrect headcode, through Surbiton station. On the left, behind the deserted goods yard, can be seen the former Carter Paterson depot established in 1936, which became a British Road Services parcels depot between 1959 and 1971.

A BR-built Southern Railway design 4EPB, No. 5228, arrives at Surbiton station on a headcode 42 Guildford to Waterloo via Cobham New Line service.

Passengers board and say their farewells on a Windsor side platform at Waterloo. The 4COR unit, No. 3124, waits to have its indicator blinds changed pending departure on a Reading line service. These platforms and ornate canopies were part of the original Waterloo station built in 1860. They later made way for the Waterloo 'Eurostar' International Terminal. The Eurostar terminal has been superseded by St Pancras International station, and has since been brought back into use for domestic South Western train services.

Passengers have alighted from 4SUB 4635 at Thames Ditton and are busy finding their tickets for checking as the train continues on its way towards Hampton Court.

Through a line of Southern Railway concrete lamp posts and modern signs, Warship diesel-hydraulic No. D817 *Foxhound* leans to the curve as it arrives at Basingstoke on an Exeter St David's to Woking and Waterloo service on 6 June 1971. In the right, background building work is in progress on the site of the old Basingstoke steam locomotive shed. The west signal box can also be glimpsed.

4REP No. 3005 hauls the 10.18 semi-fast service from Basingstoke to Waterloo on 4 July 1971. That morning there was a significant derailment at Surbiton station. Two wagons of an engineer's train derailed on the slow lines and were run into by a fast Waterloo to Portsmouth service at around 70 mph. Much disruption ensued. Because of the derailment this train was diverted via Byfleet, Virginia Water, Staines and Hounslow, not arriving at Waterloo until 11.43, just over half an hour late.

4VEC unit No. 044 is seen at Ryde Pier Head on 4 July 1971 as passengers make their way down the platform to board the train. Since the 1920s these diminutive trains had put in years of service with London Transport before being ferried over to the Isle of Wight (Roman name Vectis) for the 1967 electrification of the Ryde–Shanklin line.

On 4 July 1971 Hunslet diesel mechanical shunter No. D2554 awaits its next duty at Ryde works on the Isle of Wight in the company of a Southern Railway 'pillbox' goods brake van. The loco was transferred to the island from Parkestone Quay on the Eastern Region, being brought over from the mainland by low-loader on the Portsmouth to Fishbourne car ferry.

A very spick and span 3TIS unit, No. 034, awaits departure from Ryde Pier Head for Shanklin on the same date. Originally painted plain blue, as here, the 4VEC and 3TIS units later received the blue and grey livery. They allowed the venerable class O2 Adams 0-4-4 tank locos and carriages to be withdrawn in 1967. In the 1990s these trains were replaced by London Transport 1938 Tube stock.

I was travelling home from Portsmouth Harbour that evening, 4 July, and caught the service shown above, headed by 4COR No. 3105. The train departed at 18.11 and travelled via Guildford, then being diverted via Leatherhead and Epsom due to the derailment at Surbiton. Note the Mark 2 stock of a loco-hauled inter-regional train on the left.

The service also called at Wimbledon later that evening. After one of my last Portsmouth Direct Line runs in a train of COR stock, the service is seen in the twilight heading on to Waterloo with 4COR No. 3158 at the rear. The roof of Wimbledon signal box can just be glimpsed above the second from last coach.

In the New Forest near Beaulieu Road station on summer Saturday 10 July 1971, an Up train of 4VEPs in blue livery is about to pass a REP and TC formation in blue and grey on a Down service.

On the same date, E6101, one of the 2,500 hp high-power electro-diesels, is seen with an additional train to Weymouth comprised of loco-hauled coaching stock. The fifth coach is one of the Mark 2a Corridor firsts allocated to the Southern. These locos suffered from a number of failures of their sophisticated electronic control systems and all were withdrawn by 1977.

Brush Type 4 No. 1732 is hauling a cross-country train from the Midlands as it traverses the Down line towards Bournemouth, also on 10 July 1971.

At Wareham, Dorset, junction for the Swanage branch, Western Region Hymek No. 7061 is arriving with a Cardiff to Weymouth cross-country service on 10 July 1971. Hampshire DEMU No. 1107 waits in the bay platform with the connecting service to Corfe Castle and Swanage. Wareham station opened in 1847 and was rebuilt in 1887. It served the Swanage branch from 1885.

An 8TC formation propelled by a Crompton diesel locomotive is about to traverse the level crossing at Wareham on a Weymouth to Waterloo service on the same date in July 1971. Note the signalman in the ex-LSWR signal box keeping an eye on the level crossing, and the line of oil tankers in the Up-side sidings, presumably provided to serve the BP Furzebrook oil terminal. The oil industry in the Isle of Purbeck started in 1936 but BP's Kimmeridge oilfield was not discovered until the 1960s.

The end of the line at Swanage station, on 10 July 1971. Passengers are disembarking with their holiday luggage from Hampshire unit No. 1107, which will later return to Wareham. Since steam operation finished the run-round loop on the right had been lifted. However it has been replaced in more recent times by the Swanage Railway, which now runs steam-operated services on this popular branch line.

A quiet interlude at Swanage station with DEMU No. 1107 occupying the platform. By good fortune the station buildings and canopy were still in place when the Swanage Railway Preservation Society took over operation of the line with steam locomotives.

Out of the early evening sun on 10 July 1971, the unique 8VAB EMU No. 8001 enters Bournemouth station from the sidings to make a semi-fast service for Waterloo. The 8VAB was formed from three 4VEP motor coaches giving 3,300 hp, four 4VEP driving trailer composites and a loco-hauled Restaurant-Buffet Car through-wired for multiple-unit operation. Initially the former 4VEP vehicles were in plain blue and the restaurant car in blue and grey livery, as seen here. Behind, the old Bournemouth loco depot is giving way to a new car park.

A couple of BR-built, SR-style 2HAP EMUs hasten down into the evening sun past New Malden signal box towards Surbiton. The branch for the Kingston, Strawberry Hill and Shepperton lines diverges down to the left.

A dramatic view of a REP and TC formation on a Bournemouth and Weymouth fast service speeding past New Malden station. The station was opened in 1846 as Malden and was known by several different names until it became New Malden in 1957. At the time this photograph was taken the middle platforms serving the fast lines were no longer in regular use.

A 4SUB, No. 4743, arrives at Shepperton station, the terminus of its headcode 24 service from Waterloo. Another train of 4SUB units is berthed in the sidings on the right.

Here we see 4SUB No. 4743 following arrival at Shepperton station, which was opened in 1864. In time-honoured fashion, the guard is changing ends and walking down to what will now become the rear of the train with the all-important tail lamp.

A 4VEP approaches out of the setting sun on the Up fast line at Raynes Park station. At this station, opened in 1871, the platforms were staggered, hence there is no platform directly opposite.

With the evening sun behind it, an Up Portsmouth line semi-fast service formed of CIG and BIG stock powers through Raynes Park as it speeds on its way up to Waterloo. This station is the junction for the Chessington South, Epsom, Leatherhead and Horsham lines.

From where I took the two previous pictures, behind me there was this long footbridge diagonally spanning all four main line tracks. Both platforms are islands, each serving the main and branch routes. Raynes Park signal box is visible as a 4SUB approaches on the Down slow line. Raynes Park and New Malden signal boxes were each of timber construction in elevated, exposed locations, and had brickwork built around their lower floor interlocking rooms as protection against wartime enemy action.

Leaving Winchester station is 4REP No. 3007 hauling a formation of 4TC units, heading for Waterloo on a semi-fast service calling at Basingstoke and Woking. The station was known as Winchester City for many years to differentiate it from the erstwhile Winchester Chesil station on the Didcot, Newbury & Southampton line.

Alton station, seen here, is the end of the electrified line from Waterloo and the interchange for the connecting Hampshire DEMU service to Winchester via Alresford. Prior to closure of the Alresford route by BR we see blue 4VEP No. 711 waiting to leave on a stopping service north to Waterloo while DEMU No. 1122 awaits departure towards Winchester.

Seen through lineside foliage, Hampshire DEMU No. 1122 leaves Alton on its journey south-west towards Alresford, Winchester and Southampton. Following closure by BR in 1973, the Watercress Railway took over operation between Alton and Alresford from 1975.

Two Hampshire DEMUs pass in Alresford station. This station is now the headquarters of the Watercress Railway. Watercress began to be grown commercially in the chalk streams and rivers in this area and when the railway came in 1865 the perishable watercress could be on sale in Covent Garden market the day after it was picked.

A travel-stained 4REP arrives at Eastleigh station at the front of a semi-fast service to Winchester, Basingstoke and Waterloo. The Down side buildings were rebuilt in the 1960s but the old Up-side station building, seen here, remained in place together with the original footbridge.

On a winter trip to the Swanage branch before it closed we were bedevilled by mist and fog. Here Hampshire DEMU No. 1104 waits in the bay platform at Wareham on 4 December 1971 to form the service to Corfe Castle and Swanage. A member of staff is closing the doors ready for departure.

Hampshire DEMU No. 1104 arrives at a misty Corfe Castle station, which almost has a haunted and surreal air about it. Luckily the station avoided demolition after closure by BR. It used to be the site of a couple of camping coaches, well placed for visits to the Norman castle at Corfe and by train to the seaside at Swanage.

Hampshire unit No. 1104 departs from Corfe Castle station on the same date and heads into the fog towards Swanage. The station dates from the opening of the Swanage branch in 1885.

Also on 4 December 1971, the local Western National bus service No. 419 from Swanage to Worth Matravers waits outside the station while passengers board. It is provided by a Bristol and Eastern Coachworks single-deck bus operated by Southern National. Note the white steering wheel denoting an 8-foot-wide vehicle.

Push-pull-fitted Crompton diesel loco No. 6519 waits to propel a Waterloo service between Weymouth and Bournemouth on 4 December 1971 while a Western Region Gloucester RC&W three-car cross-country DMU (with W51092 visible) sits at Weymouth station awaiting its next duty.

A British Railways-built Class 03 diesel mechanical shunter, No. D2086, rests at Weymouth coupled to a 4TC unit. Note the waist-height brake hoses fitted to the shunter to enable it to couple to the 4TC stock. A rather nice Triumph Herald sits in the right foreground.

Two 4TC units are coupled together at Weymouth to form an eight-car train back to Bournemouth. This will be attached to a 4REP at Bournemouth station to form a twelve-car train through to Waterloo. Until the Second World War these tracks were covered by a glazed overall roof.

A Western region cross-country DMU awaits departure from Weymouth for Bristol. A Wolseley 1500 car is parked alongside. Branch lines to Portland and Weymouth Quay left the main line just north of the station.

In the late afternoon, a diesel mechanical shunter traverses the tramway between Weymouth station and Weymouth Quay. It is hauling what appears to be an enthusiasts' excursion comprised of 4TC units in contrasting states of cleanliness. The loco has a flashing orange light and a bell above the front bufferbeam to give warning of its approach on the tramway.

Hastings 6B Buffet Car DEMU No. 1034 has arrived at Weymouth station on a Southern Region Central Division 'Pleasure Seeker' excursion. 'Pleasure Seekers' were the equivalent of 'Merrymaker' excursion trains on other regions. It would have originated from Hastings and run via Lewes, calling at other Central Division stations en route. A good display of corporate image station signage is visible.

Hastings 6B DEMU 1034 is seen again over the buffers at Weymouth station. The well-sited poster display shows some of the early Awayday adverts encouraging day travel to London and other places served by direct train services. Pre-dating the Bournemouth to Weymouth electrification, 'Ride Dorsetway' was a campaign run by the Southern Region South Western Division to promote local travel on the Bournemouth to Weymouth line in a similar manner to the campaigns promoting the Portsmouth to Brighton and Hastings 'Coastway' route and Reading to Redhill, Gatwick and Tonbridge line.

Here we visit the site of my early trainspotting days at Winklebury, just west of Basingstoke. A twelve-car REP and TC formation takes the slow line towards Worting Junction on a headcode 92 semi-fast service to Bournemouth and Weymouth.

Also at Winklebury, a 4VEP approaches Basingstoke on a Bournemouth to Waterloo (headcode 93) stopping service. This four car unit will join at Woking with a 4VEP from Alton to form an eight-car service for the run up to Surbiton and Waterloo. In the distance, round the curve in the far left, two silos can just be made out that mark out the 'Blue Peter Retreads' car tyre remould factory at Worting. I doubt that such tyres would be suitable for today's high-speed motoring.

Slightly further west, a 4VEP is heading over Battledown Flyover towards Basingstoke on a stopping service from Bournemouth to Waterloo. The line to Salisbury and Exeter, which diverges from the Bournemouth line at Worting Junction, passes on a curve under the flyover.

Under a threatening sky, a train of empty oil tankers is being hurried down past Battledown Flyover towards Fawley refinery, double-headed by a couple of Crompton diesel locos. The load includes three 100-ton bogie tankers that appeared on the scene in the mid- to late 1960s and were something of a novelty at this time.

At Battledown Flyover a Crompton Type 3 diesel locomotive whisks an afternoon parcels and empty stock train up towards Basingstoke and most likely on to Clapham Junction sidings.

With Battledown Flyover almost in silhouette, another Crompton Type 3 diesel heads a train from Exeter St David's east towards Basingstoke and Waterloo under the flyover. The first carriage bears a waist-level destination board while the second is a Restaurant Buffet Car (RB).

4REP No. 3010 hauls its train into Basingstoke on a semi-fast service to Woking and Waterloo. The white building in the right background was the factory of Eli Lilly, a pharmaceutical company. The building was completed just before the Second World War and was once connected to the railway network by a private siding.

On 6 May 1972 the train crew are strolling down the wooden platform as 3D unit No. 1307 reverses at Brighton en route to, or from, St Leonards Depot. At this time the units that worked the Oxted line services from London to East Grinstead and Uckfield were maintained at St Leonards Depot, near Hastings, entailing lengthy empty stock workings.

Following arrival at Brighton alongside a pair of 4VEPs on the adjacent line, 4COR unit No. 3151 is now ready to form a headcode 16 service to Lewes, Eastbourne, Hastings and Ore on 6 May 1972. The corridor connection leans forwards in typical 4COR fashion.

On the same date, 6 May 1972, a contrast between the new and the old regimes is seen under the magnificent overall roof of Brighton station with 4VEP No. 7782 alongside 4COR No. 3151.

With a fine array of semaphore signals on display a 4COR unit arrives at Hastings from Ore on 6 May 1972. The signal box opened in 1930 just prior to the rebuilding of the station.

While a 3D unit waits to leave for Ashford, a train comprised of 4BIG No. 7048 and a 4CIG awaits departure from Hastings for Eastbourne on 6 May 1972. There it will reverse to continue its journey to Lewes, Haywards Heath, and up the Brighton main line to Victoria. The 4BIG buffet cars were famed for their seemingly unique ability amongst BR catering vehicles to supply freshly made buttered toast!

As passengers wait to board, luggage in hand, 6L Hastings line DEMU No. 1019 enters Hastings station on 6 May 1972, ready to saunter up to Charing Cross on its headcode 22 service via Battle and Tonbridge.

A 3D unit leaves Hastings for Ore and Ashford on 6 May 1972. Unlike the Hampshire DEMUs, where the first class accommodation was in the driving trailer vehicle, in these units the first class seating was in the centre coach – as denoted by the yellow cantrail stripe.

With the Edwardian town of Hastings in the background, a 4COR unit forms an east Coastway service from Hastings to Eastbourne and Brighton on 6 May 1972.

An early morning shot taken into the rising sun at Basingstoke of a Crompton diesel on a Waterloo to Exeter St David's service. The cranes in the background are busy building the office blocks for which Basingstoke would soon rival places such as Croydon. The line to Reading can be seen forking to the left behind the panel signal box.

On the eastern side of Victoria station, 4CEP No. 7209 is ready to depart on the 11.00 Boat Train service for Dover Western Docks. The date was 21 June 1972 and this was the first stage of a journey via Ostend to Austria to photograph the Stern & Hafferl system in Upper Austria and Austrian Federal Railways steam, diesel and electric trains.

On 4 February 1973, the end of the BR service on the Alton to Winchester 'Mid Hants' line is nigh. Hampshire DEMU No. 1131 on an Alton to Southampton service waits in the passing loop at Alresford for a train north to Alton to come off the single line from Winchester Junction.

On the same date in February 1973, crowds swarm around the station at Alresford to pay their last respects to the Southern Region service as Hampshire DEMUs on Alton and Southampton services pass.

Hampshire DEMU No. 1131 departs from Alresford station on 4 February 1973 and heads south towards Winchester and Southampton.

The next few pictures were taken on the summer Saturday of 10 June 1973 in the New Forest, near Beaulieu Road station. This picture shows two 4VEPs heading westbound towards Bournemouth Central.

The high seating capacity of the 4VEPs, i.e. 222 seats per four-car unit, is being put to good use as two of the units head towards Waterloo with returning holidaymakers. Note the Southern Railway concrete platelayer's hut. With the chimney removed these were designed to fit the loading gauge when loaded on a flat wagon.

An unusual sight here as three Western Region three-car DMMUs pass on an excursion working making its way towards Bournemouth.

A reverse formation of two 4TCs with a 4REP propelling from the rear is seen heading towards Waterloo with returning holidaymakers.

A 2,500 hp high-power 6100 series electro-diesel speeds towards Weymouth while a REP and TC formation heads up to Waterloo.

Heading west towards Bournemouth and Weymouth is a twelve-car REP and TC formation, this time with the 4REP in the middle.

A 4VEP is seen working the stopping service between Waterloo and Bournemouth. A couple of the chimneys at the Esso Petroleum Company's Fawley refinery are visible on the horizon. The refinery was started in 1925 and has been considerably rebuilt and enlarged since.

An inter-regional service from Birmingham to Weymouth heads west in the charge of a Brush Type 4, still in green livery.

A Southern Region push-pull fitted Crompton Type 3 diesel heads two 4TC units on a summer-Saturday-only service towards Weymouth.

A 4VEP is seen making its way east towards Southampton and Waterloo on an Up stopping service.

En route west to Weymouth with Southern Region loco-hauled stock we see one of the small 1,600 hp electro-diesel locomotives.

Here we visit my trainspotting roots at Winklebury, just west of Basingstoke again, this time on 27 April 1974. A 4REP and 8TC formation heads west on the fast line on a headcode 91 limited stop service. At Worting Junction it will switch to the slow line for Southampton, Bournemouth and Weymouth. There are five tracks here, the nearest being a non-electrified Up relief line.

A Crompton Type 3 diesel heads towards Basingstoke on a service from Exeter St David's to Waterloo on 27 April 1974. It has come under Battledown flyover and remained on what here has become the Up fast line. The area to the right was open fields in my youthful trainspotting days but is now taken up by housing development.

Also on 27 April 1974, another REP and TC formation with the 4REP leading heads eastwards to Basingstoke, Woking and Waterloo on a headcode 92 semi-fast service. This train will have come over the flyover at Battledown and remains on what has here become the Up slow line as far as its next stop at Basingstoke.

And here is a real reminder of my very earliest trainspotting days. After relaxation of BR's main line steam locomotive ban in the early 1970s, we see preserved Merchant Navy class No. 35028 *Clan Line*, which hauled one of the Southern Region's official 'Last Steam Specials' on 2 July 1967. This picture, taken on 27 April 1974, shows the return leg of *Clan Line's* first main line special in preservation between Westbury and Basingstoke. Much more of a crowd is present compared with just me and my brother in our early teenage years!

A 1,600 hp electro-diesel hauls a train of miscellaneous vans westward at Winklebury on the same date. The western extent of the old market town of Basingstoke can be seen in the background. However, the landscape behind the trees is rather different now, with the Milestones Museum and an ice rink among other modern developments.

Not far from Worting Junction a Hampshire DEMU trundles down from Basingstoke towards Overton, Whitchurch, Andover, Grateley and Salisbury.

A Crompton Type 3 diesel heads towards Andover, Salisbury and stations to Exeter St David's on a service from Waterloo.

Engineering work must be planned as a Crompton Type 3 loco, in charge of a train of SR bogie 'Walrus' hopper wagons, heads away towards Andover and Salisbury with a ballast working. Fifty Walrus hopper wagons for carrying and laying track ballast were built in the early 1950s. The Civil Engineer's wagons tend to be named after sea creatures, probably as codes or abbreviations for telegraphic messages in times past.

Baking

2nd Edition

by Wendy Jo Peterson, MS, RDN

A Wiley Brand

Baking For Dummies®, 2nd Edition

Published by: **John Wiley & Sons, Inc.,** 111 River Street, Hoboken, NJ 07030-5774, www.wiley.com

Copyright © 2023 by John Wiley & Sons, Inc., Hoboken, New Jersey

Published simultaneously in Canada

For general information on our other products and services, please contact our Customer Care Department within the U.S. at 877-762-2974, outside the U.S. at 317-572-3993, or fax 317-572-4002. For technical support, please visit https://hub.wiley.com/community/support/dummies.

Wiley publishes in a variety of print and electronic formats and by print-on-demand. Some material included with standard print versions of this book may not be included in e-books or in print-on-demand. For more information about Wiley products, visit www.wiley.com.

Library of Congress Control Number: 2023934609

ISBN 978-1-394-17246-7 (pbk); ISBN 978-1-394-17247-4 (ebk); ISBN 978-1-394-17248-1 (ebk)

SKY10045194_033023

Contents at a Glance

Introduction 1

Part 1: Baking Essentials 5

CHAPTER 1: Bake, For Goodness' Sake!. 7

CHAPTER 2: Stocking Up 11

CHAPTER 3: Going Over the Gear. 39

Part 2: Basic Training for Baking 63

CHAPTER 4: Familiarizing Yourself with Your Oven 65

CHAPTER 5: Focusing on Basic Techniques 71

CHAPTER 6: Considering Allergies and Insensitivities When Baking 87

CHAPTER 7: Getting Ready to Bake 93

Part 3: Ready, Set, Bake!... 107

CHAPTER 8: Understanding the Ins and Outs of Baking Cookies. 109

CHAPTER 9: Baking Moist Cakes. 149

CHAPTER 10: Fixing Fabulous Frostings 183

CHAPTER 11: Preparing Perfect Pies and Tarts 205

CHAPTER 12: Creating Crisps, Cobblers, and Other Delights 237

CHAPTER 13: Making Quick Breads, Muffins, and Biscuits 247

CHAPTER 14: Rising with Yeast Breads 269

CHAPTER 15: Going Savory with Baked Goods 295

CHAPTER 16: Baking with Mixes and Premade Doughs. 309

Part 4: Dealing with Other Important Stuff................ 319

CHAPTER 17: Storing Your Creations. 321

CHAPTER 18: Making the Ordinary Extraordinary. 333

Part 5: The Part of Tens 341

CHAPTER 19: Ten Ways to Boost Nutrition When Baking 343

CHAPTER 20: Ten Ways to Get Kids Baking. 347

Appendix A: Glossary of Baking Terms 351

Appendix B: Metric Conversion Guide 357

Index 361

Recipes at a Glance

- Crispy Chocolate Chip Cookies 114
- Chocolate Drop Cookies 115
- Classic Oatmeal-Raisin Cookies 116
- Everything Cookies 117
- Chocolate-Coconut Macaroons 118
- Butterscotch Drops 119
- Poppy Seed Cookies 120
- French Macarons 121
- Peanut Butter Cookies 124
- Snickerdoodles 125
- Rolled Sugar Cookies 126
- Crisp Sugar Cookies 127
- Gingersnaps 128
- Lebkuchen 129
- Lemon Cookies 130
- Apricot-Date Half-Moons 131
- Rosemary Shortbread Cookies 132
- Russian Tea Balls 133
- Anisette Biscotti 134
- Basic Cookie Press Cookies 136
- Gingerbread Cookies with Royal Icing 140
- Tender Sugar Cookies 142
- Dense Chocolate Brownies 144
- Black-and-White Brownies 145
- Lemon Bars 146
- Crunchy Granola Bars 147
- Light and Fluffy Yellow Cake 152
- Martha's Chocolate Cake 153
- Texas Chocolate Sheath Cake 154
- Carrot Cake 155
- Applesauce Cake 156
- German Apple Kuchen with Streusel 157
- Banana-Sour Cream Bundt Cake 158
- Classic Pound Cake 161
- Chocolate Swirl Pound Cake 162
- Chocolate Cupcakes 164
- Lemon Cupcakes 165

⏱ Angel Food Cake 168
⏱ Jelly Roll 170
⏱ Tres Leches with Mango 171
⏱ Lemon Rosemary Almond Cake 173
⏱ Gluten-Free Chocolate Hazelnut Cake 174
⏱ Molten Lava Cake 175
⏱ Classic Cheesecake 178
⏱ Pumpkin Cheesecake 179
⏱ Lemon Curd Cheesecake 180
⏱ Cream Cheese Frosting 186
⏱ Mocha Frosting 187
⏱ Basic Vanilla Buttercream Frosting 188
⏱ Sweetened Whipped Cream Frosting 190
⏱ Chocolate Frosting 191
⏱ Martha's Sweet and Creamy Frosting 192
⏱ Quick Apricot Glaze 196
⏱ Classic Sugar Glaze 197
⏱ Old-Fashioned Pie Dough 211
⏱ Stir-and-Roll Pie Pastry 212
⏱ Pumpkin Pie 217
⏱ You'll-Be-Glad-You-Tried-It Apple Pie 218
⏱ Cinnamon Apple Dumplings 219
⏱ Blueberry Pie 220
⏱ Cherry Crumb Pie 221
⏱ Rhubarb Pie 222
⏱ Pecan Pie 223
⏱ Chocolate Cream Pie 225
⏱ Banana Cream Pie 226
⏱ Coconut Cream Pie 227
⏱ Sour Cherry-Berry Pie 229
⏱ Cran-Apple and Pear Pie 230
⏱ Tart Lemon Tart 232
⏱ Ginger-Spiced Key Lime Yogurt Pie 233
⏱ Wonderful Pear Tart 234
⏱ Plum Galette 235
⏱ Apple Crisp 239
⏱ Blueberry Crunch 240
⏱ Peach Cobbler 241
⏱ Pumpkin Custard 243

Rich Chocolate Pudding 244
Bread Pudding with Bourbon Caramel Sauce 245
Sticky Date and Toffee Pudding 246
Pumpkin Bread. 250
Banana Bread. 251
Chocolate Zucchini Bread. 252
Cranberry-Orange Bread 253
Crumbcake 254
Sweet Chocolate Chip Pull-Apart Bread. 255
Boston Brown Bread. 257
Southern Corn Bread 258
Blueberry Muffins 261
Lemon Poppy Seed Muffins. 262
Buttermilk Biscuits. 265
Cheesy Cheese Biscuits. 266
Lemon Blueberry Scones 267
Bacon Cheddar and Chives Scones 268
Basic White Buttermilk Bread 282
Braided Egg Bread. 283
Honey-Oatmeal Bread 285
Jeff's Potato Bread 286
Basic Hamburger Buns 288
No-Fail Rolls. 290
Crescent Rolls 291
Fluffy Dinner Rolls 292
Sesame-Topped Rolls 293
Molly's Sweet Cardamom Rolls 294
Cheese Soufflé 297
Chicken Potpie. 300
Potato-Beef Potpie 301
Goat Cheese and Tomato Tart. 302
Weeknight Pizza Dough 304
Calzones 305
Broccoli and Cheese Quiche with Potato Crust 307
Super Chocolate Cake. 312
Crazy-Good Pineapple Upside-Down Cake 313
Super-Easy Veggie Party Pizza 315
Cinnamon Spiced Cheesecake Bars 316
Apple Turnovers. 317
Cream Cheese and Cherry Danishes 318

Table of Contents

INTRODUCTION 1
    About This Book. 1
    Foolish Assumptions. 3
    Icons Used in This Book 3
    Beyond This Book 4
    Where to Go from Here 4

PART 1: BAKING ESSENTIALS. 5
CHAPTER 1: **Bake, For Goodness' Sake!** 7
    Knowing How to Get Started 8
        Getting organized 9
        Familiarizing yourself with baking techniques 9
        Practicing and practicing some more. 10
    Enjoying What You Bake. 10

CHAPTER 2: **Stocking Up** 11
    Flour: Focusing on the Main Ingredient 12
        Identifying the main types of flour 13
        Storing flour 15
    Sugar: Getting Sweet. 15
    Salt: Adding Some Seasoning 16
    Eggs: Yolking It Up 17
    Leaveners: A Baker's Best Pick-Me-Up .18
        Baking soda 19
        Baking powder. 19
        Cream of tartar 20
        Yeast 20
        Sourdough starter. 21
        Beaten egg yolks and egg whites .22
    Fats: Ramping Up Flavor and Mouthfeel 22
        Butter 22
        Shortening 24
        Lard 24
        Oil. 25
        Nonstick cooking spray. 25
    Liquids: Including Some Moisture. 26
    Chocolate and Cocoa: A Chocoholic's Dream 27
        Chocolate 28
        Cocoa. 29
    Add-Ins and Flavorings: Enhancing the Taste 29

Nuts 29
Raisins and other dried fruits 31
Oats 32
Peanut butter 32
Coconut 32
Liquors 32
Maple syrup and extract 33
Molasses 33
Spices, herbs, and extracts 33
Fresh fruits and veggies 35
Baking with Extras That Are Nice to Have on Hand 37

CHAPTER 3: **Going Over the Gear** 39
Familiarizing Yourself with Baking Pans 40
Baking (cookie) sheets 40
Baking (muffin) tins 41
Bundt and tube pans 41
Cake pans 42
Loaf pans 42
Pie plates (pans) 43
Springform pans 43
Including Basic Pots in Your Kitchen 44
Saucepans 44
Double boiler 44
Dutch oven 45
Utilizing Electric Tools to Bake 45
Air fryer 46
Blender 46
Food processor 46
Handheld mixer 47
Instant Pot or multicooker 48
Stand (table) mixer 48
Considering Other Essentials 49
Cooling racks 49
Cookie and biscuit cutters 50
Cutting boards 50
Knives 50
Measuring cups 52
Mixing bowls 53
Measuring spoons 53
Potholders and oven mitts 53
Rolling pin 54
Rolling mat 54
Scale (metric) 54
Spoons 55

Adding Other Great Gadgets 55
   Apple corer 55
   Box grater 55
   Cake tester 56
   Citrus juicer (reamer) 56
   Flour sifter 57
   Funnel 57
   Kitchen scissors 58
   Microplane 58
   Oven thermometer 58
   Pastry bags and tips 58
   Pastry blender 59
   Pastry brush 59
   Pie weights 60
   Sieve (strainer) 60
   Silpat 61
   Spatulas 61
   Timer 62
   Tongs 62
   Trivets 62
   Vegetable peeler 62
   Wire whisk 62

PART 2: BASIC TRAINING FOR BAKING 63

CHAPTER 4: **Familiarizing Yourself with Your Oven** 65
Knowing the Difference among the Three Types of Ovens 65
   Gas ovens 66
   Electric ovens 67
   Convection ovens 68
Positioning Your Racks 68
Preheating Your Oven — More Important Than You May Think 69
Gauging and Adjusting the Heat 70

CHAPTER 5: **Focusing on Basic Techniques** 71
Measuring Ingredients 71
   Nailing the measurements with a scale 72
   Measuring with teaspoons and tablespoons 73
   Measuring dry ingredients 73
   Measuring fats and other solids 73
   Measuring liquids 74
Preparing Pans 75
   Using solid shortening 75
   Lining a pan 76

Working with Eggs...78
    Separating an egg 78
    Whipping egg whites.....................................79
Whipping Heavy Cream 80
Working with Fruits...81
    Peeling and pitting fruits 81
    Zesting and sectioning citrus fruits...................82
Melting Chocolate 84
Scalding Milk 85
Toasting Nuts..86

CHAPTER 6: **Considering Allergies and Insensitivities
When Baking** 87
Examining Gluten- and Wheat-Free Baking...................88
    Gluten-free flours 88
    Gluten-free and wheat-free recipes 89
Moving beyond Eggs...89
Skipping Out On Nuts..90
Being Aware of Dairy Allergies..............................91
    Identifying dairy-free alternatives......................91
    Making dairy-free recipes..............................92

CHAPTER 7: **Getting Ready to Bake**.............................93
Preparing Your Kitchen......................................93
    Inspect your oven 94
    Organize your space 94
Working with Recipes 95
    Consider your skill level 95
    Understand the instructions 96
    Read the recipe all the way through before you start 96
    Check how many people it serves.......................97
    Take inventory 98
    Use the right tools for the job 98
Timing It Right 101
Baking at High Elevations...................................101
Keeping Your Kitchen Cool with Baking Alternatives.............102
Cleaning As You Go 104

PART 3: READY, SET, BAKE! 107
CHAPTER 8: **Understanding the Ins and Outs of Baking
Cookies** 109
Making Cookies like a Pro 110
    Measuring accurately 110
    Understanding the effect of fats.......................110
    Knowing the proper mixing technique..................110

Choosing the right pan 111
Spacing your cookies far enough apart 112
Starting with Drop Cookies 112
Shaping Shaped Cookies 123
Pressing Pressed Cookies. 135
Baking Rolled Cookies. 137
Rolling as easy as 1, 2, 3 138
Keeping in mind other tips. 139
Mastering Brownies and Bar Cookies .143

CHAPTER 9: **Baking Moist Cakes** 149
Focusing On Butter Cakes 149
Making Pound Cakes. 159
Creating Cupcakes. 163
Adding a Little Air: Sponge Cakes 166
Angel food cake 166
Rolling with the jelly rolls 169
Creating Cheesecakes. 176

CHAPTER 10: **Fixing Fabulous Frostings** .183
Finding Out More about Frostings 183
Knowing How Much to Make. 185
Making Quick Frostings 185
Trying Cooked Frostings. 189
Ready, Set, Frost!. 193
Frosting a cake. 194
Glazing a cake 195
Getting Fancy with Decorating 198
Choosing a pastry bag 198
Frostings for decorating 199
Tinting frosting. 199
Choosing a tip 199
Filling your bag. 201
Using your pastry bag. 202

CHAPTER 11: **Preparing Perfect Pies and Tarts**. 205
Picking the Proper Pie Plate. 206
Making Perfect Piecrusts 206
Mixing the dough. 206
Cutting in the fat 207
Choosing the right flour 207
Chilling the dough 208
Rolling out the dough 208
Transferring the crust to the pie plate 209

Getting Double-Crust Pie Ideas..................................213
    Solid top crust 213
    Lattice crust 213
    Cutout top crust...214
Making Simple Pastry Edges and Decorations 215
Creating Tantalizing Pies and Tarts...........................215
    Fruit and nut pies 216
    Cream pies 224
    Double-crust pies 228
Making To-Die-For Tarts..231
Troubleshooting Common Pie Problems............................236

CHAPTER 12: **Creating Crisps, Cobblers, and Other Delights** 237
Baking with Fruit 238
Making Custards and Puddings...................................242

CHAPTER 13: **Making Quick Breads, Muffins, and Biscuits** 247
Quick Tips for Quick Breads....................................248
    Sweet breads...249
    Savory breads 256
Making the Perfect Muffin 259
    Preparing the pans 259
    Going mini 260
    Magnificent muffins 260
Focusing on Biscuit Basics 263
    Mixing biscuit dough.......................................263
    Forming your biscuits 264
    Storing your biscuits 264

CHAPTER 14: **Rising with Yeast Breads** 269
Understanding the Role of Yeast Bread Ingredients 270
    Yeast 270
    Flour 272
    Sweeteners...274
    Salt...274
    Fat 274
    Eggs 275
    Liquids..275
Mixing and Kneading Breads.....................................275
    Getting a hold on mixing 275
    Preparing your work surface 276
    Kneading as easy as 1, 2, 3 276
Encouraging Bread to Rise — Yes, You Can Do It! 278
    Getting dough to rise in four easy steps 278
    Knowing when the dough is ready 279

Shaping and Baking the Loaves. 279
Baking Yeast Bread Recipes. 281
    Loaves 281
    Buns and rolls 287

CHAPTER 15: Going Savory with Baked Goods 295
Whipping Up Soufflés 295
Baking Tasty Potpies and Tarts 299
Going Italian — Calzones and Pizzas 303
Getting Creative with Quiches 306

CHAPTER 16: Baking with Mixes and Premade Doughs 309
Baking with Mixes 310
Baking with Refrigerated and Frozen Dough 314

PART 4: DEALING WITH OTHER IMPORTANT STUFF. 319
CHAPTER 17: Storing Your Creations. 321
Wrapping Your Baked Goods 321
    Plastic wrap 322
    Beeswax wraps 322
    Aluminum foil. 323
    Waxed paper 323
    Glassware or plastic 323
    Tins 324
Storing at Room Temperature. 324
    Cookies 325
    Cakes. 325
    Pies 326
    Bread 326
Keeping Things Cool 326
    Baked goods that should be chilled 327
    Cookies 327
    Pies 327
    Breads. 328
Freezing Your Baked Goodies 328
    Cookies 328
    Cookie dough 328
    Bread dough. 329
    Cakes. 329
    Pies 330
    Avoiding freezer burn 331

CHAPTER 18: **Making the Ordinary Extraordinary** 333

   Cutting Your Baked Goods Neatly and Evenly 333

      Cutting cakes and pies into even slices 334

      Cutting cheesecakes cleanly 335

      Cutting sheet cakes, bar cookies, and brownies 336

      Cutting loaves and rolled cakes 336

   Presenting with Flair 336

   Creating Quick, Spiffy Garnishes 337

      Garnishes for cakes 337

      Fruit garnishes 338

      Whipped cream and flavored creams 339

      Decorating plates 340

PART 5: THE PART OF TENS 341

CHAPTER 19: **Ten Ways to Boost Nutrition When Baking** 343

   Adding in Seeds 343

   Ramping Up the Nuts 344

   Exploring Whole Grains 344

   Scaling Back the Sugar 345

   Stirring in Fruits 345

   Grating in Greens 345

   Baking with Beans 346

   Focusing On Quality over Quantity 346

   Swapping in Fermented Foods 346

   Making Peace with Enjoying Desserts 346

CHAPTER 20: **Ten Ways to Get Kids Baking** 347

   Grocery Shopping 347

   Reading Recipes 348

   Working through the Math 348

   Crafting Science Experiments 348

   Encouraging Knife Skills 348

   Letting Kids Set the Pace 349

   Encouraging Explorations and Mistakes 349

   Finding Kid-Friendly Kitchen Tools 349

   Expanding Vocabulary 349

   Experiencing with Recipes 350

APPENDIX A: GLOSSARY OF BAKING TERMS 351

APPENDIX B: METRIC CONVERSION GUIDE 357

INDEX 361

Introduction

At some point in your life — maybe now because you're reading this book — the mystery of baking has attracted you. The desire to create becomes stronger than the desire to pick up a pack of cookies at the store, and you think, "Hey, I'm a smart person. I can do this!" And you can!

Knowing how baking works and which role each ingredient plays enables you to understand how to *bake* instead of how to just follow a recipe (there is a difference). When you understand how to bake and master the various techniques used in baking, you'll gain confidence in the kitchen and become a proficient baker. You'll also find yourself confidently experimenting with some recipes, too! So, roll up your sleeves, clean off the countertop, and get ready to bake.

About This Book

The purpose of this book is to fill you in on how to become a proficient and independent baker. You may feel like you know nothing now, but as you dive into this book, you'll become competent in the kitchen and realize baking skills are something you can easily master. This book acquaints you with familiar, as well as unfamiliar, ingredients, and also tells you a few things you may not know, such as the secret to flaky pastry crusts and how to zest a lemon. From organizing your kitchen to an efficient workspace to storing your baked good properly, this book gives you the tools you need to become a successful baker and plenty of tantalizing recipes to practice with.

This book introduces you to the *hows* and *whys* of baking. From mixing a batter to putting the finishing touches on your baked goods, you'll discover all kinds of information in this book. This book also explains various techniques for all kinds of baking situations — and with good technique, the sky is the limit. Practice makes perfect, so the more familiar you become with baking and handling your ingredients, the more proficient you will become as a baker.

Since the first edition of this book 20 years ago, the world of baking has exploded, from new techniques, trendy ingredients, and a newfound appreciation for old world recipes. Here's what you can find in this updated edition:

>> **More than 20 new recipes:** These new recipes address some of the recent trends in baking. In addition, recipes now have weighted measurements. Many bakers work with a metric scale to ensure accuracy with a recipe. Whether you're a beginner or an expert baker, a scale is an essential tool in your kitchen.

>> **New equipment:** Many kitchens are now equipped with Instant Pots (multi-cookers) and air fryers. Recipes that can be baked in some of these nifty tools have been updated with additional cooking instructions.

>> **Allergy considerations:** Ingredients also have come a long way, and although this book isn't an allergy-free book, I've taken time and consideration into recipes that are perfect for loved ones following a specific diet or have a need for an allergen-free recipe.

The recipes in this book are very straightforward and easy to understand. But here are a few notes on the ingredients, which apply to all the recipes:

>> All oven temperatures are given in Fahrenheit.

>> Unless specified in the ingredient list, you can use any degree of fat in milk (whole through skim cow's milk). You can also substitute dairy alternatives.

>> All eggs are large.

>> All flour is all-purpose flour, unless specified otherwise in the ingredients list.

>> All sugar is granulated sugar, unless specified otherwise in the ingredients list.

>> If a recipe calls for butter and not margarine, don't use margarine. A few recipes just won't taste good if margarine is substituted.

>> All dry ingredients are measured using nestled dry measuring cups (not the glass ones with the graded amounts on the side), and all ingredients are measured level, unless specified.

>> *Lemon zest* or *orange zest* refers to the outer colored peel, not any of the white pith.

>> Generally, canned, fresh, or frozen fruit can be substituted, unless the recipe specifies one or the other.

And keep in mind:

>> If you don't know about an ingredient or technique in a recipe, be sure to check in Parts 1 or 2 for an explanation.

>> Make sure you have all the equipment you need. Double-check that the pans you have are the right size before you get started.

>> You can double most recipes in this book, unless the recipe states otherwise.

The recipes are basic but delicious and interesting. All of them can be embellished a little with additional ingredients, frostings, whipped cream, or powdered sugar. They use easy-to-find ingredients and simple instructions for extraordinary results.

Foolish Assumptions

This handy guide is a tool for both beginning and experienced bakers. No matter which group you fall in, this book will open you up to new ideas, techniques, and recipes. Here are some assumptions I do make about you:

>> You already know your way around a kitchen, but you probably favor the top of your stove more often than the oven.

>> You may rely too often on the grocery store or local bakery for your baked goods.

>> You love to bake or you love the idea of baking. You don't have any prior baking knowledge to use this book. You won't get lost either because I explain every technique and ingredient in plain English.

>> You want to become a better baker, no matter your skill level. You'll discover your untapped talent and also master a lifetime of skills, tips, and shortcuts to keep you baking for years to come.

Icons Used in This Book

Look for these icons peppered throughout the book to help you find helpful bits of information:

WARNING

This icon staves off potential mistakes or mishaps in the kitchen. Heed the warning to avoid a kitchen calamity.

REMEMBER

I use this icon when you need to keep a "baking basic" in mind so nothing bad happens.

TECHNICAL STUFF

This icon is used to identify information that may be just a little more than you actually need to know for successful baking, but that is interesting nonetheless. If you're in a hurry and just want to get the information you absolutely need, you can skip the paragraphs marked by this icon and come back to them later when you have more time.

TIP

Here you'll find little gems of information that you may not have known about the recipe or technique you're using. This icon points to information that will make things just a little bit easier to do or save you time.

Beyond This Book

This book is chock-full of tips and other pieces of helpful advice you can use as you're baking to your heart's content. In addition, check out the book's Cheat Sheet at www.dummies.com and search for "Baking For Dummies Cheat Sheet" for information and resources to reference on a regular basis.

Where to Go from Here

Pick your favorite spot and begin. Perhaps you want to brush up on some technique know-how in Chapter 5 or dive right into your first batch of cookies in Chapter 8. Because you don't have to read this book cover to cover to make the most of it, you can start anywhere.

Above all, enjoy yourself. Baking should be fun and an activity you share with your loved ones. Whether the inspiration for baking is remembering a birthday, making a sweet treat for the family or friends, bringing dessert for a dinner party, or welcoming a new neighbor or co-worker, you can certainly taste a difference when something is baked with love. You're saying that the people you're baking for are important enough that you took the time to do something special. Happy baking!

1
Baking Essentials

Build upon your foundation of baking.

Discover some common ingredients that you should consider keeping in your kitchen and their role in baking.

Create a well-stocked kitchen, from appliances to gadgets.

Chapter **1**

Bake, For Goodness' Sake!

So you've decided you want to find out how to bake? Congratulations! Perhaps you have tinkered in the kitchen but feel uncertain about what you're doing, or maybe your attempts at creating something in the oven have not been very successful. Or perhaps you just have some general questions about baking. Reading this book is a good start for getting answers to the fundamental questions that arise when you bake. Soon you'll be well on your way to becoming a better baker!

Baking is rewarding in many ways. First and most basic, it allows you to feed yourself and provides you with the ability to choose what you eat. You can give up the ammonium alginate, disodium guanylate, and guar gum you find in cake mixes. Your breads will no longer be preserved with sodium propionate. And your pies will be heptylparaben-free. Welcome to the world of butter, sugar, flour, and vanilla.

There's something deeply satisfying about taking those basic ingredients and turning them into something that everyone loves, such as cakes and cookies. Freshly baked treats say "You are special to me" to the people you share them with. And recipients feel special because you took the time to create something for them. Welcome a new neighbor with fresh bread, surprise your office workers with a crumbcake for their coffee break, or treat your children to homemade cookies.

Baking is a way to enjoy the simple pleasures of life. An afternoon spent in the kitchen baking bread or making cookies to pack in lunches for the rest of the week is a nice gift to give yourself or your family. Mixing up a batch of cookies with your children, roommates, or loved ones is a great activity that doesn't cost a lot of money and that will give you lasting memories.

Baking really is a lot of fun when you feel comfortable in the kitchen and at ease with what you're making. Unfortunately, baking can also be a source of great anxiety and frustration when you're not sure what you're doing or feel like the ingredients are staging a rebellion against you. But it's time to calm the troops. This chapter serves as the jumping-off point to the world of baking.

Knowing How to Get Started

If baking is so great, then why does it sometimes seem like it's so hard? Did you ever get a chance to practice the basics? How many bad experiences have you had in the kitchen with burned cookies or dry cakes? You can forget about all that you don't know (and perhaps your past kitchen disasters) and look toward a new horizon. You're about to equip yourself with the knowledge of how to bake.

Baking differs dramatically from other forms of cooking. It involves a kind of magic. From mixing up batters to working bread doughs firmly but gently to watching your dough rise, baking brings a spectacular feeling. Other forms of cooking are more about sustenance — feeding hunger. But baking is something special. It's both an art and a science. And the science really does count — instructions and ingredients work together to create delicious results. Wondrous aromas will waft from your kitchen, filling your home with flavors today and sweet memories tomorrow.

Sometimes it's hard to know where to start when you're trying something new. Chapters 2 through 7 are a good start. They not only help familiarize you with *what* you're baking but also explain *how* to bake. Knowing how to bake involves more than knowing how to read a recipe and following the instructions; it's also about understanding the following:

>> The variety of ingredients available

>> The roles of the various ingredients in a recipe

>> What happens when you combine certain ingredients

>> Various baking techniques

When you equip yourself with this knowledge, you'll discover how easy and fun baking can be!

Getting organized

As you set out to bake, the most important thing is to get organized. Kitchen counters are often dumping grounds for dirty dishes, yesterday's mail, car keys, or stray kitchen items that haven't been properly put away. Take the 5 minutes it takes (if that much!) to clean off the space you need. Visit Chapter 7 for more tips and ideas for organizing your baking space.

TIP

Before you crack your first egg, be sure that you have all ingredients on deck. Nothing is more frustrating than thinking you have a full box of raisins on hand and then finding that you have only half the amount you need when you go to pour them out. Read more about stocking up on staple ingredients in Chapter 2.

And one more thing: Do you know where both your beaters are for your electric mixer? Are you sure you have both the top and the sides for the springform pan you want to use? How about all the parts for your food processor? One thing I've learned over the years is that you can never be too prepared when you start to bake. Sometimes I tear my kitchen apart looking for my square pan, only to remember that I lent it to my neighbors. Or I search high and low for parts to my mixer, only to find them on the drainboard or put away in a different drawer. Have the tools you need in front of you before you start baking. Check out Chapter 3 for more details.

Finally, make friends with your oven. If you haven't paid much attention to it lately, read some helpful advice in Chapter 4 to make sure that your oven is in proper working order. No matter how good the recipes are, if your oven is off, there is little hope for baking success.

Familiarizing yourself with baking techniques

If your eyes glaze over after reading a recipe, make a quick stop at Chapter 5 to get to know the common, and not so common, baking terms and techniques. There, you discover how to zest, fold, cut in, and whip. You should be aware that sometimes cooking terms dictate the kitchen tool you use.

For example, you whip or whisk eggs with a wire whisk, you cut in butter with a pastry blender, and you fold with a rubber spatula. If a recipe uses equipment you don't have, you have time to consider alternatives or choose another recipe. So understanding the techniques not only helps you know what to do but also lets you know whether you need a specific tool to do it properly.

Practicing and practicing some more

If you ask any professional bakers or cooks whom you respect how they acquired all their baking talent, I'm sure that you'll discover they spent a lot of time practicing their craft. The more you practice baking, the more you'll get a feel for it and the more successful you'll be.

Eventually, you'll know by the look and feel of certain foods what's going on with your dough or batter. You'll find yourself adding a pinch of this or that or kneading the dough a little more or less just because you know how it *should* feel or behave. Practice is the key to successful baking, and Part 3 is full of recipes to practice with. You'll discover what a good cake batter should look like, how bread dough should feel, and what to do if your recipes aren't turning out the way you want.

Practicing baking is lots of fun, too, because the results are usually delicious and people are always happy to participate in your experimenting. I was quite popular with family and friends as I was developing and testing the recipes for this book, so I know that you, too, will be just as popular as you try these recipes.

Enjoying What You Bake

Who doesn't get excited when a co-worker or family member bakes up a treat? Everyone is happy when homemade desserts are brought in to be shared. The reason you bake dozens of cookies or multiple loaves of bread is to share the results. There never was a baking book titled *Baking for One or Two* because baked goods are meant to be shared.

Cakes will last for days, and cookies can stick around for a week or so if stored properly. So be sure to read Chapter 17 to pick up some great tricks and hints on how to keep every last bite of pie tasting as good as the first ones.

If you want to really wow your fellow friends, turn to Chapter 18 for some easy and neat ideas to spruce up your finished product. You can find some tips on how to package your baked goods or add some extra special touches that elevate the ordinary to the extraordinary.

Chapter 2

Stocking Up

A well-stocked pantry really makes a difference when it comes to baking for several reasons:

» It's a huge time-saver because it eliminates a trip to the grocery store.

» It enables you to create delicious treats whenever the mood strikes.

» If you happen to run out of one ingredient, a well-stocked pantry will ensure that you have a substitute or an extra ingredient on hand.

You don't need a lot of room to have a good pantry, but you need to be organized and store your ingredients well to maximize not only space but also the ingredients' shelf life. This chapter presents a list of staples you should have on hand when you begin baking. Of course, you don't have to purchase everything all at once, but you may be surprised at how quickly you'll build your pantry and how accommodating it will be to have a well-stocked kitchen for future baking.

STORING BULK FOODS

TIP

If your supermarket or natural-foods store has a bulk section, purchasing ingredients there is an economical choice. However, never store items in the plastic bags for more than a week. Instead, save your jars and containers! Washed, clean jars or containers from spaghetti sauce, salsa, yogurt, peanut butter, and applesauce make great containers to hold items you purchase in bulk. Baby food jars, in particular, recycle into great spice jars. Don't forget to mark your jars with masking tape and permanent marker. (Don't use nonpermanent marker — it can rub off, and you'll be left wondering what you put in those jars!) You may someday need a reminder of what's in them and when you bought it! Labeling and dating each product as you get it is a good idea.

When shopping for your pantry, be a smart shopper. Look for items on sale at your local grocery store. If space is not an issue, buy two or three popular items when they go on sale (my theory is you can never have enough baking soda or sugar). Also, take a look in discount stores and those ever-popular dollar stores. Recently, I found nonstick cooking spray at the dollar store and stocked up, because one can costs double or triple that amount in my local grocery store. This also goes for spices; I almost always purchase spices "loose" at a local store that sells them prebagged. I never spend more than 75 cents for what most people pay $3 to $4 in a supermarket. You may be surprised at how inexpensively you can stock your pantry when you shop around.

If you hope to bake a lot or the holidays are coming, it is good to purchase flour, sugar, chocolate, and nuts in bulk at warehouse clubs. Of course, do this only if you will go through the ingredients quickly. If you're a part-time baker, I find that the "bulk section" of my food store is good if I need smaller amounts of ingredients. I can purchase just what I need, and there is no waste — perfect for unusual spices you may only need during holiday baking, too!

Your dry pantry can be in the cabinets, on shelves, in a cupboard or in a designated pantry or closet. Make sure to keep the floor clean. Remove everything and wipe down the shelves at least twice a year (spring and fall are good times for this type of cleaning). And, of course, if you spill anything, clean it up right away to avoid any sort of animal or insect infestation.

Flour: Focusing on the Main Ingredient

Flour is the primary ingredient for most cakes, cookies, pastries, and breads. Although it is one of the most basic baking ingredients, it also can be the most confusing, because of the wide variety available on grocery store shelves. Some flours are perfect for bread baking but disastrous for piecrusts or tender pastries. What makes a flour good for one recipe and bad for another? The amount of protein it contains. The more protein a flour has, the more gluten it will produce when it's kneaded. And the more gluten you have, the less tender your baked good will be.

Gluten is the protein that forms weblike structures present in wheat and other flours. When the flour is moistened and the bread is kneaded, or doughs and batters are mixed together, gluten forms and adds an elastic and cohesive nature to the food. This elasticity allows the dough to expand and trap the carbon dioxide, produced by the leavening, which makes the dough rise and stretch. Gluten makes it all possible!

Here I touch on flour using in baking and what you need to know about storing your flour.

Identifying the main types of flour

Several different kinds of flour are available for baking; all-purpose, cake, bread, self-rising, and whole wheat flour are just a few. Become acquainted with three basic types of flour: all-purpose flour, cake flour, and bread flour.

>> **All-purpose flour:** It's a blend of hard and soft wheat flours. The presence of more and tougher gluten in the hard wheat results in a rather elastic product. This produces the texture you want for cakes and cookies.

Bleached and unbleached all-purpose flours can be used interchangeably, but unbleached flour has a higher nutritional value. Southern flours, such as White Lily, are made with a softer wheat, which means that they have cake flour–like qualities. Southern flour is great for tender biscuits and piecrusts.

>> **Cake flour:** This flour is made with soft wheat, producing less gluten when mixed, so your cake will be more delicate, with a slightly crumbly texture. When purchasing cake flour, don't buy self-rising cake flour unless the recipe specifically calls for it. If you do buy it by mistake, omit the baking powder or baking soda and salt from the recipe.

>> **Bread flour:** It has a higher gluten-forming protein content, making the dough nice and elastic. This makes it ideal for making bread.

GOING BEYOND WHEAT FLOUR

In the United States wheat is king, and it's the only flour type you'll find in many grocery stores. However, should you travel to Europe, you can find a large section of flours, from spelt, rye, einkorn, and semolina within each grocery store you visit. Each of these flours are used in cakes, cookies, and breads all throughout Europe, yet for some reason this appreciation of old-world grains was lost in the United States during the Industrial Revolution.

In this new edition I have added suggestions in some recipes on how to use or integrate more of these flours into your recipes. Rye is technically a grass and lower in gluten. Spelt, or *dinklmehl* in Germany, is also a lower gluten old-world grain. That means these grains will yield more dense baked goods.

If you're curious about adding in more of these grains and having a wider variety of grain baked goods, start by cutting ¼ to ½ of the wheat-based flours and adding in ¼ to ½ of a different grain flour. For instance, if you're making the Peanut Butter Cookies from Chapter 8, try using half spelt flour in the recipe or replacing ¼ cup all-purpose flour with ¼ cup rye flour. Look for these suggestions throughout the book and give them a whirl!

If you're baking gluten-free, you can try using a gluten-free oat flour or a gluten-free all-purpose flour blend, now available at many grocery stores or online, such as Bob's Red Mill Gluten Free Flour.

In addition to grain-based flours, nut flours like almond flour, hazelnut flour, and peanut flour are now being used in cakes and cookies. Check out the Lebkuchen recipe in Chapter 8 or the Gluten-Free Chocolate Hazelnut Cake in Chapter 9. Nut flours are full of flavor and offer a delicious grainy texture in each bite.

TIP

If your recipe calls for cake flour and you have only all-purpose flour on hand, you can substitute 1 cup *minus* 2 tablespoons all-purpose flour for 1 cup of cake flour. If you need all-purpose flour and have only cake flour on hand, substitute 1 cup *plus* 2 tablespoons of cake flour for 1 cup of all-purpose flour. The texture will be different, but if you have no other choice, using it is okay. If you have instant flour on hand, such as Wondra, combine 2 tablespoons in the cup measure, then add enough all-purpose flour to make 1 cup (which would be about ¾ cup plus 2 tablespoons). That will also give you a flour-like cake flour.

Storing flour

Don't store any of your flours in the paper sacks you buy them in. Instead, transfer them into airtight canisters and store them in a cool, dry place to make sure your flour won't absorb any odors or off-flavors. Label the containers to ensure that you can tell the difference between the different varieties (they tend to look the same out of their bags). Flour can last up to six months if stored properly in the pantry and indefinitely if stored in the freezer. If you bought the flour from a natural food store, place it in the freezer for a few days to make sure nothing will hatch.

If you use flour slowly, you can store your flour in the freezer. Double-bag the flour in sealable freezer bags and be sure to label it. Flour stored in the freezer can last for several years.

Sugar: Getting Sweet

Sugar, another basic in baking, gives tenderness and sweetness to doughs and batters. Sugar also causes browning because it *caramelizes* (turns brown) when heated. Sugar also is a food source for yeast, making it rise.

In baking, you need to have three different types of sugar on hand: granulated sugar, confectioners' sugar, and brown sugar (light or dark).

>> **Granulated sugar:** It's the standard white sugar, either from sugar cane or sugar beets, and is the most popular and readily available sweetener in baking. Superfine sugar is a form of granulated sugar that dissolves easily in liquid. You can make your own superfine sugar: Place 1 cup of granulated sugar in the blender, cover, and process for 1 minute. Let it sit for about 1 minute longer to let the "smoke" settle. This produces 1 cup of superfine sugar. Sometimes superfine sugar is used in frostings and certain cakes. It dissolves quickly, so it doesn't need much cooking time.

>> **Confectioners' (powdered) sugar:** This sugar has been refined to a powder and contains a small amount of cornstarch to prevent lumping. Confectioners' sugar dissolves instantly in liquid and has a smoothness that makes it a popular choice for frostings, icings, and whipped toppings. It's also perfect for dusting cake tops and brownies. If your confectioners' sugar becomes lumpy, you can sift it.

>> **Brown sugar:** Both light and dark is a mixture of granulated sugar and molasses. Brown sugar has a deeper flavor than granulated sugar. The color of brown sugar depends on the amount of molasses mixed in; dark brown

sugar has more. Light brown sugar is the most common type used in baking, but the more assertively flavored dark brown sugar is also used. Recipes specify which brown sugar to use when it makes a difference; otherwise, you can use whichever you have on hand.

>> **Demerara sugar:** It's a sugar made from the first pressing from the sugar cane. The large sugar crystals and light brown color have a unique molasses-like flavor. This sugar can add texture to baked goods, both baked inside and as a topping.

REMEMBER

When measuring brown sugar for recipes, be sure to pack it into the measuring cup for accurate measuring.

TIP

When exposed to air for an extended amount of time, brown sugar tends to harden. If this happens to your sugar, there's a quick fix: Place the hardened brown sugar in a heatproof bowl and place the bowl in a baking pan containing about an inch of water. Tightly cover the entire baking pan with aluminum foil and place it in a 200-degree oven for 20 minutes or until softened. Use the softened brown sugar immediately, because it will re-harden when it cools. You can also use your microwave to soften brown sugar. Place the hardened sugar in a microwavable dish. Add a wedge of apple. Cover and microwave on high for 30 to 45 seconds. Let stand for about 30 seconds, then use normally.

Store all your sugars in airtight containers in a cool, dry place.

Salt: Adding Some Seasoning

Salt is invaluable in the kitchen. It not only adds its own flavor but also helps bring out the flavor of the other ingredients. When used in baking, following the precise amount called for in the recipe is important.

Three types of salt are available for baking:

>> **Table salt:** This is by far the most popular variety.

>> **Kosher salt:** This salt has less of a salty taste than table salt and can be coarser.

>> **Sea salt:** This salt has a fresher taste and is usually used in salt grinders.

All these salts can be used measure for measure in baking.

TIP

Most table salt has an anticaking agent added to help prevent it from clumping. However, on humid days (especially during the summertime) salt still tends to stick or clump. To prevent this, add about a teaspoon of rice to your saltshaker. The rice will absorb the moisture and keep your salt free-flowing. You never want to add the rice to anything you bake, though. If you need to get the rice out of your salt, run the salt through a fine-mesh strainer.

Eggs: Yolking It Up

Eggs thicken custards and sauces, help cakes to rise and be tender, and enrich and add sheen to baked doughs. Eggs come in two different colors — white and brown — but there's no nutritional difference between them.

Eggshell color and color of the yolk (light yellow to deep orange) are the results of the breed and diet of the chicken and say nothing about the nutritional value or quality of the eggs.

Always buy large, fresh eggs. All the recipes in this book were tested with Grade A large eggs. Egg sizes are determined by their weight and volume, so substituting one egg size for another can affect the outcome. For example, two large eggs equal approximately ½ cup. It takes three medium eggs to equal the same ½ cup. Feel free to use free-range or organic eggs in any of the recipes in this book, as long as they're the right size.

REMEMBER

How do you know your eggs are fresh? An easy way to tell is to place the egg in a bowl of tap water. If the egg sinks to the bottom, it's fresh. If the egg stands up and bobs on the bottom, it isn't so fresh. If it floats, it's likely to be rotten. What makes the eggs float? Eggs naturally have a small pocket of air. As they age, this pocket increases, which causes the eggs to float in water. Check the expiration date on the box to ensure that your eggs are the freshest available.

WARNING

Do not store your eggs in the refrigerator door. This is the warmest part of the refrigerator, and you want your eggs to be cold. Keep the eggs in the carton and store them in the refrigerator. That way, you'll always know the expiration date on the carton, and you'll know which eggs to use first. Keep them away from strong odors as well.

TAKING CARE WITH EGGS

You need to handle your eggs with TLC because they can carry *salmonella,* a bacteria that can cause dangerous food poisoning. Although salmonella is rare, prevention is the best cure. Of course, pregnant women, young children, the elderly, and those with a compromised immune system should not eat anything that contains raw or under-cooked eggs. Here are some tips that can help:

- **Always buy the freshest eggs possible.** Buy only the number of eggs you will use within two weeks' time to ensure the freshness of your supply. If you don't use eggs that often, try to buy them by the half-dozen.

- **Be sure to wash your hands with hot, soapy water before and after handling raw eggs.** If you use a bowl to hold raw eggs, wash and dry the bowl before reusing it for another purpose.

- **Don't store eggs in the egg holder on the door of the refrigerator.** It might be convenient, but it's also the warmest part of the refrigerator. Salmonella doesn't grow in temperatures cooler than 40 degrees. And it's killed at temperatures above 160 degrees.

- **Never use an egg with a cracked shell.** If you detect an off-odor after you have cracked an egg, discard it immediately.

- **If a recipe calls for eggs at room temperature, allow the eggs to sit at room temperature for 20 minutes to reach room temperature.** Never use eggs left at room temperature for more than two hours.

- **If you're using farm-fresh eggs, store on the counter and don't wash the eggs.** Fresh eggs can be stored in a cool spot for one week without refrigeration. Most places in Europe only sell fresh eggs at room temperature, so if you're traveling and can't find the eggs, look beyond the refrigerated cases.

Leaveners: A Baker's Best Pick-Me-Up

Leaveners cause a dough or batter to rise by producing carbon dioxide, which rises throughout the batter and gives it a light, porous texture. There are two types of leaveners: chemical and yeast. Chemical leaveners include baking soda, baking powder, and cream of tartar. Yeast is just that, yeast — which, if you want to get technical, is a fungal leavener. Here I delve into the most common leaveners.

Now for a quick bit of Chemistry 101: When an acid and an alkaline are combined in the presence of a liquid, carbon dioxide is formed. All three elements are needed to produce the rise. When they're combined, the reaction is immediate, and, thanks to the heat of the oven, the gases in the batter expand, acting as another rising agent. Of course, too much rise is not desirable, because then the cake or bread or whatever you're baking will fall.

Baking soda

Otherwise known as *sodium bicarbonate*, baking soda is an alkali that must be mixed with something acidic (such as lemon juice, buttermilk, chocolate, or molasses) to react. Because baking soda reacts immediately, you should place the batter in the oven as soon as you've finished putting it together. If you taste baking soda, you will feel it tingle on your tongue.

When mixed with an acidic ingredient such as sour milk, buttermilk, yogurt, or citrus, baking soda acts as a leavening agent for cookies, cakes, and muffins. But baking soda has many other uses in and around the kitchen (listed here), so keeping a couple boxes on hand is always a good idea. Here are some other uses for baking soda:

>> **Removing coffee stains from metal pots or ceramic mugs:** Just sprinkle a tablespoon or two inside the pot, rub with a dishcloth, and watch the stain disappear.

>> **Destroying odors and keeping your refrigerator and freezer fresh:** Arm & Hammer now makes a special design just for the refrigerator and freezer.

>> **Putting out grease fires:** Keep a box of baking soda near the stove in case of an emergency.

>> **Softening your skin in a hot bath.** I like to have a box in the bathroom to add to my bath after a day of baking in the kitchen — it softens my skin and keeps me fresh-smelling!

Don't substitute baking soda and baking powder for one another.

Baking powder

Baking powder usually comes in a small, round, sturdy container with an airtight lid. Baking powder is essential for cakes, cookies, muffins, and quick breads and acts as the leavening agent. Choose double-acting baking powder, which is the most readily available.

Baking powder contains both an acid and an alkali (which is almost always baking soda), so just the addition of liquid is necessary to create a rise. Double-acting baking powder is true to its name — it reacts twice: once when the liquid is mixed in and then again when the batter is placed in the oven. Today, almost all baking powder sold in the United States is double-acting; however, should you travel to Europe most baking powder is single-acting and doesn't produce the same rising effect.

WARNING

Although baking powder contains baking soda, don't substitute one for the other. Too much baking powder will make your baked goods taste acidic and may cause the product to collapse.

Baking powder can be stored in its own container, but if your baking powder has been sitting around for several months, be sure to test it for potency. Dissolve 1 teaspoon in ¼ cup of hot water. If it doesn't foam within a few seconds, it's time to get a new container. Be sure to check expiration dates on baking powder before purchasing or using.

TIP

In a pinch, you can make your own baking powder. Combine ¼ teaspoon baking soda and ½ teaspoon cream of tartar to equal 1 teaspoon baking powder. Or you can use 1 teaspoon baking soda plus 2 teaspoons cream of tartar for each cup of flour called for in the recipe. If you do make your own baking powder, make just what you need for the recipe; it can't be stored.

Cream of tartar

After the manufacturing of wine, the acid left in the wine barrels is made into cream of tartar. Not widely used in baking, cream of tartar is generally added to egg whites when whipping to help stabilize them and keep their shape. Cream of tartar is sold with all the other spices in the supermarket. It's good to have on hand because you can mix it with baking soda if you run out of baking powder (see the preceding section). It's also often used in candy making.

Yeast

Yeast is the leavening agent for breads and rolls. Mostly used in bread making, yeast gets its rising power from the combination of the right amount of warmth, food for it to eat (sugar), and liquid, which causes the yeast to release carbon dioxide.

In general, here are the two types of yeast:

>> **Active dry yeast,** which I use for all the recipes in this book, is available in most supermarkets in premeasured packets, containing ¼ ounce (or about

1 tablespoon). You can also buy active dry yeast in jars that contain larger amounts.

TIP

Dissolve it in lukewarm water, no hotter than 110 degrees, which is actually just slightly warmer than lukewarm. Test the water on the inside of your wrist or run the tap over a candy thermometer until you reach this temperature. If you're unsure, it's better to err on the side of cooler water than hotter because all yeast will die if exposed to temperatures over 120 degrees.

>> **Fresh compressed yeast** is moist yeast, available in 0.6-ounce squares. A square of fresh yeast can be substituted for one package of active dry yeast.

You can also find bread machine yeast, which I don't recommend for any of the recipes in this book. It's a special strain of fine-granulated, dehydrated yeast, specially designed to dissolve during the kneading and mixing processes of bread machines. Another type of yeast is rapid-rise or quick-acting yeast, which is just another strain of dehydrated yeast. Although this type of yeast can be substituted for active dry yeast measure for measure, I don't often use it. I haven't found it to significantly reduce rising time for my breads and am somewhat wary of its sustained rising power. If you do choose to use this variety of yeast, be sure not to *proof* it (to dissolve it in water and sugar before mixing it into the flour mixture to make sure that it's working). It may expire before your dough finishes rising.

REMEMBER

Before starting any recipe, be sure to check the expiration date on your package of yeast. Don't bother trying to use yeast that has passed that date. I like to store active dry yeast in the refrigerator to ensure its freshness, although you don't have to. You must store compressed cake yeast in the refrigerator or freezer because it's highly perishable. You can also proof your yeast to make sure that it's still alive.

Sourdough starter

Sourdough starters are made by fermenting flour and water. It takes about two weeks to grow your own, and you can purchase one through King Arthur Flour's website (https://shop.kingarthurbaking.com/) or pop onto your local neighborhood app or Facebook group and see if someone would be willing to share their starter.

Starter can be used to replace dry yeast. One cup of bubbly starter can replace 2 teaspoons of dry yeast. Additionally, you'll need to reduce the amount of flour and liquid used in the recipe. One cup of starter is 300 grams, so typically I reduce the flour by 150 grams and the water by 100 to 150 grams. Dry yeast has powerful rising power, quickly growing and releasing gasses in an hour, whereas sourdough starter has a slower rising process, from 6 hours to 12 hours. To find out more about growing your own starter or baking with sourdough starter, check out my other book, *Bread Making For Dummies* (John Wiley & Sons, Inc.).

Beaten egg yolks and egg whites

Beating egg yolks or egg whites can provide leavening power in a recipe. Cakes such as sponge cakes only use the leavening power of eggs to give the cake a beautiful, light, and spongy rise. Remember the following:

» Egg yolks need to be beaten with a whisk, either by hand or with a mixer with sugar until light yellow in color, and they produce ribbon-like batter when the whisk is pulled from the batter.

» Egg whites, also beaten with a whisk attachment by hand or mixer, can be beaten to different stages. Egg whites used in leavening often are beaten until stiff peaks form. When the whisk is pulled from the batter, the peaks stand straight up and don't flop over (soft peak stage).

Be sure not to overwhip the egg whites because they'll break, losing their leavening power and weeping liquid. The Tres Leches Cake with Mango in Chapter 9 is a perfect example of a sponge cake.

Fats: Ramping Up Flavor and Mouthfeel

In baking *fat* is just a generic way of referring to butter, margarine, lard, oil, and shortening. How rich a cake, pastry, cookie, or other baked item tastes depends largely on the type of fat used in it and how the fat was incorporated. Although fat has gotten a bad reputation, it really does play an important role in baking, adding tenderness and flavor to baked goods. It also retains moisture and helps the leaveners in batters.

Several different types of fats are used in baking, which I discuss in the following sections. Although butter, stick margarines, and shortenings are pretty interchangeable, using the ingredient the recipe calls for is always best.

Butter

Of all the fats, butter has the best flavor for baking. Most professional bakers wouldn't think of baking with anything else. It's made from the richness of cream and gives a wonderful melt-in-your-mouth taste to baked goods. Here I break down what you need to know about butter.

Butter varies in taste from brand to brand, so finding the brand you like is important. Because butter can be expensive compared to your other choices (margarine, oil, shortening, and so on), your best choice is usually the brand that's on sale.

Taking a closer look at butter

At the market, butter comes in two forms:

>> **Whipped in tubs:** Whipped butter gives a much different texture to baked goods because it has air whipped into it.

>> **Sticks:** For baking, choose the stick form.

You also have another choice:

>> Salted

>> Unsalted

For the recipes in this book, it doesn't really matter which one you use, although you may want to choose unsalted butter for less salt content in your baked goods. Most professional cooks are butter purists and use only unsalted butter for baking. They vow that salty butter will alter the taste of their recipes, so they like to control that by choosing only unsalted. Personally, I haven't yet found a recipe where the salted or unsalted butter has made or broken a recipe, but I'm sure that many would passionately disagree. I respect their choices, but I believe that the choice is yours. No need to get too fussy here.

Storing and using butter

Keep butter wrapped in the refrigerator, away from strong odors (the butter compartment of your refrigerator is always a good choice). You can also freeze butter (which is a great reason to load up when there's a sale). Just remember that butter is a sponge for odors, which can dramatically change its flavor. So wrap your butter in aluminum foil or seal it well in plastic wrap or plastic bags before freezing and rotate your stock (first in, first out). Think about storing your butter near an open box of baking soda, too.

Butter will keep frozen for up to one year, and in the refrigerator for several weeks. If you're in doubt about freshness, just give it a taste. It should taste like nothing but butter. When butter goes bad, it becomes rancid, which is indicated by a bad odor and taste. If it has picked up refrigerator odor, you will also be able to easily detect that.

One stick of butter or margarine weighs 4 ounces (114 grams) and equals 8 table-spoons or ½ cup.

There's nothing like butter, which imparts its own fresh, creamy flavor to baking. But stick margarine can be substituted in recipes where butter is called for, unless otherwise stated.

European butters are all the rage in markets these days, but what is the difference between American butters and European butters? European butters are cultured butters, often with slightly higher butterfat, around 82 to 85 percent. The color is a deeper yellow hue, and the flavors may have a slight tang. American butters are monitored and have at least 80 percent butterfat. Even though you may think the two butters can be easily swapped for one another in baking, I don't recommend it when making American cookie recipes. Higher butterfat may create more spread and unusual outcome in baking.

Shortening

Shortening is 100 percent fat and is great for creaming and whipping because it doesn't break down or melt (like butter can) from the friction created by creaming fats. Many bakers swear by vegetable shortening for the flakiest piecrusts. Solid vegetable shortening is great for incorporating air into the batter, which gives added volume to cookies and cakes and makes them softer and spongier.

Unfortunately, shortening doesn't impart much flavor to baked goods (although its lack of flavor makes it ideal for greasing cookie sheets and pans). Although there are butter-flavored shortenings, they still fall short of the real thing. Shortening is a good choice when the flavor of the fat isn't that important. For example, you may want to use shortening for a spice or chocolate cake, and it makes a great choice for crunchy chocolate chip cookies. It's a bad choice for sugar cookies, however, because butter is an important flavoring ingredient in that recipe. Substitute shortening for butter, measure for measure. You also can use half butter and half shortening in some baking recipes.

Solid vegetable shortening comes in cans and, unopened, can be stored indefinitely. Once opened, it will last for several years if it's stored in an airtight container.

Lard

Lard is rendered pork fat, which is 100 percent animal fat. Lard makes for a great flaky piecrust, and the pork fat gives good flavor, especially good for savory recipes, and is inexpensive. You usually can find lard in the supermarket where the shortening is kept. You also can get lard from a butcher. Piecrusts aside, lard isn't recommended for cakes, cookies, or other baked goods because of the strong flavor of the pork fat. When serving, you may want to inform your guests that there is lard in the crust in case there are any vegetarians in the crowd.

Oil

Oils impart a tenderness and moistness to baked items. Mild-flavored vegetable oils such as corn, canola, or peanut are often called for in quick-bread, muffin, and some cake recipes. Oil also can be used to grease baking sheets or pans.

Vegetable oils are a good choice in baking because they're low in saturated fats and contain no cholesterol. When oil is called for in a recipe, be sure to choose one with a very mild flavor, such as safflower, canola, vegetable, peanut, or corn. I learned this the hard way. When I was a beginning baker, I once decided to make fresh blueberry muffins for guests visiting from Russia. The only oil I could find in the kitchen was extra-virgin olive oil, so I used it. Although the muffins looked fine, the assertive flavor the olive oil gave to the muffins made them pretty unpleasant-tasting (although the jolt was better than coffee!). Our guests were extremely gracious and even sampled one or two, but in the end we used the muffins to feed the birds. However, you can use light or pure olive oil for baking because it doesn't have the same flavor qualities that extra-virgin olive oil has.

You don't have to refrigerate vegetable oils. Refined oils will keep for a year or longer in an airtight container, whereas, unrefined oils, such as unrefined coconut oil are best used within a couple months or stored in the refrigerator. You'll know that it's gone rancid if it tastes stale or smells oddly pungent.

When baking, use oil only when a recipe calls for it. Because oil mixes up differently than solid fats, the outcome of using it when it isn't called for may be undesirable.

Nonstick cooking spray

I love nonstick cooking spray for one-shot super-easy greasing action. It's especially great for greasing Bundt pans because the molded design makes it particularly difficult to grease. You can also find a product called Baker's Joy, which "greases and flours" your baking pans for you.

REMEMBER

Fat adds flavor, texture, and rising power to baked goods. For many years, fats were on the chopping block and debated relentlessly about their health attributes. Consider the following:

>> Trans fats, which are liquid vegetable fats that have had hydrogen added to them to create a solid fat, are now banned in U.S., Canadian, and European foods.

» *Saturated fats* (animal-based fats such as butter) have long been villainized, but now research is showing saturated fats may not be the root of heart disease.

» *Mono- and polyunsaturated fats,* such as olive oil and nut and seed oils, are revered for their health attributes and benefits to cardiovascular disease.

So what do you do? Bake with fats! As a dietitian, I don't shy away from fats. Fats are satiating and tasty and provide a necessary texture and taste to baked goods. If you want to add in more health to baked goods, check out Chapter 19. *Hint:* It's more about adding in good and less about taking away!

Liquids: Including Some Moisture

Liquids are added to a batter to help dissolve the salt and sugar and to create steam, which helps a cake rise and adds to its texture. Liquids also moisten the leavener, which helps to activate it. Although liquids include everything from water to fruit juice, the liquids I define here are dairy liquids because these are the ones you'll come in contact with most often:

» **Fresh milk:** When a recipe calls for milk, it refers to cow's milk. Several varieties of fresh milk are available in the market: whole, low-fat, and skim. Although all the recipes in this book were tested with whole milk, unless otherwise specified, you can substitute the milk of your choice.

TIP

Fresh milk without the fridge? Keep a constant supply of milk on hand in your pantry. Parmalat makes a boxed milk that can be stored in the pantry for months without refrigeration. Open it, use what you need, and then store it in the refrigerator. Its flavor is slightly sweeter than traditional milk, but that's undetectable when it's used in baking. You can find this milk in your grocery store's baking section.

» **Buttermilk:** This milk contains no butter but was once a by-product of butter-making. Most commercial buttermilk is fermented from milk mixed with lactic acid (like yogurt and sour cream). Buttermilk adds a tangy flavor to doughs and batters, and it is lower in fat than whole milk.

TIP

If a recipe calls for buttermilk and you don't have any on hand, you can substitute 1 cup of regular milk plus 1 tablespoon vinegar or lemon juice for 1 cup of buttermilk. Let it sit for a few minutes before using. You can also substitute plain yogurt, measure for measure.

If you purchase buttermilk and you don't use the whole container, freeze it! Pour the buttermilk in 1-cup yogurt containers, and then you'll always have a small amount ready when you need it.

>> **Cream:** Cream is produced when the butterfat of milk is separated out of the liquid. The different types vary depending on the amount of butterfat in them.

- **Heavy (whipping) cream** is the richest of all the creams, containing between 36 and 40 percent butterfat. It's used to make whipped cream and for some cooked frostings. Ultra-pasteurized heavy cream has been sterilized and will keep for several weeks in the refrigerator. Regular heavy cream will keep for up to one week.

- **Light cream** is only about 20 percent butterfat. It's much richer than milk and can be substituted for milk in many recipes. It's good for making sauces or baking when you don't want all the richness of heavy cream. It's also tasty in coffee. Light cream will not whip up, though.

- **Half-and-half** is a mixture of light cream and milk and contains between 10 and 12 percent butterfat. If you ever run out of milk, half-and-half makes a great substitute.

>> **Evaporated milk:** Available in small cans, evaporated milk is whole milk with half the water removed. The mixture is slightly thicker than whole milk. Skimmed evaporated milk is widely available and can be used interchangeably with regular evaporated milk.

Keeping a can of evaporated milk on hand is always a good idea. If you ever run out of fresh milk while baking, just mix equal parts evaporated milk and water to make up the amount of milk you need.

>> **Sweetened condensed milk:** Also available in small cans, this is similar to evaporated milk with sweetener added. It's often used for cream pies and candy making.

Chocolate and Cocoa: A Chocoholic's Dream

Chocolate comes from cocoa beans that have been fermented, roasted, and crushed into nibs. These nibs are then reheated and ground into a paste called *chocolate liquor*, which contains at least 53 percent cocoa butter. All chocolate and cocoa start out this way but are made into many different products. Here I explain chocolate and cocoa in greater detail.

Chocolate

Solid chocolate used for baking and eating comes in many varieties. Their differences lie not only in their varying proportions of chocolate liquor, sugar, and cocoa butter, but also in the addition of vanilla and sugar.

Usually, baking chocolate comes in individually wrapped 1-ounce squares (usually in 8-ounce boxes). Many varieties of chocolate are available, including the following:

>> **Unsweetened chocolate** is pure chocolate liquor, containing at least 50 percent cocoa butter and no added sugar.

>> **Bittersweet, semisweet, dark, and sweet chocolate** vary from one another by the amount of sugar added to the chocolate liquor.

>> **Milk chocolate** has dried milk powder, cocoa butter, and sugar added.

>> **Ruby chocolate** is the newest chocolate category, patented in 2017 in Belgium. Ruby chocolate is pink in color with a bit more acidity, with a sweet and sour taste.

>> **White chocolate** isn't really chocolate because it doesn't contain chocolate liquor, but most brands of white chocolate have cocoa butter in them. Make sure that the brand you choose contains cocoa butter. Without it, the flavor is inferior. White chocolate is also called *vanilla chips* or *vanilla baking bar*.

WARNING

When a recipe calls for a specific type of chocolate, such as unsweetened chocolate, don't substitute any other type, such as milk chocolate. You run the risk of a bad baking outcome.

Store chocolate in a cool, dark place (don't refrigerate). It should remain at a constant temperature, between 65 degrees and 78 degrees, and stored well wrapped in aluminum foil or plastic wrap. If stored at a high temperature or exposed to air for a long period of time, the chocolate will *bloom,* meaning that it will have a whitish haze or may become crumbly. What has happened is the cocoa butter has separated from the solids, and your chocolate gets a grayish exterior color. Not to worry, though — the quality of the chocolate isn't affected. Stored properly, chocolate has an extremely long shelf life — up to one year.

When melting chocolate, never do so over direct heat. It's very delicate and burns easily. See Chapter 5 for the correct chocolate-melting procedure.

Cocoa

Unsweetened cocoa comes from pure chocolate liquor that has been separated into cocoa butter and solid cocoa cakes. These cakes are ground into cocoa powder, which is used often in baking cakes, cookies, and commonly used to make brownies. Unsweetened cocoa is much different than cocoa for hot chocolate drinks, which have milk powder and sugar added. They can't be substituted for one another, although you can add sugar and milk to cocoa to make hot chocolate.

You may notice that you now have a choice between Dutch process cocoa powder and regular cocoa powder. Simply put, the Dutch process treats the cocoa beans with an alkaline solution, and it has a different pH (about 7 or 8) than regular cocoa (about 5.5) before grinding the nibs. The result is a darker color and milder flavor than regular cocoa powder. This Dutch process finds favor with many pastry chefs.

Cocoa powder comes in a tin with a fitted lid. Cocoa powder is great if you bake a lot with unsweetened chocolate because it makes a good substitute and you don't have to melt it. Many people also feel that cocoa powder gives a more intense flavor than unsweetened chocolate.

Add-Ins and Flavorings: Enhancing the Taste

Many times, you don't want just plain baked goods, so you stir in a little fun. Nuts, coconut, raisins, and other ingredients make fine additions or toppings for many recipes. Extracts and syrups also add flavor to baked goods. These ingredients may come in small packages, but they're essential for good flavor.

Nuts

Nuts add a wonderful flavor to baked goods, and they can also double as decorations. Here's a list of the nuts most commonly used in baking (see Figure 2-1):

>> **Almonds:** Almonds are oval-shaped with a light brown exterior. They're available in or out of the shell, *blanched* (skinned) or *unblanched* (raw), halved, sliced, slivered, toasted, smoked, buttered, or salted. Whew!

TIP

Blanching your own almonds is easy. Just place the almonds in boiling water for 30 seconds to 1 minute. Drain and run under cool water to cool, and then rub them in a clean kitchen towel to loosen the skins. Or you can pop them straight out of their skin by just squeezing them a little.

>> **Hazelnuts:** Also called *filberts,* hazelnuts are incredibly popular in Europe and less so in the United States. You can find just about anything flavored with this nut, from coffees to gourmet desserts. Their round shape makes them perfect for garnishing, too. Hazelnuts have a light-brown skin and can be used whole, ground, chopped, or as a paste to flavor fillings for desserts.

TIP

To skin hazelnuts, spread them out on a baking sheet and bake at 350 degrees for 10 minutes, or until the skins begin to crack. Rub the nuts in a clean kitchen towel to remove the skins.

>> **Pecans:** Pecans are an American original, made famous in such dishes as pecan pie and pecan cookies and grown primarily in the southern part of the United States. They're in season from September to November and are largely available shelled, in pieces. Whole halves are the most expensive and used largely for decorating.

>> **Pine nuts:** Also called *piñon,* these buttery-tasting nuts are popular because of their starring role in pesto, but they're delicious in cookies, piecrusts, and breads. Shaped like a tiny ivory teardrop, these little nuts have a high oil content, so they should be stored in the freezer and used within six months of purchase. Although the pine nut is grown worldwide and many varieties are available, don't purchase the Chinese pine nut, which has a strong, piney flavor.

>> **Walnuts:** The most common variety of walnut is the English walnut, which has a wonderful mild flavor and is usually found in cookies, pies, and brownies. Walnuts are available in halves or in pieces (which is usually the least expensive way to buy them). Less well known is the black walnut, which has a very assertive, almost bitter flavor. All the recipes in this book that call for walnuts use the English walnut.

TIP

Be sure to get the freshest nuts possible. Store all your nuts in airtight containers in a cool, dry place if you'll use them in less than a month. Otherwise, pop them into your freezer, away from strong odors, where they can keep for up to one year. Because most nuts have a high oil content, they can go rancid quickly if they're not frozen. You can still chop and grind frozen nuts without any defrost time, so there really isn't any reason not to freeze them.

FIGURE 2-1:
An assortment
of nuts used
in baking.

Raisins and other dried fruits

Raisins are essential ingredients in many breads, cookies, and quick breads or muffins. I love to have them around to throw into something that may need a touch of sweetness.

You also can use dried currants, blueberries, cherries, and cranberries in place of or in addition to raisins. They're a wonderful flavor burst and can be used measure for measure as a substitute.

TIP

For moist, chewy raisins, soak them in hot water or alcohol for a half hour or so. Just place them in a small bowl and add hot water to cover (you can also soak in coffee, rum, brandy, or bourbon if you like). When they become plump, drain the raisins and use as directed in the recipe. The brandy or rum version offers a nice cocktail while you bake!

Oats

Rolled oats are essential for oatmeal cookies and an important ingredient if you're making any sort of streusel or crumbly pie or cake topping. I also like to use them for making oatmeal bread.

Old-fashioned and quick oats generally come in a large cardboard container with a tight-fitting lid, which is fine to keep them in for storage. You can also find oats in the bulk section of many supermarkets. Don't store the oats in the plastic bag; instead, transfer the oats to an airtight container. If you don't use your oats often (for example, only a couple times a year), store them in the freezer. Also, never use instant oats for baking (which are different from quick oats). Instant oats absorb the water immediately and cook, which then turns your baked good into cement.

Peanut butter

Peanut butter is great for peanut butter cookies and peanut butter pie, among other things. Peanut butter will store for many months in the pantry. If you purchase an all-natural brand, be sure to stir in the oils and then store it in the refrigerator so that it won't separate. Don't be alarmed if the oil separates from the ground peanuts. That's normal for unprocessed (natural) peanut butter to do.

You can also find lots of other nut butters — cashew, almond, and soy. Although you can interchange them with peanut butter for baking, the flavor of your baked goods will be very different.

Coconut

Coconut is great for decorating cakes and cookies and is the essential ingredient for coconut cream pies and meringue cookies. Your recipe should specify whether you should use sweetened or unsweetened coconut. (If a recipe calls for unsweetened and you can't find it at your grocery store, look for it in a whole-foods or natural grocery store.) Store it in an airtight container or a sealable bag. Unopened coconut will keep for six months. Opened, it will keep for several weeks. You can refrigerate or freeze coconut if you don't use it very often.

Liquors

Liquors (bourbon, rum, brandy, and so on) add a nice flavor to many cakes, pies, and cookies. The alcohol evaporates during cooking, so unless a cake is soaked in the liquor or is uncooked, there isn't much of a chance to overindulge. Always choose a moderate-quality alcohol when baking — the quality will be passed on to your finished product.

Maple syrup and extract

Maple syrup is the boiled sap from the maple tree. I always use pure maple syrup, but it's quite expensive (unless you live in Maine or Vermont, where it's much cheaper — if you travel or live there, look for it in grocery stores for the most reasonable price).

REMEMBER

Keep your maple syrup in the refrigerator. Trust me when I say this — I once lost a whole gallon of pure maple syrup to mold because I didn't refrigerate it. It may turn darker in the refrigerator, but that darker color won't affect the flavor. Also, believe it or not, it takes quite a bit of syrup to impart maple flavor to baked goods or even frosting, so pick up some maple extract and try that before using your precious syrup, which I like to drizzle over cakes, cookies, and breads.

Molasses

Molasses is a strong-flavored syrup and comes from what is left over after granulated sugar has been extracted from sugar cane. It comes in light or dark varieties and is used to make gingerbread and to flavor cakes and muffins. Molasses will keep for a long time and should be stored in tightly closed jars in a cool place.

Spices, herbs, and extracts

Spices, herbs, and extracts lend a wonderful flavor accent to all baked goods. They should never overwhelm a dish and should be as fresh-tasting as possible.

Spices

Spices come from the seeds, bark, roots, and nuts of different plants and add flavoring to baked goods. The most common spices used in baking are

>> Allspice

>> Cardamom

>> Cinnamon

>> Cloves

>> Ginger

>> Mixed spice (also called *apple pie spice*)

>> Nutmeg

Recipes usually call for ground spices. When spices are ground, the oil that gives them their fresh flavor evaporates over time. For best results, buy small quantities of ground spices to ensure a high turnover in your own cupboard. Store them in tightly closed containers (glass is best) and keep them in a cool, dry place (not near the stove) to minimize the loss of the oil. Still, you should consider replacing spices you've had for more than one year, after which the flavor will have dissipated.

TIP

Buying spices loose is much less expensive than buying them in jars at grocery stores or supermarkets. Find out if your local natural-foods store or baking supply shop carries loose spices so that you can scoop just the right amount (usually ¼ ounce is plenty). Just don't forget to label the jars you store them in.

Herbs

Fresh or dried herbs add interesting flavor dimensions to baked goods, such as shortbread cookies or cakes. The most common spices used in baking are

- » Lavender
- » Mint
- » Rosemary
- » Thyme
- » Sage

Recipes usually call for dried or fresh herbs. Check out the Rosemary Shortbread Cookies in Chapter 8.

Extracts

Extracts often are the essential oils of many foods or plants. They're extracted as a concentrated oil, such as orange, lemon, or almond, and then mixed into an alcohol base. The most common extract used in baking is vanilla.

At the market, you have a choice of pure or imitation extracts. For the best flavor, always choose pure extract if you're baking it in a simple recipe that contains few ingredients. Although pure extract can cost almost twice as much as imitation, it's a smart investment because the flavor it gives your baked goods is so much better than that of imitation.

Because alcohol evaporates, be sure to keep the lids of extract bottles on tight and store your extracts in a cool, dry place. If you do, they will keep indefinitely.

Fresh fruits and veggies

Cakes, pies, and tarts made with fresh fruit make a wonderful ending to any meal. The better the fruit you choose, the better the end result will be. Always buy fruit in season, at the peak of ripeness. The following guidelines can help you select the best of each season's crop:

REMEMBER

>> **Apples:** Choose apples that have a fresh, bright look and smooth, tight, unbruised skin. They should be firm and crisp. The best apples for baking are the more tart or sturdy varieties, such as Granny Smith, Winesap, McIntosh, and Golden Delicious. Keep in mind that Red Delicious apples may look pretty and are great for snacking, but they aren't a good choice for baking.

Always store apples in the refrigerator. At room temperature, they ripen up to ten times faster and turn mealy. Yuck!

>> **Avocados:** Avocados create a solid fat and can often be used when baking cakes, cookies, or brownies. Try using mashed avocado for ½ of the fat in a recipe. You may see a light green color peak through, so try it within a chocolate recipe first.

>> **Bananas:** Bananas should be lightly firm and golden yellow with speckles of black spots; you don't want green stems or tips. If your bananas have green tips, let them ripen at room temperature for a few days.

>> **Berries:** All berries, especially raspberries, are highly perishable and should be refrigerated and used within a day or two of purchase. Don't wash berries until you're ready to use them. Inspect packages of berries carefully; you should see no sign of mold. Fresh berries should give off a pleasant, fresh aroma. If they don't have much of a smell, they won't have much flavor either.

>> **Carrots:** Carrots add a dose of nutrition and color to baked goods, from muffins to cakes to quick breads. Carrots are available all year long.

>> **Cherries:** Unfortunately, cherries have an extremely short season — July and August — so grab them while you can. Look for firm, plump, glossy cherries with a dark maroon color. Avoid soft or brown cherries; they're overripe. Wash cherries only when you're ready to use them (within a few days of purchase).

>> **Citrus fruits:** This category includes lemons, limes, key limes, grapefruits, and oranges. Choose fruits that are firm and feel heavy for their size. (The heaviness comes from the fruit being juicy.) Avoid lemons and oranges that have tinges of green skin. Always wash the fruit if you plan on using it for *zest* (the colored skin, not the white pith underneath). ***Note:*** Key limes are smaller in size and have a more pronounced sweeter flavor than the typical large limes found in a market.

Keep lemons on hand for freshly grated zest and for their juice. These bright, cheery fruits will keep for several weeks in the vegetable crisper.

>> **Cranberries:** You can usually find cranberries only in the autumn, and they're often sold in plastic packaging. Look for bright, plump, glossy cranberries. Shriveled or soft berries are a sign of age — and certainly steer clear of any brown or moldy packages. Rinse fresh cranberries before using them. Cranberries freeze very well, so consider stocking up on them for a year-round supply. Just don't defrost them before baking.

>> **Mangoes:** Purchase your mango while it's still slightly firm but gives a bit when pressed. Look for smooth skin with red and yellow coloring. A little touch of green is okay but avoid mangoes that are all green.

>> **Nectarines and peaches:** Choose fruits with an orange-yellow or creamy-yellow skin, a nice red blush, and a fragrant smell. Any green on the skin means that the fruit was picked unripe and will never sweeten. If the fruits have nice color but are slightly hard, set them out at room temperature for a few days to ripen. Refrigerate peaches and nectarines when they're ripe.

>> **Pears:** A good pear has a nice pearlike fragrance. Because pears bruise so easily, choose your fruits slightly firm. They'll ripen at room temperature in a few days. Avoid very green or bruised fruit.

>> **Pineapple:** Choosing a good pineapple can be tricky because the fruits won't continue to ripen, or sweeten, after they're picked. Some pineapples are labeled *field ripened,* and these should be your first choice. Otherwise, look for fresh-smelling, deep-green leaves. Pineapples should be firm but give slightly when squeezed.

REMEMBER

Pulling a leaf from the center of the pineapple isn't a good indicator of the fruit's freshness or sweetness (a popular misconception). Avoid pineapples that are soft or smell like they're beginning to ferment.

>> **Pumpkin:** Nothing says fall like fresh baked pumpkin bread! You can use either canned or fresh, baked, and mashed pumpkin in recipes.

>> **Zucchini:** In the height of summer zucchini crops are popping! It's a great time to grate, squeeze, and add zucchini to your favorite baked cake or quick bread. Check out Chapter 13 for the Chocolate Zucchini Bread recipe.

USING FROZEN FRUIT

In the summertime, I love to go to pick-your-own farms and stock up on all kinds of fresh fruit. Then I freeze my harvest for the winter months, when a fresh blueberry pie lifts my spirits. You can also keep frozen berries and fruits on hand (you can pick them up at the supermarket if you like) for pies, muffins, pancakes, and other desserts.

Baking with Extras That Are Nice to Have on Hand

Although the following ingredients are not must-haves, you'll come across them every once in a while when you're baking. A well-stocked pantry keeps many of these ingredients at your fingertips so that you'll be ready to bake on a moment's notice:

» **Cornmeal:** I'm a lover of corn breads and spoonbread, and cornmeal is great for keeping pizza crusts from sticking to the baking sheet, so I always keep some on hand. Cornmeal can be white or yellow — where you live will probably dictate the availability and choice or preference. White cornmeal is a bit lighter and more delicate but doesn't give you as chewy or strong a flavor as yellow cornmeal does. Store cornmeal like you would flour — in an airtight container in a cool, dark place.

» **Cornstarch:** Cornstarch is used in baking to thicken the juices in pies and in gravies and sauces. Cornstarch keeps forever — just make sure to store it in an airtight container in a cool, dry place.

» **Decorative frostings:** Tubes of different colors of decorative gels or frostings make adding spur-of-the-moment decorations to cakes and cookies easy. They keep forever and are always ready to turn the ordinary into something extraordinary.

» **Dried beans (for pie weights):** Dried beans may seem like a strange thing to keep in the kitchen for baking, but they act as inexpensive pie weights when you're baking a piecrust without a filling.

» **Food coloring:** Food coloring is great to keep on hand to tint coconut or frostings and to make colored hard-boiled eggs. Be careful when using it, though — it can stain!

» **Frozen dough:** Piecrust, well wrapped, keeps for up to a year in the freezer. Just defrost the dough before rolling it out. You also can keep puff pastry and bread doughs on hand in the freezer.

» **Instant tapioca:** Tapioca comes in several forms: pellets, flour, and granules. I love to use instant tapioca (which consists of small pellets and is found where puddings and flavored gelatin are sold) when I bake fruit pies. It acts much like cornstarch does, thickening fruit juices, but I think it give the pies a better overall flavor.

» Yogurt: Plain yogurt is often used in quick breads and muffins. Its tangy flavor and richness add a nice component to baked goods. You can substitute Greek yogurt for sour cream in many recipes as well. Unless a particular type is specified, you can use nonfat, lowfat, or whole-milk yogurt in any recipe. *Note:* Greek yogurt is thicker in texture and often higher in protein.

» **Recognizing the machines you'll use to bake with**

» **Identifying the tools and utensils for every task**

Chapter **3**

Going Over the Gear

aking is a good activity because there is relatively little startup cost. If you have a bowl, a mixing spoon, and some baking sheets, you don't need much more to make cookies or even bread. I'm a huge lover of kitchen gadgets, but I live in a tiny apartment, so I have to streamline what I buy in the interest of having walking-around room. Because I love to bake, I've put together a list of the basics you need in order to use this book.

If you're starting from scratch, I recommend looking for bakeware and appliances on sale. Online shopping has created a competitive market and way for businesses to save money delivering goods directly to the consumer. If you prefer to touch and feel items before you buy, you can also see if a store will price match an online price. Department stores usually have a good sale every few weeks in their house-wares section, so keep an eye out for quality products at reasonable prices. Outlet malls are also a good place to find discounted stuff for the kitchen. If you aren't fully committed to the idea of baking, you can always find heavy-duty aluminum foil baking pans in just about every shape and size at the grocery store. You can usually use the pans only once, so they're not an economical choice, but they're perfect if you don't bake often or are bringing a baked good to a friend's house — you don't have to worry about getting the pan back.

REMEMBER

Cost isn't always the best indicator of value. Look for sturdy pots and pans; despite the price tag, if something feels flimsy, it is. Your bakeware should feel sturdy and heavy. They'll be going in and out of a hot oven throughout their lifetime, so you want to choose equipment that won't warp and will withstand the wear and tear of baking. Before using any new bakeware, be sure to wash it thoroughly in hot, soapy water.

Familiarizing Yourself with Baking Pans

You won't get very far in baking if you don't have some baking pans. Although you don't need many, it's a good idea to acquaint yourself with the variety and sizes of pans available. In the following sections I introduce all you need to know about the pans that make baking possible.

TIP

Generously grease insides of pans with solid vegetable shortening. Use a pastry brush to spread the shortening evenly, making sure that all the inside surfaces are well covered. Refer to Chapter 5 for more information.

Baking (cookie) sheets

To keep yourself sane, I recommend owning at least two cookie sheets so that you can always have a batch of cookies ready to go into the oven. I recommend four baking sheets for an avid baker. Choose heavy, shiny aluminum baking sheets.

WARNING

Thin baking sheets will warp in the oven, so make sure that yours are sturdy. Avoid dark baking sheets — they tend to burn cookies faster.

Cookie sheets either are flat (with no sides) or have a lip running around all four sides (see Figure 3-1). I prefer a baking sheet with a lip because I can use it for many things, such as placing it under juicy pies as they bake so that it catches the juice and the juice doesn't drip into the oven.

FIGURE 3-1:
Baking sheets can be flat or have a lip running around all four sides.

© John Wiley & Sons, Inc.

TIP

If you find that your baking sheets with nonstick coating are browning your cookies too fast, reduce the oven temperature by 25 degrees. You also can buy insulated baking sheets — they're a little pricey, but they keep your cookie bottoms from getting too brown. You may find that you need to increase your baking time by a few minutes if you use insulated sheets.

You can create your own insulated baking sheets instead of spending extra money to buy them. If your cookies are burning on the bottom but raw on top, stack two baking sheets together (one on top of the other) and continue baking as usual. This should prevent further burning.

Baking (muffin) tins

Muffin tins are little cups, usually 6 or 12 cups per pan, pressed out of one sheet of metal. They're used for making muffins, cupcakes, or rolls or for baking small cakes. Like other baking tins, the best muffin tins

>> Are sturdy

>> Are made of heavy aluminum

>> May have a nonstick coating

Specialty muffin tins are also available in mini-muffin size, as well as muffin-top pans (from which you get only the crunchy tops of the muffins and not the cakey bottoms).

Bundt and tube pans

Bundt and tube pans allow a hurried cook to make a beautiful, tall cake without the worry of layers. The secret is the funnel, which cooks the cake from the inside out. Bundt pans (check out Figure 3-2) almost always have some sort of cut-crystal design molded into the pan and have tall sides with a hollow tube in the center.

FIGURE 3-2:
Bundt pans let you make fancy cakes, sculpted cakes.

BUNDT PAN

© John Wiley & Sons, Inc.

A tube pan (shown in Figure 3-3), or angel food cake pan, has a funnel in the center, too, but the sides of this pan are smooth, which allows the batter to climb up the walls of the pan as it bakes. Tube pans often have *feet,* which are little metal nubs that stick out above the rim of the pan, allowing the pan to be flipped over while it cools without smashing the cake inside. If your tube pan doesn't have feet, chances are the tube center is higher than the sides of the pan, which will give you the same clearance that feet would. Angel food cakes need to cook this way so that they don't collapse in the pan.

FIGURE 3-3:
The funnel in the middle of this tube pan helps your cake bake evenly.

TIP

If you don't know how many cups of batter your Bundt or tube pan holds, fill the pan to capacity with measured water to find out what its volume is. The same goes for any baking pan you need to use.

Cake pans

Cake pans come in several sizes. The most common are 8-inch round and 9- inch round. When you're buying a cake pan, make sure to get one that's at least 1½ inches deep. You'll need two 9-inch-round baking pans for making a layer cake. I recommend heavy aluminum pans, with or without a nonstick coating, and with straight sides. Be sure your pans are sturdy; you don't want them to warp and produce an uneven cake.

REMEMBER

These pans will mold the batter you put into them, so you want them to be straight and flat.

Loaf pans

Loaf pans come in two standard sizes: 9 x 5 x 3 inches and 8½ x 4½ x 2½ inches. Either size is fine for the recipes in this book. You can find loaf pans made of glass, shiny metal, and nonstick aluminum. Glass pans and dark, non-stick pans have a tendency to brown your breads a bit faster than shiny metal, so you may have to lower the oven temperature by 25 degrees.

Always have two loaf pans for bread baking because most recipes make two loaves of bread, and you'll need both pans to put the bread in to rise; you can't really bake one loaf of yeast bread at a time. I also don't recommend baking quick breads one at a time. The leavening will become active when the wet ingredients are mixed together, and if the batter sits around for too long, the leavening may become inactive.

Pie plates (pans)

The most common sizes for pie plates are 8 inches and 9 inches. Pie plates can be a bit tricky because the size refers to the diameter, not the depth, of the plate, so they vary in the amounts they hold, even if they're the same diameter. Pie plates come in a variety of materials:

>> **Glass:** A glass pie plate is often the best choice for pies that bake for 30 to 50 minutes. The glass radiates and conducts heat at the same time, so it cooks the crust quickly. If you have only glass pie plates and you need to cook a pie for more than an hour, lower the oven temperature by 25 degrees so that the crust won't burn in the pan.

>> **Aluminum:** A thick aluminum pie plate gives you a more evenly baked crust than a thin plate does. Dull metal or dark pans also absorb heat faster and cook faster than shiny pans. Be sure to adjust the cooking time and temperature accordingly.

A shiny pie plate reflects heat, so your pie will end up with a soggy bottom crust if you bake your pie for less than an hour.

>> **Ceramic:** Ceramic pie plates are less popular, but they're available. They behave like thick aluminum pie plates, baking crusts evenly and slowly. They're a good choice for quiches and double-crust pies that require a longer cooking time.

Springform pans

Springform pans are clever contraptions. They allow the cake to bake, but then you can remove the sides of the pan (there is a clasp on the side) without having to invert it, and you're left with a lovely cake ready to be cut and served (see Figure 3-4). They're the perfect pans to make cheesecakes in. The most common sizes of springform pans are 8 inches, 9 inches, and 10 inches. Finding sets of springform pans sold in these three sizes is common.

When shopping for a springform pan, make sure that the bottom fits in tightly and the clasp is strong. Carrying a cake to the oven and having your clasp give out on you, bottoming out the whole pan and leaving you wearing the cake, isn't a pleasant experience. Even worse is when this happens when you're carrying the finished cake to the cooling rack!

FIGURE 3-4:
The sides
spring off of a
springform pan
so you don't
have to disturb
your cake.

© John Wiley & Sons, Inc.

TIP

To make sure that your springform doesn't spring a leak, place it on a baking sheet when you place it in the oven. The baking sheet will help catch any drips and allow you to transport your cake without any risk of the bottom falling from the cake pan.

Including Basic Pots in Your Kitchen

You don't need that many pots and pans for baking. However, you may have to melt chocolate for a cake or cook a filling for a potpie or even a pudding for a pie. This section presents a very short list of essential pots you need to have in the kitchen. For all pots, I recommend heavy, stainless steel cookware (with or without a nonstick coating).

Saucepans

TIP

You should have at least a 1-quart saucepan and a 2-quart saucepan on hand for stovetop procedures such as scalding milk and melting chocolate. Heavy-bottomed saucepans are better conductors of heat, and you're less likely to burn or scald the bottom than if you use thinner metals. I prefer stainless steel saucepans because they're *nonreactive* (they don't react with acidic ingredients, which can cause discoloration) and durable. They also don't pick up food odors or stain easily.

Double boiler

If you melt chocolate, you need a double boiler. A double boiler consists of two nesting saucepans or a saucepan with a fitted bowl inside. To use a double boiler, heat water in the lower pot until it steams with the upper pot in place. This warms the bottom of the upper pot or bowl. Make sure that the bottom of the bowl doesn't touch the simmering water. Then the chocolate can melt with no risk of burning. This method of indirect heating also is used for making some creams and sauces. If you don't have a double boiler, check out the nearby sidebar for a workaround.

WHAT? NO DOUBLE BOILER?

If you're in a pinch and need to make a double boiler, take two saucepans of different sizes or a saucepan and a stainless steel or tempered glass bowl to fit on top. Fill the larger saucepan with about 2 inches of water and rest the smaller saucepan on top of the water (it doesn't matter whether the second saucepan touches the water, because the bottom of a regular saucepan is sturdier than the bottom of a double boiler) or insert the bowl in the saucepan. Use as you would a regular double boiler.

Warning: Because the two pans won't be fitted, you need to make sure that none of the simmering water gets into the top saucepan. Also, be very careful when removing the top bowl if you're using a bowl. It will be hot!

Or you can use a stainless-steel bowl large enough to sit on top of the pan of simmering water. What's nice about this setup is that there's no danger of the water mixing in with your melting chocolate. Just remember that the bowl will be very hot to touch, so use an oven mitt.

REMEMBER

Never use the top saucepan of a double boiler over direct heat because the metal used to make the upper pan isn't as sturdy as the bottom saucepan.

Dutch oven

Its name is said to have come from its Dutch ancestry, dating back to the 1700s. These large pots or kettles are good for going from the stovetop to the oven, which is great if you're making potpie or stew and dumplings. Make sure that your Dutch oven has a tight-fitting lid and is flameproof (oven safe). This includes the handles and lid knobs.

Utilizing Electric Tools to Bake

Although most baked goods don't require electric gadgets, these convenience tools certainly speed up the baking process. Electric mixers enable you to speedily beat sugar and butter, whip egg whites, and mix together batters. Food processors and blenders can chop and puree in no time.

Air fryer

An air fryer is a small convection oven, circulating hot air around a food. Air fryers are a great baking tool when the weather is hot, you only need to bake a small amount of items, or you have a small living space. Air fryers are great for

>> Hand pies

>> Cakes baked in custard cups, such as mug cakes or molten lava cakes

>> Small batch cookie baking

If you have limited storage space, an air fryer may be hard to store. They're often bulky in size. If you have the space, they can be a fun additional electric tool to keep on hand. Check out *Air Fryer Cookbook For Dummies* by yours truly and Elizabeth Shaw (John Wiley & Sons, Inc.) for some inspiration.

Blender

A blender is great for a number of tasks, such as

>> Pureeing fruits

>> Making cheesecake

>> Crushing crackers or cookies for a crumb crust

>> Grinding or chopping nuts

There's no better tool than a blender when you need superfine (quick-dissolving) sugar and have only granulated sugar on hand. Just dump the amount you need into the blender and whiz it for a minute or so, and — voilà! — superfine sugar. (I once tried this in my food processor and the results weren't the same.)

Food processor

A food processor (shown in Figure 3-5) is a wonderful kitchen tool because it's strong, simple to use, and pretty quiet — but it's also quite expensive. I absolutely love my food processor and use it all the time. You can use a food processor to do the following:

>> Make pastry dough with the dough blade.

>> Chop nuts or citrus zest with the metal blade.

>> Puree fruit with the metal blade.

>> Juice lemons or limes with the juicer attachment.

>> Shred carrots with the shredder attachment.

>> Slice apples with the slicing attachment.

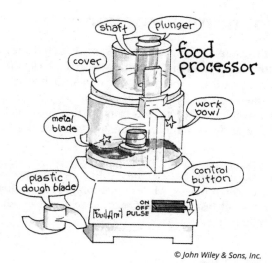

© John Wiley & Sons, Inc.

FIGURE 3-5:
A quality food processor comes with numerous blades for a variety of tasks.

Food processors can do these tasks and more — all in a fraction of the time required to do it by hand.

If you're considering purchasing a food processor, don't skimp on quality. Make sure that you purchase a reputable brand with a good, durable motor. The money you spend on it upfront will save you money and time in the long run.

Handheld mixer

A handheld mixer is relatively inexpensive and great to have on hand. You can use a handheld mixer for

>> Whipping up cake batters and light cookie doughs

>> Whipping cream and egg whites

Handheld mixers have three speeds: slow, medium, and fast. They are portable and easy to clean (the beaters just pop off when you're finished), which can save you a great deal of time and frustration.

Although the motor in a handheld mixer isn't as strong as the one in a standing mixer, you can find sturdier, more expensive models that come with attachments for creaming thick cake batters and dough hooks for bread doughs. The advantage of a handheld mixer is that it's portable, which means that you can use it wherever you need it (as long as you can plug it in).

Instant Pot or multicooker

Pressure cooking became a trend with the Instant Pot, and they're a nifty tool to use. The trick with baking in an Instant Pot is to use the rack at the base of the pot, so a baked good isn't sitting in the water. For items, such as cheesecake or sticky pudding, I recommend a small 8-inch springform pan. Wrap the bottom tightly with foil and up the sides to keep liquid from getting into the baked good. Most cheesecakes require 25 to 35 minutes under pressure with a 10-minute natural release.

TIP

Start with boiling water at the base so the multicooker comes to pressure quicker. It's a great tool to use on hot days, while RV camping, or in kitchens where storage isn't an issue. Check out *Instant Pot Cookbook For Dummies* by Elizabeth Shaw and me (John Wiley & Sons, Inc.).

Stand (table) mixer

A good stand mixer (shown in Figure 3-6) has been called the most efficient tool known to man. It can handle just about any workload you dish out because the motor is about six times stronger than that of any handheld mixer. It also has a wider range of speeds than a handheld mixer.

A stand mixer generally comes with its own bowl attachment, which is usually generous in size, and three standard attachments, including

>> **A paddle,** which blends batters and creams ingredients together

>> **A wire whisk,** which incorporates air into batter and whips egg whites

>> **A dough hook,** which kneads dough

You also can purchase special attachments for some models, including a pasta maker, a grinder, a shredder, a slicer, and a juicer.

Stand mixers aren't quite as convenient and don't disassemble as neatly as handheld mixers, so you'll more than likely store yours on the countertop or in an easy-to-access place.

Stand Mixer

motor head
flat beater
speed control lever
wire whip
bowl
dough hook

FIGURE 3-6: A sturdy stand mixer can tackle many of the toughest baking tasks.

© John Wiley & Sons, Inc.

A wide range of stand mixers are available in a wide assortment of prices. My best advice is to determine how much baking you'll be doing. If you bake about once a month, I recommend investing in a quality mixer, such as a KitchenAid. It's expensive but well worth the money. My mother has had hers for more than 25 years and has never had problems with it — and I plan on having mine for that long or even longer!

Considering Other Essentials

You need bowls, racks, and cutting boards for preparing doughs and batters. Then, when your finished creations come out of the oven, you need cooling racks to help them cool quickly. This section describes the essentials for a good baking kitchen.

Cooling racks

Cooling racks are wire racks that allow air to circulate around baked goods while they cool, preventing them from having a soggy or moist bottom. A wide variety of shapes and sizes are available; just make sure that your rack has feet on it so that it won't lay flat against the countertop, thereby defeating the purpose of circulation. Also, look for the rack's wires to be close together. This will prevent delicate cakes from sinking too much and smaller cookies from slipping through the spaces between the wires.

Cookie and biscuit cutters

Cookie cutters come in all shapes and sizes. They're generally made of plastic or metal. When choosing your cutters, look for somewhat simple shapes that won't cut your cookies into a variety of thicknesses. For example, a cookie cutter that cuts out giraffes may be tricky because the small head might burn before the body is done cooking. Avoid cutters that are too detailed.

Biscuit cutters generally are nothing more than 1- or 2-inch-round cutters. If you don't have a biscuit cutter, you can use a clean soup can with both top and bottom removed instead.

Cutting boards

Cutting boards offer smooth, even surfaces for tasks such as chopping, cutting, peeling, and rolling out doughs. You can choose from a few different materials:

>> **Wood:** A wooden cutting board is your best choice for preserving the sharp edges of knives because they don't blunt as quickly as they do on plastic, metal, or marble. Don't place your wooden cutting board in the dishwasher or let it soak in water for any length of time. The heat from the dishwasher will warp your board, and the water will soften the board's bonded sections. Keep one side of your cutting board knick-free and smooth so that it's suitable for rolling out cookie or pastry dough.

>> **Polyurethane:** Polyurethane boards won't warp and are soft enough for knives to be used without dulling. They also can be sterilized in the dishwasher.

>> **Thin plastic:** My new favorite cutting boards are very thin, flexible chopping surfaces. They are bendable, are so easy to use, and take up hardly any space, plus they seem easier to clean and don't retain odors. I promise that if you purchase one, you'll use it time and time again.

Knives

A good sharp knife can be your best friend in the kitchen. Just be sure to hold it carefully! (See Figure 3-7.) Good, professional knives are quite expensive and not really necessary for the home baker. Still, you should have four basic knives in your kitchen:

>> **A large cleaver:** This knife is perfect for chopping, and its side is ideal for crushing things.

- **A serrated knife:** This knife is great for slicing breads and delicate cakes.

- **A medium-sized knife (chef's knife):** This knife is best for slicing cakes, cutting pastry, and for less heavy work than the cleaver.

- **A paring knife:** This knife is ideal for cutting small foods, peeling fruits, hulling strawberries, and performing many other detail tasks.

FIGURE 3-7:
The proper grip ensures safe cutting.

© John Wiley & Sons, Inc.

WARNING

Although a knife's sharp edge can be dangerous, dull knives are even more dangerous. You need to apply more pressure to cut with a dull knife, therefore increasing your chances of slipping and injuring yourself. Always tuck your fingertips under when cutting with a knife so that if your knife does slip, it will cut your knuckle, not your fingertip (see Figure 3-8).

FIGURE 3-8:
Curling your fingertips under enables you to work quickly without risking your fingertips.

© John Wiley & Sons, Inc.

Measuring cups

Measuring cups are essential for every kitchen. You won't find many recipes that don't require measurements of some kind. Measuring cups come in two basic types:

>> **Graded:** Graded cups (see Figure 3-9) range in sizes from ¼ cup to 1 cup and can range from 4 to 6 cups in a set. Use graded cups to measure dry ingredients and solid fats, such as shortening.

>> **Glass:** Glass cups (see Figure 3-10) are available in a wide range of sizes, the most common being 1 cup, 2 cups, and 4 cups. Use these cups for measuring liquids. Make sure that you read your measurement at eye level, with the cup on a flat surface.

FIGURE 3-9:
Every baker needs a set of measuring cups.

dry measure cups

FIGURE 3-10:
Use a glass measuring cup to measure and pour liquids.

liquid measure cup

© John Wiley & Sons, Inc.

TIP

When measuring thick, sticky liquids such as honey, molasses, and corn syrup, spray the inside of the measuring glass with nonstick cooking spray or grease it a little with oil. The liquid will then be much easier to remove.

Mixing bowls

You don't have to go out and purchase new bowls — you can use any bowl you have on hand to make the recipes in this book. However, if you plan to buy bowls, this section offers some tips for selecting the best ones.

For mixing cake batters and cookies, I like a wide stainless steel mixing bowl. These come in a variety of sizes, but look for bowls with flat bottoms and wide, sloping sides. They make mixing easier and are less likely to tip over if you leave a whisk or spoon in them than a narrower bottomed bowl. Stainless steel is also durable, unbreakable, and *nonreactive* (it won't react with acidic ingredients, turning the bowl different colors).

When I make bread, I like to let the dough rise in a heavy ceramic bowl. The ceramic bowl keeps my dough well insulated and at a more consistent temperature.

REMEMBER

When choosing a mixing bowl, make sure that you'll have enough room to fit all the ingredients and still have space to mix them up. Also consider what ingredients will be going into it. That's especially important when you're whipping egg whites or cream because egg whites can grow up to six times their original volume, and cream will at least double.

Measuring spoons

Graded measuring spoons usually come in sets of four or six, ranging from ¼ teaspoon to 1 tablespoon. Sometimes sets have ⅛ teaspoon and 1½ tablespoon, too. You use these measuring spoons for both dry and liquid measures.

Potholders and oven mitts

Potholders and oven mitts enable you to hold hot baking sheets and pans without burning yourself. I like to have both an oven mitt and potholders (generally square pads) on hand for different tasks. I use the mitt if I'm reaching into the oven and run the risk of burning my whole hand. I choose the square pads when I need to hold the sides of a dish, such as a soufflé.

I highly recommend that you forgo the decorative potholders that are so commonly found in stores' housewares sections. If you have them, use them for display. Few of these decorative potholders provide adequate protection from heat. Make a special trip to your kitchen supply store and purchase insulated potholders. They're slightly more expensive than regular potholders, but I trust them in every situation — whereas the decorative holders wear in strange spots and inevitably end up burning your hands.

Always have two sets of potholders. No matter what kind of potholder you have, if it gets wet, stop using it until it dries. It can no longer protect your hands.

Rolling pin

You use a rolling pin to roll out pastry dough. Many types are available, but I recommend a relatively heavy pin with handles, such as the one shown in Figure 3-11. The weight of the pin helps distribute the dough evenly, so don't push down on the pin when using it.

FIGURE 3-11: Heavy wooden rolling pins are best for rolling out pastry dough.

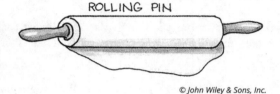

© John Wiley & Sons, Inc.

There are such things as *cool pins,* made of plastic or marble. Some you can even fill with water and freeze. These rolling pins ensure that your dough stays cool while you're working with it. I don't recommend buying a cool pin unless you've worked with one and prefer it to the traditional wooden pin. The marble variety is too heavy for my liking. The plastic is too light. And the frozen pins are a waste of money in my opinion. Not only are they awkward to work with, but the frozen center sweats as the water comes to room temperature, so it can make your dough sticky. So stick with a sure thing: wood.

To minimize sticking, always dust your rolling pin with flour before using it and wipe it clean when you're finished. Never put your rolling pin in the dishwasher.

Rolling mat

A fantastic tool for easy cleanup and quick measuring is a rolling mat. Rolling mats typically are made from silicone for easy cleaning and are marked with a ruler and circular measurements. When you're whipping up a piecrust, you know exactly large to roll it out by following the guide on the rolling mat.

Scale (metric)

Most bakers recognize the importance of accuracy in measurements for successful baked goods. A metric scale allows you to measure to the gram, which is a small unit and helps you find greater success when baking. A metric food scale generally costs between $15 and $25, making it an affordable tool to invest in.

Spoons

You should have two types of spoons in your kitchen:

>> **Metal:** You want at least two metal spoons, one solid for stirring and one slotted for lifting foods from liquids.

>> **Wooden:** Wooden spoons are great for stirring custards and sauces made in nonstick pans and for stirring batters and doughs. Nothing beats a sturdy wooden spoon. They're inexpensive, so you may want to get two or three.

Adding Other Great Gadgets

This section provides a list of helpful tools for the kitchen. Although you don't need to go out and purchase each and every one of these items, it's good to know that they're out there to help make your life in the kitchen that much easier.

Apple corer

Apple corers (see Figure 3-12) come in two basic types:

>> One is a wooden handle attached to an elongated curved metal cylinder with a cutting edge. This tool is indispensable when you want to core an apple or pear without slicing through it, making it perfect when you want baked apples or pears. You just press down vertically into the apple at the stem with a slight twisting motion until you reach the bottom.

>> Another version cores the apple and slices it into segments. This tool has sets of metal spokes that meet in the circle in the center. Press directly over the apple and it slices and cores the apple easily.

Box grater

Graters are usually made of metal (although plastic is available) and usually have four sides, offering a choice from fine to coarse grating, as well as a slicing blade that I like to use for cheese and carrots. If you don't own a box grater, choose a sturdy one with four sides and comfortable handle. You also can find a flat grater, which usually offers a choice of only two holes, but I find them cumbersome to use and unsteady. In their favor, flat graters take up less space and are easier to clean than box graters.

© John Wiley & Sons, Inc.

FIGURE 3-12:
Some apple
corers remove
the core whereas
others also slice
the apple into
wedges.

TIP

Clean your box grater from the inside out. Scrub the inside with a stiff brush, under running water, to push food from the back through to the front. Then hang the grater to air-dry.

Cake tester

Thin plastic or metal needlelike instruments, sometimes with a round handle, are sold as cake testers. You insert the tester into the center of the cake to determine whether it's done. If dough clings to it, the cake is not yet finished. If the tester comes out clean, the cake is finished. But I find that a wooden toothpick or even a thin, small knife works just as well.

Citrus juicer (reamer)

A citrus juicer is a hand tool that enables you to juice a lemon without getting too much pulp or seeds. Some are handheld; some you place over a bowl and strain out the seeds and pulp so that only the juice falls into the bowl; and others collect everything at their base. Citrus juicers come in many different shapes and sizes, so choose one that works well for you.

TIP

If you don't have a citrus juicer and you need to get more juice out of a lemon than squeezing will allow, try this: Squeeze the lemon — roll it on the counter while mashing down with the palm of your hand — before cutting. Then insert a teaspoon and gently squeeze again while twisting the spoon around the inside of the lemon. This will help release additional juice.

Flour sifter

A flour sifter (see Figure 3-13) removes any lumps or debris from your dry ingredients by sifting them through a fine mesh. Although most of the flour you find today is presifted, it has a tendency to settle during storage, so sifting flour or just stirring it up with a spoon before measuring it is a good idea so that the flour isn't so densely packed. This is especially important with cake flour. Sifting also is a good way to blend all dry ingredients evenly and aerate dry ingredients.

FIGURE 3-13:
Use a flour sifter when you want smooth, evenly textured flour.

If you don't have a sifter and you need sifted flour for a recipe, you can use a wire mesh strainer instead (see Figure 3-14 for instructions).

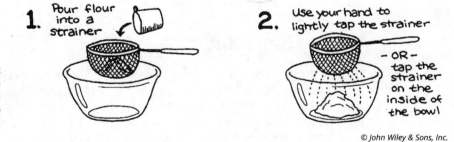

FIGURE 3-14:
In a pinch, you can always use a strainer to sift flour.

Funnel

Funnels come in handy in the kitchen in many ways. They're ideal for hanging an angel food cake pan over or for filling salt shakers. They're also helpful if you need to return liquids to containers without spilling. You may not reach for a funnel every time you bake, but when you need one, you'll be glad you have it.

Kitchen scissors

Keeping a pair of scissors in the kitchen for food-related jobs is a good idea. Kitchen scissors are perfect for trimming pastry dough, cutting paper to line a pan, opening plastic bags, cutting fresh herbs, and snipping strings. The heavier and stronger the scissors you have, the better they will help you in the kitchen — heavy-duty scissors can easily cut through doughs or frozen items in one try. Also, the weight of sturdy scissors makes the cut more precise.

TIP

When cutting up fruits, especially sticky ones like dates, figs, apricots, and so on, lightly oil or butter the scissors first.

Microplane

A microplane is a small, handheld grater and an incredibly versatile tool. You can grate nutmeg, chocolate, garlic, citrus peels (making zest), and ginger.

Oven thermometer

If you were to run out immediately and purchase just one item for the kitchen, I recommend an oven thermometer. A good oven thermometer is inexpensive and can save you from ruining your baked goods. Because you rely on your oven for baking, you need to be sure that the heat is accurate. Many home-oven thermostats aren't always accurate, so the best way to monitor your oven's temperature is with a thermometer. Look for one with a hook for hanging. I hang my thermometer on the oven's center rack and can easily double-check the temperature. Installing an auxiliary oven thermostat is the best thing you can do for your oven and the success of your baking. Flip to Chapter 4 for more on oven thermometers.

Pastry bags and tips

I like a sturdy nylon cloth or silicon pastry bag for decorating cakes. If you're going to purchase one, I suggest getting one slightly larger than you think you need (it's always better to have more room than you need). Pastry tips are hard little metal cones that are either dropped into the pastry bag (coming out the small end) or screwed onto the coupler on the outside of the bag (making switching tips quite easy). The tip you use determines the pattern you pipe onto the cake. For more on using a pastry bag, see Chapter 10.

TIP

For small, quick piping jobs, use a small zipper-top plastic bag rather than digging out the pastry bag. Fill it with icing, remove the excess air, seal the top, and snip off a tiny bit of one corner. You're now ready to pipe away!

Pastry blender

A pastry blender is a handheld tool with a set of steel cutters (see Figure 3-15). The most common use for a pastry blender is to cut fats into flour quickly so that the fats won't melt and your dough remains tender. When shopping for a pastry blender, be sure it's sturdy and not flimsy like a whisk. To use a pastry blender, mix the ingredients while cutting into the fats with the blender using a rocking, up-and-down bouncing motion. If you don't have a pastry blender, you can use two knives or two forks to cut in the fat.

FIGURE 3-15:
Using a pastry blender to cut fat into flour makes the job quick and easy.

© John Wiley & Sons, Inc.

Pastry brush

A pastry brush (see Figure 3-16) is a small tool that makes life in the kitchen a lot easier — there's no substitute for a brush. You use it to spread melted butter, glaze pastries, and brush breads with egg wash. If you enjoy working with phyllo dough or pastry, you may want to purchase a pastry brush. Look for one with very soft bristles. Rough or stiff brushes will tear your pastry, so avoid them if you can. Wash your brush with hot, soapy water after each use and hang to dry. Do not store with the weight on the bristles or you will cause them to curve and not brush effectively anymore.

FIGURE 3-16:
A pastry brush.

© John Wiley & Sons, Inc.

Pie weights

When you prebake an empty pie shell, sometimes you'll need to weigh down the crust with pie weights to prevent it from bubbling up. Pie weights are available at any kitchen supply store and are usually ceramic or metal round pellets. To use them, pour them onto an unbaked, foil-lined piecrust and then place the crust in the oven, as shown in Figure 3-17. About 5 to 10 minutes before the crust has finished baking, remove the weights by lifting out the foil and return the crust to the oven to finish browning.

1.
TO USE PIE WEIGHTS, POUR THEM INTO AN UNBAKED, FOIL-LINED PIECRUST. PLACE IN THE OVEN.

2.
ABOUT 5 TO 10 MINUTES BEFORE THE CRUST HAS FINISHED BAKING, REMOVE THE WEIGHTS BY LIFTING OUT THE FOIL AND RETURN THE CRUST TO THE OVEN TO FINISH BROWNING.

FIGURE 3-17: Using pie weights when baking an empty piecrust.

© John Wiley & Sons, Inc.

TIP

If you don't have pie weights, you can use dried beans instead. Follow the same directions as for the pie weights. Keep the beans in a special jar — you can reuse them many times. Unfortunately, after you've used beans in place of pie weights, the beans can no longer be cooked — they'll have dried out too much.

Sieve (strainer)

A sieve is great for sifting flour, dusting cakes with confectioners' sugar, or straining liquids from solids. A sieve generally has a bowl-shaped bottom made of fine mesh and a long handle. You also can mash soft fruits through the mesh to make a puree, which is especially good for removing all the seeds from a raspberry puree.

Silpat

Silicon baking sheets are used to line cookie sheets for an easy, nonstick, reusable sheet cover. They're great for baking macaroons, Parmesan crisps, lacy cookies, and most other baked goods. The silicon sheets aren't for temperatures above 500 degrees. Be sure to follow care instructions for a longer lifespan.

Spatulas

Two kinds of spatulas are important in baking: rubber and metal. A rubber spatula (shown in Figure 3-18) is great for scraping down the sides of bowls during mixing, getting all the batter into pans, and folding together ingredients. Choose a spatula with a flexible, but stiff, blade. The stiffness in the blade gives you more scraping control. Don't expose your rubber spatula to heat because most will melt or crack.

FIGURE 3-18:
Rubber spatulas are great for scraping every bit of batter from a mixing bowl.

A metal spatula (see Figure 3-19) has blunt edges and a rounded tip and is the perfect tool for spreading frostings and fillings. These are available in a wide range of sizes, but for finished cakes, you may want to have a 10-inch blade so that you can sweep across the entire top of the cake for a smooth finish. Make sure that the blade fits snugly in the handle and that the handle is comfortable to hold.

FIGURE 3-19:
Metal spatulas are especially useful for spreading frostings.

Timer

Many people use their smartphones to keep time, but you may still want a kitchen timer. A timer is an inexpensive item that can save you money in the long run by reminding you when to take your baked creations out of the oven, therefore preventing wasted batches.

REMEMBER

Always set your timer for the minimum amount of time given in a recipe, and check for doneness. You can always leave your goodies in the oven for a few more minutes — just don't forget to reset the timer!

Tongs

Think of tongs as an extension of your hands. Tongs are great for retrieving foods from hot water, flipping cooking foods, and lifting hot lids.

Trivets

A trivet can be made of wood, cork, or ceramic. It's usually round or square and is placed underneath the bottom of a hot pot or pan to prevent it from burning the surface it's placed on. Trivets also protect glass and ceramic baking dishes from the sudden shock of cold surfaces, which can cause them to break.

Vegetable peeler

There's nothing like a comfortable vegetable peeler for removing the skins of fruits and vegetables. A vegetable peeler also makes great chocolate curls. Look for a stainless steel blade so that it won't react with acids.

Wire whisk

Not a week goes by when I don't use my wire whisk. It has many purposes: It mixes, blends, and aerates batters and ingredients. It's essential if you want to make puddings, smooth lumpy liquids, or blend liquids into solids. If you don't have a whisk, I recommend that you get one. Purchase a stainless steel whisk that's comfortable to hold and use. Avoid a narrow handle because your hand might get tired holding it. And look for one that's well manufactured so that food doesn't get stuck in it.

2
Basic Training for Baking

Discover the variety of ovens and how to use them.

Understand basic techniques frequently used in baking.

Identify allergens in recipes and how to craft an allergy-free dessert.

Unlock kitchen mysteries, from lingo used in baking to baking in an Instant Pot.

Chapter **4**

Familiarizing Yourself with Your Oven

Most people take their oven for granted — it has always been there and it always will be in the kitchen. Some people don't think twice about their oven. They just put food in and it cooks. Others find that they're constantly battling the demons that live inside. If you have a love-hate relationship with your oven, read on to discover how to uncover the quirks of your oven and overcome common oven issues. Even if you don't have a worrisome oven, in this chapter I tell you how to make sure that your oven remains in tiptop working order.

Knowing the Difference among the Three Types of Ovens

You can imagine how important a properly working oven is. Three different types of ovens are on the market: gas, electric, and convection ovens. Gas and electric are the most common varieties found in homes, and convection ovens are generally found in professional or top-of-the-line kitchens.

Before conventional ovens were in homes (the first gas stove was introduced into American homes in the 1850s), the majority of cooking was done over open fires, and the baking was done in beehive-like ovens usually above or behind an open fire. Temperature was gauged by touch — how long your hand could remain in the oven. Judging when an oven was hot enough was one of a baker's most difficult challenges. Bakers today have it easy — they even have choices. The next time you have to purchase an oven, consider the information in the following sections.

Gas ovens

Gas ovens generally have a constantly running pilot light, and the heat comes from a perforated bar that runs down the center or in a T shape in the bottom of the oven. This bar is usually covered by a false bottom of the oven. An advantage of this false bottom is that you can set pans of water on the bottom of the oven floor if you want to make your oven "moist" for baking bread. Another advantage to a gas oven is that it tends to be warm because of the pilot light (although many modern ovens have eliminated this constant burning pilot and replaced it with a "self-starting" pilot). If you have the older type, inside the oven is the perfect place to let bread dough rise because it's warm and draft free.

WHAT'S GOING ON IN THERE?

Everyone knows what an oven is, but have you ever given much thought to how your oven works? Food cooks in an oven because it's surrounded by hot, dry air. How quickly or evenly the food cooks depends on the temperature of the oven. The way food is baked in the oven is due to *conduction,* or transfer, of energy (heat, in the case of baking) from the air to the batter or dough.

The foods you bake are made up of many elements: proteins, starches, sugars, water, and fats. Heat has an effect on all these elements, each producing a specific and necessary reaction. Slowly, the heat from the air inside the oven is transferred to and penetrates the food from the outside inward (that's why the outside of a cake may look cooked, even though it's still wet and gooey inside). The metal pan helps to retain the heat from the oven and acts as an insulator for the heat. Heat affects the batter in several ways:

- The proteins (eggs and gluten) begin to lose moisture, shrink, and coagulate.

- The liquid in the starches begins to become gelatinous and firms up (for example, the flour begins to absorb the liquids and becomes firm and dry).

- The sugars begin to caramelize, which is why baked goods turn golden brown. The type of sugar used affects how brown the food becomes.

- Water also evaporates, which can happen rapidly as the internal temperature of the food increases.

- Fats begin to melt.

- The air that has been incorporated into the batter — either because of beating it or because of the gases produced by the chemical leaveners — begins to expand, which gives cakes and cookies rise.

So, basically, the food enters the oven; the surface begins to lose the moisture and firms up; and the food browns, which completes the cooking process. Pretty neat, huh?

Electric ovens

Electric ovens have large, exposed coils placed in the top and bottom of the oven, so they heat from both areas (unless you broil, in which case only the top element does the heating). Because electric ovens heat from the top and bottom and gas ovens heat only from the bottom, many people claim that electric ovens supply more even heat, which results in more even cooking. Also, gas ovens will surge on and off with the heat to maintain the temperature, and electric ovens don't. I like electric ovens because you can broil items in the same space that you bake them. This is great if you want to brown the top of a cake or custard and you don't have to worry if the pan will set into the broiler section of the gas oven area.

WHAT HAPPENS IF YOUR OVEN TEMPERATURE IS INACCURATE?

If the temperature of your oven is too cool, the surface of a cake will dry out too quickly, leaving the middle still uncooked. When it does cook through, the cake will be too dry because it will have evaporated too much of the moisture. If the temperature of your oven is too hot, all the chemical reactions happen too quickly. A cake can rise unevenly, or too quickly, and the outside of the cake will be cooked and browned while the inside is still raw batter.

Convection ovens

Convection ovens use an internal fan to circulate the hot air, so every part of the oven is the same temperature and it can cook lots of food at one time. These ovens are almost always free-standing and have many racks. In general, convection ovens cook food faster than conventional ovens, so if you're using one, you may have to reduce the heat called for in a standard recipe by 25 to 50 degrees or reduce the baking time by 25 percent.

Positioning Your Racks

Although it may sound odd to you, the position of the racks within your oven affects the way your foods cook. The center of your oven is where the temperature is most moderate, giving your baked goods what I consider the best placement for even cooking. Depending on the placement of the heating elements inside your oven, you're likely to have hot spots. In general, the lower third of your oven is hotter than the middle (because generally the source of heat is located in the bottom of the oven), and the top third of your oven is also hotter (because heat rises) than the middle but not as hot as the floor.

If your oven heats from the top *and* bottom, you may find your oven to be equally hot at the top and bottom and moderate in the middle. This is why it's important to bake items in the center of the oven. It's where the temperature is most consistent. You can bake in the top and bottom thirds, but you'll have to rotate the items from top to bottom and turn the pans 180 degrees to ensure even baking.

REMEMBER

Hot spots in the oven result in uneven cooking. You can't really do anything about that, but if you notice that you need some extra protection, try placing all your pans on baking sheets before you put them in the oven. The baking sheet will actually help insulate the pans and help bake things more evenly. If it seems that your oven cooks your food unevenly, give the food a half-turn halfway through the baking time, so what was in the back is now in the front and what was on the left is now on the right.

If you need to adjust the racks in your oven, do so while the oven is cool. Racks usually don't just slide in and out easily because most are designed to pull out and still support the weight of the baked good on it without tipping forward. So there is usually some sort of up-and-over motion you have to finesse when removing the racks from each level. You certainly don't want to be trying to manipulate tricky racks when they're hot.

TIP

I recommend using only one rack, the center rack, when you bake. However, if you want to use two racks, position the racks as close to the center of the oven as possible (usually that means one rack will be in the center and one rack will be positioned directly below). Don't place the pans one on top of the other, but position them off-center so that air can circulate around both pans (see Figure 4-1). Halfway through baking, rotate the top and bottom pans and turn them back to front so that they'll bake most evenly. You may notice with two pans in the oven at the same time that you'll need to increase the baking time. Of course, if you have a convection oven, you won't need to rotate the pans or worry about rack placement since every inch of the oven is the exact same temperature.

FIGURE 4-1:
Staggering pans
for even baking.

© John Wiley & Sons, Inc.

Preheating Your Oven — More Important Than You May Think

You'll notice that almost all recipes say to preheat the oven. You may think that this step is frivolous, but it's actually very important.

A preheated oven allows the ingredients to react properly, ensuring a good finished product. If you place anything to bake in a cold oven, the ingredients will react much differently with each other and the results are most undesirable. Preheated ovens contribute a lot to your finished product:

>> They give breads their final growth spurt.

>> They give soufflés a good push up.

>> They give cakes a good rise.

>> They keep cookies from spreading all over the pan.

REMEMBER

Whether baking with an electric or convection, allow the oven to preheat for 10 to 15 minutes before you plan to use it to allow time for it to fully heat to baking temperature.

Gauging and Adjusting the Heat

If you've been baking and the results aren't what you expected, it may not be the recipes, but your oven's temperature. Don't trust the oven dial with which you set the temperature. Even ovens that may have been tried and true for many years may suddenly become uncalibrated and, without warning, increase their temperature by 25 to 50 degrees!

An unsuspecting baker wouldn't know that their oven has become uncalibrated — unless they've placed an additional auxiliary thermometer in the oven. You can find oven thermometers in any kitchen-supply store or hardware store; they should cost only a few dollars. The time and frustration an oven thermometer will save, and the peace of mind it gives even a casual baker are worth every dime. Place your oven thermometer in a central location in your oven. You can hang it off the center of your oven if you like (don't place it on the floor of the oven — it gives you an inaccurate reading). If you're convinced you have a tricky oven, you may want to invest in two thermometers — one for the front of the oven and one for the back — to make sure that the temperature is even throughout your oven.

REMEMBER

No peeking: Every time you open the oven door, you lower the oven's temperature. If you keep the door open, you can lower it by 25 to 50 degrees, so constantly checking on your items can be detrimental. Always check after the minimum baking time given. If you need to peek, turn on your oven light and look from the outside. It's the best way to keep your oven the right temperature.

IN THIS CHAPTER

» Getting your measurements just right

» Keeping your goodies from sticking to your pans

» Separating eggs

» Whipping egg whites and heavy cream into shape

» Peeling, zesting, and sectioning fruits

» Working with chocolate

» Scalding milk — it's not cruel, really!

» Bringing out the flavor of nuts by toasting them

Chapter **5**

Focusing on Basic Techniques

When you read a recipe and it calls for scalding milk or tempering chocolate without providing further explanation, it can cause your head to spin. This chapter walks you through some basic techniques that are good to familiarize yourself with.

Measuring Ingredients

You probably know someone who bakes a lot, and it seems like they just toss this in and that in and presto, out come cookies or a pie or something delicious. It seems like magic, so you may wonder how important accurate measuring is. The answer is: *very important.* Proper measuring is critical to baking. Baking is a science, and when you mix together ingredients, you're creating chemistry, albeit edible chemistry, so being precise is important. There is balance with flour, leaveners, fats, and liquids.

WARNING

Extra salt or baking soda can ruin otherwise perfect cookies. Too much flour makes muffins taste dry and flavorless. No beginning cook should be nonchalant about measuring. The success of your recipe depends on it.

As you begin to feel more comfortable with baking, you may feel inclined to experiment a bit, maybe add some chocolate chips to peanut butter cookies, or throw some nuts or dried cranberries into oatmeal cookies, or substitute pecans for walnuts. That's all well and fine but give it time. You're never too good or experienced to measure.

Nailing the measurements with a scale

Baking is all about precision and accuracy, so I suggest measuring your ingredients. Even expert bakers use scales when making their favorite baked goods.

While teaching culinary arts I always kicked off the class with a quick measurement challenge, beginning with each student measuring a cup of flour. Then we weighed each student's cup of flour, and guess what? Not a single student had 120 grams (the correct weighted measurement of all-purpose flour), and one student had more than 200 grams of flour. Imagine making a cake or cookies with so much extra flour. Having that much flour can drastically throw off the results of your baked goods.

PACKING IT IN

Sometimes ingredients, such as brown sugar, shredded cheeses, coconut, or herbs, are called for as lightly or firmly packed. Why pack? Generally, these ingredients are bulkier and can form big air pockets if you use the traditional spoon-and-level method of measuring. If you apply light or slightly firm pressure to the ingredients, you eliminate some of the air pockets and get a more accurate measurement. Never push the ingredients in so much that you actually crush them or pack them in so tightly that you have difficulty getting them out the of cup measure.

If you do so, you'll overmeasure, adding too much of the ingredient. A good visual cue that you have lightly packed something is that after you pour it out of the measuring cup, it will lose the shape of the cup it was in. If it's firmly packed, it will slightly retain the shape of the measuring cup after it's dumped out into the bowl, but it will be easy to stir apart.

Investing in a scale is a smart move. You can purchase a scale relatively inexpensively — around $15 to 25 — and they take up minimal space in your kitchen. Be sure to get a weighted scale that measures with the metric measurements of grams and kilograms.

Measuring with teaspoons and tablespoons

Teaspoons and tablespoons are pretty simple, and you can use the same measuring tools for both liquids and dry ingredients. For liquids, fill the spoon until it's full. For dry ingredients, pour or scoop into the spoon until it's full, leveling off the spoon with the straight side of a spatula or knife.

WARNING

Never measure over the bowl of ingredients you're using for the recipe. If you overpour or level extra into the bowl, your measurements won't be accurate.

Measuring dry ingredients

To measure flour, sugar, breadcrumbs, and other dry ingredients (with the exception of brown sugar in many cases), spoon the ingredients lightly into the measuring cup. Then level off the cup with the straight side of a butter knife — don't use the cutting side (see Figure 5-1). Leveling it off gives you one level cup. If the recipe calls for a heaping cup, don't level off the cup. Instead, leave a small, mounded top of ingredients.

To measure chopped nuts, shredded cheese, fresh herbs, and coconut, spoon the ingredients into the measuring cup and pack down lightly.

Measuring fats and other solids

To measure shortening, spoon the ingredients into a cup and pack down firmly with a spoon or rubber spatula to eliminate any air holes. Lucky for bakers, you don't often have to measure fats because butter and margarine come in conveniently measured sticks. One stick equals 8 tablespoons. Two sticks equal 1 cup. You still have to measure solid shortening, but now they make shortening sticks, so even that task has been greatly simplified.

TIP

If you're measuring fats, an easy way to keep the cup clean (and save yourself time by not having to wash it) is to place a piece of plastic wrap in the measuring cup first. Then, after you measure the shortening, pull the ends of the plastic out of the cup. The measuring cup stays clean and you have perfectly measured shortening.

Accurate Measuring

FIGURE 5-1:
Measuring dry
ingredients.

Measuring liquids

Always use a glass measuring cup for measuring liquids. For an accurate reading, always rest the cup on a level surface and read at eye level (see Figure 5-2).

FIGURE 5-2:
Measuring liquids
at eye level.

Sometimes the container in which you purchase an ingredient might be labeled in ounces when your recipe calls for cup or spoon measurements (or vice versa). Check out Table 5-1 for some common equivalencies.

TABLE 5-1

Measurement Equivalents

If a Recipe Calls for This Amount	You Also Can Measure It This Way
Dash	2 or 3 drops (liquid) or less than ⅛ teaspoon (dry)
1 tablespoon	3 teaspoons or ½ ounce
2 tablespoons	1 ounce
¼ cup	4 tablespoons or 2 ounces
⅓ cup	5 tablespoons plus 1 teaspoon
½ cup	8 tablespoons or 4 ounces
1 cup	16 tablespoons or 8 ounces
1 pint	2 cups or 16 ounces or 1 pound
1 quart	4 cups or 2 pints
1 gallon	4 quarts
1 pound	16 ounces

Preparing Pans

For many basic recipes, you need to grease the pan, so always prepare your pan before you start mixing the batter. The only exception is if you use nonstick spray. Then just quickly spray the pan just before you pour the batter into it. That way, the coating won't slide down the sides of the pan while you mix up the batter. You also can dust the greased pan with flour for an added barrier of protection. When you grease a pan, you're essentially creating a thin barrier that keeps the cake from sticking to the pan. These sections explain different ways to ready your pans when baking.

Using solid shortening

When you grease a pan, use solid shortening. Many people use the residue of butter or margarine wrappers, which is okay, but if you have shortening, use it. Shortening doesn't contain water, which can cause the batter to stick to the pan, and it also can withstand higher temperatures without burning. Flour you use to dust with also adheres better to shortening than to butter or margarine.

Place about ½ tablespoon of shortening in the pan that is to be greased and spread it into a thin layer with your fingers or a piece of waxed paper. Professional bakers use a medium-stiff pastry brush to apply grease, but I think fingers work just as well, and you already have them at the ready. If your recipe tells you to dust with flour, place about 1 tablespoon of flour in the bottom of your pan. Rotate and tap the flour around in the pan until it clings to the bottom and sides of the pan (this is also a good way to see that you have completely coated the pan with grease because the flour won't cling if you missed a spot).

If you're making a chocolate cake, dust your pans with sifted cocoa. Then you won't have the telltale marks of flour on your cake when you turn them out of the pans.

Nonstick cooking spray is a baker's best friend, particularly if you're making muffins (greasing a muffin tin can be cumbersome) or greasing a decorative Bundt pan that has lots of nooks to get into. Nonstick sprays contain emulsified oil beads that literally rest on the pan's surface creating a barrier between the batter and the pan. A nonstick flour/oil spray on the market called Baker's Joy does two jobs with the press of a button.

REMEMBER

If a recipe calls for greased pans, always do it even if the pans you're using have a nonstick coating. It's up to you which method of greasing you use. Nonstick spray is quick and easy, but I enjoy the ritual of greasing and flouring pans by hand. Plus, it's the perfect task to give the little ones when they want to help out in the kitchen.

Lining a pan

Occasionally, a pan has to be lined with parchment, waxed paper, or other liner to prevent a cake from sticking to the pan. Sometimes liners are used if the batter is very sticky and greasing the pan won't be sufficient. Other times, you won't want to grease the pan, but you want to ensure that the baked item won't stick. Many professionals prefer to line their pans because doing so is the surest of ways to prevent baked goods from sticking to the pans. If you need to line a pan, the recipe will tell you. To hold the liner in place, place a dab of shortening on the pan, and then place the liner on top. Figure 5-3 shows you how to line a variety of pans, which I also discuss in the following list:

>> **To cut a liner to fit a round pan:** Place the pan on a sheet of parchment or waxed paper and trace the shape of the pan onto the paper. Cut out the circle and place it in the pan. You can grease and flour the paper and the sides of the pan, too, to ensure that it will not stick to the cake once it is baked and it will be easy to remove.

TIP

To prevent paper liners from slipping out of place, grease the pan with shortening or butter and then insert the paper. The liner will stick in place.

>> **To cut a liner to fit a loaf pan:** Take two long pieces of parchment or waxed paper. Cut one to fit the length of the pan and the second to fit the width of the pan. Allow extra for overhang. Grease the pan, then fit both pieces of paper.

>> **To line a jelly roll pan:** Trace the pan onto a piece of waxed paper or parchment. Secure the paper onto the jelly roll pan by greasing it first, and then flatten the liner onto the pan to fit.

>> **To line a tube pan:** Trace the pan on a piece of waxed or parchment paper. If possible, stick the pencil inside the tube and draw around its base. If you can't reach, hold the pan upside down and press the paper onto the base to mark the outer and inner edges of the pan. Cut out the paper and ring. Don't line the sides of a tube pan if it's a sponge cake or an angel food cake. Those batters need to climb the walls of the pan.

PREPARING PANS

FOR A ROUND PAN:
PLACE THE PAN ON A SHEET OF
PARCHMENT OR WAXED PAPER.
TRACE THE SHAPE OF THE PAN
ONTO THE PAPER....

...CUT OUT THE CIRCLE AND PLACE IT
IN THE PAN. YOU CAN GREASE AND
FLOUR THE PAPER AND THE SIDES
OF THE PAN TOO!

FOR A LOAF PAN:
TAKE 2 LONG PIECES OF PARCHMENT.
OR WAXED PAPER. CUT ONE TO FIT THE
LENGTH OF THE PAN AND A SECOND TO
FIT THE WIDTH. GREASE THE PAN, THEN
FIT BOTH PIECES INTO THE PAN!
(THEY WILL OVERLAP AND THERE
WILL BE SOME OVERHANG)

FIGURE 5-3:
Making liners for
baking pans.

© John Wiley & Sons, Inc.

The simplest and most common liners are those that you use when you prepare cupcakes or muffins. You can purchase muffin cup liners at the grocery store to fit the cup and pour the batter directly into the paper cup.

Working with Eggs

Eggs are important ingredients in baking. They add leavening, texture, color and richness. Plus, they also add an element of nutrition. Eggs help with binding and hold batters together, and the protein in eggs helps the structure of the dough hold its shape. The following sections explain what you need to know about working with eggs.

Separating an egg

Baked goods often call for egg whites or egg yolks without their counterpart. You can buy egg whites without the yolks, but separating the eggs yourself is nearly as fast and is much cheaper.

Eggs separate best when they're cold. Not having any egg yolk in the whites is important, but it's okay if the whites get mixed into the yolks. If you're separating many eggs, minimize your risk of leaking egg yolk into the whites by doing one at a time over a small bowl and then adding the clean white into a large bowl. Transfer the egg white after each separation to prevent any accidental egg yolk breakage from contaminating the whole batch of whites.

WARNING

When working with raw eggs, keep in mind that eggs can carry a bacteria that may be present in the porous shells of the eggs, which can cause salmonella poisoning. Although this is rare, it's helpful to know that nearly every carton of eggs sold in the United States has a toll-free number on it as well as an expiration date for the eggs. You can call the supplier to see if any cases of salmonella have been reported. (Not many have.)

That said, you can choose how you want to separate your eggs. Look at Figure 5-4 to see these methods in action.

> » The most common practice is to crack the egg cleanly in half over a bowl and pass the yolk from one shell to the other, allowing the white to gradually fall into the bowl below. This method can be a bit messy, and you run the risk of the yolk getting punctured. Don't let any yolk contaminate the whites because egg yolk will prevent the whites from whipping to their full volume. Also, some whites will be lost to the shell.
>
> Note that most food safety experts don't recommend this practice because of the risk of introducing salmonella into the egg product even though the risk is quite small and people have been doing this safely for decades. If you do use this technique, make sure your eggshells, particularly eggs from a farm stand, don't have any foreign matter sticking to the shells.

» My favorite method is to crack and break the egg into your cupped hand held over a bowl. Gently relax your fingers, which allows the white to spill through and drop into the bowl below. After all the white has separated, you're left with a perfect, round yolk. Wash your hands thoroughly before and after using this method.

» You can also separate an egg by using an egg separator. Place the egg separator over a small bowl or glass. Crack the egg open, and let it fall into the center of the separator. The whites will slip through the slots of the separator and into the bowl, and the yolk will stay in the separator, which can be transferred easily into another bowl.

FIGURE 5-4:
A few ways to separate an egg.

© John Wiley & Sons, Inc.

Whipping egg whites

The purpose of whipping egg whites is to incorporate as much air as possible into the whites, which gives good lift to your cakes or meringues. If you have good arm strength, the best tools are a copper bowl and a whisk with a large balloon. The most common method of whipping egg whites is with a mixer with a whisk attachment. A pinch of salt helps break up the gelatinous texture of egg whites; a pinch of cream of tartar helps to stabilize them. If you use a copper bowl, you don't need the cream of tartar or salt because the copper of the bowl helps stabilize the egg whites naturally.

REMEMBER

Egg whites increase their volume best if they come to room temperature first. They can expand up to six times their natural volume, so make sure the bowl you choose can accommodate them. Also, be sure the bowl and whisk you use are perfectly dry and clean; any amount of moisture, egg yolk, or other debris will prevent the egg white from whipping up properly.

Beating whites to *soft peaks* means the whites flop gently over when the beater is removed; *stiff peaks* hold their shape when the whisk is lifted (see Figure 5-5).

FIGURE 5-5:
Soft and stiff peaks.

© John Wiley & Sons, Inc.

WARNING

Pasteurized egg whites are being sold in the refrigerated sections of many grocery stores. *Don't* use these egg whites if the recipe you're using requires you to beat them. The pasteurization process breaks down the egg whites' ability to whip up and hold their shape. If you try to do this, you'll end up with a frothy top and liquid on the bottom of your bowl.

WARNING

Don't overbeat the egg whites or they'll become dry. If you're nervous about overbeating egg whites, you can always stop using the electric mixer when the whites reach soft peaks and finish beating them by hand with a wire whisk. Also, be sure not to beat the egg whites until you're ready to use them. If you let them stand around, they'll deflate.

Whipping Heavy Cream

Many types of cream are on the market. The best cream for whipping is called heavy whipping cream (which is different from plain whipping cream, which has less fat — only 30 percent — and will whip up but won't hold its shape well). Heavy whipping cream contains 36 to 40 percent butterfat and will whip up and hold its form without much effort. Remember, it doubles in volume, so if a recipe calls for 2 cups of whipped cream, you just need to whip up 1 cup of heavy whipping cream.

Use a whisk or handheld or electric mixer. Pour the cream into a chilled metal bowl and whip until it thickens and just forms soft peaks (don't overbeat). Add 2 tablespoons of granulated sugar or 4 tablespoons of confectioners' sugar and 1 teaspoon of vanilla when the cream begins to thicken but before it forms soft peaks.

TIP

To prevent whipped cream from deflating, store it in the fridge with a paper towel covering the container. Tupperware containers work great for this if you put the paper towel under the lid before closing. You'll be amazed at how long you can keep whipped cream this way.

WARNING

Don't overwhip heavy cream, or else it will turn into butter. This will happen suddenly, especially with electric mixers, so be careful. To avoid overbeating your cream, if you use an electric mixer, stop beating the cream when it begins to thicken, and finish whipping it by hand with a wire whisk.

Working with Fruits

Fresh fruits are a wonderful filling for pies, cakes, and many baked desserts. Refer to this section the next time you're working with a recipe that calls for fruit.

Peeling and pitting fruits

Keep these tips in mind to get the best fruit for your recipes:

» **Apricots or nectarines:** You don't need to peel apricots or nectarines. Just slice them in half and pop out the pits.

» **Apples and pears:** Peel off the skin with a standard vegetable peeler, cut the fruit into quarters, then remove the core and stem bits from the center.

   If you need the fruit to stay whole, remove the stem and core using an apple corer, which has a handle attached to an elongated curved piece of metal with a cylindrical bottom and a cutting edge (see Chapter 3). Just press down vertically with a slight twisting motion until you reach the bottom.

>> **Cherries:** While cherry pitting can be tedious, it's actually quite easy. Simply make a slit, north to south, around the circumference of the cherry and pull it apart, and then pop out the pit with the tip of a paring knife or your finger. This method will result in the cherries being both pitted and halved, which is the way most recipes require them. You don't need a cherry pitter tool unless you're preparing large quantities for canning or jam.

>> **Peaches:** If your peach is perfectly ripe, sometimes the skin will slip right off, without even so much as a knife, but that's not always the case. This method will make peeling peaches a snap, leaving the beautiful flesh unmarked.

TIP

Have ready a medium-sized bowl of ice water. Set a 2-quart pan on the stove to boil. While you wait for the water to boil, lightly cut a small X on the bottom of each peach. Try not to cut into the flesh, but just the skin. When the water is boiling, gently drop the peach into the water. Wait about 30 seconds (you'll see the cut skin start to loosen and flutter a bit in the water). Remove the peach from the water and plunge it into the ice water for 1 minute. The skin should slip right off. If not, return the peach to the hot water for 30 more seconds. This method also works for plums and tomatoes.

Zesting and sectioning citrus fruits

The *zest* of citrus is the colored part of the skin, which contains essential oils. The *pith* is the white membrane between the skin and the fruit, which is bitter. You want to get the zest and not the pith when zesting citrus fruits.

The most common citrus fruits used for zesting are lemons and oranges. Here are the two ways to zest a citrus fruit:

>> You can use a *citrus zester,* a kitchen tool that removes the zest of the fruit and leaves the pith behind. Hold the fruit in one hand and the zester in the other; run the citrus zester along the length of the fruit. The peel should come off in thin little strips. You can either dice the strips or use them whole (the recipe will call for one or the other). You can see what this looks like in Figure 5-6.

FIGURE 5-6:
A citrus zester.

© John Wiley & Sons, Inc.

» You can also use the coarse, sharp-edged holes of a grater (not the large holes used to grate cheese). Rub the fruit against the sharp edges, rotating the fruit after a few rubs, until the peel grates off and the desired amount is grated (see Figure 5-7). Be careful of your knuckles and fingers when using a grater because the holes are very sharp.

FIGURE 5-7: Using a grater to zest citrus fruits.

WARNING

Using a vegetable peeler to remove the zest can be tricky business and isn't recommended. I speak from experience. Unless you have a very dull peeler, the chances you'll remove zest and pith together are very high. Then you'll have wasted the zest you did remove. Remember, the white pith is bitter and should be avoided.

You probably won't run into too many recipes that call for sectioned fruit, but this is a handy technique to know, and sectioned fruit always makes a nice garnish.

Citrus fruits, particularly oranges and grapefruits, have a tough skin that can be difficult to chew. When you section a citrus fruit, remove the fruit from the tough membrane, making it easier to eat.

To section an orange, follow these simple steps:

1. **Cut off the top and bottom of the fruit and cut to the fruit.**

   Don't leave any white pith on the fruit.

2. **Lay the fruit on its cut end.**

3. **Being careful not to cut too deeply, cut away the peel and the white pith, following the shape of the fruit.**

4. **Hold the fruit in one hand.**

   It will be juicy, so you may want to do this over a bowl. You'll see the membranes that hold the fruit together.

5. **Make a cut parallel and right next to the membrane, cutting toward the center to release the fruit.**

   When you get to the center, turn the knife and cut away, next to the other membrane, following the shape and size of the section of fruit and continue cutting until the section of fruit is free.

6. **Repeat until all the sections are free.**

   Figure 5-8 shows you how to do this.

Sectioning an Orange to Eliminate Membranes

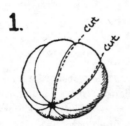 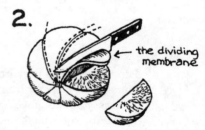

FIGURE 5-8: Sectioning an orange isn't as difficult as you may think.

Melting Chocolate

There is nothing so versatile or universally welcomed as melted chocolate. You can stir it into recipes, drizzle it over finished baked goods, dip cookie bottoms into it, or stir it into frosting for a flavor burst. Melting chocolate is easy, but you do need to pay attention when you're doing it.

Never melt chocolate directly over a heating element. Chocolate burns very easily and must be melted over low heat. Because quality varies from brand to brand, follow the manufacturer's instructions for best results. If none are given, here are some guidelines:

1. Cut the chocolate into pieces smaller than a 1-ounce square.

2. Place the chocolate pieces in the top part of a double boiler, and set it over simmering, not boiling, water.

3. As the chocolate melts, stir it often; remove it from the heat when almost all of it has melted.

4. Continue stirring until all the pieces have melted and the chocolate is smooth.

The microwave is also a great tool for melting chocolate. Chocolate melts very easily, so set your temperature to medium-low and follow the manufacturer's directions for time (usually 1 to 2 minutes). Check the chocolate after 1 minute. It won't melt the same way it does over a double boiler, so you'll have to stir it and keep a close eye on it because it will burn easily. White chocolate needs particularly close attention and very low heat.

TIP

To melt chocolate, place it in a metal bowl and put the bowl in the oven with the temperature turned on the lowest possible setting. Close the door. After about 5 minutes, turn the oven off. In about 10 minutes, the chocolate should be melted.

Scalding Milk

Scalding has fallen out of favor among many cooks because now that milk is pasteurized, it is an unnecessary step to retard the souring of milk. However, it's also a good idea to scald milk that you use for bread baking to enhance the sugars, which will promote better texture in your breads. To scald, you heat the milk to just below its boiling point. Follow these steps:

1. Measure the milk into a saucepan and place it over medium heat.

2. Heat the milk, stirring occasionally.

3. As soon as the surface of the milk begins to bubble, remove the pan from the heat.

    If the milk does boil, it might form a thick film on top. Remove the film before using the milk underneath.

TIP

Here's a trick that I learned at the bakery: Rub some butter along the inside edge of the pan. Even if the milk does foam up when it's heated, it will stop foaming when it reaches the butter.

Toasting Nuts

Toasting nuts helps to bring out their wonderful flavor and removes some of their raw taste. To toast nuts, place them in a shallow baking dish and bake in a 350-degree oven, stirring often, until they're golden brown and smell toasted, about 5 to 10 minutes, depending on the nut (pine nuts take the least amount of time; almonds and hazelnuts take a bit longer). Don't overbake them or their flavor will become bitter.

You can also toast nuts in a dry skillet over medium heat. Stir the nuts frequently until they become golden brown and smell toasted, about 5 to 10 minutes, depending on the nut.

TIP

If I have a small amount of nuts to toast, I use my toaster oven. I spread the nuts on the small tray and set the toaster to the lowest setting. After the nuts finish toasting, I let them sit for a few minutes and then check to see if they're golden brown. If they aren't, I just push down the toast button again. The second time around, I closely monitor them to make sure that they don't brown too much.

If you've burned your nuts, discard them — they'll ruin the flavor of your baked item.

goods

» **Understanding ingredients that are high allergens**

» **Discovering store-bought alternatives for high allergen ingredients**

Chapter **6**

Considering Allergies and Insensitivities When Baking

Whether it's an allergy to eggs or a wheat intolerance, more than likely you know someone living with an allergy. Even though this chapter doesn't replace an extensive book on baking with allergies, I do strive to help you bake recipes for those living with allergies.

This chapter covers wheat, eggs, nuts, and dairy because these four foods can significantly affect baking outcomes. I look where allergens can be hidden and why you need to understand substitutions and how to bake your favorite recipes with those substitutions. Baking for someone living with allergies doesn't need to be scary, although I understand the fears involved. When you take the time, those living with allergies will thank you for it.

Examining Gluten- and Wheat-Free Baking

Gluten is a protein in wheat, and not only is gluten found in wheat, but it's also found in many other products. Here's a simple list of common grains that contain gluten:

>> Wheat (including wheatberries, durum, emmer, semolina, spelt, farina, farro, graham, khorasan [also called Kamut], and einkorn)

>> Rye

>> Barley

>> Triticale

>> Malt

>> Brewer's yeast

>> Wheat starch

When baking gluten-free, using the right products is essential. These sections explore some common gluten-free flours, as well as information on how to make your own blend.

Gluten-free flours

Food marketers and manufacturers have recognized the importance of gluten-free and wheat-free living and have created amazing products to support a gluten- and wheat-free lifestyle. Your options are endless: You can find everything from pizza crusts to cookies to breads all without gluten and wheat.

King Arthur Flour and Bob's Red Mill are two leaders in making products for baking or cooking gluten and wheat free. The Gluten Free Measure for Measure Flour from King Arthur is a great choice as well as Bob's Red Mill's 1 to 1 Baking Flour. Each company tests for gluten, and their products are made from wheat-free products; however, they can't guarantee that the flour hasn't been contaminated with any wheat products. Look at the nearby sidebar to make your own flour. You can also check out the latest edition of *Living Gluten-Free For Dummies* by Danna (Korn) Van Noy for more ideas (John Wiley & Sons, Inc.).

MAKING YOUR OWN WHEAT-FREE FLOUR BLEND

If you need to make your own blend here is a simple recipe to try:

- 1 cup white rice flour
- 1 cup potato starch flour
- 1 cup soy flour
- 1 cup oat flour (grind gluten-free oats in a blender to create oat flour)
- ¼ cup tapioca starch

Whisk these ingredients together and use as a 1:1 flour replacement.

Gluten-free and wheat-free recipes

Are you ready to bake? If so, you can use a flour alternative in Dense Chocolate Brownies or the Oatmeal Raisin Cookies in Chapter 8 and the Chocolate Zucchini Bread in Chapter 13 and Carrot Cake in Chapter 9. You can make the cheesecakes, like in Chapter 9, with a nut crust or using a wheat-free cookie for the crumbs. I love a good pecan crust for the Pumpkin Cheesecake in Chapter 9. The Gluten-Free Chocolate Hazelnut Cake and the Lemon Rosemary Almond Cake both use nuts for the flour and are gluten- and wheat-free. Just make sure any additional ingredients used are made in a wheat-free space; you can find this information on the food label.

WARNING

Avoid cross contaminating while baking. Be sure your baking items have been properly cleaned and haven't touched any wheat or gluten surfaces. I recommend giving all your tools a quick, soapy wash before using just to be on the safe side.

Moving beyond Eggs

Eggs are a major allergen and are often found in many baked goods. Here are the five items I consistently use as a 1:1 egg replacement when baking egg-free:

- ➤ ¼ cup mashed bananas
- ➤ 1 tablespoon chia or flaxseeds with 3 tablespoons water (mix and let sit for ten minutes to thicken)

>> 2 tablespoons water + 2 teaspoons baking powder + 1 teaspoon vegetable oil (whisked together)

>> ¼ cup Aquafaba — the water from the chickpea can (you can whip it and use it in place of whipped egg whites)

>> ¼ cup carbonated water — this performs the best in quick breads and muffins

REMEMBER

The key is what you have on hand when baking. This list gives you options, and some may be easier to find in your pantry. Start with muffins, quick breads, and cookies when using these ingredients. Avoid recipes where egg is the star of the recipe like frittatas, soufflés, and egg-centric cakes.

Skipping Out On Nuts

Of all allergens, nuts seem to get the biggest spotlight, and the reason is that a nut allergy can be deadly. If you're baking for someone who requires dishes to be nut-free, find out which nuts a person is reactive to. Some have a peanut allergy (which technically is a legume), whereas some have an allergy to all tree nuts, and some are allergic to all, which can include peanuts, pecans, macadamias, almonds, walnuts, pistachios, cashews, pine nuts, and hazelnuts.

If that's the case, the best choice is to bake recipes that are naturally nut-free. Many recipes only stir in nuts, so you can either omit or replace them with another mix-in, like dried fruit or seeds. Seed and legume butters can be used in place of peanut or nut butters; however, the flavor will be different.

In January 2023 the FDA has now required sesame seeds to be labeled as an allergen on food labels. Allergic reactions to seeds are on the rise in the United States. Make sure you check with your nut-free friends to see if they also need to be seed-free.

WARNING

Avoid any cross contaminants with anything that has touched nuts. A nut allergy often has a highly reactive, and even deadly response, so clean all surfaces before baking a nut-free recipe.

REMEMBER

If you are baking for others, like at a school event or potluck, keep the foods nut-free so everyone can safely enjoy your goodies! If you do include nuts, make sure you clearly label everything with a note like "Includes nuts." Include nut-free options, particularly for school events.

Being Aware of Dairy Allergies

A dairy allergy can mean anything with casein or whey, which can include cow's milk, goat's milk, or sheep's milk. (*Casein* and *whey* are the proteins found in milk, which are often the culprits behind a food allergy.) Products that are frequently used in baking and contain dairy include milk, cream, sour cream, yogurt, chocolate, condensed or evaporated milk, butter, buttermilk, and cheeses. Here I delve deeper into dairy-free options and dairy-free recipes.

Identifying dairy-free alternatives

When baking, here are my top dairy-free baking alternatives:

>> **Butter:** Replace with coconut oil, lard, or vegetable-based shortening.

>> **Buttermilk:** Use 2 teaspoons of lemon juice in 1 cup of nut milk and let the mixture thicken for ten minutes.

>> **Cheese:** A dairy-free cheese can be used in place of cheese.

>> **Chocolate:** Chocolate often contains milk, so look for dairy-free dark chocolate or cacao nibs. Cocoa powder is dairy-free.

>> **Condensed milk:** Coconut milk–based, sweetened, condensed milks are a perfect replacement for sweetened condensed milk. If a specialty market doesn't carry it, check Amazon.

>> **Cream cheese:** Cashew or soy cream cheese is a good replacement for cream cheese. Silken tofu can also be used in place of cream cheese in cheesecakes.

>> **Cream or whipping cream:** Coconut milk and coconut cream are great alternatives for cream. Be sure you're using canned coconut milk or cream and not the variety from a box or coconut water. Place a can of coconut milk in the refrigerator for 30 minutes and then whip the solid coconut fat for frostings.

>> **Milk:** Nut, seed, pea, oat, rice, soy, or hemp milk can be used in recipes that call for milk.

>> **Yogurt or sour cream:** A dairy-free yogurt can be swapped for yogurts or sour cream.

Making dairy-free recipes

You have endless options for baking dairy-free recipes. Cookies are a great place to start. You can replace the butter with vegetable-based shortenings. If a recipe calls for milk, you can usually use a nut milk. Consider these other dairy-free substitutions when baking:

>> **Frosted cookies:** Use coconut products in place of cream and butter.

>> **Brownies, cobblers, and crisps:** Use dairy alternatives that I mention in the previous section. Cobblers and crisps in Chapter 12 are great recipes to try by swapping out coconut oil for butter.

>> **Cakes:** Use almond milk or a blend of oat and nut milks.

>> **Fruit pies:** Swap out lard when making a crust and you're ready to bake. Try the Rhubarb, Cherry, or Blueberry Pies in Chapter 11, along with the Plum Galette and Wonderful Pear Tart.

>> **Breads:** Use oils in place of butters and use a dairy alternative in place of milk. The Pumpkin Bread and Cranberry Orange Bread are dairy-free recipes in Chapter 13.

> » **Reading and understanding recipes** *before* **you start baking**

> » **Having the right tools for the job**

> » **Timing recipes correctly**

> » **Cleaning up as you bake**

Chapter **7**

Getting Ready to Bake

aking, like cooking, is just a series of different techniques. Be familiar with the ingredients and know their different variables. Knowing how ingredients react together is a great way to understand baking and to prevent disaster.

The best way to become comfortable with baking is to practice and practice some more. At first, don't overchallenge yourself when you select recipes. Choose ones that call for familiar ingredients and involve familiar techniques. After you master them, move on to more challenging recipes — maybe try a recipe for which you have to pick up an unfamiliar ingredient or try one new technique. If you continue progressing in a slow and steady manner, you'll soon become a proficient baker, and you may wonder why you ever bought a cake from a grocery store. This chapter focuses on the basics to ensuring you and your kitchen are raring to go.

Preparing Your Kitchen

One of the best first things to do when you're getting ready to bake is to look around your kitchen because that's where all your baking will take place. If you don't spend a lot of time there, take stock of the equipment you have. These sections identify the basics to setting up your kitchen.

Inspect your oven

Take a peek in the oven — the tool without which you couldn't bake at all. Does it need to be cleaned?

REMEMBER

So how do you know if your oven needs to be cleaned? You generally can tell that your oven needs to be cleaned if lots of spilled food has burned onto the oven's surface and smokes or gives off a burned odor when you bake. You should clean your oven about twice a year if you use it regularly, yearly if you use it occasionally. If you can't remember the last time you cleaned your oven or if it smells stale when you open the oven door, it's time to clean.

When was the last time you used your oven for baking? I know a woman who lived in her apartment for six years and never once used the oven. If you're unfamiliar with your oven or you tried baking before and it didn't work out, I strongly suggest that you purchase an oven thermometer to put in your oven — the problem may not have been what you made but how it baked (see Chapter 3 about buying a thermometer). Ovens tend to acquire minds of their own. Just recently (thanks to my oven thermometer), I discovered that my own oven interprets just about all temperatures as 350 degrees Fahrenheit, even when I set the dial at 300 degrees. I never would have discovered this problem without the thermometer, and now I know that I have to set the oven temperature lower. For more about ovens, see Chapter 4.

Organize your space

Look around your kitchen. Do you have a lot of counter space or just a little? Do you have a lot of cabinet space? I have very little counter and cabinet space in my kitchen, so I've organized things to hang on the walls just about everywhere I can. A utensil or pot or pan is within reach just about anywhere I stand in the kitchen, which simplifies my baking time immensely. Think about what you use and, as you read through this book, keep in mind what you may need to make your kitchen efficient.

Counter space is the hottest real estate in the kitchen. If you have a lot of things cluttering up your counter (spice racks, napkin holders, paper towel holders, appliances, and so on), it may be time to reorganize. Take a good look around your kitchen and decide what you can put away and what you want to leave out. If you make coffee only on the weekends, for example, tuck your coffeemaker in a cabinet so that you have more counter space during the week. If you always seem to be searching for utensils in drawers, think about organizing your most frequently used utensils in a can or small crock on the counter.

WARNING

Never store your knives with other utensils. If you reach for a spoon, you could easily cut yourself on a knife's sharp blade.

Take a look in your cabinets. Do you have a lot of opened, half-used bags of flour? Half-used boxes of brown sugar that are now rock hard? Store-bought cookies that you forgot about? Clean out your cabinets at least twice a year, once in the spring and once in the fall, to get rid of forgotten treasures — now trash — and to prevent insect infestation.

TIP

Three-tiered hanging baskets are a huge space-saver in the kitchen. You can use them in literally hundreds of ways (and not one of them has to be food related), such as storing plastic container lids, spice jars, scraps of paper, loose pens and pencils, recipes, and so on.

Take the time now to organize things so that later you won't be looking for all the parts of the food processor or the bottom plate to your springform pan. Feeling comfortable in your kitchen is a huge part of feeling comfortable with baking.

Working with Recipes

If you know how to read, you can read a recipe. However, you need to keep a few things in mind as you select and work with recipes to make sure that you won't experience any surprises along the way.

Consider your skill level

If you want to improve your baking skills, the best thing to do is practice. Start with an easy recipe — one that doesn't require a lot of ingredients or involve numerous steps. Practice beating butter and cream together. Get used to mixing, measuring, scooping, and timing. (For basic techniques, see Chapter 5.) For example, the recipe for Pumpkin Bread in Chapter 13 and the recipe for Snickerdoodles in Chapter 8 are easier recipes to start with getting experience.

After you master basic techniques, try recipes with longer lists of ingredients. Then move on to intermediate recipes, which may involve slightly more difficult techniques, such as whipping egg whites. For example, try the recipe Lemon Rosemary Almond Cake in Chapter 9.

When you feel comfortable with what you're doing, move on to even more challenging recipes. Take a stab at the recipe Tres Leches with Mango in Chapter 9 or Braided Egg Bread in Chapter 14. Before you know it, you'll be baking like a pro.

Understand the instructions

What's crystal clear to recipe writers may not be so easy for you to understand, especially if you aren't an experienced baker. If you run across any unfamiliar words as you read a recipe, be sure to look them up. Use the Glossary of Baking Terms at the back of this book or use a dictionary.

Recipe writers follow certain rules that sometimes confound beginning bakers. For example, if a recipe calls for "1 cup walnuts, chopped," you may wonder whether that means to chop the walnuts and then measure them or to measure out 1 cup of walnuts and then chop them. The answer is simple. When you're supposed to do something to an ingredient *after* you measure it, the action is listed *after* the ingredient; if you're supposed to do something to the ingredient *before* you measure it, the action is listed *before* the ingredient.

Therefore, "1 cup walnuts, chopped" means that you should measure the whole walnuts and then chop them. If you were supposed to chop the nuts before measuring them, the recipe would have called for "1 cup chopped walnuts."

Read the recipe all the way through before you start

When you find a recipe you want to try, read all the way through it carefully before you start baking. You want to preview a recipe for any of the following:

>> To make sure that you're familiar with all the terminology used in the instructions

>> To know how much prep work you'll have to do before you begin

>> To get a sense of how much time it will take you to make it

>> To familiarize yourself with all the necessary ingredients and methods the recipe requires

Look up what you don't know *before* you start baking. Leafing through a book is harder when you're up to your elbows in batter!

Keep in mind that many times it's easier for recipe writers to shorten the main recipe by including some steps in the ingredient list. For example, a recipe may call for "3 apples, peeled, cored, and diced," so you have some work to do to the apples before you get started. I've been caught in the middle of a recipe without nuts chopped, pasta cooked, or vegetables peeled and chopped because I didn't read the recipe fully — I just read it quickly to make sure that I had the necessary ingredients. Similarly, if you read through once, you'll know whether the ingredients need to be chilled or marinated, which may determine whether you can do the recipe now or later. If you develop one good habit of baking, make it this one. You'll thank me later.

Check how many people it serves

As you're deciding what to make, be sure to take the number of servings into account. It's easy enough to figure out whether four dozen cookies are enough for your needs, but you may not be sure about how many people a given pie or cake will serve. Table 7-1 gives you some guidelines.

TABLE 7-1 **How Many People Your Goodies Will Serve**

Baked Good	Yield
8-inch layer cake	8 to 10 people or more
8-inch cheesecake	10 to 12 people
9-inch layer cake	10 to 12 people
9-inch cheesecake	12 to 14 people
9-inch pie	8 to 12 people

To slice your cakes and pies so that you get an accurate yield, see Chapter 18.

KEEPING YOUR RECIPES OUT OF HARM'S WAY

The kitchen can be a dangerous place for papers, recipes, and even books. A cookbook can get into a lot of trouble on a kitchen countertop. Place the cookbook you're using in a convenient place, but not in direct contact with ingredients, especially liquids. Read the recipe several times before you start, place the book a few steps away from the action, and go back and forth to read the recipe. You can tape recipe note cards onto cabinets, at eye level, so that they're always in view but not in harm's way.

The benefit of using a tablet or a phone for recipes is the ability to wipe them clean. Be sure to have your electronics protected from electrical shock with liquids or from breaking if they get bumped in the kitchen.

Generally, the richer the dessert, the smaller the slices you want to cut. Of course, you must take your guests into consideration when choosing a dessert. If you know that someone has a particularly sweet tooth, they may want seconds. Better to have too much than too little.

If you're attending a potluck or expecting a crowd for dessert, think about making something with a high yield, like a sheet cake or cupcakes. Almost all cake recipes can be made into sheet cakes or cupcakes, which feed between 16 and 24 people.

Take inventory

After you've read through your chosen recipe, it's time to assemble all your ingredients and equipment. You don't want to remember halfway through a recipe that you polished off the brown sugar last week and forgot to pick up more at the market. You can avoid last-minute dashes to the market by doing a quick inventory check before you start baking to ensure that you have an adequate supply of all the necessary ingredients.

If you bake infrequently, your flour supply may be lower than you remember. I'm always thinking that I have more eggs and butter in the refrigerator than I really do. It takes only a second to check, and doing so will save you a lot of time in the long run. Start composing a shopping list if you need one.

During this stage, you may discover that you're out of materials. If you're baking muffins, for example, make sure that you have liners for the tins. Also, you may be low on shortening to grease the baking sheets, or you may need more nonstick spray. These things may not be listed among the recipe's ingredients, but they're just as essential as any of the ingredients you add. Assembling the tools and going over ingredients are two surefire ways to ensure that you'll have a successful baking experience. (But you can find useful substitutions on the Cheat Sheet at www. dummies.com if you get stuck without a necessary ingredient. Just search for "Baking For Dummies Cheat Sheet.")

After you've assembled all the ingredients and equipment, it's time to start baking.

Use the right tools for the job

When you read through a recipe, you also need to read about the equipment that's called for. If you have to beat together butter and sugar, you'll more than likely want to have at least a hand mixer available. If you're making rolled cookies, you'll need a rolling pin. The right tools make baking much easier and save you quite a bit of time.

PREMEASURING: MAKE IT EASY ON YOURSELF

Chances are that, at some point in your life, you have happened on a cooking show and have seen the cook dumping in bowls of this and that into bowls or pans. Although you don't see what these pro cooks do beforehand, know that they premeasure everything into these bowls, making it possible to throw together several dishes in a short time. If you premeasure everything (or, in cooking terms, prep everything), you'll make baking the easiest thing in the world to do. After you have your ingredients at your fingertips ready to be mixed together, you may wonder why you ever felt intimidated by baking. Of course, you may dirty an additional bowl or two, but the payback in pleasure and ease of baking is worth the extra few seconds it takes to wash the bowl.

If you know that you'll be pressed for time, you can even prep in advance and store your ingredients in the refrigerator overnight. You will just have to take them out so that everything can come to room temperature before you use it.

Before starting a recipe, be sure that you have the pan size that the recipe calls for. If you use a larger or smaller pan than is called for, your finished product will be different, and you run the risk of it burning or never cooking through. Certain pans can be fudged a little, though. Loaf pans, for example, come in 8½ x 4½ and 9 x 5 sizes, and, in most cases, either can be used with the same result. If the recipe calls for a covered casserole, you can create a cover with aluminum foil.

Of course, much of baking can be done with just a few simple tools, so if you want to bake, you don't have to go out and stock your kitchen with a variety of expensive pans and tools. The following is a list of what I consider the essential tools for baking (flip to Chapter 3 for more detailed descriptions and for a more comprehensive list of baking tools and gadgets):

- Measuring cups/spoons
- Wooden spoon
- Rubber spatula/plastic spatula
- Whisk
- Mixing bowls (at least two sizes)
- Knives (at least a cleaver and a paring knife)
- Pots/skillet (at least a 1-quart, a 2-quart, a stockpot, and a 10-inch skillet)
- Baking sheets

>> Cake/pie pans

>> Cooling racks (two racks are a good start)

If you look around your kitchen, I'm sure you'll find a lot of these items already there. I baked for several years without any electrical appliances; you don't have to spend a lot of money when you're just starting out. Hand mixers, stand mixers, and food processors certainly make quick work of preparing and mixing ingredients and are the workhorses in the kitchen, so if you really start to enjoy baking, invest in one or more of those appliances. They really do make baking a breeze.

However, if you're a simple kind of person or can't fit too many more appliances in your kitchen, try out these recipes from this book. They use a minimum of tools and don't require special machinery to get the job done:

>> Crisp Sugar Cookies (Chapter 8)

>> Crispy Chocolate Chip Cookies (Chapter 8)

>> Granola Bars (Chapter 8)

>> Martha's Chocolate Cake (Chapter 9)

>> Blueberry Muffins (Chapter 13)

WHEN IN DOUBT, USE A SCALE!

Using a metric scale helps you ensure that your brownies don't turn out cakey or your cookies too dry. A metric scale is a means for accuracy and a fast way to prep ingredients. Why? Metric measurement is more finite than using ounces or pounds. Getting down to grams is incredibly helpful with baking, where you may only be using 4 grams of yeast or 127 grams of sugar. An inaccurately measured ingredient can drastically throw off a recipe. Baking involves finite chemical reactions and having accurately measured ingredients will help achieve the best baked goods.

Additionally, if you're following a European recipe, more than likely the recipe will be in weighed measurements, not volumetric. If you don't have a scale, but you're using a European recipe you want to try, you can search out the weighted measurement in volumetric. Just search online for the weight of the ingredient and the measurement converted to volume. For example, in this book I list both weights and volumetric measurements.

When measuring with a scale, place the mixing bowl onto the scale and zero out the weight. Then begin adding in ingredients, zeroing the scale after each addition.

Timing It Right

The recipes in this book include preparation times as well as baking times. However, not everyone bakes at the same pace, so be sure to give yourself ample time to prepare your baked goods. You'll find it much more relaxing when you don't have to play beat-the-clock.

Certain times are *not* included, such as the 15 to 20 minutes it will take for a cake to cool enough to handle. If you want to frost the cake, you'll need to allow even more time for the cake to cool so that you can frost it. What if you run out of an ingredient and have to run to the store? Allow for such mishaps. Even if you don't need additional time, you'll be better off having planned for it. I've cooked under relaxed conditions and flustered conditions alike, and when I'm under the gun in regard to time, the recipes inevitably reflect my rushed approach.

Baking at High Elevations

People who live at elevations above 3,500 feet face some interesting cooking challenges. Because baking is a science, the higher altitude (thanks to the change in air pressure and humidity) causes different reactions in baking. You may notice that once-dependable recipes baked at sea level become a bit out of whack up in the mountains.

Air pressure is lower at higher altitudes, so water boils at a lower temperature and liquids evaporate much faster. Gases also expand more rapidly, so you may find that your cakes rise so much that they actually collapse on themselves. This means that your tried-and-true recipes may start behaving poorly when the altitude increases.

REMEMBER

You have to adjust recipes to compensate for differences in altitude. Unfortunately, you're left to trial and error for the most part. If you're new to high-altitude cooking, you can contact your local U.S. Department of Agriculture Extension Service. Colorado State University's Food Science and Human Nutrition Department consistently is working on recipe development; you can find their information at https://extension.colostate.edu/topic-areas/nutrition-food-safety-health/high-altitude-food-preparation-p41/#3k, and also King Arthur Flour has useful information at www.kingarthurbaking.com/learn/resources/high-altitude-baking.

Here are some things to keep in mind if you're baking at a higher altitude:

>> If you're boiling foods, they'll take longer to cook because the temperature at which water boils is between 203 and 207 degrees, not the usual sea level 212 degrees.

>> You need to cream butter and sugar less and beat eggs less so that less air is incorporated into your finished products and they won't rise as much.

>> Most baked goods made with baking powder or baking soda will be better off if you make the following adjustments: Increase the liquid by 1 to 4 tablespoons, decrease the leavening by ¼ (so if the recipe calls for 1 teaspoon, you should use ¾ teaspoon), decrease the sugar by 1 to 3 tablespoons per cup, and/or use a larger pan size (for example, if the recipe calls for an 8-inch square pan, use a 9-inch square). For butter-rich cakes, decrease the butter by 1 to 4 tablespoons.

>> You may want to increase the oven temperature by 25 degrees and shorten the baking time to compensate for the loss of moisture.

>> If egg whites are your primary leavener, beat them only to soft peaks so that less air is incorporated into them.

>> Quick breads, cookies, biscuits, and muffins require the fewest adjustments. Experiment with increasing the liquid by ¼ to ½ cup and decreasing the leaveners and sugar by ¼ if necessary.

>> Yeast breads rise more rapidly at higher altitudes, so shorten the rising time and be watchful of your breads because they may overrise. Also, they may dry out faster, so use the minimum amount of flour called for in the recipe, decrease the amount of flour by ¼ to ½ cup, or increase the liquid by ¼ to ½ cup.

>> Cooked frostings become concentrated more quickly because of the faster evaporation of the water. Watch very closely and reduce the recipe temperature by 2 degrees for every 1,000 feet you are above sea level.

Keeping Your Kitchen Cool with Baking Alternatives

With the rise of energy costs, some people may venture away from baking in large ovens. Here are three tools to consider when baking in hot environments or where energy costs are concern:

» **The compact air fryer can mimic convection ovens.** Air fryers are tiny convection ovens, so baking in them can come with great results, but remember that the heat is more intense, so the general rule is to decrease the temperature by 25 degrees and also decrease the baking time by one-fourth. So, if you're baking cookies that use an oven temperature of 350 degrees for 12 minutes, decrease the temperature to 325 degrees and bake for 8 minutes.

Every air fryer is different, so play around with yours. Most air fryers now come with a cookbook or a cooking guide; reference the manufacturers recommendations for the best help. Refer to Chapter 3 about including one in your kitchen.

» **Cooking under pressure with a multicooker can decrease bake times.** A multicooker (such as an Instant Pot) cooks foods under pressure in a moist environment; therefore, baking items like flan, custards, cakes, cheesecakes, and quick breads can be successful. Tricks to baking in a multicooker, like an Instant Pot, include the following:

- Preheating the pot with boiling water

- Using the right size baking pan, like an 8-inch round cake pan

- Covering with foil to keep from adding in extra moisture to the baked item

- Lining your baking pans with parchment paper for easy cleaning and removing of the baked goods

Chapter 3 discusses including one in your kitchen.

» **Outdoor grills can achieve great results, too.** When the temps climb and you want to fire up the grill outside, let the grill serve double duty by baking up a dessert, too. Cookies, flatbreads, pizza, rustic galettes, crisps, and cobblers all work great on a grill. Consider the following when baking on a grill:

- Bump up the temperature by 25 degrees and be sure to preheat the grill.

- Use indirect heat when baking cookies, galettes, or crisps, and cobblers, which means you fire up one side of the grill. Leave the other side on low or turned off, allowing the heat to circulate around the food, but not burn the bottom.

- Don't open the grill too often, so the heat can stay tucked in the grill, keeping the temperature constant.

Cleaning As You Go

When I was younger and would bake at home, I was always amazed at the large mess I'd end up with. I seemed to dirty every single bowl, spoon, countertop, and article of clothing that came near me. When I entered college, I catered to earn a living. A huge sign in the kitchen read: *Clean as you go.* Why hadn't I thought of that? I began that practice and wow, what a difference it made! Not only did I use fewer utensils, but my mess wasn't nearly as large.

Now, I have one of the world's smallest kitchens, and I always seem to be getting in my own way. So, when I bake, I have no other choice than to clean as I go. Doing so not only makes my life easier (I'm not saddled with a huge pile of dishes at the end) but also frees up space on my counters.

TIP

Here are some tips for cleaning as you go to make your baking easier and your cleanup time at the end shorter:

>> **Recycle bowls and utensils as you bake.** If you use a spatula to scrape down the sides of the bowl while you're mixing, use it again to scrape the batter into pans. If a bowl had sugar in it and you need to beat eggs, either give the bowl a quick rinse or just use it as is. You might be amazed at how few utensils you really need, and you'll save time in washing the dishes.

>> **Make use of your downtime.** If you have to mix dough for 5 minutes, wash the bowls that held the ingredients for the dough while your electric mixer does the work. If the dough needs to chill, wipe down the appliances you used and put them away if you won't be using them anymore. I always find it convenient to have a container of hot, soapy, clean water ready in the sink to wipe down counters, rinse off utensils, or soak things.

>> **Wash your hands often — not only for sanitary purposes at the start of baking, but also because your hands will become dirty or sticky while you bake.** If you don't wash them often (a quick rinse in soapy water usually does the trick), you'll find batters and dough stuck to your refrigerator handle, on your appliances, and all over your clothes or whatever else you touch, which means more cleaning for you later.

>> **Keep a vegetable or fruit waste bowl** when baking with fruits or vegetables. When you're baking crisps, cobblers, and pies, a waste bowl to catch the peels and waste can be a time-saver. Then be sure to toss the scraps into the compost when you're finished to help keep the fruit flies at bay and your space clean while prepping.

>> **Keep cutting boards clean.** The flavor of one food can be transferred to another if the foods share the same space. For example, if you chop onions or garlic, be sure to wash and dry (and even flip over) the cutting board before you set out to slice your strawberries; otherwise, your berries might taste like onions.

>> **Wipe down your countertops often.** They're the most likely things to have ingredients spilled on them and be messy. A quick wipe every so often will help keep whatever you put on them clean, too.

>> **Always check to see whether your garbage needs to be emptied before you begin baking.** You may be amazed at the amount of trash you can produce, and you don't want to pile the garbage so high that you run the risk of spilling it onto the floor or having to stop what you're doing to take out the trash.

>> **Put away ingredients and equipment as soon as you finish using them.** Doing so frees up quite a bit of counter space, giving you room to work with dough or spread out pans for batter, for example.

3 Ready, Set, Bake!

Make mouth-watering cookies to serve your family or give away to friends and family.

Create cakes for all occasions, from the festive Tres Leches with Mango to cheesecakes.

Skip the store-bought frostings and make your own.

Bake the perfect pie, from cream pies to rhubarb pie.

Discover how easy crisps, cobblers, and custards can be.

Jump start your day with muffins and whip up simple biscuits for dinner.

Slow down and savor fresh baked breads.

Craft your own homemade pizza or pot pie.

Discover recipes that tap into ready-made crusts and premade doughs.

Chapter **8**

Understanding the Ins and Outs of Baking Cookies

RECIPES IN THIS CHAPTER

🍪 **Crispy Chocolate Chip Cookies**

🍪 **Chocolate Drop Cookies**

🍪 **Classic Oatmeal-Raisin Cookies**

🍪 **Everything Cookies**

🍪 **Chocolate-Coconut Macaroons**

🍪 **Butterscotch Drops**

🍪 **Poppy Seed Cookies**

🍪 **French Macarons**

🍪 **Peanut Butter Cookies**

Finding someone who didn't like cookies in some form or another would be a difficult task. Cookies come in any shape or size, and they're portable treats that are appropriate for just about every event. They can be dressed up or eaten plain, drowned in milk or quietly accompanied by a cup of tea. Most cookies are pretty easy to make and not at all intimidating when you're just starting out. Cookies don't need much equipment, they have a relatively high yield (as long as you don't snack on too much of the dough for quality control), and you probably have most of the ingredients on hand — you may even have all the ingredients ready to go in your kitchen right now.

Just as there's a cookie for everyone, there's an opinion about cookie making, too. Some people like thin, crunchy cookies; some like softer cookies; some like a crispy drier cookie; and some prefer them to be soft and gooey. You know who you are, so just take the time to find the perfect cookie for you.

- ⏱ Snickerdoodles
- ⏱ Rolled Sugar Cookies
- ⏱ Crisp Sugar Cookies
- ⏱ Gingersnaps
- ⏱ Lebkuchen
- ⏱ Lemon Cookies
- ⏱ Apricot-Date Half-Moons
- ⏱ Rosemary Shortbread Cookies
- ⏱ Russian Tea Balls
- ⏱ Anisette Biscotti
- ⏱ Basic Cookie Press Cookies
- ⏱ Gingerbread Cookies with Royal Icing
- ⏱ Tender Sugar Cookies
- ⏱ Dense Chocolate Brownies
- ⏱ Black-and-White Brownies
- ⏱ Lemon Bars
- ⏱ Crunchy Granola Bars

Despite the simplicity of making cookies, you do need to be aware of a few basics so you get the most from your cookie-baking experience. Some things can go wrong — maybe your cookies spread too much, maybe they spread too little, or maybe they're too crunchy. Because you're baking such small amounts of batter, it's easy to see when the dough is not quite right — maybe it spreads too much or too little or it isn't behaving the way you want it to. In this chapter, I explain the fundamentals of what makes your cookies crumble — in addition to providing lots of recipes to get you started.

Making Cookies like a Pro

Cookies are crowd pleasers on many levels. Also, if you're a beginner baker, cookie recipes are a surefire way to experience success — just keep the information in the following sections in mind as you bake.

Measuring accurately

Always measure your ingredients carefully when making cookies. Too much or too little of just one ingredient will affect the outcome of your cookie. Because cookies are miniature baked goods, you'll see right away if something is off. Remember, test your dough first and always bake a test cookie.

Understanding the effect of fats

You can interchange stick butter or shortening when you make cookies. Use vegetable oil only when it's specifically called for in the recipe. Cookies baked with butter or margarine will flatten out more than cookies baked with shortening, but the ones with butter or margarine have a richer taste. Sometimes I call for half butter and half shortening when I want a round cookie with good flavor.

Knowing the proper mixing technique

If you like your cookies dense, mix the dough by hand. An electric mixer will incorporate more air into your cookie dough, giving it a lighter and crispier texture. Either way, be sure not to mix the cookie dough too much; it will toughen the cookies.

Choosing the right pan

Nonstick coatings are a boon for any cook, but you may find they brown your cookies on the bottom a bit faster than desired. If that's happening to your cookies, lower the oven temperature by 25 degrees, and bake as instructed. If your cookies are still browning too quickly on the bottom, use two cookie sheets (one on top of the other) to create an insulated cookie sheet. If a recipe calls for a greased cookie sheet, don't grease with butter or margarine. Use shortening instead; otherwise the area in between the cookies will burn onto the sheet, and it will be next to impossible to clean. No shortening? Then use a piece of parchment paper instead to prevent them from sticking to the sheet.

WARNING

When you're baking cookies, be sure you have at least two sheets, so you can scoop out dough while another batch bakes. If you only have one sheet, be sure you let it cool between batches (at least 10 minutes) to prevent the cookie dough from spreading. Cookie dough placed on a hot sheet will begin to melt immediately, resulting in very flat cookies.

Make sure your cookie sheets fit into your oven. You want to be able to leave at least 2 inches around all sides to ensure proper heat distribution while baking. If the cookie sheet is too big, you may find the cookies on the end of the sheet are burning, while the cookies toward the middle are too raw.

Bake only one sheet of cookies at a time so that they bake in the center of the oven where the heat is optimal. If you're pressed for time and need to bake two sheets at once, turn the sheets halfway around and switch the placement of the sheets halfway through baking.

TIP

IN PRAISE OF PARCHMENT PAPER

When I worked in a bakery, the staff used parchment paper to line the large, industrial baking sheets. Parchment paper, available in many sizes in baking-supply stores and in some supermarkets, is a wonderful tool in the kitchen. It doesn't burn or smoke like waxed paper sometimes can, and it comes in either precut sheets or in a roll. Cut the sheet to fit your pan and scoop the cookies onto it. When the cookies are done, you can slide the whole sheet of parchment paper (with the cookies on them) onto a cooling rack. Parchment paper is great because it keeps your baking sheets clean and mess-free. It also eliminates the need to grease cookie sheets.

Spacing your cookies far enough apart

When scooping cookies onto the baking sheets, be sure to leave enough room for them to spread. Most recipes will tell you the amount of space to leave, but if not, use 2 inches as your general rule. This includes space from the edge of the sheet, too. All the cookies on one tray should be the same size and shape to ensure even baking; otherwise the smaller cookies will burn while the larger cookies are still uncooked.

REMEMBER

Always bake a test cookie. A test cookie will let you see what an entire batch of cookies will turn out like before they're baked. That way, if you want to make any adjustments, you won't waste a whole batch of cookie dough in the process. If you find your test cookie has spread too much during baking, add 2 tablespoons of flour and bake another test cookie. Also try chilling the dough before baking for at least 30 minutes — it really works wonders. If you find your cookie is too dry, add 2 tablespoons of milk or water and test again.

Starting with Drop Cookies

Like their name suggests, you form drop cookies by dropping the dough onto the baking sheet. Use a regular spoon, not a measuring spoon, to drop the cookies onto the sheet, usually the teaspoons in your silverware drawer are perfect. Use two spoons — one to scoop up the dough and the second to push the dough onto the baking sheet.

When I worked in a bakery, we used spring-handle ice cream scoops to make cookies all the same size and shape (see Figure 8-1). You can use this trick at home. Ice cream scoops are sold by number; this number corresponds to the amount of level scoops you will get out of a quart of ice cream. I suggest choosing a #70 scoop if your recipe calls for dropping the dough by rounded teaspoons. It's a pretty small scoop, but you'll discover how easy it makes scooping out uniform cookies and keeping your hands clean.

TIP

If you like rounded cookies and you find your dough is spreading too much in baking, try chilling the dough for an hour or so. To speed this process, you can also scoop out the dough and place it in the refrigerator to chill for at least 30 minutes.

Always check the cookies after the minimum amount of baking time given. Also, you should remove cookies from the baking sheets with a wide spatula so that they don't break once they're done baking, unless the instructions say otherwise. Don't let cookies cool on their sheets. They become harder to remove.

FIGURE 8-1:
Use an ice cream scoop to make all of your cookies the same size.

TIP

When making drop cookies, make a large batch of dough, form into balls, and freeze on a cookie sheet. When frozen, put them into self-sealing plastic bags and store in the freezer. Later, just remove the amount you need from the freezer, place on cookie sheets, and bake while still frozen — just remember to add an extra 2 or 3 minutes to the baking time.

GIFTS FOR COOKIE LOVERS

Cookie cutters make great gifts. You can find them in just about every shape and size and for just about every occasion. Check out your local baking-supply or kitchen-supply store to come up with ideas for great cutout cookies. For a really special gift, present the cutter with a recipe and a batch of cookies. I'm sure that the recipient would like to know what nice cookies the new cutter makes.

Crispy Chocolate Chip Cookies

PREP TIME: 25 MIN	BAKING TIME: 10 TO 12 MIN	YIELD: 42 TO 48 COOKIES

INGREDIENTS

300 grams (2½ cups) flour

2 teaspoons baking soda

1 teaspoon salt

113 grams (½ cup/1 stick) butter or margarine, softened

103 grams (½ cup) shortening

200 grams (1 cup) light brown sugar, lightly packed

115 grams (½ cup) sugar

2 teaspoons vanilla extract

2 tablespoons milk

2 eggs

340 grams (2 cups) chocolate chips (one 12-ounce bag)

150 grams (1 cup) chopped walnuts (optional)

DIRECTIONS

1 Preheat the oven to 350 degrees. Combine the flour, baking soda, and salt. Set aside.

2 In a large mixing bowl, cream the butter, shortening, brown sugar, sugar, vanilla, milk, and eggs together until light and creamy, about 2 minutes. Stop as necessary to scrape down the sides.

3 In three batches, add the flour and mix together well. Stir in the chocolate chips and, if desired, the walnuts.

4 Drop the dough onto ungreased cookie sheets about 2 inches apart. Bake for 10 to 12 minutes, until the edges are a light golden brown. Remove from the oven and transfer the cookies onto a wire rack.

TIP: If you want a softer chocolate chip cookie, omit the shortening and increase the butter or margarine by ½ cup. Also, remove them from the oven after 10 or 11 minutes of baking. Just let the edges of the cookie brown and don't let them get golden brown all over.

PER SERVING: *Calories 122 (From Fat 60); Fat 6g (Saturated 3g); Cholesterol 14mg; Sodium 107mg; Carbohydrate 16g (Dietary Fiber 1g); Protein 1g.*

Chocolate Drop Cookies

INGREDIENTS

170 grams (1 cup) semisweet chocolate chips

113 grams (½ cup/1 stick) butter

50 grams (½ cup) confectioners' sugar

1 egg

240 grams (2 cups) flour

1 teaspoon baking soda

1 teaspoon salt

DIRECTIONS

1 Preheat the oven to 350 degrees. Melt the chocolate chips and butter together over low heat in a small saucepan. Set aside.

2 In a large mixing bowl, beat together the sugar and egg until creamy, about 30 seconds. Add the chocolate mixture and stir. Stir in the flour, baking soda, and salt.

3 Drop the dough by the teaspoonful onto an ungreased baking sheet about 1 inch apart. Bake for 8 to 10 minutes. Let the cookies cool on the baking sheet for a few minutes before transferring them to a rack to cool.

PER SERVING: Calories 58 (From Fat 28); Fat 3g (Saturated 2g); Cholesterol 10mg; Sodium 77mg; Carbohydrate 7g (Dietary Fiber 0g); Protein 1g.

AN AMERICAN FAVORITE IS BORN

The invention of the chocolate chip cookie can be attributed to a very smart lady, Ruth Wakefield, owner of the Tollhouse Inn in Massachusetts. Legend has it that, in 1940, she was substituting a chopped-up chocolate bar for the nuts in the butter cookies she was making. She expected the bar to melt evenly throughout the cookie, but instead she was left with a lovely chocolate-studded cookie. A guest at the inn described the cookie to a friend at a Boston newspaper, word got around, and soon the cookie became a local favorite. Then Nestle got involved, bought the recipe, and began marketing chocolate chips, offering Ruth's recipe on each package. And the rest, my friends, is history. So let that story be an inspiration to all bakers — you never know what you may invent!

🍅 Classic Oatmeal-Raisin Cookies

PREP TIME: 15 MIN PLUS 30 MIN CHILLING	BAKING TIME: 10 TO 12 MIN	YIELD: ABOUT 4 DOZEN

INGREDIENTS

226 grams (1 cup/2 sticks) butter, softened

230 grams (1 cup) sugar

200 grams (1 cup) light brown sugar, firmly packed

2 teaspoons vanilla extract

3 eggs

¼ cup milk

300 grams (2½ cups) flour

1 teaspoon salt

1 teaspoon baking soda

1 teaspoon baking powder

½ teaspoon cinnamon

270 grams (3 cups) rolled oats (not instant)

239 grams (1½ cups) raisins

150 grams (1 cup) walnuts (optional)

DIRECTIONS

1 In a mixing bowl, cream together the butter, sugar, brown sugar, and vanilla. Add the eggs, one at a time, beating well after each addition. Add the milk.

2 In a separate bowl, combine the flour, salt, baking soda, baking powder, and cinnamon. In three batches, add the flour mixture to the butter mixture. Stir in the oats, raisins, and, if desired, the walnuts. Chill the dough for 30 minutes.

3 Preheat the oven to 350 degrees. Drop the dough by the teaspoonful 1 inch apart onto an ungreased cookie sheet. Bake for 10 to 12 minutes. Let the cookies cool for 1 minute before transferring them to a cooling rack.

VARY IT! Jazz up ordinary oatmeal cookies by adding ½ cup chocolate chips, or substitute chocolate-covered raisins in place of regular raisins. Or you can update the classic by using dried cranberries or blueberries in place of the raisins.

TIP: To keep the raisins plump, I like to soak them in hot water before adding them to the batter. You can start the soaking 30 minutes before you start the recipe, for plump, moist raisins, if desired.

PER SERVING: *Calories 131 (From Fat 41); Fat 5g (Saturated 3g); Cholesterol 24mg; Sodium 91mg; Carbohydrate 21g (Dietary Fiber 1g); Protein 2g.*

Everything Cookies

| PREP TIME: 15 MIN | BAKING TIME: 10 TO 12 MIN | YIELD: ABOUT 3 DOZEN |

INGREDIENTS

170 grams (¾ cup/1½ sticks) butter or margarine, softened

250 grams (1 cup) peanut butter (creamy or chunky)

230 grams (1 cup) sugar

200 grams (1 cup) light brown sugar

2 eggs

1 teaspoon vanilla extract

240 grams (2 cups) flour

1 teaspoon baking soda

1 teaspoon salt

¼ cup milk

135 grams (1½ cups) rolled oats (not instant)

170 grams (1 cup) chocolate chips

159 grams (1 cup) raisins

75 grams (½ cup) peanuts or walnuts

DIRECTIONS

1 Preheat the oven to 350 degrees. In a mixing bowl, cream together the butter, peanut butter, sugar, and brown sugar. Add the eggs and beat well for 1 minute, stopping the mixer once to scrape down the sides. Add the vanilla and beat for 15 seconds to combine.

2 Add the flour, baking soda, and salt and blend well. Stir in the milk to blend. Add the oats, chocolate chips, raisins, and peanuts. The mixture will be somewhat thick.

3 Drop rounded teaspoons of dough 1 inch apart on an ungreased cookie sheet. Bake for 10 to 12 minutes, until lightly browned. Let the cookies cool for 1 minute before transferring them to a cooling rack.

PER SERVING: *Calories 213 (From Fat 95); Fat 11g (Saturated 4g); Cholesterol 22mg; Sodium 142mg; Carbohydrate 28g (Dietary Fiber 1g); Protein 4g.*

Chocolate-Coconut Macaroons

PREP TIME: 20 MIN	BAKING TIME: 20 TO 25 MIN	YIELD: 36 TO 42

INGREDIENTS

20 grams (¼ cup) unsweetened cocoa powder

100 grams (1 cup) confectioners' sugar

58 grams (¼ cup) sugar

3 egg whites

¼ teaspoon cream of tartar

¼ teaspoon salt

½ teaspoon almond extract

254 grams (2 cups) sweetened coconut

DIRECTIONS

1   Preheat the oven to 300 degrees. Line the cookie sheets with parchment paper. In a small bowl, sift together the cocoa, confectioners' sugar, and sugar.

2   In a mixing bowl, using an electric mixer, beat the egg whites, cream of tartar, and salt together until foamy, about 2 minutes. Beat in the cocoa mixture, about 1 tablespoon at a time, until the egg whites are stiff and glossy.

3   Fold in the almond extract and coconut. Drop the mixture by heaping teaspoonfuls about an inch apart on an ungreased cookie sheet. Bake for 20 to 25 minutes. Cool for 10 minutes and then transfer the cookies to a wire rack to continue cooling.

NOTE: The cream of tartar helps stabilize the egg whites, so don't leave it out.

TIP: Line the cookie sheets with parchment paper so the cookies won't stick as you remove them from the sheet. If you don't have parchment paper, you can use waxed paper, but it might smoke a little as you bake the cookies.

VARY IT! If you want to skip the chocolate part, omit the cocoa and sugar. If you want to double your pleasure, toss in ½ cup chocolate chips when you fold in the coconut.

PER SERVING: *Calories 39 (From Fat 15); Fat 2g (Saturated 1g); Cholesterol 0mg; Sodium 30mg; Carbohydrate 6g (Dietary Fiber 0g); Protein 1g.*

Butterscotch Drops

INGREDIENTS

300 grams (2½ cups) flour

1 teaspoon baking soda

1 teaspoon salt

226 grams (1 cup/2 sticks) butter or margarine, softened

250 grams (1¼ cups) dark brown sugar, lightly packed

1½ teaspoons vanilla extract

2 eggs

170 grams (1 cup) butterscotch chips

150 grams (1 cup) chopped pecans

DIRECTIONS

1 Preheat the oven to 350 degrees. Combine the flour, baking soda, and salt. Set aside.

2 In a large mixing bowl, cream the butter, sugar, vanilla, and eggs together until light and creamy, about 1 minute. Stop as necessary to scrape down the sides. In three batches, add the flour and mix well. Stir in the chips and pecans.

3 Drop the dough onto ungreased cookie sheets about 2 inches apart. Bake for 10 to 12 minutes, until the edges are a light golden brown. Remove from the oven and transfer the cookies onto a wire rack to cool.

PER SERVING: *Calories 156 (From Fat 81); Fat 9g (Saturated 5g); Cholesterol 26mg; Sodium 111mg; Carbohydrate 18g (Dietary Fiber 1g); Protein 2g.*

Poppy Seed Cookies

PREP TIME: 10 MIN PLUS 30 MIN CHILLING TIME

BAKING TIME: 12 TO 15 MIN

YIELD: 2 DOZEN

INGREDIENTS

113 grams (½ cup/1 stick) butter

200 grams (1 cup) sugar

1 egg

½ teaspoon lemon extract

½ teaspoon almond extract

120 grams (1 cup) flour

36 grams (¼ cup) poppy seeds

Zest of 1 lemon (about 1 tablespoon)

¼ teaspoon salt

DIRECTIONS

1 In a large bowl, cream the butter and sugar together. Add the egg, lemon extract, and almond extract and beat well. Scrape down the sides of the bowl as needed. Mix in the flour, poppy seeds, lemon zest, and salt. Mix well. Chill for 30 minutes.

2 Preheat the oven to 350 degrees. Drop heaping teaspoons of the dough 2 inches apart onto ungreased cookie sheets. Bake for 12 to 15 minutes, until the edges are very light colored.

3 Remove the baking sheet from the oven and allow the cookies to cool for 2 minutes before removing them from the cookie sheet. Transfer to a wire rack to cool further.

TIP: To speed up the softening of cold butter, slice it first; then let stand for about 10 minutes.

TIP: Because the buttery flavor of the cookie is important for overall flavor, don't use margarine for this recipe.

PER SERVING: *Calories 104 (From Fat 49); Fat 5g (Saturated 3g); Cholesterol 19mg; Sodium 28mg; Carbohydrate 13g (Dietary Fiber 0g); Protein 1g.*

French Macarons

PREP TIME: 24 HRS PLUS 45 MIN	BAKING TIME: 23 MIN	YIELD: 24 COOKIES

INGREDIENTS

100 grams egg whites (about 3 eggs)

70 grams (⅓ cup) sugar

¼ teaspoon vanilla bean paste

140 grams (1 ½ cups) sifted almond flour

130 grams (1 cup) confectioners' sugar

1 ½ cups buttercream frosting

DIRECTIONS

1 Place the egg whites into a glass bowl, cover with plastic wrap with holes poked into the plastic to allow them to dry out, and then let the egg whites sit at room temperature for 24 hours or at least 3 days in the refrigerator. This dries out the egg whites and is an important step when making macarons. Let egg whites sit at room temperature before whipping.

2 Place the egg whites into the bowl of a stand mixer and beat on medium speed until they form soft peaks, about 3 to 4 minutes. While continuing to beat the eggs, sprinkle in the sugar and vanilla bean paste. Beat the egg whites until stiff peaks form, about 3 to 4 more minutes. While the egg whites are forming stiff peaks, sift together almond flour and confectioners' sugar. Place the mixture into a food processor and process for 2 minutes. Again, sift this mixture.

3 After the egg whites have formed stiff peaks, add in a third of the almond flour mixture, folding in the mixture for about 1 to 2 minutes. Add in the next third and repeat the process. Finally add in the final amount of almond flour and continue to stir until the mixture yields a ribbon-like batter.

4 Place the batter into a piping bag with a round tip. Place parchment paper onto a heavy baking sheet. Pipe out 1-inch round circles, each 1 inch apart, onto the parchment paper. Repeat until you've piped out all the batter, about 48 cookies. Tap the baking sheets with solid pressure to release any air bubbles. Use a toothpick to pop any visual bubbles. Let the cookies rest for at least 30 minutes (and up to 24 hours) prior to baking. If the weather is humid, the cookies should rest for at least 4 hours prior to baking.

(continued)

5 Preheat the oven to 300 degrees or 280 degrees with a convection oven. Bake the cookies in batches for 13 minutes; the cookies should be dried but not browned. Cool the cookies on the baking sheets for 1 hour before removing them from the baking sheet.

6 Place a buttercream frosting of your choice into a piping bag with a round tip. Pipe frosting onto one side of the cookie and sandwich together with another cookie. Place the cookie back onto the parchment paper and continue filling the remaining cookies. Place cookies into a glass storage container, cover, and let the cookies refrigerate for 2 to 3 days before sampling (if you can resist).

PER SERVING: *Calories 149 (From Fat 46); Fat 5g (Saturated 1g); Cholesterol 0mg; Sodium 53mg; Carbohydrate 25g (Dietary Fiber 1g); Protein 2g.*

Shaping Shaped Cookies

Shaped cookies can be as simple as peanut butter cookies, with the crisscross pattern on top, or as fancy as candy-cane cookies. The dough for shaped cookies is usually richer and softer than drop cookie dough, so chilling the dough before working with it is helpful. If the dough is still too soft after chilling, mix in 2 tablespoons of flour. If it is too soft and crumbly, add 2 tablespoons of water.

The dough for shaped cookies can be rolled out, slid onto a baking sheet, refrigerated, and then cut. Or it can be shaped into a log, wrapped in plastic wrap, and then refrigerated. Use a thin, sharp knife to slice the dough. You also can make the dough ahead of time and freeze it. Thaw it in the refrigerator before using it.

If you're shaping the dough into different shapes, make sure that all the cookies are the same shape and size to ensure even baking.

TIP

Make your own slice-and-bake cookies. Properly wrapped dough will last several weeks in the freezer and up to 24 hours in the refrigerator. When you need some quick cookies, they'll be ready to pop into the oven. To make your own slice-and-bake cookies, follow these easy steps:

1. **Shape chocolate chip, peanut butter, sugar cookie, or gingerbread cookie dough in a round log shape.**

   A convenient size is 3 inches in diameter and between 9 and 12 inches long.

2. **Wrap tightly in plastic wrap, with the ends tightly twisted, and refrigerate or freeze.**

3. **When you're ready to bake, bring the dough to room temperature and slice the dough into ¼-inch-thick rounds.**

   The dough should be workable — not too soft or rock hard.

4. **Place the rounds onto a baking sheet and bake according to their instructions.**

Peanut Butter Cookies

| PREP TIME: 15 MIN | BAKING TIME: 12 TO 15 MIN | YIELD: ABOUT 4 DOZEN |

INGREDIENTS

226 grams (1 cup/2 sticks) butter, softened

330 grams (1½ cups) light brown sugar, firmly packed

100 grams (½ cup) sugar

2 eggs

1½ teaspoons vanilla extract

375 grams (1½ cups) peanut butter (smooth or chunky)

420 grams (3½ cups) flour

1½ teaspoons baking soda

½ teaspoon salt

DIRECTIONS

1 Preheat the oven to 325 degrees. Cream together the butter and both sugars until well blended. Stir in the eggs, vanilla, and peanut butter. Add the flour, baking soda, and salt.

2 Drop the dough by the teaspoonful onto an ungreased baking sheet about 2 inches apart. Flatten the tops of the cookies with the tines of a fork, if desired. (To keep the fork from sticking to the dough, dip it in sugar prior to flattening.) Bake for 12 to 15 minutes. Let the cookies rest on the baking sheet for a few minutes before transferring them to the wire rack to cool.

TIP: For a really dense, chewy cookie, mix the batter by hand.

VARY IT! If you want to go a little wild, throw in 1 cup chocolate chips for that peanut butter cup flavor.

PER SERVING: *Calories 150 (From Fat 74); Fat 8g (Saturated 3g); Cholesterol 19mg; Sodium 107mg; Carbohydrate 17g (Dietary Fiber 1g); Protein 3g.*

Snickerdoodles

INGREDIENTS

330 grams (2¾ cups) flour

2 teaspoons cream of tartar

1 teaspoon baking soda

¼ teaspoon salt

½ teaspoon ground nutmeg

300 grams (1½ cups) sugar

226 grams (1 cup) butter

2 eggs

¼ teaspoon almond extract

½ teaspoon vanilla extract

3 tablespoons sugar

1 tablespoon cinnamon

DIRECTIONS

1   Preheat the oven to 375 degrees convection or 400 degrees conventional baking. Line three baking sheets with parchment paper. In a medium bowl, sift together the flour, cream of tartar, baking soda, salt, and nutmeg.

2   In a stand mixer or with a handheld mixer, cream together the sugar and the butter. Next beat in the eggs and the almond and vanilla extracts. Then add in the flour mixture in batches until combined.

3   Stir together the sugar and cinnamon in a separate bowl. Scoop about 2 tablespoons per cookie, rolling in a ball in your hand and then rolling the mixture into the cinnamon sugar mixture. Place the cookie ball onto the baking sheet. Space cookies 3 inches apart.

4   Bake cookies for 12 to 14 minutes or until the edges are just turning golden in color. Cool for at least 5 minutes on the baking sheet before removing cookies to a cooling rack.

NOTE: This is a great recipe to get kids actively involved in baking. Have them help measure the ingredients and roll the cookie balls in the cinnamon sugar mixture.

TIP: If you don't have almond extract on hand, don't fret. Just increase the vanilla extract to 1½ teaspoons.

PER SERVING: *Calories 107 (From Fat 44); Fat 5g (Saturated 3g); Cholesterol 23mg; Sodium 19mg; Carbohydrate 15g (Dietary Fiber 0g); Protein 1g.*

🍅 Rolled Sugar Cookies

INGREDIENTS

113 grams (½ cup) unsalted butter

102 grams (½ cup) vegetable shortening (like Crisco)

300 grams (1½ cups) granulated sugar

3 eggs, room temperature

½ teaspoon salt

1 teaspoon baking soda

1 tablespoon warm water

1 teaspoon vanilla extract

600 grams (5 cups) flour

Frosting

500 grams (4 cups) confectioners' sugar, sifted

¼ cup evaporated milk

3 tablespoons melted butter

Sugar crystals for decorating

DIRECTIONS

1 Preheat the oven to 350 degrees. Line four baking sheets with parchment paper. In a stand mixer, using a paddle attachment, cream together the butter, shortening, and sugar until creamy and fluffy, about 3 to 4 minutes. Add 1 egg at a time, mixing for 30 seconds after each egg.

2 In a small bowl, stir the baking soda and warm water. Pour this mixture into the butter mixture. Then add in the vanilla and flour, ½ cup at a time. Mix just until combined.

3 Flour a flat surface for rolling out the cookie dough and flour the rolling pin. Divide the dough into five equal parts. Refrigerate the dough you aren't rolling. Roll out the dough to ¼-inch thickness and use cookie cutters to cut out desired shapes. Place cut cookies onto baking sheets, leaving about 1 inch between cookies. Bake for 14 minutes. Allow cookies to cool for 15 minutes before removing from baking sheet. Repeat rolling and baking.

4 To make the frosting, using a stand mixer and whisk attachment, whisk the confectioners' sugar, evaporated milk, and melted butter. The frosting should be thin enough to spread. Add more evaporated milk, 1 teaspoon at a time if needed. Frost cooled cookies and top with sugar crystals or cookie decorations, as desired. Allow cookies to set for at least 2 hours before storing.

NOTE: Cookie dough can be stored wrapped in the refrigerator for up to 2 days or frozen up to 1 month before baking. Cookies can be stored in an airtight container at room temperature for 1 week or frozen for up to 3 months.

PER SERVING: *Calories 160 (From Fat 38); Fat 4g (Saturated 2g); Cholesterol 16mg; Sodium 25mg; Carbohydrate 21g (Dietary Fiber 0g); Protein 1g.*

🍅 Crisp Sugar Cookies

INGREDIENTS

226 grams (1 cup/2 sticks) butter

100 grams (½ cup) sugar

63 grams (½ cup) confectioners' sugar

½ teaspoon baking soda

½ teaspoon cream of tartar

½ teaspoon salt

1½ teaspoons vanilla extract

1 egg, beaten

300 grams (2½ cups) flour

Sugar, for dipping

DIRECTIONS

1 Preheat the oven to 375 degrees. In a large mixing bowl, cream together the butter and both sugars until light and creamy. Add the baking soda, cream of tartar, salt, and vanilla, and mix to blend. Then add the beaten egg and flour.

2 Shape the dough into balls the size of a small walnut and place them on a baking sheet.

3 Dip the bottom of a glass into additional sugar; press on each cookie, flattening to about ¼-inch thickness. Bake for 10 minutes, until lightly brown. Cool on a wire rack.

NOTE: I like these cookies because you don't have to roll them out. You just roll the dough into balls and press them with the bottom of a glass. Try to make all the cookies the same shape to make sure that they bake evenly.

PER SERVING: *Calories 73 (From Fat 36); Fat 4g (Saturated 2g); Cholesterol 15mg; Sodium 39mg; Carbohydrate 8g (Dietary Fiber 0g); Protein 1g.*

Gingersnaps

PREP TIME: 15 MIN PLUS 1 HR FOR CHILLING	BAKING TIME: 8 TO 10 MIN	YIELD: ABOUT 5 DOZEN

INGREDIENTS

200 grams (1 cup) sugar

170 grams (¾ cup/1½ sticks) butter or margarine, softened

65 grams (¼ cup) molasses

1 egg

270 grams (2¼ cups) flour

1½ teaspoons baking soda

¼ teaspoon salt

1 teaspoon cinnamon

½ teaspoon cloves

½ teaspoon ginger

¼ teaspoon nutmeg

Sugar, for rolling

DIRECTIONS

1 In a large bowl, cream the sugar and butter until light, about 1 minute. Add the molasses and egg and continue beating until light and fluffy. Stir in the flour, baking soda, salt, cinnamon, cloves, ginger, and nutmeg. Cover the bowl and chill for 1 hour.

2 Preheat the oven to 350 degrees.

3 Place about ½ cup of sugar on a plate; add more sugar if needed. Shape the dough into 1-inch balls. Roll the balls in sugar and place them on a baking sheet about 2 inches apart. Bake the cookies for 8 to 10 minutes or until set. Cool the cookies on a wire rack.

NOTE: Not only do these cookies make a great snacking treat, but you also can save a dozen or so in the freezer and use them the next time you want to make a crumb crust for a cheesecake. They'll last up to 6 months frozen.

PER SERVING: *Calories 56 (From Fat 22); Fat 2g (Saturated 2g); Cholesterol 10mg; Sodium 43mg; Carbohydrate 8g (Dietary Fiber 0g); Protein 1g.*

Lebkuchen

INGREDIENTS

Forty 70mm back oblaten (communion wafers)

5 eggs

220 grams (1 cup) packed brown sugar

60 grams (¼ cup) honey

1 teaspoon cinnamon

½ teaspoon cloves

⅛ teaspoon nutmeg

⅛ teaspoon allspice

¼ teaspoon cardamom

⅛ teaspoon ginger

192 grams (2 cups) almond flour

224 grams (2 cups) hazelnut flour

½ teaspoon salt

½ teaspoon baking powder

100 grams (1 cup) finely chopped candied orange peel

60 grams (¾ cup) finely chopped candied lemon peel

250 grams (2 cups) confectioners' sugar

¼ cup milk or water

½ teaspoon vanilla extract

DIRECTIONS

1 Preheat the oven to 300 degrees. Place parchment paper onto two baking sheets. Place 20 back oblaten papers down onto each baking sheet. The cookies won't spread when baked, so the papers can be close to one another, but not touching.

2 In a medium mixing bowl, whisk together the eggs, brown sugar, and honey until well combined. In a separate large mixing bowl, stir together the cinnamon, cloves, nutmeg, allspice, cardamom, ginger, almond flour, hazelnut flour, salt, and baking powder. Add the whisked egg mixture to the dry ingredients and the chopped citrus. Stir the mixture until combined. Using a cookie scooper, place a rounded scoop onto each back oblaten paper. Using your fingers, gently spread the mixture to the edges of the paper. Bake the cookies for 25 minutes and allow to cool for 30 minutes on baking sheets.

3 In a small bowl, stir together confectioners' sugar, milk (or water), and vanilla extract and drizzle on the cookies.

NOTE: You can find back oblaten paper on Amazon or look for communion wafer papers.

NOTE: The glaze should be thin enough to drizzle onto the cookies; if not add more liquid, 1 teaspoon at a time. You can either drizzle the glaze onto the cookies or dip the tops of the cookies into the glaze. Let the glaze dry for about 10 minutes. Cookies made with milk can be stored for up to 1 week in the refrigerator.

PER SERVING: *Calories 135 (From Fat 52); Fat 6g (Saturated 1g); Cholesterol 26mg; Sodium 43mg; Carbohydrate 19g (Dietary Fiber 2g); Protein 3g.*

Lemon Cookies

INGREDIENTS

226 grams (1 cup/2 sticks) butter, softened

100 grams (½ cup) sugar

110 grams (½ cup) light brown sugar, packed

3 tablespoons fresh lemon juice

1 egg

480 grams (4 cups) flour

½ teaspoon baking soda

1 tablespoon grated lemon zest

48 grams (½ cup) finely chopped almonds

DIRECTIONS

1   In a large mixing bowl, beat together the butter and both sugars. Add the lemon juice and egg and beat well.

2   Sift the flour and baking soda together and add to the butter mixture. Add the lemon zest and nuts and mix until well blended.

3   Shape into 4 rolls, 2 inches in diameter, and wrap tightly in plastic wrap. Chill until firm, about 1 hour.

4   Preheat the oven to 375 degrees. Cut the dough into ⅛-inch slices and place them about 1 inch apart on a cookie sheet. Bake for 9 minutes or until lightly browned. Cool the cookies on a wire rack.

PER SERVING: *Calories 56 (From Fat 24); Fat 3g (Saturated 1g); Cholesterol 8mg; Sodium 4mg; Carbohydrate 7g (Dietary Fiber 0g); Protein 1g.*

Apricot–Date Half–Moons

PREP TIME: 35 MIN	BAKING TIME: 10 TO 12 MIN	YIELD: 2½ DOZEN

INGREDIENTS

42 grams (⅓ cup) confectioners' sugar

170 grams (¾ cup/1½ sticks) unsalted butter

122 grams (¾ cup) small-curd cottage cheese

2 teaspoons vanilla extract

210 grams (1¾ cups) flour

Pinch of salt

88 grams (½ cup) chopped dates

95 grams (½ cup) chopped dried apricots

50 grams (¼ cup) sugar

2 tablespoons water

2 tablespoons brandy

1 egg, beaten (optional)

DIRECTIONS

1 In a large mixing bowl, cream together the confectioners' sugar, butter, and cottage cheese (it won't get completely smooth like only butter and sugar would). Add 1 teaspoon of the vanilla. Add the flour and salt and continue mixing until the dough just comes together. Gather the dough into a ball and chill for 2 hours.

2 When the dough has almost finished chilling, combine the dates, apricots, sugar, water, and brandy in a small saucepan and cook, stirring frequently, over low heat until thickened. Transfer to the bowl of a small food processor and pulse several times to blend (it will be thick and sticky). Stir in the vanilla.

3 Preheat the oven to 375 degrees. Divide the dough in half and roll out one of the halves to about ¼-inch thickness. Using a drinking glass or a cookie cutter, cut out 2½-inch round circles. Place about ½ teaspoon of the filling in the center of the dough, fold it in half, and pinch closed. Repeat with the remaining dough. Brush each half-circle with the beaten egg, if desired.

4 Bake for 10 to 12 minutes, until golden brown. Transfer to a wire rack to cool.

NOTE: Adding cottage cheese to a cookie recipe may sound kind of funny, but it was all I had in the fridge at the time, and it really makes these cookies yummy.

TIP: For the filling, I find dates and apricots difficult to cut into small pieces, and you don't want a lumpy filling, so I just simmered them for a while in some brandy and sugar and then gave them a few whirls in the food processor until I liked their consistency.

VARY IT! You can use straight apricots or go wild with dried cranberries, blueberries, or even raisins — whatever you please.

PER SERVING: *Calories 99 (From Fat 44); Fat 5g (Saturated 3g); Cholesterol 13mg; Sodium 27mg; Carbohydrate 12g (Dietary Fiber 1g); Protein 2g.*

🍅 Rosemary Shortbread Cookies

| PREP TIME: 10 MIN | BAKING TIME: 35 TO 45 MIN | YIELD: 10 SERVINGS |

INGREDIENTS

240 grams (2 cups) flour

67 grams (⅓ cup) sugar

1 tablespoon chopped fresh rosemary (2 tablespoons if you prefer a more pronounced flavor)

2 teaspoons lemon or orange zest

1 teaspoon sea salt

226 grams (1 cup/2 sticks) cold, unsalted butter

65 grams (½ cup) dried cranberries

Cooking spray

DIRECTIONS

1 In a food processor, add the flour, sugar, and rosemary, pulsing to mince the rosemary. Cut butter into 1-inch pieces and add to the flour mixture. Pulse until the dough resembles crumbles. Pour the flour mixture into a bowl and add in the dried cranberries. Use your hands to knead the dough into a ball. Cover with plastic wrap and refrigerate for 30 minutes.

2 Preheat the oven to 325 degrees. Place a baking sheet or stone in the oven as it preheats. Spray a round 9-inch pie or tart pan with cooking spray.

3 Using your hands press the chilled dough into pan. Place the pie pan onto the heated baking sheet. Return to oven and bake for 35 to 45 minutes or until the edges are golden brown in color and set in the center. Cool in the pan for 30 minutes before slicing. Slice into 10 wedges.

TIP: Store in an airtight container at room temperature for up to 3 days or in the freezer for up to 3 months.

NOTE: You can also try to place a cutting board over the pan and invert to release the cookie from the pan. Invert again before slicing and serving.

PER SERVING: *Calories 295 (From Fat 68); Fat 19g (Saturated 12g); Cholesterol 49mg; Sodium 190mg; Carbohydrate 30g (Dietary Fiber 1g); Protein 3g.*

Russian Tea Balls

INGREDIENTS

226 grams (1 cup/2 sticks) butter, softened

63 grams (½ cup) confectioners' sugar

1 teaspoon vanilla extract

270 grams (2¼ cups) flour

½ teaspoon salt

93 grams (¾ cup) finely chopped walnuts

Additional confectioners' sugar, for dusting

DIRECTIONS

1 Preheat the oven to 400 degrees. In a large mixing bowl, beat together the butter, confectioners' sugar, and vanilla. Stir in the flour, salt, and chopped nuts.

2 Roll into 1-inch balls and place on an ungreased baking sheet. Bake for about 10 minutes, until set but not brown.

3 While the cookies are still warm, roll them in additional confectioners' sugar; let cool on a wire rack. Roll in the confectioners' sugar again.

TIP: Finding cookie dough sticking to your hands? Wet your hands with cold water first, and you'll find that they won't be as sticky.

TIP: If you use an electric mixer, don't crank up the speed too quickly. Otherwise, you'll be left in a puff of confectioners' sugar.

PER SERVING: *Calories 72 (From Fat 46); Fat 5g (Saturated 3g); Cholesterol 10mg; Sodium 25mg; Carbohydrate 6g (Dietary Fiber 0g); Protein 1g.*

🍅 Anisette Biscotti

PREP TIME: 25 MIN	BAKING TIME: 60 MIN	YIELD: 2 TO 3 DOZEN

INGREDIENTS

3 eggs

200 grams (1 cup) sugar

113 grams (½ cup/1 stick) unsalted butter, melted

2 teaspoons anise extract

360 grams (3 cups) flour

¼ teaspoon salt

3 teaspoons baking powder

127 grams (1 cup) coarsely chopped walnuts or almonds, optional

DIRECTIONS

1 Preheat the oven to 350 degrees. Line a baking sheet with parchment or waxed paper.

2 Using an electric mixer, beat the eggs on high speed about 2 minutes, until light and frothy. Keep the mixer on high speed and slowly add the sugar, ¼ cup at a time, and drizzle in the melted butter. Add the anise extract.

3 Reduce the speed to low and add the flour, salt, and baking powder, and mix just until blended (the dough won't be stiff, but rather glossy from the melted butter).

4 Divide the dough in half and form the dough into 10- to 12-inch logs, 2 to 3 inches high. If the dough seems sticky, dust your hands with flour. Place the logs on the baking sheet (they should both fit sideways). Bake for 30 minutes, until firm but not hard. Remove from the oven.

5 Reduce the oven temperature to 300 degrees.

6 Let the logs cool for 20 to 30 minutes before slicing them on the diagonal into half-inch slices. Return the slices to the baking sheet (you'll need two sheets for all the slices) and return to the oven for 30 more minutes, or until they're dry and crispy.

NOTE: The biscotti will bake all the way through after 30 minutes, and you don't have to rebake it if you don't want to. It's a lovely, tender cookie baked just once.

PER SERVING: Calories 89 (From Fat 28); Fat 3g (Saturated 2g); Cholesterol 25mg; Sodium 54mg; Carbohydrate 14g (Dietary Fiber 0g); Protein 2g.

Pressing Pressed Cookies

Pressed cookies are a holiday favorite. You can make a large amount of pressed cookies in a short amount of time, so they make holiday baking a breeze. What's a pressed cookie? It's made using a cookie press, which is a device that forces dough down a hollow tube and through a die-cut disk, resulting in shaped cookies. You can come up with many variations by using one standard recipe and simply decorating the cookies in different ways or changing the pressing disk. Shop for a cookie press that's easy to use and clean and that comes with several disk attachments.

THE HISTORY OF THE SPRITZ COOKIE

A classic pressed butter cookie is the Spritz cookie, which has been around since the 16th Century and has been found throughout Germany and the Nordic countries. My husband's family is from Sweden and my family from Germany, so both of our families have some type of pressed butter cookie, with only the subtle differences in flavors.

With the Swedish Spritz, one often uses a small amount of almond extract (¼ teaspoon), and with German Spritzen or Spritzgebäck, one may use lemon zest and vanilla sugar. Other variations can include dipping in chocolate, coloring the dough, dusting in powdered sugar, or using orange zest in the dough. This chapter gives you a basic recipe (Basic Cookie Press Cookies); you can decide which flavor profile you desire.

Basic Cookie Press Cookies

PREP TIME: 20 MIN | BAKING TIME: 12 MIN | YIELD: 6 DOZEN

INGREDIENTS

226 grams (1 cup/2 sticks) butter, very soft

150 grams (¾ cup) sugar

⅓ teaspoon salt

2 egg yolks

1 teaspoon vanilla extract

280 grams (2⅓ cups) flour

1 egg, beaten

Decorating sugar or colored sprinkles

DIRECTIONS

1 Preheat the oven to 350 degrees. In a large bowl, beat together the butter, sugar, and salt with an electric mixer until light and fluffy. Beat in the yolks and vanilla until smooth. Add the flour gradually, beating the dough until just combined well. The dough will be soft.

2 Pack the dough into a cookie press fitted with the disk of choice and press about 1 inch apart onto ungreased baking sheets. Gently brush the cookies lightly with the beaten egg and sprinkle with decorating sugar.

3 Bake the cookies until the edges are pale golden, for about 12 minutes. Cool the cookies on sheets for 2 minutes and transfer to racks to cool completely.

TIP: This dough usually passes well through a cookie press. If you find it too thick, stir in a tablespoon or two of milk. If it has no body to it and doesn't hold its shape, stir in a tablespoon or two of flour.

VARY IT! Divide the dough in half or in thirds and color with a few drops of food coloring. Add a teaspoon of almond or lemon extract to the dough. Decorate your cookies with bits of chocolate, candied fruit, poppy seeds, cinnamon dots, dollops of jam, or sprinkles of sugar before you bake them, if you like.

PER SERVING: *Calories 52 (From Fat 25); Fat 3g (Saturated 2g); Cholesterol 16mg; Sodium 10mg; Carbohydrate 6g (Dietary Fiber 0g); Protein 1g.*

Baking Rolled Cookies

When making rolled cookies, you need something to cut the dough with; however, you don't need cookie cutters. You can use a glass or a clean tuna can with both sides cut out, or you can just cut the dough with a knife. Traditionally, cookie cutters are used to make the job quite easy and fun. When choosing a nontraditional shape, avoid those with intricate designs or lots of "fingers." You run the risk of burning the thinner part of the cookie before the bigger parts have fully cooked. Here I discuss just what you need to know about making rolled cookies.

MAKING YOUR COOKIES LOOK MAG-NI-FIQUE

Cookies make the perfect gift for special occasions. Whether you're taking them to an informal work function or they are decking the halls at holiday time, there will be times when you will want your cookies to shine a little more than usual. Here are some super-easy tips to dress those masterpieces up when the need arrives:

- If you're going to a picnic and decide to bring cookies for a portable dessert or snack (which is always a good idea), jazz up the presentation by lining the container with clean linen napkins or bandanas.

- Personalize your basic sugar cookie or gingerbread cookie recipe by decorating the dough with cinnamon hearts, chocolate chips, colorful candy-coated chocolates, chopped nuts, or raisins (or even chocolate-coated raisins!) before baking.

- Melt some chocolate and dip half the cookie into it. Set the cookie on a rack until the chocolate hardens. You can even sprinkle some colored sprinkles or finely chopped nuts on top of the chocolate before it hardens.

- Sandwich a scoop of ice cream between two homemade cookies and watch them disappear. (Who doesn't like ice cream sandwiches?)

- Buy some tubes of frosting or use the recipes in Chapter 11 to frost your cookies. Any cookie looks good wearing a bit of frosting.

- Press your thumb into the center of each cookie to make a little depression and then fill it with chocolate chips or jam before baking.

- Decorate the plates or trays you serve the cookies on with colorful napkins or pretty doilies.

- Dust the tops of chocolate brownies with confectioners' sugar. Confectioners' sugar not only makes the brownies look more appetizing but also covers up any imperfections.

- Place a brownie square in the bottom of a bowl, top with ice cream and your favorite sundae toppings, and serve. Brownie sundaes are always a hit.

Rolling as easy as 1, 2, 3 . . .

Rolled cookie dough is much like pastry dough, and it follows many of the same baking principles. Rolled cookie dough usually requires some chilling time to re-harden the butter and to let the dough rest, so it's easier to roll out. When you chill the dough, divide the dough in half or in thirds. Take out a piece of the dough to work with and leave the remaining pieces in the refrigerator so they stay nice and chilled.

TIP

Make sure that the dough is the right temperature. If it's too cold, it will crack and fall apart. If it's too warm, it will stick to everything in sight. Remove the dough from the refrigerator about 15 minutes before you plan to use it. That will take the chill out of it but leave it with firmness to give your cookies good shape. The more you practice with rolled cookies, the better you'll become. Rolling out cookie dough can be quick and easy if you follow these steps.

1. **Before rolling out your dough, lightly dust the work surface with flour.**

   I like to use a flat, large, nick-free wooden cutting board, but any countertop is fine. You can also lightly dust the work surface with flour and sugar. The sugar does a great job of not allowing the dough to stick, and it won't toughen your cookies the way too much flour will. However, don't be too generous with either ingredient when dusting.

2. **Roll out your dough.**

   Roll out the dough to the same, even thickness so that your cookies will bake evenly.

3. **Cut out your shapes.**

   When you're ready to cut out the shapes, dip your cutter in flour, sugar, or confectioners' sugar to prevent the dough from sticking to the cutter. Tap off any excess before cutting the dough so that you won't get clumps of flour on your cookies. When you cut through the dough, give the cookie cutter a tiny twist to be sure you've cut all the way through the dough. The twist should be subtle, just a fraction of an inch.

   As you cut out your cookies, try to cut as many as possible out of one sheet. If you have an odd-shaped cookie cutter, such as a candy cane or Christmas tree, sometimes turning the cookie cutter upside down on every other cut or creatively angling the cutter enables you to cut out more cookies by using the whole dough surface.

4. **When you've cut out all your cookies, carefully lift up the scrap dough and put it aside.**

   On your work surface, you'll have all your cutout cookies.

5. **Use a pancake turner or metal spatula to transfer your cookies to a baking sheet.**

   The dough is quite delicate, and you wouldn't want to stretch it or tear it by transferring the cookies by hand. Save all the scraps from each section of dough. Then gather all the scraps together to re-roll again. This will eliminate excessive re-rolling.

Keeping in mind other tips

When you're rolling out the cookies, remember these helpful tips:

» Avoid rolling out the dough more than once if possible. The dough will toughen up if you roll it out too many times. That's why you want to cut out as many cookies as possible the first time.

» If you really need to re-roll scraps of cookie dough, dust the surface with equal parts flour and confectioners' sugar. This will help keep the dough from getting tough.

» If you don't have a rolling pin or don't want to be troubled by rolling out the cookie dough, you can "unroll" cookies. Scoop out a heaping tablespoon of cookie dough and roll it into a ball. Place the ball onto a cookie sheet. Dip the bottom of a drinking glass (2-inch diameter) into granulated or confectioners' sugar and gently press down the dough into a ¼-inch-thick round. Repeat until you have filled the tray (9 to 12 cookies) and then bake as directed.

» When your cookies have baked, let them cool for a few minutes on the cookie sheet before transferring them to a cooling rack. This will let delicate shapes harden, so no gingerbread people will leave any limbs stuck onto the sheet.

Gingerbread Cookies with Royal Icing

PREP TIME: 35 MIN PLUS 2 HRS OR OVERNIGHT FOR CHILLING	BAKING TIME: 12 MIN	YIELD: 3 DOZEN

INGREDIENTS

420 grams (3½ cups) plus 30 grams (¼ cup) flour, divided

2½ teaspoons ginger

1 teaspoon cinnamon

¾ teaspoon baking soda

¾ teaspoon salt

154 grams (¾ cup) vegetable shortening

150 grams (¾ cup) sugar

2 eggs

1 teaspoon vanilla extract

93 grams (⅓ cup) dark molasses

Royal Icing

INGREDIENTS

1 egg white

125 grams (1 cup) confectioners' sugar

2 drops glycerin (optional)

DIRECTIONS

1   In a medium bowl, combine the 3½ cups flour, ginger, cinnamon, baking soda, and salt. Stir to combine and set aside.

2   In a mixing bowl, cream together the shortening and sugar, about 30 seconds. Add the eggs and vanilla, stopping once to scrape down the sides of the bowl, about 1 minute. Add the molasses and beat until well blended, about 30 more seconds. Add the dry ingredients and beat on low speed to mix together. The dough should come off the sides of the bowl and hold together. If the dough is too loose, stir in the additional ¼ cup flour, 1 tablespoon at a time, until the dough comes away from the sides of the bowl. (I use a stand mixer, so the dough hangs onto the paddle. If you're using an electric mixer, the results may be different. Do not add more than ¼ cup additional flour.)

3   Gather the dough together into a ball and cut it in half. Wrap each half in plastic wrap. Chill for 2 hours or overnight. Remove the dough from the refrigerator and let stand at room temperature for 15 minutes.

4   Preheat the oven to 350 degrees. Lightly dust your work surface and rolling pin with flour. Roll out the dough until it's ¼-inch thick. Using a cookie cutter or juice glass, cut out the cookies. Place them on the cookie sheets about ½ inch apart. Repeat with the second ball of dough. Gather the scraps and roll out again.

5   Bake the cookies for 12 minutes. Transfer to a wire rack to cool.

6   To make the icing, in a mixing bowl, beat the egg white until frothy. Add the confectioners' sugar in two batches, beating well after each addition. Mix in the glycerin, if using. Transfer to a small bowl. Cover with a damp paper towel if you won't use it immediately, but don't let it sit for more than 1 hour. Frost the cookies with the icing.

NOTE: These cookies are perfect if you want crunchy gingerbread. It's a good recipe to use if you want to make a gingerbread house; just double it and omit the baking soda so it won't rise. Royal icing dries to a hard, white icing. It is also the "cement" in the food world; you can stick cookies together with it. You can find the glycerin for the icing in baking supply stores or vitamin stores. The recipe doubles or even triples quite well.

PER SERVING: *Calories 126 (From Fat 42); Fat 5g (Saturated 1g); Cholesterol 12mg; Sodium 81mg; Carbohydrate 19g (Dietary Fiber 0g); Protein 2g.*

STORING YOUR COOKIES

Cookies can be stored at room temperature if they'll be eaten within a few days; in the refrigerator if they'll be eaten within a week; or in the freezer for several months (freezing cookies is a good idea so you always have cookies on hand). Some cookies (usually ones with frosting) need to be refrigerated after they're cooled — the recipes will let you know if this is necessary.

Cookies should be allowed to cool completely before they are stored. If cookies are stored in an airtight container while they're still warm, they will give off heat, create condensation, and then become soggy.

Crisp, thin cookies actually do better if they're wrapped in an airtight container. If your crisp cookies soften a bit, re-crisp them by placing them on a baking sheet and popping them into the 250-degree oven for 5 to 7 minutes. Freezing crispy cookies and then defrosting them before eating also helps them retain their crispiness.

Soft, moist cookies should also be stored in an airtight container. You can also put in the container a slice of bread (a trick I learned from my friend Martha) or a slice of an apple (which you need to change daily) to help your cookies stay moist and chewy. You can also microwave cookies to make them tender again. Wrap them in a clean paper towel and heat for 15 to 20 seconds on High.

Frosted cookies should be stored in a single layer or with a sheet of waxed paper between layers, depending on how soft the frosting is. Also, if you have delicate shaped or rolled cookies, consider storing them in single layers or with waxed paper between the layers.

Bar cookies are easy to store — just wrap the top of the baking pan with aluminum foil or plastic wrap, and you're done. They also can be removed from the pan and transferred to a container or serving plate. Seal the container or just wrap the plate with aluminum foil or plastic wrap to keep the brownies or bar cookies fresh.

⌖ Tender Sugar Cookies

PREP TIME: 15 MIN PLUS 30 MINS OR OVERNIGHT FOR CHILLING	BAKING TIME: 12 MIN	YIELD: 3 DOZEN

INGREDIENTS

420 grams (3½ cups) flour

1 teaspoon baking soda

2 teaspoons cream of tartar

1 teaspoon salt

½ teaspoon nutmeg

226 grams (1 cup/2 sticks) butter (not margarine)

300 grams (1½ cups) sugar

2 eggs

½ teaspoon vanilla extract

½ teaspoon almond extract (optional)

DIRECTIONS

1 Sift together the flour, baking soda, cream of tartar, salt, and nutmeg. Set aside.

2 In a mixing bowl, mix together the butter and sugar until light and fluffy, about 1 minute. Add the eggs, vanilla, and, if desired, the almond extract, and continue beating, stopping once or twice to scrape down the sides, about 1 minute more. Blend in the flour mixture, just to incorporate.

3 Gather the dough together and wrap in plastic. Refrigerate for 30 minutes, or up to 24 hours.

4 Preheat the oven to 375 degrees. Have ready two baking sheets. Remove the dough from the refrigerator and let rest for about 10 minutes to take the initial chill off the dough. Lightly dust your work area with flour or sugar (or a combination).

5 Roll out the dough until it's ¼-inch thick. Using a cookie cutter or juice glass, cut out the cookies. Place them on the cookie sheets about ½ inch apart. Gather the scraps and roll out again.

6 Bake for about 12 minutes or until pale golden. Transfer to a wire rack to cool.

TIP: If you're a purist and only roll once, gather all your cookie dough scraps together and mold them into a 2-inch round log and slice and bake the scraps. The real secret to keeping rolled cookies tender is to use the least amount of additional flour necessary on your work surface.

PER SERVING: *Calories 127 (From Fat 50); Fat 6g (Saturated 3g); Cholesterol 26mg; Sodium 104mg; Carbohydrate 18g (Dietary Fiber 0g); Protein 2g.*

Mastering Brownies and Bar Cookies

Brownies and bar cookies are different than other cookies because they're baked in one pan and then cut into squares (or whatever shape you desire) before serving.

If you use a glass baking pan rather than metal, remember to reduce the baking temperature by 25 degrees. For more information about baking pans, see Chapter 3.

WARNING

Always use the correct pan size. If you substitute a larger pan, your brownies will be too thin and may dry out when you bake them. If the pan is too small, it will take a much longer time to bake, and the inside may still be raw when the outside is done cooking.

Cut your bar cookies into their shapes only after they've been cooled completely, unless otherwise instructed. If you cut them when they're too warm, they're difficult to cut cleanly and may crumble much easier than when they have cooled completely. You can also chill them before cutting if you have a really moist top, such as a cream cheese topping.

TIP

A great trick for cutting brownies and bars evenly, and eliminating dirty pans, is to line the baking pan with aluminum foil. When the brownies have cooled completely, just lift out the aluminum foil, place them onto a cutting board, and remove the foil. You can then cut the bars and place them on a serving plate or even back into the pan. Another incredibly easy way to slice up bar cookies is to use a pizza cutter rather than a knife.

Dense Chocolate Brownies

PREP TIME: 15 MIN | BAKING TIME: 20 TO 25 MIN | YIELD: 18 TO 24

INGREDIENTS

336 grams (1⅔ cups) sugar

170 grams (¾ cup/1½ sticks) butter

2 tablespoons strong brewed coffee, water, or milk

3 eggs

2 teaspoons vanilla extract

160 grams (1⅓ cups) flour

118 grams (1 cup) cocoa powder

½ teaspoon baking powder

¼ teaspoon salt

255 grams (1½ cups) chocolate chips

63.5 grams (½ cup) chopped walnuts (optional)

DIRECTIONS

1 Preheat the oven to 350 degrees. Grease a 9-x-13-inch pan.

2 In a mixing bowl, combine the sugar, butter, and coffee in a large bowl and beat well. Add the eggs and vanilla and mix well, stopping once to scrape down the sides of the bowl.

3 Stir in the flour, cocoa, baking powder, and salt. Stir in the chocolate chips. Pour into the prepared pan and sprinkle the top with the walnuts, if desired. Bake for 20 to 25 minutes. Do not overbake. A cake tester won't come out clean. Let cool completely before cutting.

NOTE: This recipe creates brownies that are big with chocolate and light on flour, giving them a dense, deep chocolate flavor.

NOTE: See the color insert for a photo of this recipe.

PER SERVING: *Calories 199 (From Fat 91); Fat 10g (Saturated 6g); Cholesterol 42mg; Sodium 43mg; Carbohydrate 28g (Dietary Fiber 2g); Protein 3g.*

🍑 Black-and-White Brownies

| PREP TIME: 30 MIN | BAKING TIME: 60 MIN | YIELD: 25 BROWNIES |

INGREDIENTS

200 grams (1 cup) sugar

3 eggs

59 grams (½ cup) cocoa

226 grams (1 cup/2 sticks) butter or margarine, melted

1 teaspoon vanilla extract

90 grams (¾ cup) flour

½ teaspoon salt

½ teaspoon baking soda

Topping

One 8-ounce package cream cheese (Neufchâtel is okay to use)

½ cup sugar

2 eggs

1 teaspoon vanilla extract

DIRECTIONS

1 Preheat the oven to 300 degrees. Spray a 9-inch baking pan with nonstick cooking spray.

2 In a mixing bowl, beat together the sugar and 3 eggs until light and frothy, about 1 minute. Add the cocoa, butter, and 1 teaspoon vanilla, and stir together. Stir in the flour, salt, and baking soda. Pour into the baking pan.

3 In a blender or small bowl, add the cream cheese, ½ cup sugar, 2 eggs, and 1 teaspoon vanilla. Blend until smooth. Carefully spread the mixture on top of the chocolate layer (for easier spreading, chill the bottom chocolate layer first).

4 Bake for about 60 minutes, or until the topping is set. Remove from the oven and cool. Cut into 5-x-5-inch rows. Refrigerate the remaining squares.

NOTE: Serve them at room temperature but store them refrigerated in an airtight container.

VARY IT! If you want to make them double chocolate, melt 2 ounces bittersweet, milk, or German chocolate and stir it into the cheesecake topping.

PER SERVING: *Calories 208 (From Fat 134); Fat 15g (Saturated 9g); Cholesterol 82mg; Sodium 140mg; Carbohydrate 16g (Dietary Fiber 1g); Protein 3g.*

Lemon Bars

INGREDIENTS

240 grams (2 cups) plus
30 grams (¼ cup) flour,
divided

226 grams (1 cup/2 sticks)
butter, softened

63 grams (½ cup)
confectioners' sugar
4 eggs

400 grams (2 cups) sugar

1 teaspoon baking powder

Zest from one lemon

Juice from 3 large lemons

DIRECTIONS

1 Preheat the oven to 350 degrees. Mix together the 2 cups flour, butter, and confectioners' sugar. Pat the mixture into the bottom of a 13-x-9-inch baking pan. Bake the crust for 20 minutes.

2 While the crust is baking, beat together the eggs, 4 tablespoons flour, sugar, baking powder, and lemon zest and juice. Remove the crust from the oven and pour in this mixture. Return the pan to the oven and bake for 20 to 25 minutes more, until set. Cool the bars in the pan on a wire rack. Cut them when they have cooled. Garnish with additional confectioners' sugar, if desired.

PER SERVING: *Calories 197 (From Fat 77); Fat 9g (Saturated 5g); Cholesterol 56mg; Sodium 28mg; Carbohydrate 28g (Dietary Fiber 0g); Protein 2g.*

Crunchy Granola Bars

PREP TIME: 10 MIN	BAKING TIME: 30 TO 40 MIN	YIELD: 16 BARS

INGREDIENTS

113 grams (½ cup/1 stick) butter, softened

110 grams /(½ cup) brown sugar, lightly packed

120 grams (1 cup) flour

45 grams (½ cup) rolled oats (not instant)

40 grams (¼ cup) raisins, dried cranberries, or dried cherries

43 grams (¼ cup) chocolate chips

32 grams (¼ cup) chopped walnuts or pecans (optional)

1 teaspoon cinnamon

¼ teaspoon salt

DIRECTIONS

1 Preheat the oven to 350 degrees. Spray a 9-x-9-inch square baking pan with nonstick spray. In a mixing bowl, cream together the butter and brown sugar. Stir in the flour, oats, raisins, chocolate chips, nuts (if desired), cinnamon, and salt. Press the dough into the pan.

2 Bake for 30 to 40 minutes, until golden brown on the edges. Cool in the pan for 15 minutes and then cut into 4 x 4 rows.

VARY IT! You can add in what you like or take out either the raisins or the chocolate chips.

PER SERVING: *Calories 149 (From Fat 72); Fat 8g (Saturated 4g); Cholesterol 16mg; Sodium 40mg; Carbohydrate 19g (Dietary Fiber 1g); Protein 2g.*

Chapter **9**

Baking Moist Cakes

RECIPES IN THIS CHAPTER

- Light and Fluffy Yellow Cake
- Martha's Chocolate Cake
- Texas Chocolate Sheath Cake
- Carrot Cake
- Applesauce Cake
- German Apple Kuchen with Streusel
- Banana-Sour Cream Bundt Cake
- Classic Pound Cake
- Chocolate Swirl Pound Cake
- Chocolate Cupcakes
- Lemon Cupcakes
- Angel Food Cake
- Jelly Roll
- Tres Leches with Mango
- Lemon Rosemary Almond Cake

Anyone can bake cakes. There's no magic to it — although you may think that there is when you watch a simple mixture of eggs, butter, flour, and sugar turn into a thick, creamy batter, and then bake into a yummy treat that melts in your mouth. Although magic isn't involved, chemistry and technique are. Both can be explained and mastered. If you're feeling at all apprehensive about making a cake, don't. You can feel like a complete klutz in the kitchen and still turn out a respectable cake. My premise is everyone can, and should, bake cakes.

When you've decided to bake a cake, you need to choose the kind of cake you want to make. In this chapter, I introduce the categories of cakes so that you can size them up for yourself. Whichever you choose, I include lots of tips and hints to help you bake a great cake.

Focusing On Butter Cakes

The most popular and best-known type of cake is the butter or shortening cake. These are the classic layer cakes, the cakes you associate with birthday parties and festive occasions, loved for their moist sweetness and high-stacking layers filled with delicious frostings and topped with decorations.

🍰 Gluten-Free Chocolate
   Hazelnut Cake

🍰 Molten Lava Cake

🍰 Classic Cheesecake

🍰 Pumpkin Cheesecake

🍰 Lemon Curd Cheesecake

What makes butter or shortening cakes different from other varieties of cakes is they have a lot of fat (butter, shortening, or oil) in relation to the number of eggs used. Making a good butter cake isn't difficult, but you do need to know how to correctly mix the ingredients together to produce a silky batter that includes the right amount of air. Butter cakes rise from the air whipped into the batter as well as from the addition of baking powder or soda.

I recommend purchasing cake flour when you bake cakes. It really does make a difference with the final product, and you can freeze flour (label it first!) if you don't use it often.

Because the fat is the essential ingredient in butter cakes, selecting the best fat for your purposes is critical. Many professionals say unsalted butter is the best choice. Salt was originally added to butter as a preservative, but with modern refrigeration we no longer really need the salt. If you bake without it, you have more control over the salt content of your foods. If, however, you have only salted butter on hand, don't worry — it won't affect the flavor of your cake.

An often forgotten ingredient in good butter or shortening cakes is air. Solid vegetable shortening is great for incorporating air into the batter, which gives added volume to cakes and makes them softer and spongier. Solid vegetable shortening is the densest and will cream better than any other fats. Unfortunately, the flavor is not as rich as if you were to use butter (or even margarine), which can be disappointing. In all the butter/shortening recipes, feel free to substitute half shortening and half butter to get the best of both ingredients. For more on fats, see Chapter 5.

TIP

If you find your cakes continually come out with domed centers, decrease the flour in your cake recipe by ¼ cup and spread the batter from the center to the sides of the pan. Domed centers are caused by thick batters cooking the edges first, allowing the centers to continue to rise higher than the sides.

A well-prepared butter cake is moist and has a tender crumb. For the best results, make sure the fat you choose is softened. Shortening is ready to go from the can, but if you choose butter, you'll have to let it soften. If the butter yields slightly to your touch, but is still solid and not melted, it's just right. If you have to press hard, it's still too cold. Let it sit out for 15 more minutes and test again. If the butter is melting inside of the wrapper, it's too soft; pop it in the fridge for about 15 minutes to harden slightly before using. Butter taken directly out of the refrigerator should be ready to use in 20 to 30 minutes.

TIP

If you are pressed for time and need your butter to soften pronto, cut the butter into 10 to 12 pieces and leave it at room temperature. It will be softened and ready to use in about 5 minutes.

The proper technique for preparing butter cake batter is to have all the ingredients at room temperature. Cream the butter or butter/shortening blend with the sugar until light and smooth. If you use an electric mixer, begin on medium-low speed and then increase to medium speed. This will allow air to be incorporated into the fat without overheating and melting it — an important thing to keep in mind when working with all-butter cakes. Then add the eggs, followed by the dry ingredients, oftentimes alternated with the liquids to keep the batter creamy and smooth. Bake and — voilà! — perfect cakes!

TIP

If your cake falls in the oven, cut it into chunks and dip it in a chocolate fondue. The texture will be uneven, but that won't matter. You can use the cake for a custard bread/cake pudding. Or crumble up the cake and use it in a trifle.

TESTING FOR DONENESS

You can do several things to make sure that your cake is thoroughly baked. Some visual clues can tell you whether the cake is done:

- The color of the top should be golden brown.

- The edges should be just beginning to pull away from the pan.

- The cake should appear to be firm and should not jiggle when lightly shaken.

Touch the top surface lightly with your finger; the cake should spring back, and your finger should not make a dent. To be absolutely sure your cake is done, insert a cake tester into the center of the cake. (A product called a cake tester actually exists, but save your money — a toothpick, thin wooden skewer, or butter knife will do nicely.) The tester should come out clean and dry, indicating that the cake is done. If the tester comes out wet and covered in batter, bake the cake for a couple more minutes, then retest.

Be sure you set your timer to the minimum baking time given and try not to peek while the cake is baking. As exciting as it is to watch, you make the oven temperature fluctuate each time you open the door, and that could affect the way the cake bakes — in the worst-case scenario, the cake could fall. The only exception to the cake-test rule is cheesecake, which has its own set of rules (see the "Baking Cheesecakes" section).

Light and Fluffy Yellow Cake

PREP TIME: 20 MIN | BAKING TIME: 25 TO 35 MIN | YIELD: 16 SERVINGS

INGREDIENTS

288 grams (2½ cups) cake flour

1 teaspoon baking soda

1 teaspoon baking powder

½ teaspoon salt

1 teaspoon ginger

225 grams (1 cup/2 sticks) butter

250 grams (1¼ cups) sugar

3 eggs

2 teaspoons vanilla extract

180 grams (¾ cup) sour cream, plain Greek yogurt, or buttermilk

DIRECTIONS

1 Preheat the oven to 350 degrees. Grease two 8- or 9-inch cake pans.

2 In a medium bowl, combine the flour, baking soda, baking powder, salt, and ginger. In a separate mixing bowl, cream together the butter and sugar using an electric mixer. Add in the eggs and vanilla. Scrape down the sides of the bowl occasionally.

3 Alternate adding the flour mixture and the sour cream to the butter mixture, beginning and ending with the flour. Stir just enough to combine, but don't overmix. Divide the batter evenly between the pans.

4 Bake until golden brown around the edges and the center springs back when you touch it, 30 to 35 minutes for the 8-inch pans, 25 to 30 minutes for the 9-inch pans. Cool for 10 minutes before removing the cakes from the pan. Cool completely before frosting.

VARY IT! You can add cinnamon, nutmeg, or cardamom.

TIP: Substitute half shortening for half of the butter during mixing, not prior to serving if you need to refrigerate the cake. Pure butter cakes will toughen in the refrigerator.

PER SERVING: Calories 263 (From Fat 134); Fat 15g (Saturated 9g); Cholesterol 76mg; Sodium 195mg; Carbohydrate 30g (Dietary Fiber 0g); Protein 3g.

Martha's Chocolate Cake

PREP TIME: 15 MIN	BAKING TIME: 25 TO 30 MIN	YIELD: ONE 9-INCH LAYER CAKE OR ONE 8-INCH LAYER CAKE AND 6 CUPCAKES

INGREDIENTS

240 grams (2 cups) flour

1 teaspoon salt

1 teaspoon baking powder

2 teaspoons baking soda

89 grams (¾ cup) unsweetened cocoa powder

400 grams (2 cups) sugar

225 grams (1 cup) vegetable oil

235 grams (1 cup) hot coffee

240 grams (1 cup) milk

2 eggs

1 teaspoon vanilla extract

DIRECTIONS

1 Preheat the oven to 325 degrees. Grease and flour either two 9-inch cake pans or two 8-inch cake pans and 6 muffin cups.

2 Sift together the flour, salt, baking powder, baking soda, cocoa, and sugar into a large mixing bowl. Add the oil, coffee, milk, eggs, and vanilla. With an electric mixer, beat at medium speed for 2 minutes (the batter will be thin).

3 Pour the batter evenly into both 9-inch cake pans or fill the 6 muffin cups halfway with batter and divide the remaining batter between both 8-inch pans. Bake for 25 to 30 minutes, until a wooden toothpick inserted into the center of the cake comes out clean (check the cupcakes after 15 minutes). Let the cakes cool for 15 minutes before removing them from the pans. Let them cool completely on the wire racks before frosting.

PER SERVING: *Calories 404 (From Fat 186); Fat 20g (Saturated 2g); Cholesterol 38mg; Sodium 458mg; Carbohydrate 53g (Dietary Fiber 2g); Protein 5g.*

Texas Chocolate Sheath Cake

INGREDIENTS

230 grams (2 cups) cake flour

300 grams (1½ cups) sugar

1 teaspoon baking soda

95 grams (½ cup) vegetable shortening

113 grams (½ cup) unsalted butter

240 grams (1 cup) water

30 grams (¼ cup) cocoa powder

121 grams (½ cup) buttermilk

2 eggs, slightly beaten

1 teaspoon vanilla extract

Frosting

30 grams (¼ cup) cocoa powder

108 grams (7 tablespoons) whole milk

113 grams (½ cup) salted butter

454 grams (3½ cups) confectioner's sugar

1 teaspoon vanilla extract

109 grams (1 cup) chopped pecans

DIRECTIONS

1 Preheat the oven to 350 degrees. Grease and flour or cocoa dust a 9-x-13-inch cake pan. In a heat-safe mixing bowl, mix the flour, sugar, and baking soda.

2 In a 4-quart saucepan, bring vegetable shortening, butter, water, and cocoa to a rapid boil over medium high heat. Pour the boiling mixture into the flour mixture, whisking to combine. Add in vanilla and buttermilk and stir. Add in eggs and mix well. Pour the cake batter into the prepared baking dish. Bake for 30 minutes.

3 When the cake has 5 minutes left in baking, begin making the frosting. In the same 4-quart saucepan bring cocoa powder, milk, and butter to a boil over medium high heat. Remove from heat and add confectioner's sugar, whisking to combine and break up clumps of confectioner's sugar. Add pecans and vanilla extract, stirring to combine. Pour hot frosting over cake as soon as it is removed from the oven. Allow the cake to rest for 1-hour before slicing and serving or serve hot.

NOTE: Growing up in Texas this was a traditional cake we'd bring to potlucks, parties, and yes, funerals. There's long been a debate about the name; is it "sheath" or "sheet" cake? Well, I grew up calling it Sheath Cake, and this is the recipe my family has made for decades, so I'm sticking to it. Regardless, this sheet cake is indeed special.

PER SERVING: Calories 616 (From Fat 287); Fat 32g (Saturated 13g); Cholesterol 78mg; Sodium 83mg; Carbohydrate 83g (Dietary Fiber 3g); Protein 5g.

Carrot Cake

INGREDIENTS

338 grams (1½ cups) vegetable oil

400 grams (2 cups) sugar

4 eggs, beaten

1 teaspoon vanilla extract

240 grams (2 cups) flour

3 teaspoons cinnamon

2 teaspoons baking soda

1 teaspoon salt

348 grams (3 cups) grated carrots

124 grams (1 cup) walnuts, coarsely chopped (optional)

DIRECTIONS

1 Preheat the oven to 325 degrees. Grease and flour three 8- or 9-inch cake pans.

2 In a large mixing bowl, beat together the oil and sugar. Add the eggs and vanilla and mix to combine.

3 Sift together the flour, cinnamon, soda, and salt, and add to the creamed mixture. Stir in the carrots and walnuts, if desired. Pour into prepared pans and bake for 30 to 40 minutes. Let the cakes cool completely on a wire rack before frosting.

TIP: If you don't have three pans, bake two of the layers and then wash and reuse one of the cake pans.

PER SERVING: *Calories 485 (From Fat 263); Fat 29g (Saturated 3g); Cholesterol 71mg; Sodium 435mg; Carbohydrate 53g (Dietary Fiber 2g); Protein 5g.*

LET THEM EAT CAKE!

Birthday cakes have a long history. The Roman emperors celebrated their birthdays with offerings of cakes to the gods and to the common people. In the Middle Ages, people celebrated with a cake on the feast day of their name saint instead of their birthday.

It is believed that the first birthday cake candles were used in Germany during the Middle Ages as symbols of earlier religious votive candles. The candle in the center of the cake was called the Lebenslicht, or "light of life"; today we call this the "one to grow on."

⊙ Applesauce Cake

PREP TIME: 20 MIN	BAKING TIME: 1 HR AND 15 MIN	YIELD: 12 TO 14 SERVINGS

INGREDIENTS

240 grams (2 cups) flour

200 grams (1 cup) sugar

1 teaspoon baking powder

1 teaspoon baking soda

1 teaspoon salt

1 teaspoon cinnamon

½ teaspoon cloves

½ teaspoon nutmeg

½ teaspoon allspice

120 grams (½ cup) vegetable oil

125 grams (½ cup) applesauce

2 eggs

124 grams (1 cup) chopped walnuts or pecans

DIRECTIONS

1 Preheat the oven to 350 degrees. Grease a 9-x-5-inch loaf pan. Sift together the flour, sugar, baking powder, baking soda, salt, cinnamon, cloves, nutmeg, and allspice into a large mixing bowl.

2 Add the oil and applesauce and mix for 2 minutes. Add the eggs and mix for 2 minutes longer.

3 Fold in the nuts and turn into the prepared loaf pan. Bake the loaf for 1 hour and 15 minutes, or until a toothpick inserted into the center comes out clean. Cool the loaf in the pan for 10 minutes. Remove from the pan and finish cooling on a metal rack.

VARY IT! I've used pear applesauce and even peach applesauce for this recipe.

PER SERVING: *Calories 304 (From Fat 150); Fat 17g (Saturated 2g); Cholesterol 35mg; Sodium 269mg; Carbohydrate 36g (Dietary Fiber 2g); Protein 5g.*

🍎 German Apple Kuchen with Streusel

PREP TIME: 45 MIN	BAKING TIME: 55 MIN	YIELD: 12 SERVINGS

INGREDIENTS

450 grams (2¾ cups) flour

1½ teaspoons baking powder

1 teaspoon salt

200 grams (1 cup) sugar

112 grams (1 cup/2 sticks) unsalted butter

2 eggs

650 grams (6½ cups) peeled and thinly sliced apples

1 tablespoon lemon juice

3 tablespoons brown sugar

1½ teaspoons cinnamon

¼ teaspoon nutmeg

62 grams (½ cup) walnuts, chopped (optional)

DIRECTIONS

1 Grease a 9-inch round springform pan or 9 x 9 baking dish. In a food processor, pulse together the flour, baking powder, salt, sugar, and butter until it looks combined and resembles coarse crumbles. Add in the eggs and blend until combined, about 30 seconds to 1 minute. Remove dough and wrap in plastic wrap. Refrigerate dough for 30 minutes.

2 Place sliced apples in a bowl with lemon juice, stirring to toss the apples to help with browning. Sprinkle brown sugar, cinnamon, and nutmeg over apples.

3 Place a baking sheet into the oven and preheat the oven to 350 degrees. Remove the dough from the refrigerator and divide into three equal parts. Using your hands, spread two parts of the dough across the bottom of the pan and up the sides about 1½ inches or 4 centimeters. Pour apples over the crust. With the remaining dough, crumble mixture and mix with walnuts. Spread crumbles over the top of the apples. Bake for 35 minutes, remove from oven, and cover with foil. Continue to bake apple cake for an additional 20 minutes until the crumbles are deep golden brown and apples are bubbling. Allow the cake to cool for at least 1 hour before removing the springform pan.

NOTE: After living in Germany for numerous years, I finally figured out some key baking secrets when making their recipes. Germany uses different flour, butter, baking powder, and grows different apples. If you're baking the in United States or Canada, you'll appreciate this recipe as I use North American products to meet that authentic flavor. Most Germans allow this cake to rest for 24 hours before slicing, but I'll let you decide when to slice and serve. See the color insert for a photo.

NOTE: Use a mixture of tart Granny Smith, Jonagold, Pink Lady, or Braeburn.

PER SERVING: *Calories 315 (From Fat 80); Fat 9g (Saturated 5g); Cholesterol 55mg; Sodium 208mg; Carbohydrate 55g (Dietary Fiber 2g); Protein 5g.*

🍅 Banana–Sour Cream Bundt Cake

PREP TIME: 20 MIN	BAKING TIME: 45 MIN	YIELD: 12 SERVINGS

INGREDIENTS

113 grams (½ cup/1 stick) butter, softened

250 grams (1¼ cups) sugar

2 eggs

300 grams (1 cup) mashed very ripe bananas (about 2 bananas)

½ teaspoon vanilla extract

127 grams (½ cup) sour cream

240 grams (2 cups) flour

1 teaspoon baking powder

1 teaspoon baking soda

¼ teaspoon salt

62 grams (½ cup) chopped walnuts

½ teaspoon cinnamon

DIRECTIONS

1 Preheat the oven to 375 degrees. Grease well a 6½-cup capacity ring mold or Bundt pan. In a large bowl, beat the butter until light, about 1 minute. Slowly beat in 1 cup of the sugar. Beat in the eggs, one at a time. Add the mashed bananas, vanilla, and sour cream.

2 Sift together the flour, baking powder, baking soda, and salt. Fold the flour into the creamed mixture, stirring just to blend (do not overbeat).

3 In another bowl, combine the chopped walnuts, the remaining ¼ cup sugar, and cinnamon. Sprinkle half of this mixture over the bottom of the prepared ring mold. Spoon in half of the batter.

4 Sprinkle in the remaining walnut mixture and cover with the rest of the banana and sour cream batter.

5 Bake for 45 minutes or until the cake is brown and starts to pull away from the sides of the mold. Let the cake cool in the pan for 10 minutes before turning it onto a wire rack to cool further.

PER SERVING: *Calories 308 (From Fat 127); Fat 14g (Saturated 7g); Cholesterol 60mg; Sodium 203mg; Carbohydrate 42g (Dietary Fiber 1g); Protein 5g.*

Making Pound Cakes

The pound cake got its name because it traditionally contained 1 pound each of flour, butter, eggs, and sugar. It's a staple for bakers because it's easy to make, reliable, delicious, and keeps for a long time. Today's pound cakes aren't restricted by the original recipe and can be glamorized with bits of chocolate, poppy seeds, fruits, and raisins, just to name a few. The old-fashioned plain pound cake is still a classic, though.

For a truly dense cake, mix the batter by hand. For a lighter texture, use an electric mixer to cream the butter and sugar, then finish mixing by hand. This is supposed to be a dense cake, so be careful not to overmix the batter by beating it too long with the mixer. Otherwise, it may come pouring over the sides of the pan when it bakes.

TIP

Bake pound cakes in loaf, tube, or Bundt pans, preferably of shiny metal rather than dark steel. Dark pans cause the outside of the cake to brown before the inside is baked through. For more on baking pans, see Chapter 3.

Don't fret if the top of the cake splits — this is normal, caused by steam escaping during baking.

COOLING A CAKE

Cakes need to cool properly before they're handled. First, allow cakes to cool in their pans for a while. If a cake hasn't cooled enough, it will be quite reluctant to leave the pan — some of the cake may stick to the pan, or half of the cake will come out, and the other half will stay attached. Wire racks are perfect for cakes to cool on after they're removed from baking pans, because the wire racks allow air to circulate all around the cake while it cools. Some kinds of cakes require specific cooling techniques, such as

- **Cheesecakes:** Allowing the cheesecake to fully set before removing the springform pan is important. Cool the cheesecake to room temperature. Then cover the top of the pan with plastic wrap and place it in the refrigerator to set for at least four hours; overnight is ideal. After the cheesecake is completely chilled, run a butter knife between the cake and the edge of the pan and gently release the springform ring, bringing it over the top of cake.

- **Sponge or angel food cakes:** Sponge and angel food cakes are leavened with air, so they have to cool hanging upside down or they will collapse into themselves. The easiest way is to use a pan that has feet attached to the pan. Just flip around the feet and turn the cake upside down. If your pan doesn't have feet, don't worry — just turn the pan over onto the neck of a wine bottle or long, heatproof funnel. If those aren't handy, balance the edges of the pan on inverted mugs or cups. Allow the cake to completely cool for several hours. Then remove the pan from the bottle and slide a sharp knife with a long, thin blade between the cake and side of the pan to free any sticking crumbs. Place a plate over the top of the tube pan, flip it over, and remove the pan.

Classic Pound Cake

INGREDIENTS

210 grams (1¾ cups) flour

¾ teaspoon baking powder

¼ teaspoon salt

169 grams (¾ cup/1½ sticks) butter, at room temperature

150 grams (¾ cup) sugar

3 tablespoons milk

3 eggs

1½ teaspoons vanilla extract

DIRECTIONS

1 Preheat the oven to 350 degrees. Grease and flour a 9-x-5-inch loaf pan.

2 Sift together the flour, baking powder, and salt in a medium-sized bowl. Set aside.

3 Using an electric mixer, cream together the butter and sugar on medium speed until well incorporated, about 1 minute. Add the milk, eggs (one at a time), and vanilla and continue beating to mix well. Slowly add the flour, about ½ cup at a time, mixing on low speed until just blended.

4 Scrape the batter into the prepared loaf pan. Bake for 55 to 60 minutes, or until a wooden toothpick inserted into the center comes out clean. Let the cake rest for 10 minutes before inverting it onto a cooling rack.

PER SERVING: *Calories 179 (From Fat 88); Fat 10g (Saturated 6g); Cholesterol 64mg; Sodium 69mg; Carbohydrate 20g (Dietary Fiber 0g); Protein 3g.*

Chocolate Swirl Pound Cake

PREP TIME: 25 MIN	BAKING TIME: 50 MIN TO 1 HR, 10 MIN	YIELD: 20 TO 24 SERVINGS

INGREDIENTS

600 grams (3 cups) sugar

338 grams (1½ cups/3 sticks) butter, at room temperature

5 eggs

254 grams (1 cup) sour cream

2 teaspoons vanilla or almond extract, or 1 teaspoon each

360 grams (3 cups) flour

1½ teaspoons baking soda

½ teaspoon salt

28 grams (1 ounce) semisweet or bittersweet chocolate

1 tablespoon butter

DIRECTIONS

1 Preheat the oven to 350 degrees. Grease and flour a 12-cup Bundt or tube pan.

2 Using an electric mixer, cream together the sugar and the 1½ cups butter, about 1 minute. Add the eggs, sour cream, and vanilla and blend, stopping once to scrape down the sides of the bowl. Stir in the flour, baking soda, and salt. Reserve 1 cup of the batter. Pour the remaining batter into the prepared pan.

3 In a small saucepan over very low heat, melt the chocolate and 1 tablespoon butter. Stir into the reserved cup of batter.

4 Spoon the chocolate batter around the center of the pan. With a knife, gently swirl the two batters together with an S motion. Don't overmix.

5 Bake for 50 minutes to 1 hour and 10 minutes, until a wooden tester inserted into the center of the cake comes out clean. Let cool for 15 minutes. Remove the cake from the pan and cool completely.

TIP: I recommend using butter to achieve the rich flavor you want in this cake. Even without the chocolate swirl, this dense cake is very tasty.

PER SERVING: *Calories 302 (From Fat 141); Fat 16g (Saturated 9g); Cholesterol 81mg; Sodium 148mg; Carbohydrate 38g (Dietary Fiber 1g); Protein 3g.*

Creating Cupcakes

Like pound cakes, which originally contained a pound of each ingredient, cupcakes are so-called because all the ingredients were originally measured out by the cup: 1 cup of butter, 2 cups of sugar, 3 cups of flour, and 4 eggs. The individual tins came later, so the name really derived from the recipe, not from the baking pans.

Any recipe for layer, butter, or pound cake makes a fine cupcake. Coffee cake recipes can also be used, as can recipes for fruit cakes, nut cakes, and tea cakes. Cupcakes are baked in muffin pans. As a general rule, the pans are prepared for baking by spreading them with shortening or spraying them with a nonstick coating. They may also be lined with paper or foil baking cups, which ensure that the cakes won't stick to the pan, making cleanup a snap. The liners also help keep moisture in the cakes, keeping them fresher longer.

TIP

Flat-bottomed, wafer ice cream cones can be used as baking containers for cupcake batter. Children are particularly fond of them. To make them, fill the cones two-thirds full with batter (about 2 generous tablespoons). Place the filled cones on a flat baking sheet or in muffin tins and bake for about 25 minutes, or until a cake tester inserted in the center of the cupcake comes out clean. Eat the cake and its container.

Chocolate Cupcakes

INGREDIENTS

95 grams (½ cup) shortening, at room temperature

200 grams (1 cup) sugar

1 egg

180 grams (1½ cups) flour

59 grams (½ cup) unsweetened cocoa powder

½ teaspoon salt

1 teaspoon baking soda

113 grams (½ cup) buttermilk

118 grams (½ cup) hot water

1 teaspoon vanilla extract

DIRECTIONS

1 Preheat the oven to 375 degrees. Grease or line 12 muffin cups. In a medium mixing bowl, cream together the shortening and sugar until light and creamy, about 1 minute. Beat in the egg.

2 In a small bowl, combine the flour, cocoa, and salt. Stir the baking soda into the buttermilk and stir to dissolve. Add the flour mixture alternately with the buttermilk to the shortening mixture, beginning and ending with flour and mix just to combine.

3 Add the hot water and vanilla. Pour the batter into the muffin tins and bake for 20 minutes or until a toothpick inserted into the center comes out clean. Cool the cupcakes on a wire rack completely before frosting them.

VARY IT! If you like, you can use ¼ cup shortening and ¼ cup butter (½ stick). Just make sure that both are at room temperature.

NOTE: You can frost them with vanilla or chocolate frosting, or just a dusting of confectioners' sugar.

NOTE: See the color insert for a photo of this recipe.

PER SERVING: *Calories 216 (From Fat 87); Fat 10g (Saturated 3g); Cholesterol 18mg; Sodium 146mg; Carbohydrate 31g (Dietary Fiber 2g); Protein 3g.*

☙ Lemon Cupcakes

INGREDIENTS

230 grams (2 cups) cake flour

2 teaspoons baking powder

½ teaspoon salt

150 grams (⅔ cup/1¼ sticks) butter, at room temperature

200 grams (1 cup) sugar

3 eggs

160 grams (⅔ cup) milk

2 teaspoons lemon extract

½ teaspoon vanilla extract

Zest from 1 lemon (about 1 teaspoon)

Lemon Frosting

Lemon Frosting

454 grams (two packages [8 ounces]) cream cheese

170 grams (¾ cup/1½ sticks) butter, at room temperature

57 grams (¼ cup) fresh lemon juice (about 2 lemons)

511 grams (4½ cups) confectioners' sugar

1 teaspoon lemon extract

1 teaspoon vanilla extract

1 teaspoon grated lemon zest (optional)

DIRECTIONS

1 Preheat the oven to 350 degrees. Line two 12-cup muffin tins with paper liners.

2 In a small bowl, prepare the cupcake batter: Combine the flour, baking powder, and salt. In a mixing bowl, beat together the butter, sugar, and eggs. Add the milk, lemon extract, vanilla extract, and lemon zest. Scrape down the sides of the bowl occasionally. Stir in the flour mixture.

3 Fill each muffin cup two-thirds full. Bake for 15 to 20 minutes, or until a wooden tester inserted into the center comes out clean. Let the cupcakes cool slightly before removing them from the tin. Cool completely, about 1 hour.

4 While the cupcakes are cooling, prepare the frosting: Combine the cream cheese, butter, and lemon juice and beat until smooth and creamy. Add the confectioners' sugar, lemon extract, vanilla, and lemon zest, if desired. Beat until creamy. Chill the frosting until the cupcakes have cooled and are ready to be frosted. Frost the cupcakes and keep them refrigerated until ready to serve.

PER SERVING: *Calories 316 (From Fat 166); Fat 18g (Saturated 11g); Cholesterol 78mg; Sodium 149mg; Carbohydrate 35g (Dietary Fiber 0g); Protein 3g.*

Adding a Little Air: Sponge Cakes

Sponge cakes are light and airy. The primary reason they rise so high is the air beaten into egg whites. Sponge cakes are both lighter and dryer than butter cakes. They're dryer (in a good way, not like an overbaked cake) because they don't have the fat that adds to the moistness of butter cakes.

Butter cakes blend sugar into the fat to make the air pockets. In contrast, sponge cakes whip the eggs with sugar until light in color (lemon-colored), thick, and at the ribbon stage (when the batter forms a flat ribbon falling back upon itself when the beater is lifted). At this stage, a line drawn with your finger through the batter will remain visible for at least a couple seconds. Whisk-type beaters, not paddles, are always used to make sponge cakes. The air whipped into the egg-sugar mixture at this stage contributes to the rising of the sponge.

TECHNICAL STUFF

When the sponge cake is placed in the oven to bake, the second essential factor is the heat of the oven. Basically, what happens is this: The liquid in the batter becomes steam, which rises and escapes through the foam. The heat also causes the air in these bubbles to expand, which contributes to the rise. This same principle is what makes croissants flaky and puff pastry puffy.

Angel food cake

An angel food cake is a light, fluffy, high-rising cake that is basically a sponge cake without egg yolks or fat. To make a good angel food cake, you just need to know a few basic tricks:

- » **Whip the egg whites properly.** Angel food cake is made with a large quantity of egg whites, which are whipped into a foam; this foam provides all the cake's leavening (for instructions, see Chapter 5).

- » **Don't grease the cake pan.** The rising batter must cling to the pan sides and hold itself up. The sides of a greased pan will be too slippery for the cake to rise.

- » **Preheat the oven.** The cake shouldn't be sitting around waiting to rise, allowing the air cells to deflate while the oven heats up. The oven must also be the correct heat: The ideal temperature is 325 degrees.

- » **Test for doneness.** Use something long and thin to test the cake for doneness, such as a clean broom straw, a long thin knife, or a thin bamboo skewer.

>> **Invert the pan.** As soon as the cake is done baking, turn the pan upside down and stand it on its feet or hang it upsided own over the neck of a bottle or tall funnel. What you want to do is invert the cake until it has completely cooled to ensure it will be firm enough to hold its rise.

>> **Saw, don't cut.** To cut angel food cake, use a sawing motion with a serrated knife or a pronged *angel-food cutter* (a tool that looks like a row of thin nails attached to a bar). Just remember that if you try to cut the cake with a regular straight-blade knife, you'll end up pushing down on the cake, which will flatten it. Freeze it first for easier slicing.

Angel Food Cake

PREP TIME: 15 MIN | BAKING TIME: 40 TO 45 MIN | YIELD: 10 TO 12 SERVINGS

INGREDIENTS

115 grams (1 cup) cake flour

170 grams (1½ cups) confectioners' sugar

446 grams (2 cups) egg whites (about 6 to 8 eggs)

¼ teaspoon salt

1 teaspoon vanilla extract

¼ teaspoon almond extract

200 grams (1 cup) sugar

DIRECTIONS

1 Preheat the oven to 350 degrees. Sift the cake flour with the confectioners' sugar twice. Set aside.

2 With a wire whisk or the whisk attachment of an electric mixer, beat the egg whites, salt, vanilla, and almond extract together until they are foamy and just begin to form soft peaks. (See Chapter 5 for instructions on beating egg whites.) Gradually add the sugar, about 2 to 3 teaspoons at a time, and continue beating until stiff peaks form. Do not overbeat.

3 Add the flour mixture to the egg whites in thirds and gently fold with a rubber spatula to combine (about four turns) after each addition.

4 Carefully pour the mixture into a 10-inch tube pan. Bake the cake for 40 to 45 minutes. It will be golden brown and spring back when you touch it. Remove the cake from the oven and turn it upside down over a funnel or the neck of a bottle or rest it on the feet of the tube pan, if available. Let the cake cool inverted. Remove it from the pan and serve.

NOTE: This light and airy cake calls for cake flour. Don't purchase self-rising cake flour by mistake (it will be marked on the package). You can double-check if you aren't sure by reading the ingredients. If any leavening agent, such as baking soda or powder, is present in the flour, it's self-rising and *not* the kind you want.

PER SERVING: *Calories 156 (From Fat 0); Fat 0g (Saturated 0g); Cholesterol 0mg; Sodium 76mg; Carbohydrate 36g (Dietary Fiber 0g); Protein 3g.*

Rolling with the jelly rolls

A *jelly roll* is simply a thin sponge cake baked in a broad flat pan and then rolled up around a filling. Typical fillings include jelly or preserves, custard, or mousse. The ever-popular Christmastime treat is the Buche de Noel: a jelly roll filled with buttercream and coated in chocolate.

You want a jelly roll cake to be light and fine-grained, but it should also be a bit elastic and flexible so that it can roll without cracking. You can also use my Angel Food Cake recipe (earlier in this chapter) — just bake it in a jelly roll pan. The texture of the cake is light and flexible enough to make a delicious roll. To ensure that the jelly roll will come neatly out of the pan, spread butter or margarine on the bottom and sides of a pan. Line the bottom of the pan with waxed paper or baking parchment. (See Chapter 5 for more about lining cake pans.)

To assemble a jelly roll, as soon as the cake comes out of the oven to cool, invert the pan over a clean kitchen towel sprinkled with sugar. Lift off the pan and carefully peel off the paper. With a serrated knife, carefully slice off a ⅛-inch strip of the crisp side, which will make rolling the cake easier and prevent cracking. Fold one short end of the towel over the end of the cake, then roll up the cake. Figure 9-1 shows you how this is done.

Rolling up a jelly roll

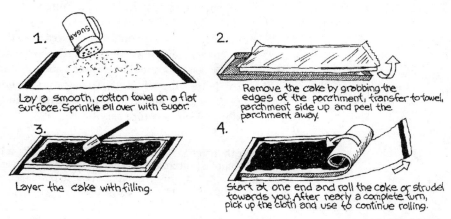

1. Lay a smooth, cotton towel on a flat surface. Sprinkle all over with sugar.

2. Remove the cake by grabbing the edges of the parchment, transfer to towel, parchment side up and peel the parchment away.

3. Layer the cake with filling.

4. Start at one end and roll the cake or strudel towards you. After nearly a complete turn, pick up the cloth and use to continue rolling.

FIGURE 9-1: Assembling a jelly roll.

© John Wiley & Sons, Inc.

Place the cake seam side down to cool. The cake can be left to cool for several hours or even overnight before unrolling and filling it. Once filled, cut the jelly roll with a serrated knife, using a sawing motion. Otherwise, you may press down too hard on the roll and squeeze out the filling.

🍅 Jelly Roll

PREP TIME: 30 MIN	BAKING TIME: 20 MIN	YIELD: 10 TO 12 SERVINGS

INGREDIENTS

90 grams (¾ cup) flour

1 teaspoon baking powder

½ teaspoon salt

4 eggs

150 grams (¾ cup) sugar

1 teaspoon grated lemon peel

170 to 230 grams (6 to 8 ounces) raspberry preserves, at room temperature

Confectioners' sugar, for dusting

DIRECTIONS

1 Preheat the oven to 375 degrees. Line a 15-x-10-x-1-inch baking pan with parchment or waxed paper. Sprinkle a clean kitchen towel with confectioners' sugar; set aside. In a small bowl, sift together the flour, baking powder, and salt. Set aside.

2 In a medium bowl, beat the eggs with an electric mixer until they thicken slightly and turn a light yellow, about 2 minutes on medium speed. Beat in the sugar, about 2 tablespoons at a time, and continue beating on medium speed for about 5 minutes. Add the lemon peel. Gently fold in the flour mixture and spread the mixture into the prepared pan.

3 Bake for 8 to 10 minutes, until the cake springs back gently when touched. Invert the cake onto the prepared kitchen towel and allow it to cool for just 2 minutes. Remove the pan and carefully peel off the waxed paper. Beginning at the narrow end, roll the cake in the towel and place on a wire rack, seam side down, to cool, about 20 minutes.

4 Unroll the cake, spoon the preserves onto the cake, and spread to cover, leaving a ¼-inch border around the cake's edges. The preserves should be spread about ¼-inch thick. Roll up the jelly roll again and place seam side down onto the cake plate; let rest about 30 minutes. Dust with additional confectioners' sugar before serving.

VARY IT! Instead of using raspberry preserves for a jelly roll, feel free to substitute a buttercream filling, sweetened whipped cream, pudding, or any flavor of jam or preserve. If you use pudding or whipped cream, be sure to keep the jelly roll refrigerated.

PER SERVING: *Calories 176 (From Fat 16); Fat 2g (Saturated 1g); Cholesterol 71mg; Sodium 158mg; Carbohydrate 37g (Dietary Fiber 1g); Protein 3g.*

🍅 Tres Leches with Mango

PREP TIME: 25 MIN | BAKING TIME: 30 MIN | YIELD: 12 TO 14 SERVINGS

INGREDIENTS

120 grams (1 cup) flour

1½ teaspoon baking powder

¼ teaspoon salt

5 eggs, divided

150 grams (¾ cup) sugar, divided

82 grams (⅓ cup) whole milk

1 teaspoon vanilla extract

Syrup

8 ounce (1 cup) can evaporated milk

8 ounce can (1 cup) sweetened condensed milk

77 grams (⅓ cup) heavy whipping cream

Frosting

300 grams (1½ cups) sugar

180 grams (⅔ cup) water

⅛ teaspoon cream of tartar

3 egg whites

1 teaspoon vanilla extract

Topping

1 large mango, thinly sliced

2 tablespoons thinly sliced mint leaves

DIRECTIONS

1 Preheat the oven to 350 degrees. Grease and flour a 9-x-13-inch cake pan. In a small bowl, sift together the flour, baking powder, and salt. In a separate mixing bowl or stand mixer, beat the egg yolks and ½ cup sugar on medium speed until pale yellow in color and fluffy.

2 In another bowl or stand mixer, whip the egg whites on medium speed. After the egg whites begin to get frothy, sprinkle in remaining ¼ cup sugar a little at a time until the egg whites form stiff peaks, about 3 minutes.

3 Pour the flour mixture, milk, and vanilla extract into the egg yolk mixture, stirring to combine. Fold in the egg white mixture, scooping and folding gently until mixed. Pour the cake batter into a prepared cake pan, using a straight-edged spatula to gently spread the batter evenly. Bake for 30 minutes or until cake is golden brown in color and a knife comes out clean when inserted into the center.

4 While the cake is baking, prepare the milk mixture. In a large liquid measuring cup, stir the evaporated milk, condensed milk, and heavy whipping cream.

5 To prepare the frosting, place the sugar, water, and cream of tartar into a 4-quart saucepan and bring to a rolling boil over medium high heat. Don't stir to avoid crystals forming. Bring this mixture to 245 degrees.

(continued)

6 While the sugar is coming to a boil, in a stand mixer beat egg whites on medium-high until soft peaks form. While the eggs are beating, drizzle in the boiling sugar. The egg whites will start to appear glossy. Add in vanilla extract and beat just until stiff peaks form. This frosting takes 5 to 7 minutes. If you overbeat the egg whites, they'll lose their shine.

7 Poke holes into the top of the baked cake. Pour milk mixture over the warm cake. Top the cake with whipped meringue frosting. Refrigerate the cake for at least 2 hours before serving. Top with mango slices and mint leaves before serving.

PER SERVING: *Calories 333 (From Fat 67); Fat 7g (Saturated 4g); Cholesterol 96mg; Sodium 205mg; Carbohydrate 56g (Dietary Fiber 0g); Protein 12g.*

🍋 Lemon Rosemary Almond Cake

PREP TIME: 20 MIN	BAKING TIME: 30 MIN	YIELD: 8 SERVINGS

INGREDIENTS

144 grams (1½ cups) almond flour

2 tablespoons lemon zest

1 tablespoon finely chopped fresh rosemary

4 eggs, separated

100 grams (½ cup) sugar

115 grams (1 cup) confectioner's sugar

77 grams (⅓ cup) lemon juice

1 lemon, thinly sliced, for garnish

1 rosemary sprig, for garnish

DIRECTIONS

1 Preheat the oven to 350 degrees. Coat a springform cake pan with 1 tablespoon of the butter and dust evenly with 1 tablespoon of the flour. In a mixing bowl, place the almond flour, lemon zest, and rosemary. In a stand mixer or with a hand-held beater, beat together the egg yolks and sugar until creamy and light yellow. Pour the mixture into almond flour and stir until combined.

2 Clean the beater attachments and bowl and beat the egg whites until soft peaks form. Fold the egg whites into the almond flour mixture.

3 Pour the cake into a prepared cake pan and bake the cake for 30 minutes or until the top is golden brown and a knife inserted into the center comes out clean.

4 Whisk together the lemon juice and confectioner's sugar. Add more juice as needed to make a thin glaze.

5 When cake is out of the oven, allow it to cool for 25 minutes. Run a knife along the edge of the pan to loosen the cake and remove it from springform. Drizzle top of the cake with lemon glaze and top with thin lemon slices and garnish with a sprig of rosemary. Serve warm or at room temperature.

NOTE: This is a gluten-free cake, which uses the eggs to leaven the cake, by beating both individually and folding them together, like a traditional sponge cake.

VARY IT! If rosemary is too strong of an herb for your tastes, try lavender or thyme.

PER SERVING: *Calories 247 (From Fat 103); Fat 11g (Saturated 1g); Cholesterol 106mg; Sodium 36mg; Carbohydrate 32g (Dietary Fiber 2g); Protein 7g.*

Gluten-Free Chocolate Hazelnut Cake

PREP TIME: 15 MIN	BAKING TIME: 35 TO 45 MIN	YIELD: 12 SERVINGS

INGREDIENTS

4 eggs, separated into whites and yolks

200 grams (1 cup) superfine or caster sugar

1 teaspoon salt

250 grams (1 cup) ground hazelnuts or hazelnut flour

1 teaspoon vanilla extract

170 grams (1 cup) semisweet or dark chocolate chips

1 tablespoon coconut oil

28 grams (¼ cup) roughly chopped, toasted hazelnuts (skins removed)

DIRECTIONS

1 Preheat the oven to 350 degrees. Grease an 8- or 9-inch springform cake pan. In a stand mixer with the whisk attachment, beat the egg whites until stiff peaks form, about 5 minutes.

2 In a separate mixing bowl, beat the egg yolks with superfine sugar until creamy and light yellow in color — when lifted, it should be ribbon-like as it falls from the whisk.

3 In a large bowl, stir together the salt and hazelnut flour. Pour in the egg yolks and mix well with a rubber spatula. Fold in the stiff egg whites until combined, careful not to overmix the cake batter.

4 Pour the batter into the prepared pan. This cake is dense and won't rise. Bake for 35 to 45 min, or until a toothpick inserted into the center comes out clean. Cool the loaf on a wire rack for 30 minutes before removing the cake from the pan to finish cooling; then use a knife to loosen the edges away from the springform pan and remove outer pan.

5 As soon as the cake has cooled, in a microwave-safe bowl melt chocolate and coconut oil in the microwave, stirring every 30 seconds until melted. Drizzle the melted chocolate over the cooled cake and sprinkle with chopped nuts.

TIP: Don't overcook the chocolate when melting. Agitating the chocolate with stirring as it melts, helps keep the chocolate from burning.

NOTE: This style of cake is popular throughout Europe, where hazelnuts grow wild in the forests.

NOTE: See the color insert for a photo of this recipe.

PER SERVING: Calories 315 (From Fat 170); Fat 19g (Saturated 5g); Cholesterol 70mg; Sodium 219mg; Carbohydrate 32g (Dietary Fiber 7g); Protein 6g.

☺ Molten Lava Cake

PREP TIME: 15 MIN | BAKING TIME: 15 MIN | YIELD: 4 SERVINGS

INGREDIENTS

Cooking spray

4 teaspoons cocoa powder

113 grams (4 ounces/⅓ cup) semisweet chocolate, chopped

113 grams (½ cup) unsalted butter

¼ teaspoon sea salt

2 egg yolks

100 grams (½ cup) sugar

2 eggs

½ teaspoon vanilla extract

DIRECTIONS

1 Preheat the oven to 400 degrees. Spray four (6-ounce) rame-kins with cooking spray and dust each with 1 teaspoon cocoa powder. In a microwave-safe bowl, melt the chocolate and butter for about 1 minute, stirring after 30 seconds. Continue to stir to fully melt chocolate. Stir in sea salt.

2 In a separate mixing bowl, beat the egg yolks with sugar until light yellow and creamy in texture. Add in whole eggs and vanilla extract and whisk to blend. Pour in the melted choco-late, whisking to combine.

3 Pour the batter into the prepared ramekins. Place the rame-kins onto a baking sheet and bake in the oven for 15 minutes or until the edges are set but the cake still has a wiggle. Cool for 1 minute, and then run a knife along the edge of the ram-ekin. Place a serving plate on top and invert the cake. The cake should remove with ease from the pan. Serve immediately.

TIP: Serve with ice cream, dusted with confectioner's sugar, or with fresh berries. Our family enjoys with a scoop of coffee ice cream or raspberries.

PER SERVING: *Calories 484 (From Fat 315); Fat 35g (Saturated 21g); Cholesterol 219mg; Sodium 145mg; Carbohydrate 45g (Dietary Fiber 2g); Protein 5g.*

Creating Cheesecakes

Who can resist the appeal of a rich, creamy, satin-smooth cheesecake? Because this is one luxury that is well within reach, easy to make, and freezes well, it is worth preparing for any occasion.

For a cheesecake to taste smooth and creamy, the batter must be smooth and creamy at all times. The best way to achieve this is to have all ingredients at room temperature before you start baking. Using a mixer with a paddle attachment, beat the cream cheese until it's smooth and soft before adding the other ingredients. If you use a handheld mixer, use it on a low speed so you don't incorporate too much air into the batter, which can cause your cheesecake to crack.

Another popular method is to dump all the ingredients into a blender or food processor and give it a whir for a minute or so; then just pour and bake. This method can incorporate a bit too much air, so if you try it, remove the blender from the motor base and thunk it on the countertop a few times to encourage the air bubbles to rise to the surface and escape.

TIP

Whichever method you choose for mixing the batter, stop several times and scrape the sides and the bottom of the container to be sure your batter is lump-free and that no ingredients are stuck to the bottom or sides.

COPING WITH CRACKS

Cracks in a cheesecake, whether they happen during baking or cooling, can be caused by several different factors: extreme temperature changes, an oven temperature that's too high, too much air in the batter, baking for too long a time, or being placed in a drafty place to cool. Sometimes cracks just happen, despite your best efforts. But worry not — the taste of the cake won't be affected. If you're serving the cheesecake to guests, and appearance is important, here are a few tips to help disguise those cracks:

- **Top the cheesecake with sliced fruit.** Any fresh fruit will do, but if you use bananas or peaches, remember to toss them in a bit of lemon juice to prevent them from browning before serving.

- **Spread the top with a thin layer of sour cream.** This will add to the richness of the cheesecake and conceal any imperfections.

- **Drizzle melted chocolate on top.** Dip a fork in melted chocolate (see Chapter 5) and drizzle a pattern on top of the cheesecake. It will give the cheesecake a new look. When didn't chocolate make everything a little bit better?

Dense Chocolate Brownies (see Chapter 8) are big with chocolate and light on flour, giving them a dense, deep chocolate flavor.

German Apple Kuchen with Streusel (refer to Chapter 9) will make your Oma proud and have your family begging for seconds.

Gluten-Free Chocolate Hazelnut Cake (see Chapter 9) is an elegant and delicious cake, worthy for any occasion.

Chocolate Cupcakes (refer to Chapter 9) with Basic Vanilla Buttercream Frosting (see Chapter 10) are the perfect addition to any birthday party.

Coconut Cream Pie (check out Chapter 11) is made with a homemade coconut pudding and topped with a fluffy meringue.

Rich Chocolate Pudding (see Chapter 12) is a rich, chocolatey pudding perfect for making with kids.

Blueberry Crunch (check out Chapter 12 for the recipe) makes for

Blueberry Muffins (see Chapter 13) are tender muffins, bursting with blueberries and perfect for breakfast.

Pumpkin Bread (refer to Chapter 13) is great for brunch. Don't wait for November to make this treasured quick bread.

Braided Egg Bread (flip to Chapter 14) is the perfect bread to start baking. Braid this loaf for a lovely appearance, or you can place it in loaf pans for a quick sandwich bread.

Make Sesame-Topped Rolls (refer to Chapter 14) into rolls or slightly larger for buns.

Bacon Cheddar and Chive Scones (see Chapter 13) make a tasty dinner or brunch addition.

Goat Cheese and Tomato Tart (refer to Chapter 15) are bursting with sun-ripened tomatoes and tangy goat cheese.

Cinnamon Spiced Cheesecake Bars (see Chapter 16) is a quick dessert baked with a ready-made dough.

A cheesecake is baked in a springform pan. (Flip to Chapter 3 to see what one looks like.) It's a good idea to place the springform on a baking sheet with a lip. A springform pan can sometimes leak, despite your best attempt to make sure it's tightly fastened. Placing the pan on a baking sheet will prevent a leaky springform from making a mess in your oven. It's also an easy and safer way to take the cheesecake in and out of the oven, preventing any surprise openings of the springform. If you don't have a baking sheet with a lip, you can wrap the bottom of the springform pan in aluminum foil to seal off any potential leaky cracks.

To tell if your cheesecake is done, observe the top surface carefully. For most cheesecakes, the edges of the cake puff up slightly and may turn faintly golden (a golden-brown cheesecake is undesirable). The top should also be dull, not shiny, and when you tap the sides, they should move, but not have the jiggle of liquid. The center should be softer than the edges. The ideal internal temperature of a cheesecake is 150 degrees. As soon as a cheesecake reaches this temperature, remove it from the oven and allow it to cool. The cake will rise slightly during baking, but when it cools, it will settle and solidify. If any cracks appear, they will get smaller as the cake cools and sinks down. You can also carefully run a butter knife around the edge of the cheesecake when it comes out of the oven. Then, as the cake shrinks as it cools, it won't stick to the side of the pan.

You can cool your cheesecake by removing it from the oven and placing it on a cooling rack. Let the cheesecake cool to room temperature before chilling it in the refrigerator for at least 3 to 4 hours, or preferably overnight, before serving.

TIP

CUTTING THE CHEESECAKE

Cutting a cheesecake can be messy. The cake tends to cling to the knife, so making neat slices can be quite a challenge. One solution is to run the knife under hot water after each slice is made. This keeps the knife clean, and the warm knife slices neatly through each piece. Of course, if you're cutting the cheesecake at the table, this method won't work. Instead, use two knives: one to cut the cheesecake and the other to scrape the knife clean after each slice.

A great trick for cutting a cheesecake is to use dental floss or heavy thread. Cut a piece of floss the diameter of the cake, plus enough to wrap around your fingers. Simply pull the thread taut between your hands and press it down all the way through the cake. Release the thread in one hand and pull it out with the other. Repeat, cutting the cake like the spokes of a wheel. It makes a great topic of conversation for your guests.

🍅 Classic Cheesecake

PREP TIME: 25 MIN PLUS 4 HOURS FOR SETTING	BAKING TIME: 1 HR, 15 MIN	YIELD: 16 SERVINGS

INGREDIENTS

240 grams (2 cups) graham cracker crumbs

57 grams (¼ cup) butter, melted

907 grams four packages (8-ounce/2 pounds) cream cheese, at room temperature

300 grams (1½ cups) sugar

5 eggs

Grated rind of 1 lemon

2 teaspoons vanilla extract

63 grams (¼ cup) heavy (whipping) cream or half-and-half

DIRECTIONS

1 Preheat the oven to 300 degrees. In the bottom of a 9-inch springform pan, combine the graham cracker crumbs and the melted butter. Press into the bottom of the pan and place the pan in the refrigerator until you're ready to fill it.

2 In a large mixing bowl or blender, combine the cream cheese, sugar, eggs, lemon rind, vanilla, and cream, and mix until well blended, about 3 minutes. Stop at least three times to scrape down the bottom and the sides of the bowl with a stiff rubber spatula.

3 Assemble the springform pan and pour the batter into the chilled crust and set on a baking sheet. Bake the cheesecake until the center is barely set, about 1 hour and 15 minutes. Shut off the oven and open it. Let the cheesecake cool like that for 20 minutes, and then finish cooling it on a wire rack. Cover and refrigerate the cheesecake for 4 hours or overnight to set. Serve chilled.

TIP: For fewer calories, you can use low-fat cream cheese, but do not use fat-free cream cheese.

PER SERVING: *Calories 397 (From Fat 243); Fat 27g (Saturated 16g); Cholesterol 142mg; Sodium 280mg; Carbohydrate 32g (Dietary Fiber 0g); Protein 7g.*

Pumpkin Cheesecake

PREP TIME: 20 MIN PLUS 6 HOURS FOR SETTING	BAKING TIME: 50 MIN	YIELD: 14 TO 16 SERVINGS

INGREDIENTS

2 cups graham or cinnamon graham cracker crumbs

5 tablespoons butter, melted

Filling

454 grams (two packages [8 ounces]) cream cheese, at room temperature

254 grams (1 cup) sour cream

200 grams (1 cup) sugar

450 grams (one can [16 ounces]) or fresh pumpkin (not seasoned pie filling)

½ teaspoon nutmeg

¼ teaspoon allspice

2 tablespoons bourbon or maple syrup

1 tablespoon vanilla extract

4 eggs

DIRECTIONS

1 Preheat the oven to 300 degrees. To make the crust, mix the cracker crumbs and the butter together until the crumbs are moistened and press them into the bottom of a 9-inch spring-form pan. Your crust should be about ¼-inch thick and a quarter of the way up the side of the pan.

2 In a blender container or large mixing bowl, make the filling: Combine the cream cheese, sour cream, sugar, pumpkin, nutmeg, allspice, bourbon, vanilla, and eggs and mix until well blended, about 2 minutes. Stop the blender or mixer several times to scrape down the sides (cream cheese tends to stick to the sides of the container). Pour the filling into the prepared pan.

3 Bake for 50 minutes or until set and not liquidy in the center. Turn the oven off and crack the door a little. Let the cheesecake cool inside the oven, 30 minutes. When the cheesecake has cooled, remove it from the oven and cover the top with plastic; chill for at least 6 hours or overnight.

NOTE: You can use a blender to make this recipe — just be sure to tap the container a few times on the countertop to release any air bubbles before you pour the mixture into the springform pan.

PER SERVING: *Calories 304 (From Fat 172); Fat 19g (Saturated 11g); Cholesterol 100mg; Sodium 200mg; Carbohydrate 28g (Dietary Fiber 2g); Protein 6g.*

Lemon Curd Cheesecake

PREP TIME: 20 MIN PLUS OVERNIGHT FOR SETTING	BAKING TIME: 45 TO 60 MIN	YIELD: 14 TO 16 SERVINGS

INGREDIENTS

180 grams (1½ cups) graham cracker or gingersnap cookie crumbs

43 grams (3 tablespoons) melted butter

454 grams (two packages [8 ounces]) cream cheese, at room temperature

254 grams (1 cup) sour cream

3 eggs

100 grams (½ cup) sugar or honey

¼ cup brandy or lemon juice

¼ teaspoon salt

Lemon Curd

3 eggs

3 egg yolks

115 grams (½ cup) lemon juice (2 large lemons)

100 grams (½ cup) sugar

57 grams (¼ cup/½ stick) butter, cold, cut into 4 pieces

DIRECTIONS

1 Preheat the oven to 325 degrees. Combine the cracker or cookie crumbs and melted butter into the bottom of a 9- or 10-inch springform pan and press into the bottom to make a smooth floor.

2 In a blender, combine the cream cheese, sour cream, eggs, sugar, brandy, and salt and process until smooth. Alternatively, use an electric mixer and blend until smooth. Pour into the prepared springform pan.

3 Bake for 45 to 60 minutes, until set and slightly golden. Remove from the oven and cool.

4 To prepare the lemon curd, combine the eggs, egg yolks, lemon juice, sugar, and butter in a small saucepan and cook, whisking constantly, over medium heat until the butter is melted and the mixture is hot. Reduce the temperature and continue whisking until the mixture begins to thicken (but don't let the mixture boil), about 2 minutes. The mixture should be thicker than custard. Pour the mixture into a sieve set over a bowl. Cool the mixture just to room temperature. Refrigerate or place the bowl in a bowl of cold water.

5 Pour the lemon curd over the top of the cheesecake still in the springform pan. Cover and refrigerate overnight. Run a knife around the edge of the cheesecake before removing the springform circle.

PER SERVING: Calories 312 (From Fat 197); Fat 22g (Saturated 12g); Cholesterol 171mg; Sodium 222mg; Carbohydrate 23g (Dietary Fiber 0g); Protein 6g.

CHEESECAKE UNDER PRESSURE IN AN INSTANT POT

If you have an Instant Pot or a multicooker, you can cook a cheesecake under pressure. In fact, cheesecakes are a perfect match for an Instant Pot because the moist environment is similar to cooking in a water bath. Here are some key pros to cooking a cheesecake in an Instant Pot:

- If the weather is hot and your goal is to keep your house cool, an Instant Pot is the perfect cooking tool. Who wants to run an oven and heat up the house? Not me!

- The Instant Pot will cook faster, so instead of taking an hour in the oven, most cheesecakes can cook in less than 30 minutes under pressure.

However, you will need a smaller baking vessel. I use a 6-inch springform pan in my 6-quart Instant Pot. When cooking, you need to have the rack inside the pot, water underneath (not touching the springform pan), and I often wrap the underside of my springform pan with foil to keep liquid from making my crust soggy. I do the same when cooking a water bath.

Stick to the following steps when making a cheesecake in the Instant Pot:

1. **Line a 6-inch springform pan with parchment paper, on the sides and on the base.**

   Wrap the base of the pot with foil.

2. **Prepare ⅔ of your selected cheesecake recipe from this chapter.**

3. **Pour 1 cup boiling water into the base of the pot. Place the cheesecake onto the rack, and lower inside the pot.**

4. **Select pressure cook high for 25 minutes with a natural release setting.**

5. **Let your Instant Pot fully release the pressure naturally.**

6. **Remove the rack with the cheesecake from the pot and place it onto the counter to cool completely.**

   After you can touch the pot, chill the cheesecake in the refrigerator for at least 6 hours.

Chapter **10**

Fixing Fabulous Frostings

RECIPES IN THIS CHAPTER

- Cream Cheese Frosting
- Mocha Frosting
- Basic Vanilla Buttercream Frosting
- Sweetened Whipped Cream Frosting
- Chocolate Frosting
- Martha's Sweet and Creamy Frosting
- Quick Apricot Glaze
- Classic Sugar Glaze

For some people, cake is just the vehicle for the frosting — frosting can never be too rich, too thick, too sweet, or too chocolaty. Personally, I prefer my frostings to enhance, not overwhelm, the cake I'm eating, but I'm sure I'm in the minority when it comes to cake eaters. Whether you like a little or a lot, when you dress a cake, you generally say you're frosting it. This chapter introduces some of the different types of frostings, explains how to frost a basic cake, and provides tips for making it all look great without a lot of fuss.

Finding Out More about Frostings

Frostings come in several varieties: buttercream frostings (made predominately with butter, confectioners' sugar and flavoring — they're thick, sweet, and spreadable), icings (usually made with confectioners' sugar and liquid — they're usually poured over a cake and harden), toppings (can be anything from flavored whipped cream to melted chocolate — usually a garnish or thick sauce), glazes (thinner and contain less sugar than icings — they'll set on a cake but not harden), and even fillings (which technically aren't a frosting but can be lumped in with frostings anyway). These types of frosting fall into two general categories:

>> **Quick frostings:** To make these frostings, you just throw all the ingredients into a bowl and beat until smooth. Quick frostings are self-explanatory. You follow the recipes, making sure that all your ingredients are sifted for the smoothest finish, and then spread the frosting all over the cake.

>> **Cooked frostings:** Although cooked frostings can be quick, too, they usually require melting something, such as butter, sugar, or chocolate. Cooked frostings need a bit more attention because you'll need to monitor the blend of sugar, cream, butter, and/or chocolate overheat. But they're just as easy to make as quick frostings.

WARNING

Never cook frostings over high heat. For best results, only use very low heat, or a double boiler placed over simmering water, and follow the recipe carefully.

TIP

A good frosting has a smooth consistency and a silky appearance. The texture should be spreadable but not runny (unless it's a glaze). Here are some tips to help you get the consistency of your frosting just right:

>> If the frosting you've made is too thick, add a few drops of milk or water to thin it. Just keep in mind that a small amount of liquid makes a big difference in consistency, so go slowly when adding milk or water.

>> For the best flavor and most spreadable consistency, use butter or margarine when preparing frostings. However, this rule has exceptions (see Martha's Sweet and Creamy Frosting recipe in this chapter).

>> Always let your butter soften to room temperature before creaming. Otherwise, your frosting will be lumpy.

>> If the recipe calls for confectioners' sugar, sift it before incorporating it into the frosting. Even the tiniest lumps will give the frosting a grainy appearance.

TIP

Adding a pinch of baking soda to icings prevents hardening and cracking so the icing stays moist.

Knowing How Much to Make

How many times have you been halfway through frosting a cake when you realized that you were running out of frosting? Panic sets in, and you start scraping bits from here or there, spreading it out thinner in spots, or, in sheer moments of desperation, taking off the top layer of cake and scraping out the frosting center. Well, worry no more. Table 10-1 gives you some general guidelines for the amount of frosting you need to adequately cover your cakes. Also, all the frosting recipes give you ample amounts to frost a 9-inch layer cake, so you have no fear about running out. As a general rule, the fluffier the frosting, the more you'll need.

TABLE 10-1   **Frosting Amounts for Various Cakes**

Type of Cake	Amount of Frosting Needed
8-inch layer cake	2½ cups
9-inch layer cake	3 cups
Bundt, tube, or sheet cake	1 cup glaze; 3 cups frosting
16 large cupcakes	2 to 2½ cups

Making Quick Frostings

As your cake cools, you can put together any of these quick frostings. These frostings are of spreadable consistency, suitable to use as fillings for the cakes and also to frost the sides and tops of the cake. When you have finished applying the frosting, "finish" by using smooth back-and-forth strokes on the top. It will give the cake a nice, even look. Your goal when frosting a cake is apply all the frosting evenly.

Cream Cheese Frosting

INGREDIENTS

340 grams (One and a half packages [12 ounces]) cream cheese, at room temperature

57 grams (¼ cup/½ stick) butter, at room temperature

325 grams (2½ cups) confectioners' sugar

1 teaspoon vanilla extract

DIRECTIONS

1   With an electric mixer, beat the cream cheese and butter together on medium speed until softened. Add the sugar gradually, ½ cup at a time, and beat until blended. Stop the mixer several times during this process to scrape down the sides of the bowl.

2   Mix in the vanilla. Cover and refrigerate if you aren't using it immediately.

VARY IT! Boost the flavor of this frosting with the addition of 1 teaspoon of grated lemon or orange rind.

NOTE: Be sure to refrigerate the cake before using this frosting. Let the cake come to room temperature before serving.

PER SERVING (1 TABLESPOON): *Calories 54 (From Fat 31); Fat 3g (Saturated 2g); Cholesterol 10mg; Sodium 21mg; Carbohydrate 5g (Dietary Fiber 0g); Protein 1g.*

Mocha Frosting

INGREDIENTS

227 grams (One package [8 ounces]) cream cheese, at room temperature

113 grams (4 ounces) unsweetened chocolate, melted

32 grams (¼ cup) cold brewed coffee

2 teaspoons vanilla extract

433 grams (3⅓ cups) confectioners' sugar

DIRECTIONS

1 Using an electric mixer, beat the cream cheese on medium speed until smooth. Beat in the melted chocolate, coffee, and vanilla.

2 Add the sugar gradually, ½ cup at a time, and beat until blended. Stop the mixer several times during this process to scrape down the sides of the bowl. Cover and refrigerate if you aren't using it immediately.

NOTE: Chocolate and coffee combine with cream cheese to make a creamy, delicious frosting. This frosting goes well with Light and Fluffy Yellow Cake in Chapter 9.

PER SERVING (1 TABLESPOON): *Calories 56 (From Fat 27); Fat 3g (Saturated 2g); Cholesterol 5mg; Sodium 14mg; Carbohydrate 8g (Dietary Fiber 0g); Protein 1g.*

🍅 Basic Vanilla Buttercream Frosting

PREP TIME: 10 MIN | **YIELD: 3 CUPS**

INGREDIENTS

170 grams (¾ cup/1½ sticks) butter, softened

650 to 780 grams (5 to 6 cups) confectioners' sugar

33 to 38 grams (6 to 7 tablespoons) heavy cream or milk, as needed

2 teaspoons vanilla extract

Pinch of salt

DIRECTIONS

1 Cream the butter in a mixing bowl. Slowly beat in 2 cups of the sugar until smooth and creamy. Alternate adding the remaining sugar and the cream in batches, and beat until smooth and creamy, about 2 minutes.

2 Add the vanilla and salt and beat until smooth. Refrigerate the frosting if you're not using it immediately.

NOTE: This all-purpose buttercream frosting is smooth and sweet. It goes well with just about any cake you make. You can add many different flavors, including almond or lemon extract, or use sour cream instead of heavy cream.

VARY IT! Beat in 4 to 6 ounces melted semisweet chocolate with the vanilla and salt if you want a chocolate buttercream frosting.

NOTE: See the color insert for a photo of this recipe on the Chocolate Cupcakes from Chapter 9.

PER SERVING (1 TABLESPOON): *Calories 50 (From Fat 26); Fat 3g (Saturated 2g); Cholesterol 8mg; Sodium 1mg; Carbohydrate 6g (Dietary Fiber 0g); Protein 0g.*

Trying Cooked Frostings

Yes, you have to turn on the stove briefly to make these frostings, but they're just as easy to make as the quick frostings and give you a little more variation. Many of these frostings are very sweet and creamy and well worth the extra effort you put into stirring, melting, and, finally, frosting. Start these frostings when your cake is baking. Then, both the frosting and the cake will be ready to use at about the same time.

TECHNICAL STUFF

Cooked (or also referred to as *boiled*) frostings have been around for centuries. They're often seen as economical because the amount of butter or cream is significantly reduced while still rendering a light, fluffy, and delicious frosting.

Sweetened Whipped Cream Frosting

INGREDIENTS

7 grams (One envelope [¼ ounces]) unflavored gelatin

2 tablespoons cold water

464 grams (2 cups) heavy whipping cream

130 grams (1 cup) confectioners' sugar, or more to taste

1 teaspoon vanilla extract

DIRECTIONS

1 Dissolve 1 envelope unflavored gelatin in 2 tablespoons cool water in a small saucepan.

2 Place the saucepan over very low heat and melt until warm. Allow the mixture to cool to lukewarm.

3 Beat the heavy cream with the sugar and vanilla until it begins to thicken. Stir in the gelatin mixture and continue beating until soft peaks form, about 3 minutes with an electric beater. Chill until ready to use, up to 24 hours. Refrigerate the cake once it's frosted.

TIP: If you want Sweetened Whipped Cream, but you don't need to frost a cake, reduce the amount of cream to 1½ cups. Add the sugar and vanilla and continue beating until soft peaks form. Don't overbeat, or you'll end up with butter.

PER SERVING (1 TABLESPOON): *Calories 39 (From Fat 33); Fat 4g (Saturated 2g); Cholesterol 14mg; Sodium 4mg; Carbohydrate 1g (Dietary Fiber 0g); Protein 0g.*

Chocolate Frosting

INGREDIENTS

454 grams (1 pound) semisweet chocolate

180 grams (¾ cup) heavy whipping cream

57 grams (¼ cup/½ stick) butter

1 tablespoon vanilla extract

DIRECTIONS

1 Cut the chocolate into small bits and place in a mixing bowl (if you're using chips, you can either chop them up or leave them whole).

2 Combine the cream and butter in a small saucepan and bring to a full boil over medium heat. Remove from the heat and pour it over the chocolate, mixing constantly. Add the vanilla and continue mixing until smooth.

3 Allow the frosting to thicken for about 1 hour in the refrigerator before frosting the cake. If you find the frosting has gotten too hard, just leave it out at room temperature until it softens.

TIP: For the best tasting frosting, invest in the highest-quality chocolate available.

PER SERVING (1 TABLESPOON): *Calories 67 (From Fat 47); Fat 5g (Saturated 3g); Cholesterol 8mg; Sodium 3mg; Carbohydrate 6g (Dietary Fiber 1g); Protein 1g.*

Martha's Sweet and Creamy Frosting

INGREDIENTS

236 grams (1 cup) whole milk

40 grams (5 tablespoons) flour

114 grams (½ cup) butter, softened

103 grams (½ cup) shortening

200 grams (1 cup) sugar

1 teaspoon vanilla extract

DIRECTIONS

1 Combine the milk and flour in a 1-quart saucepan and cook, whisking often, until thick and smooth, about 4 minutes. Cover and refrigerate until cool, about 20 minutes.

2 In a mixing bowl, beat together the butter, shortening, sugar, and vanilla until smooth and creamy, about 2 minutes. Add the chilled mixture and beat until creamy, about 10 minutes.

TIP: This frosting requires a bit of time to make, but if you do it while the cake cools, by the time you're finished, the cake will be ready to be frosted.

PER SERVING (1 TABLESPOON): *Calories 58 (From Fat 38); Fat 4g (Saturated 2g); Cholesterol 6mg; Sodium 3mg; Carbohydrate 5g (Dietary Fiber 0g); Protein 0g.*

Ready, Set, Frost!

Before you frost your cake, you must make sure that the cake has cooled completely. I learned this at a young age. I was so excited to frost my dad's birthday cake that I didn't let the cake cool much, despite my mom's warnings. I just slapped the frosting on the cake and watched as it melted into the cake and disappeared down the sides. I kept piling it on, thinking that eventually the cake would look like it should, but all I ended up with was an inedible birthday cake. So learn from my mistake and let your cake cool completely *before* you frost. Even if it seems almost cool, it won't frost as nicely as if it were totally cool or even popped in the fridge overnight.

If you're frosting a layer cake, first inspect the cake layers carefully. You want the surfaces of both cakes to be as flat as possible because you'll have to balance one layer on top of the other.

TIP

A quick and easy solution for a flat surface is to place the bottom layer upside-down, so the rounded side is on the serving plate, leaving you with a perfectly flat frosting surface. The top layer will be placed rounded side up, so the two flat layers are together with the frosting in between.

You can also even out the layers by cutting the domed tops off the cakes. Hold a serrated knife parallel with the top of the cake and gently saw off the domed top, as shown in Figure 10-1. Do this at eye level to be sure you're cutting straight, to ensure a flat top.

FIGURE 10-1:
Evening out a
cake layer.

© *John Wiley & Sons, Inc.*

Frosting a cake

Regardless of whether you're frosting a single cake or a multi-layer cake, the best utensil for frosting cakes is a thin, metal spatula with a rounded tip (see Chapter 3 for more on baking tools) or a firm but flexible plastic spatula.

TIP

To frost a layer cake, follow these simple steps:

1. **Spread between ½ cup and ¾ cup of frosting (depending on how heavily you like to frost your cake) on top of the bottom layer.**

   Be careful not to spread the frosting with hard strokes, the way you would if you were buttering bread. Using hard strokes will pick up crumbs on the cake's surface and mix it into the frosting, giving you an unevenly textured cake. Instead, gently use the spatula or knife to gently push the frosting where you want it to go. The frosting should be soft and creamy enough to do this easily. Make sure that when you frost a cake, your frosting is at room temperature or just above room temperature and isn't too cold. If the frosting is still too stiff, thin it out with just a *few* drops of water or milk.

2. **Place the second layer on the first, cut or domed side up, and brush off any crumbs.**

3. **Frost the sides of the cake with another ½ cup of frosting, or to taste.**

   Begin with a thin layer of frosting to seal in any crumbs. Then, with smooth back-and-forth strokes, frost the sides.

4. **Spread frosting on the top last, using smooth gliding strokes across the cake (see Figure 10-2).**

FIGURE 10-2: Spreading frosting on a cake, saving the top for last.

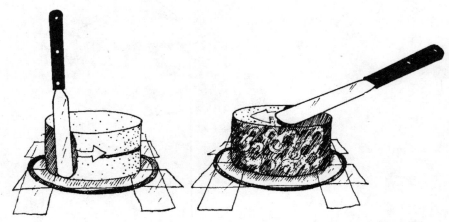

© John Wiley & Sons, Inc.

Apply a thin layer of frosting to the cake and then refrigerate until it's set before applying the final, heavier layer of frosting. This will seal in the crumbs, ensuring a clean final appearance.

Is your cake uneven or domed? You can use the frosting to cover up any imperfections in the top of your cake — just spread it a little thicker than on the sides and make it as level as you can.

If you need to refrigerate or store your cake before serving, cover with either a cake dome or an inverted mixing bowl. Make sure that the bowl is big enough that, when you place it over the cake, it doesn't touch the cake.

Glazing a cake

Glazing a cake requires a slightly different technique because the glaze is runny, not smooth and spreadable the way frosting is. One cup of glaze is sufficient for one Bundt, tube, or angel cake.

TIP

Begin the glazing process by positioning the completely cooled cake on a wire rack over aluminum foil or a baking sheet (to catch the drips). Then follow these steps:

1. **Spoon or pour the glaze, a little at a time, over the top of the cake.**

2. **With a metal spatula or the back of a spoon, spread the glaze into thin areas and to the edge of the cake, allowing some to drizzle over the side.**

3. **Continue spreading the glaze until the cake is well coated and the desired look is achieved.**

WARNING

Stop spreading the glaze as soon as it begins to set. Otherwise, the smooth finish will be lost. (Don't panic, though. You'll have several minutes before the glaze sets.)

After the glaze is set, carefully transfer the cake to a serving plate. If possible, allow the glazed cake to sit for at least 30 minutes to allow the glaze to set. If it is more than four hours before serving time, cover and refrigerate the cake.

Quick Apricot Glaze

PREP TIME: 7 MIN | YIELD: 1 SCANT CUP GLAZE

INGREDIENTS

338 grams (1 cup) all-fruit apricot preserves

DIRECTIONS

1 Place the preserves in a small saucepan over medium heat. Stir until melted. Cook and stir for about 2 minutes longer, until the fruit is boiling and slightly thickened. It should coat the back of a spoon. Cool slightly and brush over your cake or use as directed. Chill the cake to set the glaze.

NOTE: This glaze is delicious over pound cake, angel food cake, or sponge cake. It's also good to use for cake layers if you baked them too long and want to add some moisture back to them.

PER SERVING (1 TABLESPOON): *Calories 48 (From Fat 0); Fat 0g (Saturated 0g); Cholesterol 0mg; Sodium 8mg; Carbohydrate 13g (Dietary Fiber 0g); Protein 0g.*

CALLING ALL CAKE ROUNDS!

Cake rounds are a busy baker's dream. These thick cardboard circles are available in most kitchen-supply stores in a variety of sizes. They hold your cake layers while you're frosting and transporting them from your work area to refrigerator to serving plate. If you can't find cake rounds, just trace a circle, using your cake pan as a size guide, on any heavy, corrugated cardboard and cut it out. Cover your cake rounds with aluminum foil, and they become reusable.

Classic Sugar Glaze

INGREDIENTS

65 grams (½ cup) confectioners' sugar

2 to 3 teaspoons milk, warmed

¼ teaspoon vanilla extract

DIRECTIONS

1 Combine the ingredients and stir until smooth. Add more milk to thin, if desired.

VARY IT! For a chocolate glaze, melt 4 ounces of semisweet chocolate, cut up or chips, and 3 tablespoons butter over low heat, stirring frequently. Remove from heat and stir in 1½ cups sifted powdered sugar and 3 tablespoons of hot water. Drizzle over cake.

PER SERVING (1 TABLESPOON): *Calories 20 (From Fat 0); Fat 0g (Saturated 0g); Cholesterol 0mg; Sodium 1mg; Carbohydrate 5g (Dietary Fiber 0g); Protein 0g.*

Getting Fancy with Decorating

Some occasions require slightly fancier cakes. If you want to go beyond frosting and add a decorative frosting pattern, use a pastry bag with different tips to achieve the effect. *Pastry bags*, also called *decorating bags*, are plastic-coated reusable nylon bags. You stuff the frosting into the bag and then squeeze it out again. The tip you select will give you the design you want — a scalloped edge, or a thin line, or maybe a leaf petal.

TIP

When you're planning on decorating your cake, pop the frosted cake in the freezer or refrigerator for several hours to allow the frosting to harden. Then, if you make a mistake while you're decorating, the decoration will be easy to lift off the hardened frosting and you can start all over again without having ruined the frosted cake.

These sections explain how you can take your cake decorating to the next level.

Choosing a pastry bag

Pastry bags come in two varieties:

>> Ones in which the tip is dropped through the bag and comes out the narrow end

>> Ones in which a tube (called a *coupler*) is inserted, and the tips screw on the outside of the narrow end

If you want to purchase a pastry bag, I recommend the second variety (the coupler assembly). With the coupler, you can change the tips (which are usually included in the purchase of the bag) without having to empty the bag of the frosting. With the drop-in tips, you're committed to the tip you have inserted in the bag. If you need to change tips, you have to empty out the frosting, wash the bag, and then reinsert the new tip (unless you purchase several bags) — all of which can become very messy.

REMEMBER

Pastry bags come in many sizes; for all-purpose use, get a 16-inch bag. If you're not sure what size you want, remember that a bigger bag is a better choice than a smaller one.

Another type of decorating tool is a metal syringe-type tube. Although this tool is fine for writing (like when you want to write "Happy Birthday" on your cake), I think pastry bags give you more control over the amount of frosting you use and how you decorate.

Frostings for decorating

You can use any of the frostings in this book for decorating. If you want to do fancy designs, look for a thicker frosting that will hold its shape for a while. Most people use the same frosting they used to frost the cake when decorating. If you know that you want to decorate, double the recipe or just make 1½ times the recipe to ensure that you'll have enough for decorations on the cake. If you want to add a color to the frosting, choose a vanilla-base frosting so that the color will show.

Tinting frosting

Tinting frosting isn't difficult. The best idea is to choose a vanilla buttercream or basic frosting to color. You can tint frosting in one of two ways:

>> **With food coloring:** For all practical purposes, food coloring is the less expensive way to color frosting, but the paste will last a lifetime (that's no exaggeration).

To use food coloring, drop several (no more than five) drops into the frosting you plan on using. Mix thoroughly. Add two additional drops at a time until the desired color is achieved.

>> **With coloring paste, available at baking-supply shops:** To use a coloring paste, dip the tip of a toothpick into the color and add to the frosting you plan on using. Mix thoroughly. Dip the toothpick a second time, if necessary. Coloring paste is *highly* concentrated, so a very little bit goes a long way. Make sure that you mix the frosting to a uniform color and that there aren't any heavy color streaks.

WARNING

Be *very* careful when using paste food coloring. A very tiny amount will vividly color your frosting. Dip the tip of a toothpick into the paste and then dip that into the frosting. That tiny amount is usually just the right amount of color you'll need for a large bag of frosting. Remember that, as the frosting hardens, the colors will darken.

Choosing a tip

The type of tip you choose determines the decoration you make (see Figure 10-3). Hundreds of tips are available for cake decorating.

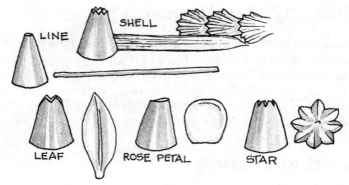

FIGURE 10-3:
Decorating tips and the designs they make.

The most important thing is to make sure that your tip fits your bag — they come in a variety of sizes for a variety of bags. Then choose the correct tip for the decoration you want to create. The following list presents five of the most popular styles of tips available:

>> **Drop flower tips:** These tips make the easiest flowers for the beginning cake decorator. The icing is dropped directly onto the cake, either just dropped on or swirled to make it look like a flower. Popular sizes include 107, 129, 190, 217, and 255.

>> **Leaf tips:** The V-shaped opening in these tips forms the pointed end of the leaf. Leaf tips can make plain, ruffled, or even stand-up leaves. String the leaves together to make an attractive border. Popular sizes include 65, 67, and 352.

>> **Petal tips:** These tips are for a more-advanced decorator and are used in making roses, violets, carnations, and other flower shapes. You can also use them to make ribbons, bows, swags, and ruffles. Popular sizes include 101, 102, 103, and 104.

>> **Star tips:** If you're going to get just one decorative tip, I recommend buying a star tip. This tip enables you to make rosettes, drop flowers, stars, scalloped borders, rope borders, and shells. Popular sizes range between 13 and 22; the larger sizes include 32 and 43.

>> **Writing tips:** Writing tips are plain, round tips. In addition to writing, you can also make polka dots, stems, vines, or just smooth lines for decoration. They're quite handy to have for decoration. Popular sizes include 1–4 (small), 5–12 (medium), and 1A and 2A (large).

Filling your bag

To fill your pastry bag, follow these steps:

1. **Place the empty bag (already with the tip in place) in a tall, narrow glass, as shown in Figure 10-4.**

    Fold back about 5 inches of a cuff over the sides of the glass.

2. **Using a spatula, fill the bag no more than halfway full with icing.**

    If you fill the bag more than halfway full, the frosting may back up out of the bag.

3. **To close the bag, unfold the cuff and gently press all the frosting down toward the tip.**

    Don't press so hard that frosting starts to come out the end, though. You just want to get the air pockets out of the bag.

4. **When the frosting is pressed down, twist the top of the bag (see Figure 10-4).**

    Continue twisting the end of the bag, being careful not to squeeze it as if it were a tube of toothpaste.

FILLING...

.... AND USING A PASTRY BAG

FIGURE 10-4:
Filling and using a pastry bag.

© John Wiley & Sons, Inc.

Using your pastry bag

The amount of pressure on the pastry bag, the size of the tip, and the consistency of the icing will determine the amount of icing flowing out of the bag. By increasing the pressure and moving the bag slowly, you can increase the size of the line being piped out. If you don't have a pastry bag, you can make one. See Figure 10-5 to find out how.

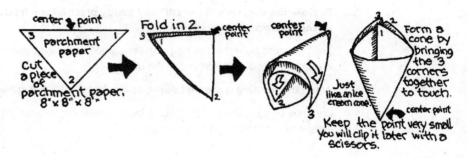

FIGURE 10-5:
Making a paper cone for decorating.

© John Wiley & Sons, Inc.

Practice your decorations on waxed paper before decorating the cake. Doing so will help you determine the type of decoration you'll be making. If your tip gets clogged while you're frosting, give the bag a little extra squeeze over a piece of waxed paper. Avoid doing this over the cake — otherwise you may end up with a big splotch of icing where you don't want it to be. If this doesn't unclog the bag, take a toothpick and poke it into the tip to release the blockage.

TIP

A turntable or lazy Susan is a cake decorator's best friend. It makes frosting and decorating cakes easier and faster.

Most designs are made by holding the pastry bag at a 45-degree angle to the surface of the cake. Support the bottom of the bag with one hand and twist the top with the other. Always begin with just a slight twisting pressure on the bag. Don't jerk the bag around too much. Instead, let the frosting just glide out and fall onto the cake.

TIP

Before making your design, lightly outline it with a toothpick. If you want to write a message on your cake, you can gently place small strips of sewing thread or dental floss on top of the cake to serve as a straight line on which to write (and then remove them when you're done).

If you make a mistake while decorating, don't panic. Everyone has messed up decorating a cake. The easiest thing to do is to get a metal frosting spatula with a rounded tip and gently lift off the mistake and scrape away any additional coloring. With the tip of the spatula, gently smooth out the area and start over again.

REMEMBER

After decorating the cake, clean the tips well in hot, soapy water. Pick out the icing in the hard-to-clean cracks with a toothpick. Always wash your pastry bag and tips by hand. A dishwasher will send your tips flying, and they may become crushed, ruining the delicate tips forever.

If you aren't feeling adventurous enough to try using a decorative bag, see the section on garnishes in Chapter 18 to find ways to add some pizzazz to your cakes without adding stress to your life.

Chapter **11**

Preparing Perfect Pies and Tarts

RECIPES IN THIS CHAPTER

Old-Fashioned Pie Dough

Stir-and-Roll Pie Pastry

Pumpkin Pie

You'll-Be-Glad-You-Tried-It Apple Pie

Cinnamon Apple Dumplings

Blueberry Pie

Cherry Crumb Pie

Rhubarb Pie

Pecan Pie

Chocolate Cream Pie

Banana Cream Pie

Coconut Cream Pie

Sour Cherry-Berry Pie

Cran-Apple and Pear Pie

Tart Lemon Tart

Ginger-Spiced Key Lime Yogurt Pie

Wonderful Pear Tart

Plum Galette

Everyone loves pies, and nothing is more American than a warm pie cooling on the windowsill. Whether that pie is filled with sweet summertime berries, hearty slices of tart apples, or thick pureed pumpkin kissed with brown sugar and cinnamon, pies are satisfying fare. Despite their love of pies, most people shudder at the thought of making the crusts that hold those delectable fillings. Often, they turn to frozen or refrigerated piecrusts to make their baking fuss-free, despite the fact those types of crusts can sometimes be flavorless and thin. But fret no more. In just a few easy steps, you'll have the confidence to make your own dough for incredibly flaky crust.

Pie doughs have simple ingredients: flour, fat (either butter or shortening), and a liquid (either water or milk) to bring everything together. The technique is what you have to master if you want tender, flaky crusts. The best method to achieve perfect pie dough is practice, practice, practice. Before long, you'll wonder why you ever hesitated to make your own.

Picking the Proper Pie Plate

When choosing your pie plate, be sure to use heat-resistant glass or dull-finished metal pie plates for good browning. Never use a shiny pan because the pan reflects heat, and the pie will have a soggy bottom crust.

WARNING

Be careful if you choose to use a nonstick pie plate. The Teflon coating doesn't hold the dough in place while it cooks (and the dough contracts), so if your crust isn't secured over the edge of the pie plate, your dough may shrink up quite a bit in the oven.

The most common pie size is 9 inches. Even though pie plates say that they are 9 inches, they can vary dramatically in the amount of filling they can hold. Make sure that your pie plate can hold the amount of filling that's called for. Keep in mind that fruit fillings shrink as they bake, so be generous.

REMEMBER

Because crusts have plenty of butter or shortening in them, don't grease the pie plate.

Making Perfect Piecrusts

Making a piecrust doesn't involve many steps. You begin with flour, maybe add a pinch of salt, cut in the butter or shortening, and then add a few drops of water and chill (not you, the dough). By cutting in the butter or shortening, you create little bits of fat mixed in with the flour and held together with water. When you roll out the dough, you'll flatten the butter even more. But when you bake the crust, the butter will melt into the flour, flavoring the flour and leaving behind little pockets where it had once been. And that is how a flaky piecrust is made.

Mixing the dough

Knowing that the butter or shortening melting into the dough and leaving little air pockets gives you a flaky crust, you can understand why overmixing the dough is so bad for a piecrust. It will incorporate the butter into the flour too much, and you won't have little pockets of butter left before the oven has a chance to melt it. Kneading the flour too much also forms gluten, which toughens the dough. If you haven't heard it before, you will hear it now: The secret to flaky piecrusts is less, not more, handling.

Cutting in the fat

Another challenge when making piecrusts is the butter. If you use your fingers to incorporate the butter into the flour, you run the risk of melting it (butter melts at 95 degrees, and your body temp is 98.6 degrees). A pastry blender (see Chapter 3) is a great help in cutting shortening evenly into the flour. If you don't have one, you can also use two butter knives, cutting parallel with one another, to cut in the butter. Another option is a fork. (See Chapter 5 for tips on cutting fat into flour mixtures.) If your hands are all you have, dip them in ice water and pat dry before working with the dough.

No matter which method you use, make sure that your butter is well chilled. You can even cut it into small pieces and toss it in the freezer for a few minutes before you add it to the flour if you like.

Many bakers swear by shortening or lard for a flaky crust. It doesn't melt at the low temperature that butter does, and it's easier to cut into the flour, resulting in less handling of the dough. But I find that shortening falls short when it comes to flavor. If the filling has good flavor, however, it can compensate for lack of flavor in the crust. You can do a mix of half butter and half shortening for the qualities of shortening and the flavor of butter.

TIP

The technique I like best for cutting in the fat is the food processor. I chill the metal blade and bowl and precut my butter into 10 to 12 pieces before adding it to the flour. After just a few quick pulses (on-and-off blasts — never let it run on the On position), my butter is incorporated into the flour, and I haven't touched a thing. I like to add the water by hand, though. I find the food processor overworks the dough when I use it.

Choosing the right flour

Very little gluten is necessary to hold a piecrust together. The flours with the least gluten are cake flours and Southern flours, such as White Lily brand. You also can find pastry flour, which is low in protein and great for tender crusts. In the bulk section of my whole-foods grocery store, I can purchase whole-wheat pastry flour, so I blend that with cake flour for some of my crusts.

There are advantages to using all-purpose flour — the piecrust will shrink less. Also, Shirley O. Corriher, the doyen of kitchen science, recommends 2 parts all-purpose flour to 1 part cake or instant flour (Wondra or Shake and Blend) for tender crusts. Without a doubt, she knows what she's talking about, so you may want to try that combination if you have the right flours on hand.

Chilling the dough

Chilling the dough is another important step in preparing pie pastry. After the butter or shortening is cut in, the dough needs to return to the refrigerator, well wrapped, for about an hour so the butter can re-harden and the dough can relax, making it easier to handle. If you have made dough for a double-crust pie, split it in half and flatten the halves into disks. Wrap tightly in plastic wrap and then refrigerate. Skimping on this step could have undesirable effects on your finished pastry, so plan accordingly. Pie dough will keep in the refrigerator for up to one week or in the freezer for up to one month. Let the dough come to room temperature before rolling it out.

REMEMBER Before baking the pies, be sure that you've preheated your oven. The initial contrast in temperature aids in the flakiness of your dough.

Rolling out the dough

After you've chilled your dough, let it sit at room temperature for 5 to 10 minutes before you roll it out to take the chill off. It will roll better if it isn't too cold, but don't let it get too warm, either. Pastry cloths, kitchen towels (not terrycloth), and a *rolling stocking* (a mesh or cloth casing that you slip over the rolling pin and gently rub with flour) are wonderful tools to have on hand because they practically eliminate sticking, and you need only a minimum of additional flour. Rubbing flour into your rolling pin and onto your work surface also works fine — just don't use too much. Two tablespoons of additional flour is all you should need. The work surface I like best is a large wooden board, at least 12 x 12 inches. It's flat and hard and gives me plenty of room to spread out.

TIP Instead of using just flour for dusting the work surface when rolling out pastry for sweet pies, use a combination of sugar and flour. The sugar acts like little grains of sand and isn't as easily absorbed into the dough as the flour is. It's a marvelous trick to keep pastry dough from sticking to the work surface, and it won't toughen the dough.

To roll out your piecrust, follow these simple steps:

1. **Begin rolling from the center of the dough outward, lifting and turning the pastry occasionally to make sure the dough isn't sticking.**

   Don't roll the dough from the outside to the center or push the rolling pin back and forth, and don't press down hard when rolling out the dough. Just let the weight of the rolling pin supply all the necessary pressure.

2. Roll the dough out to ⅛-inch thick or less.

It should be at least 2 inches larger than the pie dimensions (if you have a 9-inch pie plate, the dough should be 11 inches in diameter).

If the dough rips while you're rolling it, don't worry. You can repair it by pressing the two torn sides together. Don't ball it back up and re-roll it. Instead, moisten the edges of the torn pastry and gently press them back together again. If you re-roll the dough, you'll overwork and toughen it.

If the dough begins to stick, rub more flour into the work surface or rolling pin.

TIP

Transferring the crust to the pie plate

After you roll out the crust to the right size, the next step is to delicately transfer it into the pie plate. Doing so is not difficult, but you want to make sure that the pastry doesn't tear. Here are foolproof steps to prevent that from happening:

1. Gently loosen the pastry from the work surface and fold the pastry in half.

2. Place the pie plate right next to the pastry, gently slide the folded pastry into the pie plate, and carefully unfold it.

See Figure 11-1. Ease the dough gently into the pie plate and press it against the side of the pie plate so that no air is left between the dough and the plate, which can cause the crust to blister while baking.

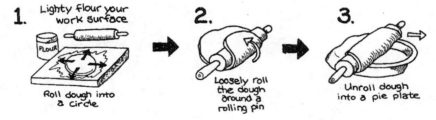

FIGURE 11-1:
Sliding the pastry into the pie plate.

© John Wiley & Sons, Inc.

3. Trim off the excess crust with a knife or kitchen shears and crimp the edges with your fingers, as shown in Figure 11-2.

See the section, "Making Simple Pastry Edges and Decorations," later in this chapter for more ideas for crimping your crusts.

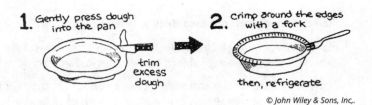

FIGURE 11-2:
Crimping around
the edges.

TIP

For juicy fruit pies, brush the bottom unbaked crust with a beaten egg white or melted butter before filling it to prevent the crust from becoming soggy.

WARNING

Don't prick the bottom crust with a fork if you're filling it with a fruit or custard filling. The liquid filling will make the crust soggy if there are holes in the crust.

☕ Old-Fashioned Pie Dough

PREP TIME: 15 MIN	CHILLING TIME: 2 HRS	YIELD: ONE 8- OR 9-INCH DOUBLE CRUST

INGREDIENTS

300 grams (2½ cups) flour

1½ teaspoons sugar

1 teaspoon salt (optional)

114 grams (½ cup/1 stick) cold unsalted butter, cut into ½-inch pieces

103 grams (½ cup) shortening, chilled and cut into ½-inch pieces

1 egg, beaten

2 tablespoons ice water or sour cream, if desired

DIRECTIONS

1 In a large bowl, using a pastry blender, combine the flour, sugar, and salt (if desired). Using your fingertips or pastry blender, cut the butter and shortening into the flour mixture until it resembles coarse meal. (You'll see a few larger or smaller pieces.)

2 Combine the beaten egg and cold water in a small bowl. While stirring lightly with a fork, pour the egg and water into the flour mixture in a fast, steady stream. Continue stirring, occasionally cleaning off the dough that collects on the fork, until the flour is almost completely mixed in but the dough does not form a ball.

3 Empty the dough onto a flat work surface. Pat and shape the dough into a 6-inch disk. Many tiny flecks of butter should be visible.

4 Wrap the dough tightly in plastic wrap or waxed paper and refrigerate it for at least 2 hours or overnight. When you're ready to use it, divide the disk in half and roll each half into an evenly rounded 13-inch circle.

PER SERVING: *Calories 370 (From Fat 228); Fat 25g (Saturated 11g); Cholesterol 58mg; Sodium 10mg; Carbohydrate 31g (Dietary Fiber 1g); Protein 5g.*

🍅 Stir-and-Roll Pie Pastry

PREP TIME: 20 MIN	YIELD: ONE 8- OR 9-INCH DOUBLE CRUST

INGREDIENTS

180 grams (1½ cups) flour

½ teaspoon salt

103 grams (½ cup) vegetable oil

3 tablespoons cold milk or water

DIRECTIONS

1 Mix together the flour and salt in a medium-sized bowl.

2 Pour the oil and milk into a mixing bowl and whisk until frothy. Pour all the liquid at once into the flour. Stir lightly with a fork until mixed and a dough is formed. Gently press the dough together to make a ball.

3 When you're ready to use it, roll out the dough between 2 sheets of waxed paper. Press the dough into an 8- or 9-inch pie pan. Flute the edges and prick thoroughly with a fork.

NOTE: The texture will be slightly denser and less flaky than a traditional piecrust because you're using oil instead of butter or shortening. One advantage to this crust is that you don't have to let the dough chill before rolling it out and using it.

VARY IT! For a prebaked crust: Preheat the oven to 425 degrees. Bake the crust for 8 to 10 minutes.

PER SERVING: *Calories 168 (From Fat 85); Fat 9g (Saturated 1g); Cholesterol 1mg; Sodium 148mg; Carbohydrate 18g (Dietary Fiber 1g); Protein 3g.*

PREBAKING PIECRUSTS

If the pie shell is to be baked without filling, prick the dough all over with a fork. To prevent the pie shell from puffing up and blistering while it bakes, place a sheet of aluminum foil or waxed paper on top of the unbaked piecrust and weigh it down with rice, dried beans, or pie weights (see Chapter 3). Then bake according to the recipe. Remove the weights from the pie shell a few minutes before the baking time is finished so that the bottom will brown a bit.

Getting Double-Crust Pie Ideas

If you're preparing a pie with a top crust, roll out the top crust as directed earlier in this chapter. You can choose from a variety of top crusts.

Solid top crust

Fold the crust in half and make several cuts along the fold, about 1 inch apart. Doing so allows steam to escape while the pie bakes. Gently transfer the folded crust to the pie plate, unfold the crust on top of the filled pie, and trim the top crust to have a 1-inch overhang. Gently press the top crust over the filling, tuck the extra top crust under the bottom crust, and seal the edges.

Lattice crust

Cut 10 to 14 ½-inch strips from the top crust pastry. Place five to seven strips on the filling, about ¾ inch apart. Fold back every other strip halfway and place a strip perpendicular over the unfolded strips. Unfold the strip. Fold back the alternate strips and place another strip ¾ inch from the first. Repeat until you've used up all the strips. (See Figure 11-3 for illustrated instructions.)

A LATTICE CRUST PIE

1. CUT 10 TO 14 ½" STRIPS FROM THE TOP CRUST PASTRY. FOLD BACK EVERY OTHER STRIP HALFWAY AND PLACE A PERPENDICULAR STRIP OVER THE UNFOLDED STRIPS.

2. UNFOLD THE STRIP FOLD BACK THE ALTERNATE STRIPS AND PLACE ANOTHER STRIP ¾" APART FROM THE FIRST.

3.

4.

REPEAT UNTIL ALL OF THE STRIPS ARE USED UP!

FIGURE 11-3:
Making a lattice crust.

When the whole pie is latticed, attach the strips loosely to the pie edge by moistening the ends and pressing down slightly into the bottom crust edge. Be careful not to pull the strips taut; allow for some shrinkage during baking. Cut off any excess from the strips and seal the edges.

For an easy lattice top, place five to seven strips over the filling, about ¾ inch apart. Turn the pie plate a quarter turn and place the remaining strips at right angles to the first set of strips, about ¾ inch apart. Don't weave the strips.

Cutout top crust

Use a small cookie cutter (no bigger than 1 inch across) to make a cutout pattern in the top crust. Work from the center of the pastry to within 1 inch of the pastry edge (make sure that the pastry is not sticking to the work surface). Gently roll the cutout pastry onto a floured rolling pin and carefully transfer the cutout top over the pie filling. By gently rolling the cutout pastry onto the rolling pin, there's less chance of it ripping while you're transferring the pastry.

Alternatively, you can cover your pie filling with the cutout shapes. A larger cookie cutter works well for this technique. Place the cutout shapes close together over the filling and flute the edges of the bottom pastry. Figure 11-4 shows you how.

A CUTOUT CRUST

USE A SMALL COOKIE CUTTER TO MAKE A PATTERN FROM THE CENTER TO WITHIN 1" FROM THE PASTRY EDGE. GENTLY ROLL THE CUTOUT PASTRY OVER A FLOURED ROLLING PIN AND TRANSFER OVER THE FILLING.

OR: YOU CAN USE A LARGER COOKIE CUTTER TO CUT THE TOP PASTRY. PLACE THE LARGE CUTOUTS ON TOP OF THE FILLING. FLUTE EDGES OF THE BOTTOM PASTRY.

FIGURE 11-4:
Making a cutout top crust.

© John Wiley & Sons, Inc.

Making Simple Pastry Edges and Decorations

To *flute* (or seal) the edges of the crust means to squeeze the edges of the pastry to make a finished, decorative edge. You want a good seal between the two crusts so that all the pie filling remains inside the pie and doesn't leak out. You can get a good seal in several ways:

» **Pinch edge:** This is the classic pie edge decoration. Place your index finger on the outside of the pastry and pinch the thumb and index finger of your other hand to form a *V* shape on the inside of the pastry. Push the pastry into the *V* shape with your index finger, along the entire edge. After you're finished, go around and pinch again to sharpen the edges. When the crusts bakes, the *V* shapes will relax, so you want them as sharp as possible.

» **Fork edge:** This edge is the best for beginner bakers. Just flatten the pastry evenly along the rim of the plate with the tines of a fork. To prevent the fork from sticking to the pastry, dip it lightly in flour.

» **Cutout edge:** Trim the overhang to the rim of the pie plate. With a tiny cookie cutter, thimble, or bottle cap, cut out decorations from the scraps of pastry. Moisten the edge of the pastry and the bottoms of the cutouts with water and press them into place.

» **Twisted edge:** Trim the overhang to the rim of the pie plate. Twist two ¼-inch strips around each other, making the twist long enough to fit around the edge of the plate. Moisten the rim of the pie plate and the bottom of the twist and gently lay it on top. Press it lightly into place. Alternatively, you can loosely braid three ¼-inch strips and lay the braid around the edge.

Creating Tantalizing Pies and Tarts

Baking fresh, flavorful pies and tarts is easier than you imagined. Would you like a slice of classic apple and blueberry pie or luscious banana cream pie? The tempting possibilities go on and on. Remember, practice makes perfect. These recipes will keep you practicing quite a bit.

Fruit and nut pies

Of all the pies out there, fruit pies have to be people's favorites. People love it when fresh pie — juicy, ripe fruits wrapped in a flaky crust — is on the menu. Cherries and berries of any type make a good pie (except strawberries, which don't hold up very well when they're baked). Feel free to mix and match fruits in these recipes. Beyond fruits, pecans also make a great filling for pies, so try your hand at that tasty recipe, too.

☙ Pumpkin Pie

INGREDIENTS

160 grams (¾ cup) light brown sugar, firmly packed

½ teaspoon salt

1 teaspoon cinnamon

½ teaspoon ginger

¼ teaspoon cloves

1 teaspoon vanilla extract

2 eggs

425 grams (one can [15 ounces]) pumpkin (not pie filling)

340 grams (one can [12 ounces]) evaporated milk

1 unbaked 9-inch piecrust

DIRECTIONS

1 Preheat the oven to 375 degrees.

2 Combine all the ingredients (except the piecrust) in a large mixing bowl and blend until smooth.

3 Pour the mixture into the unbaked piecrust and bake until a toothpick inserted into the center comes out clean, 35 to 45 minutes. Cool the pie before serving or refrigerate until ready to serve.

NOTE: Don't save this delicious pie until Thanksgiving. This pumpkin mixture, laced with cinnamon and ginger, is smooth, creamy, and delicately spiced.

PER SERVING: *Calories 282 (From Fat 109); Fat 12g (Saturated 4g); Cholesterol 65mg; Sodium 313mg; Carbohydrate 39g (Dietary Fiber 2g); Protein 6g.*

You'll-Be-Glad-You-Tried-It Apple Pie

PREP TIME: 30 MIN	BAKING TIME: 40 TO 50 MIN	YIELD: 8 SERVINGS

INGREDIENTS

Pastry for a 2-crust pie (either recipe in this chapter)

1,400 grams (8 cups) peeled, sliced apples (about 3½ pounds)

Juice of 1 lemon (about 1 tablespoon)

53 grams (¼ cup) light brown sugar, firmly packed

67 grams (⅓ cup) sugar

3 tablespoons flour

1 teaspoon cinnamon

½ teaspoon nutmeg

1 teaspoon vanilla extract

2 tablespoons cold butter, cut into little pieces

DIRECTIONS

1 Preheat the oven to 425 degrees. Prepare the pastry for a 9-inch pie plate and line the plate with half the dough, leaving a ½-inch overhang.

2 In a large bowl, toss the apples with the lemon juice. Add the sugars, flour, cinnamon, nutmeg, and vanilla and toss to coat all the apples. Place the apples in the pie plate and scatter the butter pieces over the top of the apples.

3 Roll out the top pastry and carefully lay it over the apples. Pat the pastry over the apples. Fold the edges of the bottom pastry over the top pastry and crimp the edges of the pastry. Cut six to eight slits in the top crust for vents.

4 Place a piece of aluminum foil on a baking sheet (to catch any drips). Place the pie on top of the foil and bake for 40 to 50 minutes, until the crust is golden brown and juice bubbles through the slits in the top crust. Cool the pie on a wire rack before serving.

TIP: Check your local farmers' market to get a good variety of apples, which will perk up the flavor of any pie. Keep your eyes peeled for varieties like Cortland, Macoun, Ida Red, Stayman, Mutzu, and Gravenstein. Golden Delicious and Granny Smiths are fine, too. Don't use Red Delicious apples, though — they're good for eating but turn to mush if you bake with them.

PER SERVING: *Calories 352 (From Fat 172); Fat 19g (Saturated 8g); Cholesterol 44mg; Sodium 9mg; Carbohydrate 43g (Dietary Fiber 2g); Protein 4g.*

Cinnamon Apple Dumplings

PREP TIME: 20 MIN	BAKING TIME: 50 TO 60 MIN	YIELD: 8 SERVINGS

INGREDIENTS

6 tablespoons sugar

3 teaspoons cinnamon

Pie dough for a double-crust pie

8 medium baking apples (like Granny Smith or Pink Lady), peeled and cored

4 tablespoons butter, cut into cubes

Cinnamon Sauce

400 grams (2 cups) sugar

472 grams (2 cups) water

1 teaspoon cinnamon

¼ teaspoon nutmeg

57 grams (¼ cup) unsalted butter

¼ teaspoon salt

DIRECTIONS

1 Preheat the oven to 375 degrees. Grease a 9-x-13-inch cake pan. In a small bowl, mix the sugar and cinnamon.

2 Divide the dough in half. On a lightly floured surface, roll out half the dough into a square about ⅛- to ¼-inch thick. Using a dough blade, cut the dough into four equal squares. Pat the apples dry with a tea towel and place one apple into each square. Place ½ tablespoon butter into center of apple and ¾ tablespoon of sugar into each. Wrap the pie dough up the sides and over the top of the apples, bundling them. Place into the baking dish. Repeat with remaining dough and apples. Place apple dumplings into oven and set timer for 15 minutes.

3 In a 4-quart saucepan, bring sugar, water, cinnamon, nutmeg, and butter to the start of a boil over medium high heat. Immediately remove from heat once the sauce begins to bubble. Open the oven and pour the sauce over the apples, return to the oven and continue baking for 40 to 55 minutes or until the piecrust is golden brown in color. Serve hot or let stand at room temperature until ready to serve.

TIP: Keep the apples in lemon juice and water until ready to fill. Pat dry before placing on pie dough.

NOTE: If the sauce gets to a rapid boil, it could bake up and cool like a candy, hardening to the pan. Be sure to watch the sauce closely as you cook it.

PER SERVING: *Calories 639 (From Fat 240); Fat 27g (Saturated 11g); Cholesterol 31mg; Sodium 295mg; Carbohydrate 101g (Dietary Fiber 4g); Protein 3g.*

⚘ Blueberry Pie

PREP TIME: 30 MIN	BAKING TIME: 30 TO 40 MIN	YIELD: 8 SERVINGS

INGREDIENTS

Pastry for a 2-crust pie (either recipe in this chapter)

100 grams (½ cup) sugar

30 grams (¼ cup) flour

½ teaspoon cinnamon

¼ teaspoon nutmeg

1,140 grams (6 cups) fresh or frozen blueberries (don't thaw frozen berries)

1 tablespoon lemon juice

1 tablespoon cold butter, cut into 4 pieces

DIRECTIONS

1 Preheat the oven to 425 degrees. Prepare the pastry for a 9-inch pie plate and line the pie plate with half the dough, leaving a ½-inch overhang.

2 In a large bowl, toss together the sugar, flour, cinnamon, and nutmeg. Add the blueberries and lemon juice and mix to coat. Place the blueberry mixture in the pie plate and scatter the butter pieces over the berries.

3 Roll out the top pastry and carefully lay it over the blueberries. Pat the pastry over the blueberries. Fold the edges of the bottom pastry over the top pastry and crimp the edges of the pastry. Cut 6 to 8 slits in the top crust for vents.

4 Place a piece of aluminum foil on a baking sheet. Place the pie on the foil and bake for 30 to 40 minutes, until the crust is golden brown and juice bubbles through the slits in the top crust. Transfer the pie from the baking sheet to a wire rack to cool.

TIP: Get some fresh blueberries when they're in season and put them in your freezer so that you can make fresh blueberry pie in the fall.

PER SERVING: *Calories 338 (From Fat 164); Fat 18g (Saturated 8g); Cholesterol 41mg; Sodium 12mg; Carbohydrate 41g (Dietary Fiber 3g); Protein 4g.*

🍒 Cherry Crumb Pie

| PREP TIME: 25 MIN | BAKING TIME: 40 TO 50 MIN | YIELD: 8 SERVINGS |

INGREDIENTS

Pastry for a 9-inch pie (either recipe in this chapter)

50 grams (¼ cup) sugar

57 grams (¼ cup) instant or Minute tapioca

1,008 grams (6 cups) pitted fresh or canned, drained sour cherries

½ teaspoon almond extract

2 tablespoons cold butter, cut into small pieces

Topping

120 grams (1 cup) flour

150 grams (¾ cup) sugar

114 grams (½ cup/1 stick) cold unsalted butter, cut into small pieces

60 grams (½ cup) ground almonds

DIRECTIONS

1 Preheat the oven to 400 degrees. Prepare the pastry for a 9-inch pie plate and line the pie plate with half the dough, leaving a 1-inch overhang. Crimp the edges of the piecrust.

2 Toss the sugar, tapioca, cherries, and almond extract to combine. Place the cherry mixture in the pie plate. Scatter the butter pieces over the cherries.

3 Combine all the topping ingredients and blend so that the mixture resembles coarse crumbs (you can do this in a food processor if you want to). Scatter the topping over the cherries.

4 Place a piece of aluminum foil on a baking sheet. Place the pie on the foil and bake for 40 to 50 minutes, until the crust is golden brown and juice bubbles through the top. Cool on a wire rack before serving.

VARY IT! If you don't want the crumb topping, you can make a double crust instead.

TIP: Make it in the height of summer when sour cherries are bountiful.

PER SERVING: *Calories 497 (From Fat 231); Fat 26g (Saturated 11g); Cholesterol 38mg; Sodium 153mg; Carbohydrate 64g (Dietary Fiber 4g); Protein 6g.*

ᗧ Rhubarb Pie

INGREDIENTS

Pastry for a 2-crust pie (or 2 sheets refrigerated pie dough)

500 grams (4 cups) sliced rhubarb stalks

200 grams (1 cup) sugar

30 grams (¼ cup) flour

1 egg, whisked

3 tablespoons unsalted butter, cubed

1 tablespoon cream

1 tablespoon demerara sugar

DIRECTIONS

1 Preheat the oven to 375 degrees with a baking sheet.

2 On a lightly floured surface, roll out two 10-inch piecrusts. Place one into a pie pan, gently pressing to extend up the edges.

3 In a large bowl, stir together the rhubarb, sugar, flour, and whisked egg. Pour into a prepared pie pan. Top with cubed butter and cover with piecrust. Flute the edge of the piecrust and make slits in the crust to release steam as it bakes. Brush the top with cream and sprinkle with sugar. Place pie pan on preheated baking sheet. Bake pie for 40 minutes or until golden and the filling is bubbling. Cool on a wire rack for at least 4 hours prior to slicing.

TIP: Rhubarb is a spring and early summer crop, so look for it in season! Frozen rhubarb will be heavier in weight due to absorbing more water. If you need to use frozen rhubarb, defrost and pat it dry to remove some of the excess moisture. Consider increasing flour to 45 grams.

PER SERVING: *Calories 407 (From Fat 182); Fat 20g (Saturated 7g); Cholesterol 39mg; Sodium 247mg; Carbohydrate 53g (Dietary Fiber 3g); Protein 5g.*

🍅 Pecan Pie

INGREDIENTS

Pastry for a 9-inch pie (either recipe in this chapter)

3 eggs, separated

107 grams (½ cup) light brown sugar, firmly packed

1 teaspoon vanilla extract

312 grams (1 cup) light corn syrup

125 grams (1 cup) pecans

2 tablespoons butter, softened

2 teaspoons cornstarch or flour

DIRECTIONS

1 Preheat the oven to 350 degrees. Prepare the pastry for a 9-inch pie plate and line the pie plate, leaving a 1-inch over-hang. Crimp the edges of the piecrust.

2 In a medium-sized mixing bowl, beat together the egg yolks, brown sugar, and vanilla. Add the corn syrup, pecans, butter, and cornstarch and stir to combine.

3 In a separate bowl with clean, dry beaters, beat the egg whites to stiff peaks. Fold the stiffly beaten egg whites into the egg yolk mixture. Pour the mixture into the unbaked pie shell and place the pie on a baking sheet. Bake for 45 minutes. Cool the pie on a wire rack before serving.

NOTE: Pecan pie is a great Southern tradition. The pecan is one of the few ingredients indigenous to America (blueberries, Concord grapes, and cranberries are a few others). Make this pie to serve at your next barbecue or cookout. Be sure to purchase fresh pecans for this pie.

PER SERVING: *Calories 389 (From Fat 172); Fat 19g (Saturated 3g); Cholesterol 71mg; Sodium 182mg; Carbohydrate 53g (Dietary Fiber 2g); Protein 5g.*

Cream pies

Cream pie filling is airy and delicate, surrounded by a tender crust. You get a mouthful of goodness when you eat a chocolate cream or luscious banana cream pie. Great for summer, these three chilled desserts are perfect endings to hot summer days.

Chocolate Cream Pie

PREP TIME: 25 MIN PLUS 1½ HRS FOR CHILLING	BAKING TIME: 15 MIN	YIELD: 8 SERVINGS

INGREDIENTS

¼ cup cornstarch

200 grams (1 cup) sugar

¼ teaspoon salt

476 grams (2 cups) milk, at room temperature

2 squares (1 ounce each) unsweetened chocolate, chopped into small pieces

3 egg yolks

2 tablespoons butter

½ teaspoon vanilla extract

1 prebaked 9-inch pie shell (either recipe in this chapter)

Whipped cream (optional)

DIRECTIONS

1 In the top part of a double boiler, mix the cornstarch, sugar, and salt. Gradually whisk in the milk. Cook the mixture over simmering water until it thickens, stirring constantly with a whisk, about 10 minutes. Add the chopped chocolate to the thickened mixture and continue stirring until melted through, about 3 minutes.

2 Place the egg yolks in a small bowl and beat them slightly. Slowly add a ladleful (only about ¼ cup) of the hot mixture to the egg yolks. Stir the egg yolk mixture back into the hot mixture in the double boiler. Cook for 5 minutes. Cool. Add the butter and vanilla and stir until the butter is melted and smooth, about 3 minutes.

3 Pour into the cooled baked pie shell and chill until set, about 1½ hours. Top with whipped cream, if desired.

NOTE: The only baking this pie requires is the 15 minutes it takes to pre-bake the crust, making it a great pie to make in the summertime when you don't want to heat up the kitchen. This pie needs to be refrigerated, so it's not a good choice for picnics.

PER SERVING: Calories 270 (From Fat 121); Fat 13g (Saturated 5g); Cholesterol 64mg; Sodium 171mg; Carbohydrate 35g (Dietary Fiber 1g); Protein 4g.

Banana Cream Pie

PREP TIME: 20 MIN PLUS 1½ HRS FOR CHILLING	BAKING TIME: 15 MIN	YIELD: 8 SERVINGS

INGREDIENTS

38 grams (¼ cup) cornstarch

133 grams (⅔ cup) sugar

¼ teaspoon salt

476 grams (2 cups) milk, warmed

3 egg yolks

2 tablespoons butter

½ teaspoon vanilla extract

3 ripe bananas, sliced

1 prebaked 9-inch pie shell (either recipe in this chapter)

Whipped cream (optional)

DIRECTIONS

1 In the top part of a double boiler, mix the cornstarch, sugar, and salt. Gradually whisk in the milk. Cook the mixture over simmering water until it thickens, stirring constantly with a whisk, about 10 minutes.

2 In a small bowl, lightly beat the egg yolks. Slowly add a ladle-ful (only about ¼ cup) of the hot mixture to the egg yolks and mix well. Stir the egg yolks back into the milk mixture in the double boiler. Cook for 5 minutes. Cool slightly, stir in the butter and vanilla until the butter melts, and add the banana slices.

3 Pour into the cooled baked pie shell and chill until set, about 1½ hours. Top with whipped cream.

TIP: If you're looking for a shortcut, you can substitute instant vanilla pudding, add some sliced bananas to it, chill it in a pre- baked piecrust, and top it with whipped cream.

PER SERVING: *Calories 250 (From Fat 99); Fat 11g (Saturated 3g); Cholesterol 64mg; Sodium 170mg; Carbohydrate 35g (Dietary Fiber 1g); Protein 4g.*

⏱ Coconut Cream Pie

INGREDIENTS

Pastry for a 9-inch pie (either recipe in this chapter)

476 grams (2 cups) whole milk

150 grams (¾ cup) sugar

38 grams (¼ cup) cornstarch

⅛ teaspoon salt

4 eggs, divided into yolks and whites

3 tablespoons unsalted butter, cubed

1 teaspoon vanilla extract

53 grams (1 cup) unsweetened coconut flakes

¼ teaspoon cream of tartar

2 tablespoons sugar

DIRECTIONS

1 Preheat the oven to 400 degrees with a baking sheet. Roll out the piecrust to fit into a pie pan. Poke holes in the piecrust, cover with a piece of parchment paper, and add weights or beans to pie. Bake for 12 to 15 minutes or until golden. Remove from the oven to cool and reduce oven temperature to 350 degrees.

2 In a 4-quart saucepan, heat milk, sugar, cornstarch, and salt over medium heat, whisking occasionally to keep the milk from scorching on the bottom of the saucepan. Meanwhile, whisk egg yolks until frothy in heat-safe bowl. When the milk mixture starts to boil, remove from heat and drizzle about ¼ cup of the hot milk into the egg yolks in a drizzle while whisking the yolks continuously, tempering the egg yolks. Add the egg yolks to the milk mixture and return to heat. While whisking continue to cook for 2 minutes until thickened. Remove from heat and stir in the butter cubes, vanilla extract, and coconut flakes.

3 In a separate mixing bowl, beat the egg whites with cream of tartar and sugar until stiff peaks form, about 3 minutes.

4 Remove the pie weights and parchment from the piecrust. Pour in the coconut custard. Top with meringue, making swirls with a spatula. Be sure meringue reaches the edge of the piecrust. Bake for 12 to 15 minutes or until the meringue becomes lightly golden in color. Cool on a wire rack and chill for at least 3 hours before slicing.

TIP: This pie can also be served right out of the oven, but it won't hold its shape when sliced. For my family it's too hard to resist, so it rarely ever makes it to the refrigerator.

NOTE: Flip to the color insert for a photo of this recipe.

PER SERVING: *Calories 370 (From Fat 187); Fat 21g (Saturated 11g); Cholesterol 126mg; Sodium 215mg; Carbohydrate 40g (Dietary Fiber 2g); Protein 7g.*

Double-crust pies

Double crusts let you show off the beautiful fillings of your delicious pies. Although they're a little more work than single-crust pies, they're worth the effort. If you need a primer on double-crust pies, be sure to check out the section, "Getting Double-Crust Pie Ideas," earlier in this chapter for some thoughts on how to decorate your top or crust. Use either recipe for double-crust pie at the beginning of this chapter for these recipes.

🍑 Sour Cherry–Berry Pie

PREP TIME: 55 MIN | BAKING TIME: 50 TO 60 MIN | YIELD: 8 SERVINGS

INGREDIENTS

Pastry for a 2-crust pie (or 2 sheets refrigerated pie dough)

908 grams (about 5 cups) seedless sour or tart cherries, fresh or frozen and thawed

246 grams (2 cups) raspberries, fresh or frozen and thawed

150 grams (¾ cup) sugar

2 tablespoons instant tapioca

2 teaspoons fresh lemon juice (½ lemon)

¼ teaspoon vanilla extract

½ teaspoon almond extract

2 tablespoons (¼ stick) unsalted butter, cut into 8 dots

2 to 4 tablespoons water or milk

Coarse or raw sugar (optional)

DIRECTIONS

1 Preheat the oven to 425 degrees. Prepare the pastry for a 9-inch pie plate. Line the pie plate with half the dough, leaving a ½-inch overhang.

2 In a mixing bowl, combine the cherries, raspberries, sugar, tapioca, lemon juice, vanilla, and almond extract. Place in the pie shell. Dot the top of the pie with the butter.

3 Roll out the top pastry and carefully lay it over the cherry filling. (If you have tiny cookie cutters, you can cut out 3 to 4 small shapes to vent the pie before you transfer the crust to the filling; then you won't need to cut the slits in Step 4.) Fold the edges of the bottom pastry over the top pastry and crimp the edges of the pastry.

4 Cut 6 to 8 slits in the top crust for vents if you didn't use the cookie cutters. Brush the top crust with the water and sprinkle with the coarse sugar, if desired.

5 Place a piece of aluminum foil on a baking sheet. Place the pie on the foil and bake for 50 to 60 minutes, until the crust is golden brown and the juice from the fruit is bubbling through the slits in the piecrust. Cool the pie on a wire rack before serving.

TIP: You can reduce the prep time to 20 minutes if you use refrigerated dough.

NOTE: Coarse or raw sugar are larger sugar crystals than standard granulated sugar. You can use granulated sugar, as well.

PER SERVING: Calories 362 (From Fat 172); Fat 19g (Saturated 8g); Cholesterol 44mg; Sodium 9mg; Carbohydrate 45g (Dietary Fiber 3g); Protein 4g.

🍎 Cran-Apple and Pear Pie

PREP TIME: 20 MIN	BAKING TIME: 60 MIN	YIELD: 8 SERVINGS

INGREDIENTS

Pastry for a 2-crust pie (or 2 sheets refrigerated pie dough)

3 apples, peeled, cored, and thinly sliced

2 small ripe Bosc or Bartlett pears, peeled, cored, and thinly sliced

100 grams (1 cup) fresh or frozen cranberries

150 grams (¾ cup) sugar

2 tablespoons flour or instant tapioca

65 grams (¼ cup) orange juice

½ teaspoon cinnamon

½ teaspoon nutmeg or cardamom

¼ teaspoon salt

2 tablespoons milk or water

DIRECTIONS

1 Preheat the oven to 425 degrees. Roll out or unwrap one of the piecrusts. Fix the seam (press the ends together) if separation has occurred. Place the dough in a 9-inch pie plate.

2 In a large bowl, combine the apples, pears, cranberries, sugar, flour, orange juice, cinnamon, cardamom, and salt and mix thoroughly. Pile the fruit mixture in the pie plate.

3 Roll out or unwrap the second pie pastry and fix the seam, if necessary. With a small cookie cutter or a knife, cut out 3 small shapes to vent the pie. Cover the fruit mixture with the pastry dough. Press the edges of the doughs together and flute the crust. Brush the top of the pie with milk or water.

4 Bake for 30 minutes; then reduce the heat to 350 degrees and bake until the crust is browned and the fruit is tender, about 30 minutes more.

TIP: If you shop at your local farmers' market, choose a variety of local apples to make this delicious pie. The only apple I don't recommend is Red Delicious.

NOTE: Because some peeling and chopping are involved, I call for refrigerated pie dough to make this recipe simple. If you're feeling adventurous, go ahead and make enough dough for a two-crust pie and roll the crust out to fit a 9-inch pie plate.

NOTE: Cardamom adds a wonderful spicy-sweetness reminiscent of oranges if used in this pie, but nutmeg works just as well.

PER SERVING: *Calories 253 (From Fat 86); Fat 10g (Saturated 4g); Cholesterol 7mg; Sodium 181mg; Carbohydrate 41g (Dietary Fiber 2g); Protein 0g.*

Making To-Die-For Tarts

Dessert is what guests remember most about the meal you serve them. Tarts are always festive and impressive, and they're perfect for gatherings large and small. This section includes tart recipes that use simple ingredients but convey utterly delectable results. I think you'll enjoy them.

What's the difference between tarts and pies? A thick, fluted crust can be a sure giveaway that you're about to dig into a tart. Tarts are often made in a specific pan that has a removable bottom, allowing you to serve the tart without the pan. On the other hand, pies are served in the pie pan with a thinner crust. Both pies and tarts can be sweet or savory.

🍅 Tart Lemon Tart

PREP TIME: 15 TO 20 MIN | BAKING TIME: 20 MIN | YIELD: 8 SERVINGS

INGREDIENTS

150 grams (1¼ cups) graham cracker or butter cookie crumbs

2 tablespoons butter, melted

113 grams (½ cup/1 stick) unsalted butter

168 grams (¾ cup) freshly squeezed lemon juice (about 4 lemons)

200 grams (1 cup) sugar

4 eggs

1 teaspoon vanilla extract

Zest of 1 lemon

DIRECTIONS

1 Preheat the oven to 350 degrees.

2 Combine the graham cracker crumbs and the 2 tablespoons melted butter in a small bowl and mix to moisten the crumbs. Transfer the crumbs to the bottom of an 8-inch springform pan. Press evenly to cover.

3 In a 1-quart saucepan, combine the ½ cup butter, lemon juice, and sugar. Cook over medium-low heat, stirring constantly, until the butter melts and mixes in with the sugar, 3 to 4 minutes. Stir in the eggs (one at a time), vanilla, and lemon zest. Continue stirring until the mixture just begins to thicken, 2 to 3 minutes. (Don't let it thicken too much — it should coat the back of a spoon.)

4 Remove the mixture from the heat and gently pour it into the prepared pan. Place the springform pan on a baking sheet. Bake for 15 to 20 minutes or until just set (it will not be golden brown). Cool the tart and then refrigerate it for a few hours until you're ready to serve it.

TIP: Zest the lemon before you squeeze it for the juice.

PER SERVING: *Calories 343 (From Fat 169); Fat 19g (Saturated 10g); Cholesterol 144mg; Sodium 175mg; Carbohydrate 41g (Dietary Fiber 1g); Protein 5g.*

Ginger–Spiced Key Lime Yogurt Pie

| PREP TIME: 10 MIN | BAKING TIME: 20 MIN | YIELD: 8 SERVINGS |

INGREDIENTS

128 grams (1½ cups) ground gingersnap cookies

57 grams (¼ cup) unsalted butter, melted

794 grams (Two [14-ounce] cans) sweetened condensed milk

170 grams (¾ cup) key lime juice

3 egg yolks

1 teaspoon lime zest

113 grams (½ cup) plain Greek yogurt

DIRECTIONS

1 Preheat the oven to 350 degrees. In a medium bowl, mix the gingersnap cookie crumbs with melted butter. Pour into a pie pan and use your hands to gently spread and form into the pie pan.

2 In a separate mixing bowl, whisk sweetened condensed milk, key lime juice, egg yolks, lime zest, and Greek yogurt. Pour into a pie pan.

3 Bake for 18 to 20 minutes or until the pie is still slightly jiggly in the center when you gently shake the pan. Let the pie cool for at least 30 minutes on a cooling rack and then refrigerate for 4 hours before slicing.

TIP: Personalize it! I love to bake these in heat-safe Mason jars, which makes them perfect to take on the go or bring to a picnic. I use 4-ounce Mason jars or custard cups.

NOTE: This is a spin-off of the classic key lime pie. Gingersnap cookies add a unique flavor profile that blends well with the tropical flavors of key limes. The yogurt creates a creamy finish to this tart pie.

NOTE: Refer to the color insert for a photo of this recipe.

PER SERVING: *Calories 471 (From Fat 162); Fat 18g (Saturated 10g); Cholesterol 129mg; Sodium 243mg; Carbohydrate 68g (Dietary Fiber 0g); Protein 11g.*

Wonderful Pear Tart

INGREDIENTS

150 grams (¾ cup) sugar

½ cup (1 stick) unsalted butter, softened

1 cup flour

1 teaspoon baking powder

2 eggs

2 to 3 pears, peeled, cored, and cut into ¼-inch slices

1½ tablespoons lemon juice (about ½ lemon, juiced)

1 teaspoon cinnamon, or to taste

1 tablespoon sugar, or to taste

DIRECTIONS

1 Preheat the oven to 350 degrees.

2 In a medium-sized mixing bowl, cream the ¾ cup sugar and butter until smooth, about 1 minute. Add the flour, baking powder, and eggs and mix well.

3 Spoon the batter (it will be thick) into an 8-inch springform pan and spread it around to cover the bottom evenly. Arrange the pear slices on top of the batter in a decorative fashion.

4 Drizzle the lemon juice on top, sprinkle with the cinnamon and sugar, and bake for 1 hour. Cool the tart and remove the springform pan before serving.

VARY IT! You don't have to have pears on hand — tart baking apples, peeled peaches, and fresh apricots (just cut the apricots in half and pit, but don't peel, them) also work well.

PER SERVING: *Calories 289 (From Fat 117); Fat 13g (Saturated 8g); Cholesterol 83mg; Sodium 81mg; Carbohydrate 42g (Dietary Fiber 2g); Protein 4g.*

🍅 Plum Galette

INGREDIENTS

Pastry for a 9-inch pie (either recipe in this chapter)

22 grams (¼ cup) ground hazelnuts, almonds, or walnuts

¼ teaspoon nutmeg

¼ cup sugar

3 tablespoon flour

908 grams (2 pounds) pitted and sliced plums

57 grams (¼ cup) unsalted butter

84 grams (¼ cup) plum, peach, or apricot preserves

55 grams (¼ cup) demerara sugar or course sugar crystals

DIRECTIONS

1 Preheat the oven to 375 degrees.

2 On a lightly floured surface, roll out pie dough to ¼- to ⅛-inch 12-inch circle. Transfer to a parchment lined baking sheet or jelly roll pan.

3 In a small bowl, stir the ground hazelnuts, nutmeg, sugar, and flour. Place mixture equally distributed onto piecrust. Top with thin slices of plum, leaving a 2-inch border around the edge.

4 In a microwave-safe bowl, heat butter and preserves for 1 minute. Stir to combine. Drizzle or brush the mixture over the plums. Fold the edges of the piecrust over the edges of the plums. This should look rustic and isn't meant to have a perfect shape. This can also be made in an oblong shape if it fits a baking sheet easier. Sprinkle demerara sugar over the top and bake for 45 minutes or until the fruit begins to bubble with thickened juices and the crust is golden brown. Cool for 30 minutes and then slice and serve.

VARY IT!: If plums are hard to find, try pears, apples, or peaches in this dish instead.

PER SERVING: *Calories (From Fat); Fat g (Saturated g); Cholesterol mg; Sodium mg; Carbohydrate g (Dietary Fiber g); Protein g.*

Troubleshooting Common Pie Problems

Despite your best efforts, you're not alone if your piecrusts sometimes just don't live up to your expectations. Table 11-1 provides a quick explanation of what may have happened and why, as well as how to prevent it from happening next time.

TABLE 11-1   **Figuring Out What Went Wrong with Your Crust**

Problem	Possible Cause	Solution
Pale color	Undercooked	Increase the baking time in 3-minute increments.
	Baked in a shiny pan	Choose a pan with a dull finish or a glass pie plate.
Bottom crust is soggy	Baked at too low a temperature	Increase the temperature by 25 degrees.
	Did not seal with egg white or melted butter	Seal the bottom before filling next time.
Tough, not tender	Overmixed	Handle the dough less next time.
	Too much flour	Use less flour when rolling out the dough.
Too tender	Too much shortening	Decrease the shortening by ½ tablespoon.
	Too little water	Increase the water by 1 teaspoon.
Not flaky	Overworked	Handle the dough less next time
	Cut in the butter too much	Make sure that the dough resembles coarse meal.

Chapter **12**

Creating Crisps, Cobblers, and Other Delights

RECIPES IN THIS CHAPTER

- Apple Crisp
- Blueberry Crunch
- Peach Cobbler
- Pumpkin Custard
- Rich Chocolate Pudding
- Bread Pudding with Bourbon Caramel Sauce
- Sticky Date Toffee Pudding

Crisp, cobblers, custard, and crunches (some people call these crumbles) — they may sound funny, but they're favorites for many Americans. They're down-home desserts from a slower-paced era when baking was done on a daily basis and dessert was always a finish to every meal.

Crisps, crunches, and cobblers are perfect for every beginner baker. The essence is the same for most of them: fresh fruit on the bottom and a sweet dough or crumbly topping on top. Messing them up is next to impossible because they were born of being "tossed together."

Puddings and custards are high on the list of favorite comfort foods and easy to make, too. By using basic ingredients, such as eggs, milk, vanilla, and chocolate, you end up with an extraordinary dessert.

Baking with Fruit

With fruit fillings baked warm and bubbly under a flavorful topper, these desserts build on the season's freshest fruits. Although no one is quite sure where the names originated from, they have survived in many families as recipes passed through the generations.

What I love most about these desserts is that they're easy to make, they take advantage of whatever fruit is in season, and they're much easier to put together than pies. Use peaches instead of apples, raspberries instead of blueberries. Get creative and use a little of each. Don't be afraid. They're the most forgiving of desserts. There are no mistakes — that's my favorite tip. There's just no way you can really do these recipes wrong. Like most fruit desserts, these are best if eaten the same day, topped with sweetened whipped cream (see Chapter 10 for the recipe) or vanilla ice cream.

An air fryer and an Instant Pot, also known as a multicooker, are great tools to bake crisps and puddings, especially when it's hot outside and you want to keep your house cool or you want to bake in small spaces. Be sure to check out the tips in these recipes to successfully bake in an air fryer or Instant Pot.

☞ Apple Crisp

INGREDIENTS

4 medium apples (Golden Delicious, Granny Smith, McIntosh, or a mixture) or one can (21 ounces) apple pie filling

70 grams (⅓ cup) light brown sugar, firmly packed

90 grams (¾ cup) flour

6 tablespoons butter, cut into 6 pieces

¼ teaspoon cinnamon

⅛ teaspoon nutmeg

Pinch of salt

DIRECTIONS

1 Preheat the oven to 350 degrees.

2 Peel and slice the apples (you should have about 4 cups) and arrange them in the bottom of an 8-inch square baking dish or pour the pie filling into the baking dish.

3 In a small bowl or the bowl of a food processor, mix together the brown sugar, flour, butter, cinnamon, nutmeg, and salt with a fork or pulse it a few times until it is crumbly (don't overprocess). Sprinkle the crumbly top over the filling. Bake until the top is lightly browned, 40 to 45 minutes. Serve warm.

TIP: Try out an air fryer the next time you make this recipe. Sauté the apples and brown sugar until the apples are tender, about 10 minutes. Then divide the apples into heat-safe ramekins and add the topping. Bake at 325 degrees in an air fryer for 25 minutes; then increase the temperature to 375 and continue baking for 5 minutes — this should help the topping to crisp. Every air fryer is different, so be sure to check on the crisp periodically while baking to make sure the crisp isn't browning too quickly.

PER SERVING: *Calories 246 (From Fat 107); Fat 12g (Saturated 7g); Cholesterol 31mg; Sodium 30mg; Carbohydrate 35g Dietary Fiber 2g); Protein 2g.*

Blueberry Crunch

PREP TIME: 15 MIN	BAKING TIME: 30 MIN	YIELD: 4 TO 6 SERVINGS

INGREDIENTS

444 grams (3 cups) fresh blueberries or one package (16 ounces) frozen

2 tablespoons lemon juice

142 grams (⅔ cup) brown sugar, lightly packed

60 grams (½ cup) flour

45 grams (½ cup) rolled oats

76 grams (⅓ cup) butter, softened and cut into 6 pieces

28 grams (¼ cup) chopped walnuts or pecans

1 teaspoon cinnamon

½ teaspoon almond or vanilla extract

¼ teaspoon salt

DIRECTIONS

1 Preheat the oven to 375 degrees.

2 Pour the blueberries in the bottom of an 8-inch square baking pan. Toss the berries with the lemon juice.

3 In a small bowl or in the bowl of a food processor, combine the brown sugar, flour, oats, butter, walnuts, cinnamon, almond or vanilla extract, and salt and then mix just to combine or pulse 5 times in the food processor. Sprinkle the mixture over the blueberries.

4 Bake until the topping is light brown and the blueberries are bubbly, about 30 minutes. Serve warm.

TIP: Try out an air fryer the next time you make this recipe. Divide the blueberries into heat-safe ramekins and add the topping. Bake at 325 degrees in an air fryer for 20 minutes, and then increase the temperature to 375 and continue baking for 5 minutes — this should help the topping to crisp. Every air fryer is different, so be sure to check on the crumble periodically while baking to make sure it isn't browning too quickly.

NOTE: See the color insert for a photo of this recipe.

PER SERVING: *Calories 322 (From Fat 14); Fat 14g (Saturated 7g); Cholesterol 27mg; Sodium 113mg; Carbohydrate 48g (Dietary Fiber 4g); Protein 4g.*

🍑 Peach Cobbler

PREP TIME: 20 MIN	BAKING TIME: 30 MIN	YIELD: 4 TO 6 SERVINGS

INGREDIENTS

Filling

675 grams (4 cups) sliced, peeled peaches

200 grams (1 cup) sugar

2 tablespoons butter

1 tablespoon cornstarch

1 tablespoon lemon juice

½ teaspoon nutmeg

¼ teaspoon salt

Topping

3 tablespoons butter, cut into 3 pieces

120 grams (1 cup) flour

1 tablespoon sugar

1½ teaspoons baking powder

½ teaspoon cinnamon

¼ teaspoon salt

76 grams (⅓ cup) buttermilk

DIRECTIONS

1 Preheat the oven to 400 degrees.

2 To prepare the filling, mix together the peaches, sugar, butter, cornstarch, lemon juice, nutmeg, and salt and place in the bottom of an 8-inch square baking pan.

3 To prepare the topping, in a mixing bowl or food processor, use a fork or pastry cutter to cut the butter into the flour, sugar, baking powder, cinnamon and salt (or pulse several times) until the mixture resembles coarse crumbs. Stir in the buttermilk. Drop the dough onto the filling by the tablespoonful (you can leave a little space between the drops because it spreads as it bakes).

4 Bake until golden brown, 30 minutes. Serve hot or warm.

TIP: To peel peaches, make a small, light X (don't cut through the flesh, only the skin) on the bottom of each peach. Dunk the peach in boiling water for 30 seconds. Remove from the water with a slotted spoon and plunge into iced water. The skin should slip off easily. If some is still resisting, return the peach to the water for 15 more seconds and try again.

PER SERVING: *Calories 359 (From Fat 91); Fat 10g (Saturated 6g); Cholesterol 26mg; Sodium 305mg; Carbohydrate 66g (Dietary Fiber 3g); Protein 4g.*

Making Custards and Puddings

In truth, custards and puddings aren't much more than eggs, milk, and flavoring cooked together, then baked, thickening it into a delicious satiny creamy dessert. This is comfort food at its best.

The recipes in this section are basic, but you should be aware of what you're doing scientifically, to avoid some pitfalls. You're combining ingredients and baking them until they solidify. However, baking them too long or at too high a temperature can make them dry or grainy or expel their moisture.

To avoid this, you bake custards in a water bath, which helps control the oven's heat. All you need is a baking pan with a wire rack that fits in it (try a cooling rack or a roasting pan with the rack that your turkey sits on) that comfortably fits the custard cups (see Figure 12-1).

FIGURE 12-1: Custard cups in a water bath.

© John Wiley & Sons, Inc.

TIP

You can also cover the custard cups with aluminum foil to prevent water from sloshing into the cups as you transport them to and from the oven. This also serves as an additional heat regulator, allowing the custards to cook slowly and minimizing cracking.

If finding a rack that fits your pan is too troublesome, forget it. You can place a clean kitchen towel, folded in half, in the bottom of the baking pan and place the custard cups on top. Essentially, your goal is to place the custard cups in the pan so they don't touch the walls of the baking pan (and that includes the bottom). I find it much easier to arrange the custard cups on the rack in the water bath pan, place the pan in the oven, pour the hot water around the cups, and bake. Others prefer to add the water first and then carefully transfer the ensemble to the oven to bake.

Bake the custard just until the center is a bit shaky, but no longer liquid. It should shake like gelatin. You can insert a knife into the center about halfway in. If it comes out clean or with a small smear of custard, it's done. If liquid is on the knife, bake it longer. If it's too firm, then it's likely overbaked.

Pumpkin Custard

INGREDIENTS

454 grams (one can [16 ounces]) pumpkin puree (not pie filling)

½ teaspoon salt

336 grams (1⅓ cups) evaporated milk

4 eggs

133 grams (⅔ cup) sugar

2 tablespoons butter, melted

1 teaspoon cinnamon

¼ teaspoon ginger

¼ teaspoon nutmeg

¼ teaspoon cloves

DIRECTIONS

1 Preheat the oven to 350 degrees. In a mixing bowl, combine all the ingredients and mix well. Divide the mixture into 8 custard cups or small ramekins. Place the cups on a rack in a baking pan to fit. Pour very hot water around the cups to the depth of 1 inch.

2 Bake for 30 to 45 minutes, or until a knife inserted into the center comes out clean. Cool. To serve, invert the custard cups onto a serving plate and remove the cup.

NOTE: If you're worried about pouring hot water into the custard cups, just fill the baking pan about one-third full of hot water, then add the custard cups. The water should be 1 inch deep.

TIP: If you're afraid that you cooked your custard too long, don't fret. Just remove it from the oven and transfer the cups into a cool water bath to stop the cooking (don't make the water too cold or else you may crack the custard cups). Then refrigerate the custard.

TIP: An Instant Pot is ideal to quickly baking custards. Start with 1 cup boiling water at the base of the pot, use the rack, and bake in individual ramekins. You'll need to make this in batches or you can halve the recipe. Cook under high pressure for 7 minutes with a natural release.

PER SERVING: Calories 208 (From Fat 77); Fat 9g (Saturated 5g); Cholesterol 129mg; Sodium 230mg; Carbohydrate 26g (Dietary Fiber 3g); Protein 7g.

CUSTARD 101

The word custard is derived from "crustade," which is a tart with a crust. After the 16th century, fruit creams became popular, and it was about this time that custards were made in individual dishes rather than a filling in a crust.

Rich Chocolate Pudding

PREP TIME: 20 MIN	BAKING TIME: 20 MIN	YIELD: 4 TO 6 SERVINGS

INGREDIENTS

4 ounces semisweet chocolate or ¾ cup chocolate chips

1 cup heavy (whipping) cream

3 tablespoons sugar

3 eggs

1 tablespoon vanilla extract

Boiling water

DIRECTIONS

1 Preheat the oven to 350 degrees.

2 Chop the chocolate into small bits (if using the squares). In the top part of a double boiler placed over simmering water, melt the chocolate and cream together, stirring often. After the chocolate has melted, stir in the sugar. Set aside to cool.

3 Beat the eggs and vanilla together. Gently stir ¼ cup of the chocolate mixture into the egg mixture. Slowly add the egg mixture to the remaining chocolate, stirring constantly. Carefully pour the chocolate mixture into 4 or 6 little custard cups. Cover each cup with foil. Set the custard cups on a rack in a large baking pan, and carefully pour the boiling water into the baking pan until the water comes halfway up the side of the dishes.

4 Bake for about 20 minutes or until set. Remove from the oven and let cool.

TIP: If you're afraid to pour the boiling water into the pan, you can always use a ladle and carefully transfer the water from the pot to the baking pan. Don't pour the water on top of the custard cups.

TIP: Don't overbake the pudding or else it may burn.

NOTE: Refer to the color insert for a photo of this recipe.

VARY IT: If you want to make butterscotch pudding, substitute butterscotch chips for the chocolate.

PER SERVING: *Calories 293 (From Fat 222); Fat 25g (Saturated 14g); Cholesterol 161mg; Sodium 47mg; Carbohydrate 17g (Dietary Fiber 1g); Protein 5g.*

Bread Pudding with Bourbon Caramel Sauce

PREP TIME: 25 MIN	BAKING TIME: 45 MIN	YIELD: 8 SERVINGS

INGREDIENTS

236 grams (1 cup) milk

240 grams (1 cup) heavy whipping cream

100 grams (½ cup) sugar

4 eggs

230 grams (8 ounces) day old bread (like French bread or croissants), cubed

75 grams (½ cup) raisins

57 grams (¼ cup) unsalted butter, melted

Bourbon Sauce

113 grams (½ cup) unsalted butter

100 grams (½ cup) sugar

80 grams (⅓ cup) heavy whipping cream

57 grams (¼ cup) bourbon whiskey

¼ teaspoon nutmeg

¼ teaspoon sea salt

DIRECTIONS

1 Preheat the oven to 350 degrees. Grease a 9-x-13-inch cake pan.

2 In a large mixing bowl, whisk together milk, heavy whipping cream, sugar, and eggs. Add the bread and raisins to the milk mixture. Stir to combine. Pour into baking dish. Drizzle butter over the top of the bread pudding. Bake uncovered for 35 to 45 minutes or until an internal temperature of 160 degrees is reached. Remove from oven and cool on a wire rack for 30 minutes.

3 After the bread pudding has cooled, make the bourbon sauce. In a 4-quart saucepan, heat the butter and sugar until melted and the sugar begins to become golden in color. Whisk in the whipping cream, bourbon, nutmeg, and sea salt over medium heat and continue to whisk until slightly thickened, about 3 to 5 minutes. Drizzle warm bourbon sauce over the bread pudding, slice, and serve.

NOTE: This is a great recipe to use day-old breads or bread that's about to stale. You can also serve this with ice cream or a store-bought caramel sauce.

TIP: An Instant Pot is ideal to quickly baking bread puddings. Start with 1½ cups boiling water at the base of the pot, use the rack, and bake in a 6-inch cake pan. You'll need to make this in batches or you can halve the recipe. Cover the bread pudding with foil. Cook under high pressure for 30 minutes with a natural release. Then make the sauce on the stovetop and serve hot.

PER SERVING: Calories 567 (From Fat 321); Fat 36g (Saturated 21g); Cholesterol 209mg; Sodium 313mg; Carbohydrate 51g (Dietary Fiber 1g); Protein 9g.

Sticky Date and Toffee Pudding

PREP TIME: 15 MIN	BAKING TIME: 25 MIN	YIELD: 8 SERVINGS

INGREDIENTS

300 grams (2 cups) pitted and chopped dates

227 grams (1 cup) boiling water

113 grams (½ cup) unsalted butter, room temperature

40 grams (3 tablespoons) packed light brown sugar

2 eggs, room temperature

160 grams (1⅓ cups) flour

1 teaspoon baking soda

1½ teaspoons baking powder

½ teaspoon cinnamon

½ teaspoon nutmeg

Toffee Sauce

175 grams (1 cup and 2 tablespoons) light brown sugar, packed

50 grams (3 tablespoons and 2 teaspoons) unsalted butter

225 grams (¾ cup + 2 tablespoons) heavy whipping cream

1 tablespoon molasses

½ teaspoon sea salt

DIRECTIONS

1 Preheat the oven to 350 degrees. Grease 8 ramekins. In a heat-safe bowl, add the dates and boiling water. Let this mixture sit for 10 minutes. In a separate mixing bowl, cream together the butter and brown sugar, then add eggs one at a time. In a separate bowl, stir the flour, baking soda, baking powder, cinnamon, and nutmeg. Add the dry ingredients to the creamed butter and stir to incorporate. Mash the dates and water. Stir the dates into the batter, and then pour the batter equally into the ramekins and bake for 20 to 25 minutes. Use the toothpick method to tell if the center is fully cooked.

2 Ten minutes before the cakes are done cooking, start the toffee sauce. In a 4-quart saucepan, heat the brown sugar, butter, heavy whipping cream, molasses, and salt over medium heat, whisking occasionally until sauce begins to simmer. Simmer for 2 minutes and then remove from heat. Poke holes in the tops of the hot cakes. Pour the sauce over the cakes and let them sit for 10 minutes. Invert cakes and serve.

TIP: An Instant Pot is ideal to quickly baking this sticky cake. Start with 1 cup boiling water at the base of the pot, use the rack, and bake in individual ramekins. Cover with foil and bake under high pressure for 17 minutes with a natural release. Make the sauce. Poke holes in the cake and serve the sauce over the cakes.

PER SERVING: *Calories 506 (From Fat 215); Fat 24g (Saturated 15g); Cholesterol 118mg; Sodium 152mg; Carbohydrate 72g (Dietary Fiber 4g); Protein 5g.*

Chapter 13

Making Quick Breads, Muffins, and Biscuits

RECIPES IN THIS CHAPTER

- ☺ **Pumpkin Bread**
- ☺ **Banana Bread**
- ☺ **Chocolate Zucchini Bread**
- ☺ **Cranberry-Orange Bread**
- ☺ **Crumbcake**
- ☺ **Sweet Chocolate Chip Pull-Apart Bread**
- ☺ **Boston Brown Bread**
- ☺ **Southern Corn Bread**
- ☺ **Blueberry Muffins**
- ☺ **Lemon Poppy Seed Muffins**
- ☺ **Buttermilk Biscuits**
- ☺ **Cheesy Cheese Biscuits**
- ☺ **Lemon Blueberry Scones**
- **Bacon Cheddar and Chives Scones**

Although everyone loves tender coffee cakes, muffins, scones, and hot biscuits, oftentimes people find them-selves buying them from the bakery, coffee shop, or in the refrigerated sections of the grocery store for convenience. If this sounds familiar, maybe it's because you think you don't have the time or talent to whip up a batch from scratch. As you prepare to discover the joys of home-baked goods, quick breads and muffins are the perfect introduction. The batters aren't dif-ficult to put together, most can be done in less than 15 minutes, and you can find a recipe that's right for any occasion.

Quick breads, such as banana bread, are popular favorites for many people. In this chapter, I let you know how to whip up batters for these breads. You discover how easy jazzing up quick breads with ingredients such as nuts, raisins, dried cranberries, chocolate chips, and dried fruits can be. I also offer advice on making a variety of muffins, plus give you helpful hints for making tender, flaky biscuits and scones.

Quick Tips for Quick Breads

Quick breads are quite popular because they're a snap to put together and can satisfy either a sweet or a savory desire. Because they're leavened with baking soda or baking powder, they don't require the rising time yeast breads do, which means they're fast and easy to make. Just make sure your leaveners are fresh, so they'll have optimal rising power.

What I like best about quick breads is that they're relatively indestructible when it comes to add-ins. If you want to experiment, try adding ½ cup of any of the following:

>> Nuts

>> Dried fruit

>> Chocolate chips

>> Coconut

What differentiates quick breads, muffins, and biscuits is the proportion of liquid to fat, flour, and eggs — quick breads having the most moisture and biscuits having the least.

Quick breads are generally baked in metal loaf pans. Shiny pans are best, but if you have dark, nonstick pans or glass pans, lower the oven temperature by 25 degrees if you find the breads are browning too quickly. Grease only the bottoms of the loaf pans for nut or fruit quick breads; the ungreased sides give the batter something to cling to as it rises and give you a nicely shaped loaf with a gently rounded top. For more on baking pans, see Chapter 3.

WARNING

Overmixing the batter can toughen the bread, so just mix until the ingredients are combined, unless specified otherwise by the instructions. Lumps in the batter are okay. You want to mix the breads by hand to avoid toughening the dough.

If your bread develops a large crack lengthwise down the center of the loaf, don't worry that you've done anything wrong. The crusts of quick breads are usually thinner and tend to crack. I think it gives the bread a great homemade look.

I find that many quick breads taste even better the second day or after being frozen and defrosted, although they don't always stick around until then! You can wrap the cooled loaves in plastic wrap and store them in the freezer for up to 3 months. Check out Chapter 17 for more tips on storing your baked goods.

Sweet breads

Sweet quick breads are usually made with fruits or vegetables (banana, pumpkin, zucchini, and so on) and are bursting with spice. They can be served for breakfast, an afternoon snack, or even as a not-so-sweet dessert at the end of a meal. They're great to bring as housewarming gifts and share with co-workers. They're also great batters that can easily be enhanced with chocolate chips, raisins, nuts, or other such treats. Here are some easy recipes you can try.

🍅 Pumpkin Bread

PREP TIME: 15 MIN   BAKING TIME: 1 HR   YIELD: 30 SERVINGS

INGREDIENTS

794 grams (One large [28 ounce] can) pumpkin

700 grams (3½ cups) sugar

6 eggs

267 grams (1⅓ cups) neutral vegetable oil

630 grams (5¼ cups) flour

1 tablespoon baking soda

1 tablespoon cinnamon

2 teaspoons nutmeg

2 teaspoons salt

171 grams (1½ cup) chopped walnuts or pecans (optional)

DIRECTIONS

1 Preheat the oven to 350 degrees with a baking sheet. Grease and flour three 9-x-5-inch loaf pans. In an extra-large mixing bowl, whisk canned pumpkin, sugar, eggs, and oil until blended.

2 In a separate mixing bowl, stir the flour, baking soda, cinnamon, nutmeg, and salt. Add the dry ingredients to the wet ingredients, stirring to combine. Break up any large clumps of flour, but don't overmix.

3 Pour batter equally amongst the 3 loaf pans and place on preheated baking sheet. Bake for 1 hour or until internal temperature reaches 200 degrees or a knife comes out clean after inserted into the center. Cool on wire racks for at least 1 hour prior to slicing.

TIP: This recipe can be made with whole wheat pastry flour as well. I recommend replacing only ½ of the white flour and working your way from there based on taste preferences.

NOTE: This recipe makes a large batch of pumpkin bread. You can freeze the baked bread wrapped in foil and plastic freezer-safe bags for up to 3 months.

NOTE: Flip to the color insert for a photo of this recipe.

PER SERVING: *Calories 269 (From Fat 92); Fat 10g (Saturated 2g); Cholesterol 42mg; Sodium 171mg; Carbohydrate 42g (Dietary Fiber 1g); Protein 4g.*

🍅 Banana Bread

INGREDIENTS

250 grams (1¼ cups) sugar

100 grams (½ cup) vegetable oil

2 eggs

1 teaspoon vanilla extract

210 grams (2¾ cups) flour

2 teaspoons baking powder

½ teaspoon salt

¼ teaspoon baking soda

2 medium ripe bananas, mashed

118 grams (½ cup) brewed coffee, warm or cold

113 grams (½ cup) buttermilk

113 grams (1 cup) chopped walnuts

DIRECTIONS

1 Preheat the oven to 350 degrees. Grease just the bottom of a 9-x-5-inch loaf pan.

2 In a large bowl, beat together the sugar, oil, eggs, and vanilla until light and creamy, about 2 minutes. Add the flour, baking powder, salt, and baking soda and stir together just to moisten the flour.

3 Combine the bananas, coffee, and buttermilk in a separate bowl and stir into the batter. Fold in the nuts.

4 Pour the batter into the prepared loaf pan. Bake for 55 minutes or until a wooden tooth-pick inserted into the middle of the loaf comes out clean. Remove from the pan and cool on a wire rack.

NOTE: This is a great recipe to use when you want to use overripe bananas. Don't use underripe bananas for this recipe. The mushier and riper the banana, the better the banana flavor.

PER SERVING: *Calories 375 (From Fat 153); Fat 17g (Saturated 2g); Cholesterol 36mg; Sodium 209mg; Carbohydrate 52g (Dietary Fiber 2g); Protein 6g.*

Chocolate Zucchini Bread

INGREDIENTS

242 grams (2 cups) grated zucchini

113 grams (½ cup) unsalted butter, melted

100 grams (½ cup) vegetable oil

122 grams (½ cup) plain Greek yogurt

100 grams (½ cup) sugar

2 eggs

1½ teaspoons vanilla extract

180 grams (1½ cups) flour

42 grams (½ cup) cocoa powder

½ teaspoon baking powder

½ teaspoon baking soda

½ teaspoon salt

1 teaspoon cinnamon

½ teaspoon instant coffee powder

57 grams (½ cup) walnuts, chopped (optional)

85 grams (½ cup) semisweet chocolate chips (optional)

DIRECTIONS

1 Preheat the oven to 350 degrees. Line a 9-x-5-inch loaf pan with parchment paper and grease the pan.

2 Place grated zucchini into a tea towel and wring out the moisture from the zucchini and discard liquid. In a medium bowl, add the zucchini, butter, vegetable oil, Greek yogurt, sugar, and eggs, stirring to mix.

3 In a separate mixing bowl, stir the flour, cocoa powder, baking powder, baking soda, salt, cinnamon, and instant coffee. Add the dry ingredients to the wet ingredients, stirring just to combine. Pour batter into prepared loaf pan. Bake for 1 hour or until knife inserted into the center comes out clean.

4 After the bread is removed from the oven, sprinkle the chocolate chips over the top of the hot bread. The chips will melt from the heat. Let the bread rest for 10 minutes, and then using a knife, spread the chocolate on the top of the cake. Using the parchment paper, lift the bread from the pan and place on a wire rack to cool.

TIP: Add pistachios, almonds, or dried cranberries in place of the walnuts if desired. If you want an extra pop of chocolate in the bread, stir the chocolate chips into the batter.

PER SERVING: *Calories 262 (From Fat 157); Fat 17g (Saturated 7g); Cholesterol 57mg; Sodium 100mg; Carbohydrate 23g (Dietary Fiber 2g); Protein 5g.*

Cranberry-Orange Bread

PREP TIME: 15 MIN | BAKING TIME: 60 MIN | YIELD: 12 TO 14 SERVINGS

INGREDIENTS

240 grams (2 cups) flour

125 grams (1 cup) coarsely chopped fresh cranberries

150 grams (¾ cup) sugar

57 grams (½ cup) coarsely chopped pecans or walnuts

2 teaspoons baking powder

¼ teaspoon salt

1 egg

1 teaspoon grated orange zest (peel)

124 grams (½ cup) orange juice

100 grams (½ cup) vegetable oil

DIRECTIONS

1 Preheat the oven to 350 degrees. Grease and flour a 9-x-5-inch loaf pan.

2 In a large bowl, mix together the flour, cranberries, sugar, nuts, baking powder, and salt.

3 In a small bowl, mix together the egg, orange zest, orange juice, and oil. Stir the wet ingredients into the dry ingredients and mix until just blended.

4 Pour the batter into the prepared pan and bake for 60 minutes, or until a toothpick inserted into the center of the loaf comes out clean. Cool the loaf for 15 minutes before removing it from the pan. Finish cooling the loaf on a wire rack.

TIP: The easiest way to chop cranberries is to place them in the bowl of a food processor and give them a few pulses, no more than three or four. You can use the same technique for the nuts.

PER SERVING: *Calories 254 (From Fat 120); Fat 13g (Saturated 1g); Cholesterol 18mg; Sodium 118mg; Carbohydrate 31g (Dietary Fiber 2g); Protein 3g.*

❧ Crumbcake

INGREDIENTS

Topping

1 tablespoon flour

107 grams (½ cup) brown sugar, firmly packed

2 tablespoons butter, cut into four pieces, softened

57 grams (½ cup) chopped walnuts or pecans

1 teaspoon cinnamon

½ teaspoon nutmeg

Cake

113 grams (½ cup/1 stick) unsalted butter, softened

200 grams (1 cup) sugar

1 teaspoon vanilla extract

3 eggs

240 grams (2 cups) flour

1 teaspoon baking powder

1 teaspoon baking soda

½ teaspoon salt

1 teaspoon allspice

227 grams (1 cup) sour cream or plain yogurt

DIRECTIONS

1 Preheat the oven to 350 degrees. Grease a 13-x-9-inch baking pan. In a small bowl, combine the 1 tablespoon flour, brown sugar, 2 tablespoons butter, walnuts, cinnamon, and nutmeg for the topping. Mix well and set aside.

2 In a large mixing bowl, cream together the butter, sugar, and vanilla until light and fluffy, about 1 minute. Add the eggs, one at a time, mixing well after each addition.

3 Sift together the flour, baking powder, baking soda, salt, and allspice and add to the butter mixture. Mix in the sour cream. Pour the batter into the prepared pan. Sprinkle the top of the batter evenly with the topping.

4 Bake for 45 minutes or until a toothpick inserted into the center of the cake comes out clean. Cool in the pan on a wire rack before cutting.

VARY IT! Try folding 1 cup of fresh blueberries into the batter before you pour it into the pan.

PER SERVING: *Calories 178 (From Fat 83); Fat 9g (Saturated 5g); Cholesterol 44mg; Sodium 133mg; Carbohydrate 22g (Dietary Fiber 1g); Protein 3g.*

Sweet Chocolate Chip Pull-Apart Bread

PREP TIME: 20 MIN	BAKING TIME: 30 MIN	YIELD: 16 BALLS

INGREDIENTS

240 grams (2 cups) flour

150 grams (¾ cup) sugar

1 tablespoon baking powder

½ teaspoon salt

70 grams (5 tablespoons) cold butter, cut into 5 pieces

170 grams (1 cup) semisweet chocolate chips

157 grams (⅔ cup) milk

1½ teaspoons cinnamon

3 tablespoons melted butter

DIRECTIONS

1 Preheat the oven to 350 degrees. Grease an 8-inch-square baking pan. In a mixing bowl or in a food processor, combine the flour, ½ cup of the sugar, baking powder, and salt.

2 Using a pastry blender or a few pulses of the food processor, cut the cold butter into the flour mixture until the mixture resembles coarse meal. Stir in the chocolate chips and milk to combine. Divide the dough into 16 balls and place in the prepared baking pan (the balls will touch).

3 Combine the remaining ¼ cup sugar and the cinnamon. Drizzle the balls with the melted butter and sprinkle them with the cinnamon-sugar mixture.

4 Bake for 30 minutes, until light brown. Cool in the pan set on a wire rack before removing from the pan.

NOTE: This sweet, chocolaty bread drizzled with butter and cinnamon — sometimes called monkey bread — is hard to resist. Instead of cutting it, you pull it apart with your hands — make sure to lick them clean when you're done!

PER SERVING: Calories 205 (From Fat 85); Fat 9g (Saturated 5g); Cholesterol 17mg; Sodium 150mg; Carbohydrate 29g (Dietary Fiber 1g); Protein 2g.

Savory breads

Savory breads are usually served with a meal instead of as dessert or a sweet treat. Savory quick breads are perfect for the hurried cook who wants to offer homemade bread without fussing with yeast breads. Boston Brown Bread is nice with a hearty bowl of chili or soup, and the Southern Corn Bread goes well with baked or barbecued chicken.

🍅 Boston Brown Bread

INGREDIENTS

180 grams (1½ cups) flour

150 grams (¾ cup) sugar

1½ teaspoons baking soda

1½ teaspoons salt

78 grams (½ cup) cornmeal

226 grams (2 cups) whole-wheat flour

255 grams (¾ cup) dark molasses

1 egg, lightly beaten

472 grams (2 cups) milk

113 grams (½ cup/1 stick) butter, melted

1 teaspoon vanilla extract

DIRECTIONS

1 Preheat the oven to 325 degrees. Grease two 9-x-5-inch loaf pans.

2 Sift together ½ cup of the flour, sugar, baking soda, and salt into a large mixing bowl. Stir in the cornmeal and whole-wheat flour. Add the remaining 1 cup all-purpose flour, molasses, egg, milk, melted butter, and vanilla, mixing only until all the flour is moistened.

3 Pour into the prepared pans. Bake for 1 hour or until a toothpick inserted in the center of the loaf comes out clean. Remove the bread from pans and cool on a wire rack.

VARY IT! Stir in 1 cup of raisins or walnuts (when you add the flour) to add extra flavor.

PER SERVING: *Calories 174 (From Fat 45); Fat 5g (Saturated 3g); Cholesterol 22mg; Sodium 241mg; Carbohydrate 30g (Dietary Fiber 2g); Protein 3g.*

⌀ Southern Corn Bread

PREP TIME: 10 MIN	BAKING TIME: 20 MIN	YIELD: ONE 8- OR 9-INCH CORN BREAD

INGREDIENTS

2 tablespoons butter or vegetable oil

320 grams (2 cups) finely ground cornmeal

4 teaspoons baking powder

1½ teaspoons salt

340 grams (1½ cups) buttermilk

1 egg, lightly beaten

DIRECTIONS

1 Preheat the oven to 450 degrees. Place the butter or vegetable oil in the bottom of an 8- or 9-inch square baking pan (or a 10-inch cast iron skillet) and place it in the oven while it heats for about 3 minutes (if you're using butter, keep an eye on it to make sure it doesn't burn).

2 In a large bowl, combine the cornmeal, baking powder, and salt.

3 In a separate bowl, mix together the buttermilk and egg and add it to the cornmeal mixture. Stir just to combine; don't overmix.

4 Pour the batter into the preheated skillet or pan and bake for about 20 minutes, until a knife inserted into the center comes out clean. Cool the corn bread in the skillet for 20 minutes before serving.

TIP: If you can only find coarsely ground cornmeal, you can use 1 cup of all-purpose flour and 1 cup of the coarse cornmeal in place of the finely ground cornmeal.

PER SERVING: *Calories 120 (From Fat 27); Fat 3g (Saturated 2g); Cholesterol 24mg; Sodium 456mg; Carbohydrate 19g (Dietary Fiber 2g); Protein 4g.*

Making the Perfect Muffin

Making a tender, moist muffin is really quite simple, but not knowing the proper technique can result in tough, smooth-topped muffins. The secret to bumpy rounded muffin tops and a moist inside is to avoid overmixing the dough and to use only a bowl and a spoon for mixing. Don't use a handheld or stand mixer. When you combine the flour mixture with the liquids, just give it a few (no more than five) good turns with a sturdy wooden spoon. There will be, and should be, a tiny bit of unmixed flour in your batter, and that's okay. Believe it or not, the batter will "finish mixing" in the oven, and the unmixed flour will not be present in the muffin. These sections give you the lowdown on making tasty muffins.

WARNING

If you blend your batter until it's smooth and uniform, you'll have made a cakelike batter, which will result in tougher muffins with peaked or smooth tops — not desirable for most muffins. You want to have slightly rounded, bumpy-topped muffins baked to a golden brown.

Preparing the pans

The easiest way to prepare muffin tins is to use paper liners. Just pop the liners in and fill three-quarters full of batter. You don't need liners in order to make muffins, though. Just grease only the bottoms of the muffin cups (the sides of the cup should be left ungreased), unless the recipe calls for the entire cup to be greased. Not greasing the sides actually gives you a better-shaped muffin.

REMEMBER

When you're filling muffin cups, fill the cup only three-quarters full of batter. Overfilling muffin tins will result in the batter spilling on top of the muffin tins — plus, your muffins will be oddly shaped. You may even have batter drip to the floor of the oven, which is always an unpleasant mess. Wipe off any batter that has spilled onto the top of the muffin pan before baking them.

As soon as the muffins are done baking, let them sit for just one minute to set and then remove them from the muffin pan. They should just tumble out when the pan is inverted; however, if some of the muffins are reluctant to come out, just run a butter knife or a thin metal spatula around the cup to loosen the muffin. If you leave muffins to cool in their cups, they will become a bit soggy from the trapped steam.

Going mini

The standard muffin cup is 2½ x 1¼ inches; however, almost every muffin, cake, and quick-bread recipe can be baked in mini-muffin, mini-Bundt, or mini-loaf pans. To determine the amount of baking time needed for these sizes, measure the volume of your baking pan as follows:

1. **Fill the pan to capacity with water.**

   For muffin tins, fill just one cup.

2. **Pour the water into a glass measuring cup and measure the liquid.**

   The amount of water equals the capacity of your baking pan.

When you use alternative baking pans, you not only have to adjust the amount of batter you use in each pan, but you must also alter the baking time of your recipe. Table 13-1 presents some guidelines. Bake your mini creations at 350 degrees, and always check them after the minimum time given.

TABLE 13-1   ## Adjustments for Alternative Pans

If Your Pan Holds . . .	Use This Much Batter	And Bake For . . .
¼ cup	3 tablespoons	10 to 15 minutes
⅓ cup	¼ cup	15 to 20 minutes
½ cup	⅓ cup	15 to 20 minutes
¾ cup	½ cup	20 to 25 minutes
1 cup	¾ cup	30 to 35 minutes

Magnificent muffins

The recipes in this section are sure to become favorites.

Blueberry Muffins

| PREP TIME: 15 MIN | BAKING TIME: 20 MIN | YIELD: 24 MUFFINS |

INGREDIENTS

240 grams (2 cups) flour

2 teaspoons baking powder

200 grams (1 cup) sugar

113 grams (½ cup/1 stick) butter, melted

118 grams (½ cup) whole milk

1 teaspoon vanilla extract

2 eggs, lightly beaten

475 grams (2½ cups) blueberries, fresh or frozen

DIRECTIONS

1 Preheat the oven to 400 degrees. Grease or line two 12-cup muffin cups.

2 In a small bowl, combine the flour and baking powder; set aside.

3 In a large mixing bowl, combine the sugar, butter, milk, vanilla, and eggs. Mix to combine.

4 Slowly add the flour mixture to the sugar mixture and stir just to moisten the dry ingredients. Fold in the blueberries just to combine. Don't overmix.

5 Fill the muffin cups three-quarters full of batter. Bake (both pans side by side is okay) for 20 minutes or until golden brown. A wooden toothpick inserted into the center of the muffins will come out clean when the muffins are done. Let the muffins rest for 5 minutes on the cooling rack before removing them from the pan.

TIP: If you've greased all of your muffin cups and then find your batter does not fill all of them, pour a few tablespoons of water into the greased empty cups to prevent them from burning while you bake. Just remember, when it's time to remove the muffins from the pan, not to invert the pan to release them or the water will spill out, too!

NOTE: Flip to the color insert for a photo of this recipe.

PER SERVING: *Calories 122 (From Fat 41); Fat 5g (Saturated 3g); Cholesterol 29mg; Sodium 41mg; Carbohydrate 19g (Dietary Fiber 1g); Protein 2g.*

Lemon Poppy Seed Muffins

INGREDIENTS

76 grams (⅓ cup) buttermilk

50 grams (¼ cup) vegetable oil

1 egg, lightly beaten

151 grams (⅔ cup) sour cream

2 tablespoons fresh lemon juice

1 teaspoon lemon extract

210 grams (1¾ cup) flour

36 grams (¼ cup) poppy seeds

1 tablespoon grated lemon peel

2½ teaspoons baking powder

½ teaspoon baking soda

½ teaspoon salt

DIRECTIONS

1 Preheat the oven to 400 degrees. Grease or line 12 muffin cups.

2 In a large mixing bowl, combine the buttermilk, oil, egg, sour cream, lemon juice, and lemon extract. Add the flour, poppy seeds, lemon peel, baking powder, baking soda, and salt and mix with a spoon just until moistened.

3 Fill the muffin cups about three-quarters full. Bake for about 15 minutes or until a toothpick inserted into the center comes out clean. Remove from the pans and cool the muffins on a wire rack.

TIP: When zesting the lemon, be sure to avoid the white pith, which will lend a bitter flavor to the muffin if used.

PER SERVING: *Calories 160 (From Fat 83); Fat 9g (Saturated 2g); Cholesterol 24mg; Sodium 249mg; Carbohydrate 16g (Dietary Fiber 1g); Protein 4g.*

Focusing on Biscuit Basics

Fresh, hot, fluffy biscuits are a dinnertime dream for me. I went to college in North Carolina, and living in the South for four years taught me a thing or two about making biscuits, such as using flour made from soft winter wheat to produce a more tender and lighter biscuit than those made with all-purpose flour. If you want to taste the difference, look for White Lily brand flour (their website is www.whitelily.com/products/ or call 800-595-1380 for ordering information). You can also use cake flour in place of all-purpose flour, measure for measure, for a lighter biscuit. Here I examine just what you need to know about making biscuits.

Mixing biscuit dough

Biscuits are a lot like pie pastry in that too much handling will toughen the dough, and the biscuit won't be as delicate. Because you don't want to over-mix your biscuit dough, working efficiently when making biscuits is important. Two basic steps are involved with mixing biscuit dough:

1. **Cut the fat into the flour so that it resembles coarse crumbs.**

   Cutting-in is a mixing method in which solid fat is incorporated into dry ingredients, resulting in a coarse texture. Do this by using a pastry blender, a fork, or two knifes. See Chapter 3 for tips on cutting fats into flour mixtures.

2. **Add the liquid ingredients to the flour mixture.**

   Mix these with a fork until they have just come together and the dough leaves the sides of the bowl. It's okay if your biscuits are still damp.

That's all the mixing your biscuit dough needs. Any more mixing, and you'll get tough biscuits.

THE RISE OF THE BISCUIT

Biscuits come from the French words meaning "twice cooked" *(bis cuit)* and are a far cry from the light fluffy treats we're familiar with today. They began as dry, hard crackers — the hard tack that sailors took with them on long sea voyages because the biscuits would last a long time without spoiling. Later, shortening was added to the recipe, but the biscuits were still hard because cooks mixed the batter for a long time. Ultimately, with the invention of baking powder, biscuits began their rise, and soon tender and fluffy became the norm for the biscuit.

Forming your biscuits

There is an art to a well-formed biscuit. Working with the dough too much will make your biscuits less tender. Steam is a powerful leavener for biscuits, so it's okay if your biscuits are a bit moist when you roll them out. Don't over-flour the dough to make it easier to handle. Just pat out the dough, cut it with a cookie cutter, then place the biscuit on a baking sheet.

1. **Turn your biscuit dough out onto a floured surface and either gently roll out the dough with a rolling pin or pat it out with your hands into a circle about ½ inch thick.**

2. **Use a 2-inch round cookie cutter to cut out your biscuits.**

    You can also flour the rim of a drinking glass and use this instead of a cookie cutter. The key is the thickness of the dough.

3. **Gather the scraps, pat the dough out again, and cut a few more biscuits.**

    Try not to roll out the dough any more than necessary because overhandling the dough results in tougher biscuits.

TIP

If you want biscuits with soft sides, place them in the pan so their sides are touching. If you want them to have crusty sides, place them about an inch apart on the baking sheet.

Storing your biscuits

Biscuits are best when eaten hot — fresh out of the oven. However, you can make them a day ahead if you need to, but not much more in advance than that. Store your biscuits in an airtight container when they've cooled completely or freeze for up to 1 month.

TIP

You can also make the biscuits, cut them out, and refrigerate them for up to 2 hours before baking, so that you can serve them piping hot without doing everything at the last minute.

☙ Buttermilk Biscuits

INGREDIENTS

230 grams (2 cups) White Lily brand soft white flour or cake or all-purpose flour

¼ teaspoon baking soda

1 teaspoon baking powder

1 teaspoon salt

Pinch of sugar

85 grams (6 tablespoons) cold butter, cut into 6 pieces

170 grams (¾ cup) buttermilk

DIRECTIONS

1 Preheat the oven to 425 degrees.

2 Sift together the flour, baking soda, baking powder, salt, and sugar into a large mixing bowl. Cut in the butter with a pastry blender until the texture resembles coarse meal. Add the buttermilk and mix until just moistened.

3 Pat out the dough onto a lightly floured surface until it is about ½-inch thick. Cut the dough into 2-inch circles (use a drinking glass or cookie cutter). Gather up the scraps and pat them out again. Place biscuits on an ungreased baking sheet.

4 Bake until just light brown, for 10 to 12 minutes. Serve hot.

TIP: These biscuits are easy to make — the perfect biscuit for beginners. White Lily is the most popular brand of Southern flour, but if you can't find it, you can use all-purpose flour.

PER SERVING: *Calories 100 (From Fat 41); Fat 5g (Saturated 3g); Cholesterol 12mg; Sodium 249mg; Carbohydrate 13g (Dietary Fiber 0g); Protein 2g.*

🍅 Cheesy Cheese Biscuits

PREP TIME: 15 MIN	BAKING TIME: 16 MIN	YIELD: 12 MUFFINS

INGREDIENTS

230 grams (2 cups) White Lily brand soft white flour, cake flour, or all-purpose flour

1 to 2 cloves garlic, crushed (optional)

1 tablespoon sugar

2 teaspoons baking powder

¼ teaspoon baking soda

¼ teaspoon salt

1 teaspoon black pepper

85 grams (6 tablespoons) cold unsalted butter, cut into small pieces

141 grams (1¼ cups) grated extra-sharp cheddar cheese

45 grams (½ cup) grated Parmesan cheese (about 1½ ounces)

227 grams (1 cup) chilled buttermilk

DIRECTIONS

1 Preheat the oven to 425 degrees. Lightly butter two 9-inch cake pans.

2 Combine the flour, garlic (if desired), sugar, baking powder, baking soda, salt, and pepper in medium bowl to blend. Cut in the butter until mixture resembles coarse meal. Add the cheddar and Parmesan cheese and toss to coat well.

3 Gradually mix in the buttermilk and stir just to moisten the dough.

4 Drop the dough by ¼-cupfuls (or use a 2-inch ice cream scooper) onto the prepared pans (6 for each pan); they will be touching.

5 Bake the biscuits until golden on top, about 16 minutes. Transfer to a platter. Serve warm or at room temperature.

TIP: Handle the dough as little as possible and barely stir in the buttermilk. Trust me on this. The dough will be lumpy, but it'll work itself out in the oven and you'll have delicious, tender biscuits.

PER SERVING: *Calories 196 (From Fat 101); Fat 11g (Saturated 7g); Cholesterol 32mg; Sodium 311mg; Carbohydrate 17g (Dietary Fiber 0g); Protein 7g.*

Lemon Blueberry Scones

INGREDIENTS

240 grams (2 cups) flour

1 tablespoon baking powder

3 tablespoons sugar

57 grams (¼ cup) cold unsalted butter, cubed

118 grams (½ cup) milk

1 tablespoon lemon zest

190 grams (1 cup) blueberries

45 grams (3 tablespoons) cream

3 tablespoons demerara sugar

DIRECTIONS

1 Preheat the oven to 425 degrees.

2 In a medium bowl, stir the flour, baking powder, and sugar. Using a pastry blender, cut in cold butter until the mixture is crumbly. Pour in milk and stir. Next, fold in lemon zest and blueberries. Form into a ball and gently knead on a floured surface 3 times. Don't overmix. Flatten into a 10-inch circle and cut into 8 wedges.

3 Place scones onto a parchment lined baking sheet. Brush the tops with cream and sprinkle with sugar. Bake for 12 to 15 minutes or lightly golden brown in color.

TIP: Try something different; opt for dried cranberries (½ cup) and orange zest instead.

NOTE: This is more like an English scone, than the cake-like scones you'd find at popular coffee shops. This scone is more biscuit-like and less sweet, making for a perfect afterschool snack or breakfast addition.

PER SERVING: *Calories 237 (From Fat 77); Fat 9g (Saturated 5g); Cholesterol 24mg; Sodium 11mg; Carbohydrate 37g (Dietary Fiber 1g); Protein 4g.*

Bacon Cheddar and Chives Scones

PREP TIME: 15 MIN | **BAKING TIME: 50 TO 60 MIN** | **YIELD: 16 SCONES**

INGREDIENTS

360 grams (3 cups) flour

1 tablespoon baking powder

1 teaspoon salt

113 grams (½ cup) cold unsalted butter, cubed

113 grams (1 cup) grated sharp cheddar cheese

120 grams (8 slices) cooked bacon, chopped

10 grams (¼ cup) chopped chives or 2 green onions, thinly sliced

227 grams (1 cup) buttermilk

DIRECTIONS

1 Preheat the oven to 400 degrees. Line a baking sheet with parchment paper.

2 In a medium bowl, mix the flour, baking powder, and salt. Using a pastry blender, two knives, or your hands, cut the butter into the flour until it has small, pea-sized crumbs. Stir in the cheese, bacon, and chives. Add in the buttermilk and stir to form a dough. If you live in a dryer climate, you may need a little extra buttermilk to form the dough. Don't overmix the dough; use your hands to pull it together and shape a ball.

3 Place the dough onto a floured surface and pat into a 12-inch disk for 8 large scones or into two 10-inch disks for 16 smaller scones. Cut into desired sizes and place onto prepared baking sheet. Bake for 12 to 14 minutes for smaller scones or 18 to 22 minutes for larger scones.

VARY IT!: Kick this up a notch with pepper jack cheese and cracked pepper bacon.

NOTE: Flip to the color insert for a photo of this recipe.

PER SERVING: *Calories 201 (From Fat 106); Fat 12g (Saturated 6g); Cholesterol 28mg; Sodium 240mg; Carbohydrate 18g (Dietary Fiber 1g); Protein 5g.*

Chapter **14**

Rising with Yeast Breads

RECIPES IN THIS CHAPTER

☺ **Basic White Buttermilk Bread**

☺ **Braided Egg Bread**

☺ **Honey-Oatmeal Bread**

☺ **Jeff's Potato Bread**

☺ **Basic Hamburger Buns**

☺ **No-Fail Rolls**

☺ **Crescent Rolls**

☺ **Fluffy Dinner Rolls**

☺ **Sesame-Topped Rolls**

☺ **Molly's Sweet Cardamom Rolls**

Many people get nervous about baking bread from scratch, thinking that you have to have some secret talent to make it rise or come out tasting good. And because bread is so readily available and such a staple for many people, picking up a loaf at a local grocery store or bakery is much easier than making your own from scratch. Although I'm not suggesting that you *never* pick up another store-bought loaf, I must say that, from all the baking I've done over the years, there's nothing better than baking your own bread. Making your own bread is deeply satisfying yet simple. From the relaxing repetition of kneading the dough to the slow, quiet rise to the shaping of the loaves and the heavenly smell of it baking in the oven . . . there's nothing quite like it.

Bread isn't overstated, nor is it decadent. It's simple and basic and has played a major role in history for thousands of years. With the invention of the bread machine, you can make homemade loaves in no time. But to truly experience the wonderful experience of bread making, everyone should bake at least one loaf of bread in their life. Try it once using one of the recipes in this chapter. I'm sure that the loaf you make won't be your last.

Understanding the Role of Yeast Bread Ingredients

Whole books have been dedicated to the art of bread making, and you can bake bread using hundreds of different techniques and doughs. Instead of overwhelming you with too much information, I just want you to know the basics, to lay a good solid foundation upon which you can build your bread-baking knowledge. When you feel comfortable with the mixing, kneading, and rising of basic bread doughs, you can move on to fancier types of loaves and rolls. First, you need to know how all the ingredients work together, in order to have a better understanding about the making of bread.

Yeast

Yeast is the ingredient that makes bread rise. It's a live plant, which, when dissolved in warm water (no more than 110 degrees) and given something to eat, becomes active. Yeast needs food to stay alive. Generally, the sweetener (usually sugar or honey) added to the dough is the yeast's initial food. When the bread is kneaded, more sugar is made in the starch from the flour, which sustains the yeast until it finally dies when it's baked in the oven.

REMEMBER

To ensure that your yeast stays fresh for as long as possible, store it in the refrigerator.

Several different types of yeast are available:

>> **Active dry yeast:** I like to use active dry yeast because it has a longer shelf life and is easier to store than fresh compressed cake yeast. It's available in foil packs or jars coded with an expiration date. One package of active dry yeast contains 1 scant tablespoon (*scant* means "barely"), so if you don't have yeast in the premeasured packages, measure out 1 level tablespoon and then gently shake back just a little.

>> **Bread machine yeast:** Bread machine yeast is designed to dissolve thoroughly when used in conjunction with a bread machine. If you're baking your bread without the use of a bread machine, don't use bread machine yeast.

>> **Compressed cake yeast:** Compressed cake yeast is fresh yeast; its cells aren't dried. Of all the yeasts, it's the powerhouse for rising and making wonderful breads. You can substitute 1 square of fresh compressed cake yeast (available in 0.6-ounce squares) for one ¼-ounce package of active dry yeast.

Don't use compressed cake yeast without proofing it first. (See the nearby sidebar for details on this technique.) Because fresh yeast has a considerably shorter shelf life than active dry yeast, you may find that it's already dead even though the expiration date printed on the wrapper hasn't passed. Bakery supply stores sell the freshest cake yeast.

WARNING

If you're shopping for yeast, you may come across brewer's yeast, which is available in most health-food stores. This yeast is *not* for bread making and shouldn't be substituted for active dry yeast.

OH YEAH? PROOF IT!

Proofing yeast — dissolving it in warm water, sometimes with a little sugar — was once an essential step in baking bread. The foam and distinct odor the yeast produced were "proof" that the yeast was still alive. Because yeast now comes packaged with an expiration date, much of the guesswork is eliminated, but beginning bread bakers may want a sure thing. Feel free to proof your yeast if you want to make sure that it's alive. If you use fresh cake yeast, you must proof it. Because fresh yeast has the shortest shelf life and the most punch, it's easy to proof, and finding out right from the start that the yeast is no longer alive will save you a lot of heartache later.

Don't proof rapid-rise or quick-rise yeast. Because they're designed to make dough rise faster, the proofing stage can use up a lot of their energy and leave them without enough oomph for the rising stage of the dough.

To proof yeast, follow these steps:

1. **Combine 1 tablespoon yeast with ¼ cup warm water (not higher than 110 degrees) and ½ teaspoon sugar.**

2. **Stir well to dissolve the yeast and sugar; then let it rest for about 5 minutes or until it becomes bubbly and foamy.**

   This bubbling foam is proof that the yeast is alive. Proceed with your recipe.

If you decide not to proof your yeast but discover, after many attempts to coax your bread to rise, that the yeast is dead — the dough just lies in the bottom of the bowl, unchanged — don't despair! You can save your bread by adding new yeast. This time, proof the yeast as just described and then knead it into your dead dough. You'll probably have to add some additional flour (just a couple of tablespoons) to get the right consistency again. Knead the dough for a couple of minutes and then set it in a warm, cozy place to rise again. This time, it should work.

Yeast likes to be snug and warm, but not hot. The most common mistake that first-time bread makers make is to kill the yeast by overheating it. One of the first steps in making bread is to dissolve the yeast in warm water — sometimes a temperature is given (not higher than 110 degrees). How can you tell if the water temperature is correct? The most accurate way is to use a thermometer. If you don't have one, you can measure the temperature almost as accurately by feel. Your body temperature is about 98.6 degrees, so if you run the hot water until it's just slightly warm to the touch, but not uncomfortable, that should be about right.

Flour

Flour is the main ingredient in bread. Flours made from wheat contain proteins that, when liquids are added and the dough is kneaded, form gluten. This gluten gives the dough its elasticity, allows the dough to stretch as it traps the gases released by the yeast, and causes the bread to rise. The different varieties of flour that are made from wheat have different amounts of gluten-making proteins, so it's good to know a little about your choices for bread making.

TIP

» **All-purpose enriched white flour:** This type of flour is by far the most common, although it isn't always the best choice for making yeast breads. A mix of hard and soft wheats, this flour has been chemically bleached, which aids in some of the loss of its nutrients and is why it's then enriched with additional vitamins. Because it's *all-purpose,* it's a good flour to have around if you want to make a cake, bread, or cookies, although the results may not be as good as if you chose a flour specifically intended for each purpose (cake flour for cakes and bread flour for bread).

» **Bread flour:** Bread flour is protein-rich white flour made from hard wheat. It's a good choice for bread making because it's a gluten-rich flour that makes a good, elastic dough and gives good volume when your bread rises. Loaves made with bread flour are likely to be a bit tastier, lighter, and better risen than those made with all-purpose flour.

Bread flour absorbs more liquid than all-purpose flour, so you may need less flour if your recipe calls for all-purpose flour and you're using bread flour instead.

» **Self-rising flour:** This flour is all-purpose flour with salt and baking soda mixed in it. I don't recommend it for yeast breads.

» **Unbleached white flour:** Unbleached flour is a mixture of hard and soft wheats and hasn't been chemically whitened. It has a slightly higher protein content and contains more nutrients than all-purpose flour, making it a good choice for baking bread.

>> **Whole-wheat flour:** Commercial whole-wheat flour is milled to include the flour, bran, and germ of the wheat. If a recipe calls for white flour and you want to use whole wheat, try substituting whole-wheat flour for half the amount of white flour. I've had great success substituting half whole-wheat flour for white flour in traditional loaves of bread.

WARNING

Whole-wheat flour produces a much denser loaf of bread and absorbs more liquid than white flour, so if you're substituting whole-wheat flour for white flour, add the minimum amount of flour called for in the recipe and then continue to add more slowly to make sure that you don't toughen the dough.

REMEMBER

A final word about flour: Flours (even the same type and brand) can vary in the amounts of moisture they absorb and contain. That's why you see many bread recipes give a general amount of flour (4 to 6 cups) and leave it up to you to determine how much flour to use that day. Believe it or not, even the weather — whether it's dry or humid outside — can affect how much flour you use in your bread! So pay more attention to how your dough looks than to the cup amount of flour you're adding to your dough. Good dough should have the following characteristics:

>> It should be smooth and elastic.

>> It shouldn't stick to the sides of the bowl nor should it stick to your hands or the countertop.

>> It should give when it's kneaded.

>> It shouldn't be tough.

REMEMBER

Don't pack flour into your measuring cup. Instead, spoon it into the cup to measure it. And always add flour slowly; don't dump all of it in at once.

CONSIDERING SPECIALTY GRAINS

Albeit harder to find on most grocery store shelves, flours like rye, spelt, einkorn, and khorasan (also called Kamut) have their place in bread making. These old-world grains (and grasses — rye!) are lower in gluten, so the breads will have a more dense texture. If you travel to Europe, you'll find all of these flours on the shelves and in the fresh baked breads. Wheat is king in the U.S. market, but it really needs to take seat at the knight's table because these other grains have been around longer, are healthier, and deserve to be used, too. Check out Chapter 19 for more ways to boost nutrition in baked goods.

Sweeteners

The usual sweeteners you find in bread making are sugar and honey. Although the sweetener typically doesn't make the bread sweet like a cake, it does add some flavor and feed the yeast. When the yeast eats the sugar, it begins a fermentation process, which produces the gases that cause the bread to rise. The sweetener also browns during baking, which helps produce a bread with a nice texture and golden-brown crust.

Salt

Salt is quite important in baking bread. It adds flavor, controls yeast growth, and prevents overrising. Salt was always the final ingredient added to the brioche dough we made in the bakery, and I have to admit that, on more than one occasion, we'd forget to add it. Although the omission wasn't apparent, when we went to put the dough into the bowl to rise overnight, the next morning we'd come in to find dough pouring out over the sides of the bowl and a rather flavorless, weakly structured dough. So learn from my mistakes and don't forget to add the salt. That said, don't overdo it, or the salt will inhibit the proper growth of the yeast. Just use the amount called for in the recipe.

Fat

Fat in bread recipes adds to the tenderness and texture of the bread. Fats are also flavor carriers and act as natural preservatives, helping your loaf retain its moisture and stay mold free. Butter adds a bit of color, but you can substitute shortening or lard for butter measure for measure. Some recipes also use vegetable or olive oil.

ALL FLOUR ISN'T CREATED EQUAL

If you've eaten biscuits both above and below the Mason-Dixon line, you may have noticed that the texture of the biscuits made in Pennsylvania differs from the texture of the biscuits made in North Carolina. That's because they're made with different types of wheat. Hard wheat contains more gluten-forming proteins, making it good for yeast breads. It's mostly grown in the United States in Montana, the upper Midwest, and the Southwest. Soft wheat has less gluten but more starch, making it a better choice for biscuits, quick breads, and special fine-textured cakes. It's grown in milder climates in the middle and eastern United States.

Eggs

Eggs aren't essential to baking breads, but some recipes call for them. The addition of eggs produces a richer dough and gives the dough a lovely pale yellow color.

Liquids

The liquid in a bread recipe moistens the flour, which activates the gluten. It also can feed the yeast. Typical liquids found in bread recipes are water, milk, and buttermilk. Water gives bread a brown, crisp crust. Milk gives a velvety, creamy texture to the bread. Buttermilk adds a nice tangy flavor. Yeast dissolves a bit more slowly in milk than in water.

TIP

If you use milk or buttermilk, warm it slightly (so that it's warm to the touch) to remove the chill of the refrigerator before dissolving the yeast in it.

Mixing and Kneading Breads

When you get ready to make bread, it's important to get all your ingredients assembled on the workspace. Typically, a recipe calls for you to dissolve the yeast in a liquid and then add several other ingredients (butter, salt, and sugar) to the yeast. Then you add the flour. These sections delve deeper into what you need to know about mixing and kneading.

Getting a hold on mixing

You can mix doughs in two ways: with a mixer with a dough hook or by hand, which the following sections discuss. Either way, adding the flour slowly is very important. The first 2 to 3 cups will be absorbed quickly into the dough, making a wet, loose batter. Then you start adding the flour in ½-cup intervals and continue mixing until the dough starts to come away from the sides of the bowl.

Using a mixer with a dough hook

If you have a sturdy mixer with a good motor, using it is the easy way to mix bread dough. If you're using a mixer with a dough hook attachment, knead the dough for about 5 minutes on medium speed. Remove the dough from the bowl and finish kneading by hand on a lightly floured surface.

WARNING

Don't use a handheld mixer to mix yeast bread dough. The dough will become too heavy for the motor, and you may burn it out. Unless you have a heavy-duty stand mixer with a dough hook attachment, I recommend mixing the dough by hand. Or, if you have a large enough bowl and a dough blade, you can mix it in a food processor.

Using your elbow grease — Mixing by hand

Mixing bread dough by hand is a little more work, but it has its rewards. When the dough comes away from the sides of the bowl, turn the dough out onto a lightly floured surface. A large wooden cutting board, a clean countertop, or a large slab of marble makes a good kneading surface.

Preparing your work surface

Before you begin kneading, make sure that your work surface is completely dry and that no obstacles are in your way. Put away all your ingredients except the flour, clear off a space, clean it if necessary, make sure that it's dry, and then lightly dust it with flour. Also, rub your hands with a little flour to keep the dough from sticking to them.

TIP

If you're kneading bread on a wooden board and you find that it's slipping or moving on the counter, wet a dishrag and place it between the board and the countertop. That should help steady the board.

Kneading as easy as 1, 2, 3 . . .

Kneading dough develops the gluten and incorporates tiny air pockets into the dough, all of which helps with the rising of the bread and its texture and look. As you knead the dough, you may notice that it still feels a bit sticky or tacky. If so, lightly dust the surface of the dough with additional flour and continue kneading — and dusting — until your dough is finished.

Follow these simple steps to knead dough by hand like a pro:

1. **Turn the dough onto a lightly floured surface.**
2. **Dust the top of the dough with flour.**

   Don't use more than a tablespoon or two of flour for each dusting.

3. **Press the heels of your hands into the top of the dough.**

   You need to use some arm strength, so lean into the dough and push the dough hard into the kneading surface. Sometimes, I link my fingers together, one hand on top of the other, as if I'm giving CPR to the dough. It increases my kneading strength.

4. **Fold the dough in half toward you and press down again with the heels of your hands.**

5. **Give the dough a quarter turn, fold it again, and continue the pushing and kneading with the heels of your hands, always turning the dough and folding it so that all the dough gets worked.**

6. **Continue to lightly dust the dough if it sticks to the board or your hands.**

   Keep up the kneading process for about 10 minutes (3 to 5 minutes if you've used a mixer). If you're kneading by hand, it's unlikely that you'll overwork the dough.

Kneading is a very important step in good bread making, so don't cut corners here. If you get tired and need to rest, that's okay. Just cover the dough with a clean dish towel and rest for 5 minutes. The dough will be glad to rest, too. You'll know you're done when your dough is smooth, elastic, and a bit satiny. If you press into the dough and it springs back, you've done the job correctly. Figure 14-1 shows kneading in action.

Kneading Dough

To knead dough, press down with your palm...

Fold the dough over and rotate ¼ turn

Repeat steps 1 & 2 until dough is soft and elastic.

voila!

FIGURE 14-1:
Kneading bread dough by hand.

© John Wiley & Sons, Inc.

Kneading is actually fun. You can smack, punch, toss, hammer, slam, or abuse your dough however you choose — and it will reward you with good shape and texture. Bread dough is a good thing to take your aggressions out on, and if you make it often enough, you may find that your arms are a bit more toned, and you gain arm strength. If you're a more peaceful-minded baker, you may find yourself in a pleasant rhythmic motion that gives you time to let your mind wander, look out the window, sing along to music, or just sing to yourself.

Encouraging Bread to Rise — Yes, You Can Do It!

After kneading the dough, it's time to set the bread aside to rise. I find that the best bowl for bread rising is a large, heavy ceramic bowl because they seem to be good insulators. Metal or glass bowls may fluctuate with the exterior temperature, but you can use them if you want. Yeast rises best when it's cozy warm, so preheat your bowl by rinsing it out with warm water and drying it thoroughly. Then generously grease the inside of the bowl with softened butter, margarine, or even shortening (just don't use oil). These sections discuss more specifics you need to know.

Getting dough to rise in four easy steps

To increase the chances of your bread dough rising sufficiently, follow these steps:

1. **Form the dough into a ball and place it in the bowl.**

2. **Turn the dough once around the bowl to grease the dough itself.**

3. **Dampen a *clean* dish towel with warm water and drape it over the top of the bowl.**

   If you don't have any clean dish towels available, which I often find to be the case, you can just dampen five or six paper towel squares (don't separate them into individual sheets) and double that over the top of the bowl. You also can very loosely cover (but don't seal) the top of the bowl with plastic wrap. The purpose of the cover is to keep the dough draft-free and prevent anything from entering the dough as it rises, but the dough also needs to breathe, so you don't want to seal it off from air.

4. **Place your bowl into a cold oven (meaning no heat is on) and turn on the oven light.**

   Doing so creates a draft-free place for the dough to stay warm and rise.

Many cooks agree that the best place to let dough rise is in a gas oven, turned off. The heat that the pilot light gives off creates the perfect cozy spot for bread to rise, and the oven itself should be draft-free. If you have an electric oven, you can place your bread to rise there as well. If you have two racks in your electric oven, place a pan of hot water on the bottom rack and the bowl with the bread dough on the upper rack. This creates a slightly warmer environment than the average kitchen countertop. The microwave oven, if it's large enough, is also a good, draft-free choice. First, make sure that the bowl you choose fits in there. You also can place a cup of hot water in the corner of the microwave oven, if it fits, to add a bit of warmth, but doing so is not necessary. Of course, the kitchen countertop is fine, too.

Knowing when the dough is ready

The dough needs to double in size, which usually takes 1 to 1½ hours. Always check it after the minimum amount of time. If you're using rapid-rise yeast, check it after 30 to 40 minutes.

You'll know that your bread has finished rising when you can poke your finger about a half-inch into the dough and the indentation stays. If it springs back, continue letting it rise. Don't allow the dough to more than double in size. If a recipe calls for a second rising, literally punch down the dough, give it a few quick turns in the bowl, re-cover the bowl, and allow the dough to rise again.

If you're going to shape the dough into loaves, punch down the dough and turn it out onto a lightly floured board. Knead the dough again for 2 to 3 minutes. Then divide the dough, if necessary, into the portions you need, letting the dough rest for about 5 minutes before shaping the loaves.

Shaping and Baking the Loaves

If you're making two loaves of bread from one batch of dough, pat or roll the dough out into a rectangle slightly shorter than the loaf pans. Fold the dough in thirds, like a letter, or roll it up like a jelly roll. Tuck the ends under and place it seam side down into the prepared loaf pan, as shown in Figure 14-2. Cover and allow the bread to rise until it just comes up to the side of the pan.

You also can braid bread dough (see Figure 14-3). Divide the dough into three equal portions. Roll out each portion to look like a long snake, a few inches longer than the loaf pan, and braid the three portions together. Tuck the ends under and place the braid into the prepared bread pan to rise.

In the first 15 or so minutes of baking, you'll discover that your bread has an amazing growth spurt during which the yeast gets really active and pushes up the bread before the crust begins to set. Always account for this sudden spurt of growth by not allowing your bread to rise over the top of the pan during the second rising time.

Preparing Dough for a Loaf Pan

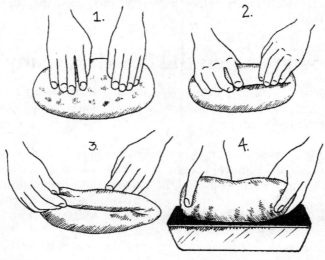

FIGURE 14-2:
Preparing dough
for a loaf pan.

© John Wiley & Sons, Inc.

Braiding Made Easy!

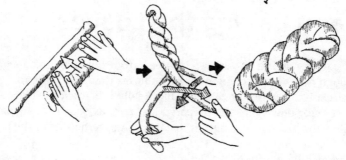

FIGURE 14-3:
Braiding
bread dough.

© John Wiley & Sons, Inc.

REMEMBER

Always bake your bread in a preheated oven. Usually, the baking time given for a recipe is accurate, but if you're unsure, give a thump on the bread (watch out, it will be hot!). If it sounds hollow, it's finished. If you still aren't sure whether it's done, you can go ahead and insert a long wooden skewer into the middle of the loaf. If it comes out clean, your bread is finished. Don't judge doneness by the color of the loaf. If you find that your bread is browning too quickly, cover it with aluminum foil for the last 15 or 20 minutes of baking.

Turn the bread out of the pans onto cooling racks when you remove them from the oven. They should slip out easily. If you want a soft crust, you can brush the top with melted butter.

Let the bread cool for at least 30 minutes before you slice it; otherwise, you run the risk of ruining the bread you've worked so hard to make. If you cut it too soon, the center will be gummy, and the bread will not be set enough to cut and can taste doughy. Always use a serrated knife — a straight edge will press and squash the loaf. If you have trouble making even slices, turn the bread on its side and cut it by using very light pressure. Pressing too hard will crush the loaf.

Baking Yeast Bread Recipes

Yeast breads are some of the most satisfying foods you can bake. Few things are as welcoming as a home filled with the aroma of freshly baked bread. Try your hand at some of the breads in this section, and you'll discover how satisfying and agreeable baking bread can be.

REMEMBER

Yeast breads do require a time commitment — usually you need to put aside a few hours to allow for the rising and baking.

Loaves

Loaves are the easiest breads to make; just shape the dough into a loaf shape and voilà! But if you want to get fancy, this section also contains a recipe for a lovely braided egg bread.

Basic White Buttermilk Bread

PREP TIME: 25 MIN PLUS 90 MIN FOR RISING	BAKING TIME: 35 MIN	YIELD: 2 LOAVES (ABOUT 24 SERVINGS)

INGREDIENTS

59 grams (¼ cup) warm water (not above 115 degrees)

7 grams (one package) active dry yeast

2 tablespoons sugar

57 grams (¼ cup/½ stick) butter, melted and cooled to lukewarm

454 grams (2 cups) buttermilk, at room temperature

600 to 720 grams (5 to 6 cups) bread flour

1 teaspoon salt

¼ teaspoon baking soda

DIRECTIONS

1 In a large mixing bowl, combine the water, yeast, and sugar. Stir with a whisk to dissolve the yeast. Add the melted butter to the buttermilk and mix it into the yeast mixture.

2 In a separate bowl, mix together 5 cups of the flour, the salt, and the baking soda; mix it into the yeast mixture to form a dough (add up to 1 cup additional flour, if necessary).

3 Knead the dough on a lightly floured surface until smooth and elastic, about 10 minutes.

4 Place the dough in a buttered bowl, cover, and set it in a warm place to rise until doubled, about 1 hour.

5 Grease two 9-x-5-inch loaf pans. Punch down the dough and knead it again for about 1 minute. Divide the dough in half and shape it into two loaves. Place them in the prepared pans, cover, and let rise in a warm place until the dough just barely reaches the edge of the pan, about 30 minutes.

6 Preheat the oven to 350 degrees. Bake the bread until it's browned and crusty, about 35 minutes. Cool the bread on wire racks.

VARY IT!: If you don't have buttermilk on hand, you can substitute whole milk.

PER SERVING: Calories 100 (From Fat 17); Fat 2g (Saturated 1g); Cholesterol 4mg; Sodium 99mg; Carbohydrate 17g (Dietary Fiber 1g); Protein 3g.

🍅 Braided Egg Bread

PREP TIME: 30 MIN PLUS 90 MIN FOR RISING	BAKING TIME: 40 MIN	YIELD: 2 LARGE LOAVES (ABOUT 16 TO 18 SERVINGS)

INGREDIENTS

590 grams (2½ cups) warm water (not above 115 degrees)

7 grams (one package) active dry yeast

168 grams (½ cup) honey or sugar

57 grams (¼ cup/½ stick)butter, melted

2 eggs

1 tablespoon salt

840 to 960 grams (7 to 8 cups) bread flour

DIRECTIONS

1 Place the water in a large bowl and sprinkle in the yeast. Whisk to dissolve. Whisk in the honey or sugar, butter, eggs, and salt. Slowly add the flour, stirring with the whisk until it gets too thick; then use your hands until a kneadable dough forms (add up to 1 cup additional flour, if necessary).

2 Transfer the dough to a lightly floured surface and knead until the dough is smooth and elastic, adding flour when necessary.

3 Place the dough in a buttered bowl, cover, and let it rise in a warm place until it doubles in bulk, about 1 hour and 15 minutes.

4 Punch down the dough and knead it for 1 minute more. Divide the dough in half. Then divide each half into 3 equal pieces. Let the dough rest for about 5 minutes.

5 Roll out the pieces into logs about 1½ inches thick.

6 Braid three of the logs together. Repeat with the remaining three logs so that you end up with two braids. Tuck the ends under and set the braids on a greased baking sheet. Let rise for another 30 to 40 minutes.

7 Preheat the oven to 350 degrees. Bake the bread for about 40 minutes, until golden brown. When you thump it, it should sound hollow. Cool the loaves on wire racks. Let them cool for at least 30 minutes before serving.

(continued)

NOTE: If you're looking to try just one bread recipe, this should be the one. It's so versatile and durable that it would be hard to make a mistake. See the color insert for a photo.

TIP: For a shiny loaf, beat an egg with a little water and brush it over the top of the loaves just before they go into the oven.

VARY IT! If you don't want to braid your bread, shape the two halves into loaves and place them in greased 9-x-5-inch loaf pans. Cover and let rise until the dough just reaches the edges of the pans, about 30 minutes. Then bake as directed.

PER SERVING: *Calories 142 (From Fat 20); Fat 2g (Saturated 1g); Cholesterol 17mg; Sodium 223mg; Carbohydrate 26g (Dietary Fiber 1g); Protein 4g.*

🍑 Honey-Oatmeal Bread

PREP TIME: 45 MIN PLUS 90 MIN FOR RISING	BAKING TIME: 35 MIN	YIELD: 2 LOAVES (ABOUT 24 SERVINGS)

INGREDIENTS

472 grams (2 cups) simmering water

89 grams (1 cup) quick-cooking oatmeal (not instant)

28 grams (2 tablespoons) butter

7 grams (one package) active dry yeast

118 grams (½ cup) warm water (not above 115 degrees)

252 grams (¾ cup) honey or maple syrup

600 to 840 grams (5 to 7 cups) flour

2 teaspoons salt

DIRECTIONS

1 Combine the water, oatmeal, and butter in a small bowl and let stand until it's cool to the touch, about 30 minutes.

2 In a small bowl, combine the yeast, warm water, and honey or maple syrup. Stir to dissolve and let stand for about 5 minutes (the water should be foamy).

3 Measure 5 cups of the flour and the salt into a mixing bowl. Add the oatmeal and yeast mixture and stir, adding more flour if necessary, until the mixture forms a kneadable dough (add up to 2 cups additional flour, if necessary).

4 Knead the dough on a lightly floured surface, adding more flour if the dough gets sticky, until the dough is smooth and elastic and springs back when you touch it, about 10 minutes.

5 Place the dough in a buttered bowl, cover, and set in a warm place to rise until doubled, about 1 hour.

6 Grease two 9-x-5-inch loaf pans. Punch down the dough and knead it again for about 1 minute. Divide the dough in half and shape into two loaves. Place them in the prepared pans, cover, and let rise until the dough barely reaches the edges of the pans, about 30 minutes.

7 Preheat the oven to 375 degrees. Bake the bread until it's browned and crusty, about 35 minutes. Cool the bread on wire racks.

PER SERVING: *Calories 112 (From Fat 10); Fat 1g (Saturated 1g); Cholesterol 2mg; Sodium 146mg; Carbohydrate 23g (Dietary Fiber 1g); Protein 3g.*

❧ Jeff's Potato Bread

PREP TIME: 35 MIN PLUS 90 MIN FOR RISING	BAKING TIME: 35 TO 45 MIN	YIELD: 2 LOAVES (ABOUT 24 SERVINGS)

INGREDIENTS

7 grams (one package) active dry yeast

118 grams (½ cup) lukewarm water (not above 115 degrees)

105 grams (½ cup plus 1 teaspoon) sugar

236 grams (1 cup) milk, warmed (not above 115 degrees)

236 grams (1 cup) warm mashed potatoes (instant is okay)

95 grams (½ cup) shortening, melted and cooled

2 eggs, beaten

2 teaspoons salt

720 to 840 grams (6 to 7 cups) bread flour

DIRECTIONS

1 Dissolve the yeast in the warm water with 1 teaspoon of the sugar and let stand for about 10 minutes.

2 In a large mixing bowl, combine the warm milk with the mashed potatoes and shortening. Add the beaten eggs to the potato mixture. Add the yeast mixture and stir to combine. Add the ½ cup sugar and the salt to the mixture. Mix in enough flour to make a kneadable dough.

3 Knead the dough on a lightly floured surface until it is smooth and elastic, adding additional flour if the dough gets sticky, about 10 minutes. Place the dough in a buttered bowl, cover, and set it in a warm place to rise until doubled, about 1 hour.

4 Grease two 9-x-5-inch loaf pans. Punch down the dough and knead it again for about 1 minute on a lightly floured surface. Divide the dough in half and shape it into two loaves. Place the loaves in the prepared pans, cover, and let rise until the dough barely reaches the tops of the pans, about 30 minutes.

5 Preheat the oven to 350 degrees. Bake the bread until it's browned and crusty, 35 to 45 minutes. Remove the loaves from the pans and cool on wire racks.

PER SERVING: *Calories 150 (From Fat 39); Fat 4g (Saturated 1g); Cholesterol 15mg; Sodium 171mg; Carbohydrate 24g (Dietary Fiber 1g); Protein 4g.*

Buns and rolls

What exactly is the difference between a bun and a roll? Is there a difference? Really it's all in what you call it. Buns are often round and are vessels for serving hamburgers, hotdogs, or sandwich toppings. Rolls are usually smaller in shape and either round or shaped into a variety of forms. You can take bread recipes, divide the dough into equal parts, and shape into round rolls for baking. In some parts of the world people say *cinnamon buns* and other places people call them *cinnamon rolls*. Whatever you prefer to call them is fine. In this book, I refer to *rolls* as something that is served alongside a meal and buns as a way to deliver the meal.

In this section, you can find recipes for a variety, ranging from hamburger buns to basic dinner rolls and sticky-sweet cardamom rolls. Yum!

Basic Hamburger Buns

PREP TIME: 25 MIN PLUS 105 MIN FOR RISING	BAKING TIME: 15 MIN	YIELD: 8 SERVINGS

INGREDIENTS

245 grams (1 cup) whole milk

114 grams (½ cup) unsalted butter

12 grams (1 tablespoon) sugar

7 grams (one package) active dry yeast

480 grams (4 cups) flour

2 eggs

8 grams (1½ teaspoons) kosher salt

DIRECTIONS

1 Place the butter into a heat-safe bowl and microwave for 1 minute; stir and heat for 30 seconds until melted. Pour the milk into the bowl of a stand mixer with dough hook attached or by hand with a rubber spatula. Add in the melted butter and stir. Mix the sugar and yeast. Let mixture rest for 5 minutes.

2 Add in the remaining ingredients. Mix on speed 2 for 8 minutes, or for 12 minutes with a dough spatula or rubber spatula. The dough will be sticky. Cover the bowl with a damp tea towel and allow the mixture to rise for 1 hour in a warm, draft-free spot.

3 Place a piece of parchment paper onto a heavy baking sheet. Remove the dough to a lightly floured surface and divide the dough into 8 portions for regular hamburger buns and into 12 for smaller sliders. Form the portions of dough into a ball shape. Gently pull a piece toward the center and then rotate the dough ¼ turn, repeating until the dough shape tightens. Pinch the seam at the top and rock the ball in a circular motion on the flat surface to smooth the ball shape. Next, flatten the dough into a 4-inch round. Place the round onto the parchment paper and repeat with remaining pieces of dough.

4 Cover the shaped buns with the tea towel and allow the breads to rise for 45 minutes.

5 Preheat the oven to 350 degrees. Bake the buns for 15 to 20 minutes or until golden brown and an internal temperature of 200 degrees is reached. Allow the bread to cool for at least 30 minutes prior to slicing.

TIP: Sticky doughs are the trick. Avoid adding too much flour. Use a scale when measuring ingredients and baking breads.

TIP: Brush the tops with an egg wash and top with sesame seeds for a sesame topped bun.

NOTE: This recipe can be used to make hotdog buns or rolls. To shape a hot dog bun, divide into 10 pieces, create a ball, and then shape into mini baguettes. I like my hotdog buns about 6 inches in length. Rise and bake like you would hamburger buns.

PER SERVING: Calories 363 (From Fat 129); Fat 14g (Saturated 8g); Cholesterol 86mg; Sodium 469mg; Carbohydrate 49g (Dietary Fiber 2g); Protein 9g.

⏱ No-Fail Rolls

PREP TIME: 20 MIN PLUS 1HR AND 20 MIN FOR RISING	BAKING TIME: 10 TO 15 MIN	YIELD: 2 TO 3 DOZEN ROLLS

INGREDIENTS

7 grams (one package) active dry yeast

236 grams (1 cup) warm water (not above 115 degrees)

2 eggs, beaten

67 grams (⅓ cup) sugar

1 teaspoon salt

67 grams (⅓ cup) oil or melted shortening

420 to 540 grams (3½ to 4½ cups) bread flour or all-purpose flour

DIRECTIONS

1   In a large bowl, dissolve the yeast in the warm water. Mix in the eggs, sugar, salt, and oil. Mix in the flour, 1 cup at a time, and stir well until a kneadable dough is formed. Knead the dough on a lightly floured surface, about 10 minutes, until it's smooth and elastic. Place the dough in a buttered bowl, cover, and let rise until doubled in size, about 1 hour.

2   Punch the center of the dough to let the air out. Form the dough into 24 to 36 rolls by pinching off pieces of dough about the size of a walnut and rolling them lightly on a floured surface. Place them about 2 inches apart on ungreased baking sheets. Cover and let rise until doubled in size, about 20 minutes.

3   While the rolls are rising, preheat the oven to 400 degrees.

4   Bake the rolls until golden brown, about 10 to 15 minutes. Serve warm.

PER SERVING: *Calories 116 (From Fat 34); Fat 4g (Saturated 0g); Cholesterol 18mg; Sodium 103mg; Carbohydrate 17g (Dietary Fiber 1g); Protein 3g.*

☙ Crescent Rolls

PREP TIME: 30 MIN PLUS 1 HR AND 40 MIN FOR RISING	BAKING TIME: 12 MIN	YIELD: 3 DOZEN ROLLS

INGREDIENTS

7 grams (one package) active dry yeast

59 grams (¼ cup) lukewarm water (not above 115 degrees)

236 grams (1 cup) milk

100 grams (½ cup) sugar

1 teaspoon salt

57 grams (¼ cup/½ stick) butter, cut into 4 pieces

600 to 720 grams (5 to 6 cups) bread flour or all-purpose flour

2 eggs

85 grams (6 tablespoons) melted butter, for brushing the dough

DIRECTIONS

1 Dissolve the yeast in the warm water with a pinch of sugar. Set aside for 5 to 10 minutes to proof, until the surface becomes a little frothy.

2 While the yeast is proofing, warm the milk (don't boil) in a 2-quart saucepan. Remove the pan from the heat and pour the milk into a large mixing bowl. Stir in the sugar, salt, and ¼ cup butter. Cool the mixture to lukewarm, about 3 minutes. Add about 1½ cups of the flour to the milk to make a thick batter. Mix well. Add the yeast mixture and eggs to the flour mixture and stir well. Add enough of the remaining flour to make a soft dough.

3 Turn the dough out onto a lightly floured surface; knead until smooth and satiny, about 10 minutes. Place the dough in a buttered bowl, cover, and let it rise in a warm place until doubled in size, about 1 hour.

4 When the dough has finished rising, punch it down and knead for about 1 minute more. Turn out the dough onto a lightly floured board. Divide the dough into three equal pieces. Let the dough rest for about 10 minutes (this makes it easier to roll out the dough). Roll each piece into a 12-inch circle. If you find that the dough is shrinking and won't hold the shape you roll it into, let the dough rest for 5 minutes more. Brush the dough lightly with melted butter and cut it into 12 pie-shaped pieces. Roll up tightly, beginning at the wide end. Seal the points firmly.

5 Place the rolls on greased baking sheets, with points underneath, about 2 inches apart. Curve to form crescents and cover. Let rise in a warm place until doubled in bulk, about 30 minutes.

6 Preheat the oven to 400 degrees. Brush the crescents lightly with the melted butter. Bake until golden brown, about 12 minutes.

PER SERVING: *Calories 117 (From Fat 36); Fat 4g (Saturated 2g); Cholesterol 21mg; Sodium 72mg; Carbohydrate 17g (Dietary Fiber 1g); Protein 3g.*

Fluffy Dinner Rolls

PREP TIME: 30 MIN PLUS 90 MIN FOR RISING	BAKING TIME: 30 TO 40 MIN	YIELD: 2 DOZEN ROLLS

INGREDIENTS

720 to 840 grams (6 to 7 cups) flour

75 grams (6 tablespoons) sugar

1¼ teaspoons salt

7 grams (one package) active dry yeast

530 grams (2¼ cups) warm water (not above 115 degrees)

38 grams (3 tablespoons) vegetable oil

DIRECTIONS

1 In a large mixing bowl, combine 6 cups of the flour, 5 tablespoons of the sugar, and the salt.

2 In a medium mixing bowl, dissolve the yeast and the remaining 1 tablespoon sugar in the warm water. Let stand for about 5 minutes until the top gets a bit foamy. Stir in the vegetable oil. Slowly add the yeast mixture to the flour mixture and mix until it's thoroughly incorporated.

3 Remove the dough from the bowl and knead, adding the remaining cup of flour if the dough gets sticky, and kneading until the dough is smooth and satiny and springs back when you touch it, about 10 minutes.

4 Place the dough in a large, buttered bowl. Cover and let rise in a warm place until the dough has doubled in bulk, about 1 hour.

5 Punch down the dough and knead it for about 1 more minute. Pinch off enough dough to make a 1½-inch ball. Roll the dough into a ball and place it in a greased 13-x-9-inch baking pan. Repeat with the remaining dough until you have about 24 balls. They can touch each other in the pan and fit snugly against the sides. Cover and let rise until doubled in bulk, about 30 minutes.

6 Preheat the oven to 350 degrees. Bake the rolls for about 30 to 40 minutes, until golden brown and fluffy.

PER SERVING: *Calories 143 (From Fat 18); Fat 2g (Saturated 0g); Cholesterol 0mg; Sodium 122mg; Carbohydrate 27g (Dietary Fiber 1g); Protein 4g.*

Sesame–Topped Rolls

PREP TIME: 30 MIN PLUS 1 TO 2 HRS FOR RISING	BAKING TIME: 20 MIN	YIELD: 4 DOZEN ROLLS

INGREDIENTS

7 grams (one package) active dry yeast (don't use rapid rise yeast)

236 grams (1 cup) warm water (not above 115 degrees)

236 grams (1 cup) warm milk

840 to 960 grams (7 to 8 cups) bread flour

1 tablespoon salt

½ teaspoon ground ginger

2 eggs, beaten

67 grams (⅓ cup) sugar

63 grams (⅓ cup) shortening, at room temperature

Melted butter or beaten egg for brushing

Sesame seeds for garnish

DIRECTIONS

1 In a large mixing bowl, dissolve the yeast in the water and warm milk. Let stand for 5 minutes. Stir 3 cups of the flour, the salt, and the ginger into the yeast mixture. Beat well; let stand covered for 20 minutes (it will be foamy).

2 Add the beaten eggs, sugar, shortening, and the remaining flour, mixing to make a kneadable dough (the dough will be somewhat soft). Knead the dough on a floured surface, adding a little more flour if it becomes sticky, until it's smooth and elastic, about 10 minutes. Place the dough in a large, buttered bowl, cover, and let it rise in a warm place for about 1 hour.

3 Punch down the dough, turn it onto a floured board, and knead it for 1 minute. Put it back in the bowl and let it rise a second time, about 40 minutes. Punch down the dough again, turn it out onto the floured board, and knead it again for about 1 minute.

4 Preheat the oven to 350 degrees. Grease two baking sheets. Pinch off pieces of dough slightly larger than a walnut. Roll out each piece into a rope, 6 or 7 inches long, and tie it into a loose knot; place the ropes on the prepared baking sheet about 2 inches apart. Brush the tops of the rolls with melted butter or beaten egg. Sprinkle with sesame seeds. Cover and let rise until doubled, about 20 minutes.

5 Bake for 20 minutes. Serve warm.

NOTE: Flip to the color insert for a photo of this recipe.

PER SERVING: Calories 102 (From Fat 22); Fat 3g (Saturated 1g); Cholesterol 15mg; Sodium 152mg; Carbohydrate 16g (Dietary Fiber 1g); Protein 3g.

🍅 Molly's Sweet Cardamom Rolls

PREP TIME: 45 MIN PLUS 2 HRS FOR RISING	BAKING TIME: 15 TO 20 MIN	YIELD: 3 DOZEN ROLLS

INGREDIENTS

14 grams (two packages) active dry yeast

59 grams (¼ cup) lukewarm water

400 grams (2 cups) sugar

472 grams (2 cups) milk, slightly warmed

27 grams (½ cup) instant mashed potato flakes

5 eggs, slightly beaten

1 teaspoon salt

1¼ teaspoon cardamom

1,080 to 1,200 grams (9 to 10 cups) flour

227 grams (1 cup/2 sticks) butter, melted and cooled

106 grams (½ cup brown sugar, lightly packed

1 tablespoon cinnamon

Additional melted butter or beaten eggs, if desired

DIRECTIONS

1   Grease two 13-x-9-inch glass baking dishes. Dissolve the yeast in the lukewarm water. Add ¼ cup of the sugar. Let stand for 8 to 10 minutes. Add the yeast mixture to the warm milk in a large, warm bowl. Add the remaining 1¾ cups sugar, potato flakes, eggs, salt, 1 teaspoon of the cardamom, and half the flour (the dough will be very loose). Cover and let stand until doubled, about 30 to 45 minutes.

2   Add the remaining flour, 1 cup at a time, and ½ cup of the butter. Knead the dough on a lightly floured surface until it's smooth and elastic, about 10 minutes. Place the dough in a buttered bowl, cover, and let rise until doubled again, about 1 hour.

3   In a small bowl, combine the brown sugar, cinnamon, and the remaining ½ teaspoon cardamom. Sprinkle your work surface lightly with flour. Divide the dough into three parts. Roll the dough into a large rectangle, about 12 x 18 and ¼-inch thick. Brush with some of the remaining melted butter; sprinkle with 2½ tablespoons of the brown sugar mixture. Fold the dough over and cut it into twelve 1-inch-thick strips. Take one end of the strip in each hand and twist. Then take each twisted strip and twist it around so that it looks like a round sticky bun.

4   Place the bun in the prepared baking dishes. Repeat with the remaining pieces of dough; fit three rows of six with sides of the rolls touching. Let them rise until doubled, about 30 minutes. Preheat the oven to 350 degrees. Brush the tops of the rolls with any remaining melted butter or beaten egg, if desired. Sprinkle the rolls with any remaining sugar mixture before baking. Bake until golden brown, about 15 to 20 minutes.

PER SERVING: *Calories 236 (From Fat 59); Fat 7g (Saturated 4g); Cholesterol 45mg; Sodium 84mg; Carbohydrate 40g (Dietary Fiber 1g); Protein 5g.*

» Turning out chicken potpies just like Grandma's

» Creating custom-made pizzas and calzones

Chapter **15**

Going Savory with Baked Goods

RECILES IN THIS CHAPTER

🍳 **Cheese Soufflé**

Chicken Potpie

Potato-Beef Potpie

🍳 **Goat Cheese and Tomato Tart**

🍳 **Weeknight Pizza Dough**

🍳 **Calzones**

🍳 **Broccoli and Cheese Quiche with Potato Crust**

When most people think of baked goods, cakes and pies generally come to mind. However, savory baked goods offer a host of options for the baker. Soufflés, potpies, vegetable tarts, and pizzas are a perfect start into savory baking — they're comfort foods for some, and long-standing favorites for others. What's great about all the recipes in this chapter is that they're basic templates for a grander foray into savories. You can enhance many of the recipes by adding whatever ingredients are your favorites. (I make a few suggestions in the recipes where appropriate, to get you started.)

Whipping Up Soufflés

If you've never made a soufflé, you should try it at least once. It isn't hard — I promise! The only special equipment you need is a straight-sided soufflé pan and an electric beater to whip up the egg whites. I used to think that it took some major talent to make a soufflé. Then I practiced a few times and made several mistakes, and now the soufflé always comes out great. I soon discovered that the soufflé is a forgiving dish — plus, it's impressive for company and inexpensive to make.

TECHNICAL STUFF

Soufflé, in French, means "to blow," which explains how soufflés rise. The egg whites capture air, and that air expands when it's heated. The straight sides of the pan allow the soufflé to rise straight up and be quite an impressive sight. If the bubbles grow too much, the soufflé can collapse on itself (the walls of the bubbles will break down and not hold its shape), but that rarely happens. However, every soufflé will deflate after it's taken out of the oven. It won't happen immediately, but if it sits out for 10 to 15 minutes, it will deflate — but it still tastes good!

In France, they say that people wait for the soufflé, but the soufflé waits for no one. This is true, so be sure that everyone is assembled around the table before taking your soufflé from the oven.

TIP

You can hold a prepared soufflé up to 2 hours in the refrigerator before you bake it.

Be sure to grease the dish well or half your dish will be ruined because it will stick to the sides of the pan. You can use flour or breadcrumbs to dust the inside of the soufflé dish for extra protection against sticking. One last thing: When you stir in the egg yolks and cheese, the mixture will be a little lumpy because the cheese won't melt entirely. That's okay. You want it that way.

WARNING

Unless you have two soufflé dishes, I don't recommend doubling soufflé recipes. They'll overflow and make a huge mess in your oven (trust me, I've tried it, and it's a big stinky mess).

Cheese Soufflé

PREP TIME: 20 MIN	BAKING TIME: 45 MIN TO 1 HR	YIELD: 3 TO 4 SERVINGS

INGREDIENTS

43 grams (3 tablespoons) butter

23 grams (3 tablespoons) flour

240 grams (1 cup) milk, at room temperature

5 eggs, separated

62 grams (¾ cup) grated Swiss cheese, lightly packed

1 teaspoon plus a pinch of salt

½ teaspoon black pepper

½ teaspoon ground nutmeg

DIRECTIONS

1 Preheat the oven to 350 degrees. Oil a 2-quart soufflé dish.

2 In a 2-quart saucepan, melt the butter over medium heat. When the butter has melted, whisk in the flour to absorb the butter. Continue whisking for 1 minute (to cook out any flour taste — it's okay if the flour browns a little).

3 Slowly add the milk in a thin stream, whisking constantly. If the mixture gets lumpy, keep whisking until smooth and the milk begins to thicken, about 2 minutes. Remove the pan from the heat. Stir in the egg yolks, cheese, 1 teaspoon salt, pepper, and nutmeg. Set aside.

4 In a large bowl, beat the egg whites with the pinch of salt until they hold stiff peaks. (See Chapter 5 for information on whipping egg whites.) Transfer about one-quarter of the egg whites to the cheese mixture and stir it in to lighten up the mixture. Fold the remaining egg whites into the cheese mixture (don't stir or else you'll deflate the whites) and transfer the mixture into the prepared soufflé pan.

5 Bake for 45 minutes to 1 hour, until the soufflé has risen and a thin straw inserted into the center of the soufflé comes out clean.

VARY IT: You can add other ingredients, such as spinach, bacon, cooked onion, or even pureed pumpkin, to the egg yolk mixture and folded into the egg whites. Just make sure that the onion and bacon are chopped finely and the spinach is wilted, squeezed dry, and chopped before you stir them in. You can add about ¼ to ½ cup of the ingredient you desire.

TIP: Figure 15-1 shows how to fold the egg whites into the soufflé batter.

PER SERVING: Calories 308 (From Fat 204); Fat 23g (Saturated 12g); Cholesterol 316mg; Sodium 779mg; Carbohydrate 9g (Dietary Fiber 0g); Protein 16g.

How to Fold Egg Whites into a Soufflé Base

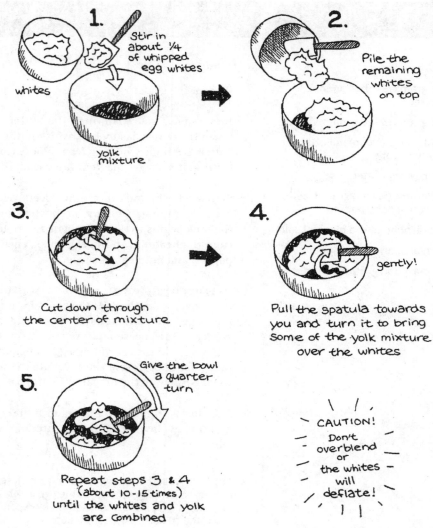

1. Stir in about ¼ of whipped egg whites

whites

yolk mixture

2. Pile the remaining whites on top

3. Cut down through the center of mixture

4. Pull the spatula towards you and turn it to bring some of the yolk mixture over the whites

gently!

5. Give the bowl a quarter turn

Repeat steps 3 & 4 (about 10-15 times) until the whites and yolk are combined

CAUTION! Don't overblend or the whites will deflate!

© John Wiley & Sons, Inc.

FIGURE 15-1: Folding egg whites into soufflé batter.

Baking Tasty Potpies and Tarts

Potpies seem to be back in fashion with the revolution of comfort foods. Potpies can be custom-made to your liking. Simply add the veggies and meat you like and make a savory sauce. The crust bakes on top. You have a hearty, filling meal without much work.

Tarts similarly use pastry crusts but on the bottom. Tarts can be both savory or sweet depending on the filling. Savory tarts are simple to pull together, elegant in aesthetics, and are the perfect addition to a brunch or serve with a salad for light meal.

Chicken Potpie

PREP TIME: 25 MIN	BAKING TIME: 45 MIN TO 1 HR	YIELD: 4 TO 6 SERVINGS

INGREDIENTS

113 grams (½ cup/1 stick) butter

60 grams (½ cup) flour

113 grams (½ cups) buttermilk

480 grams (2 cups) chicken broth

1 tablespoon olive oil

1 medium onion, diced

1 clove garlic, crushed

3 carrots, peeled and sliced on the diagonal

2 ribs celery, diced

1 small potato, peeled and chopped

12 ounces (about 2 cups) cooked chicken, shredded

73 grams (½ cup) frozen peas

87 grams (½ cup) frozen corn

1 teaspoon chopped fresh or dried rosemary

1 teaspoon black pepper

1 teaspoon salt

245 grams (½ package [17¼ ounces]) frozen puff pastry (1 sheet), thawed

DIRECTIONS

1 Preheat the oven to 375 degrees. In a large saucepan, melt the butter over medium heat. Stir in the flour with a whisk and continue whisking for 1 minute; it is okay if the flour browns a little. Turn off the heat.

2 Slowly pour in the buttermilk, followed by the chicken broth, whisking constantly, until smooth. Cook over medium heat, whisking occasionally, until the mixture begins to thicken, about 5 minutes.

3 While the sauce is thickening, heat the oil in a large skillet over medium heat. Add the onion, garlic, carrots, celery, and potato. Cook, stirring often, until the onions are just tender, about 5 minutes (the carrots and potato will still be firm).

4 In a 3- or 4-quart casserole, combine the chicken, peas, corn, rosemary, pepper, and salt, with the vegetables from the skillet. Stir to combine. Pour the thickened sauce over the chicken mixture and stir to combine.

5 Unwrap the puff pastry, roll it out, and cut it to fit the casserole, leaving a 1-inch over-hang (this will anchor the crust in place). Cover the casserole top with the puff pastry. Cut slits in the top for vents. Bake for 45 minutes to 1 hour, until the pastry is brown and the potpie is bubbly. Cool for 10 minutes before serving.

TIP: If you want to make the recipe even easier, you can use a 10-ounce package of frozen vegetables instead of the carrots, peas, and corn.

PER SERVING: *Calories 636 (From Fat 369); Fat 41g (Saturated 14g); Cholesterol 84mg; Sodium 978mg; Carbohydrate 44g (Dietary Fiber 4g); Protein 23g.*

Potato-Beef Potpie

INGREDIENTS

55 grams (¼ cup) vegetable oil

680 grams (1½ pounds) chuck steak, cut into ½-inch pieces

1 medium onion, chopped

53 grams (½ cup) chopped celery

2 medium carrots, sliced ¼-inch thick

249 grams (1 cup) red wine

508 grams (2 cups) beef broth or water

3 tablespoons cornstarch

3 tablespoons cold water

73 grams (½ cup) frozen peas

87 grams (½ cup) frozen corn

63 grams (½ cup) frozen green beans

1 teaspoon black pepper

1 teaspoon salt

2 large baking potatoes, peeled and sliced thick (½ inch)

DIRECTIONS

1 Preheat the oven to 300 degrees. Heat the oil in a large oven-proof Dutch oven over medium-high heat. Add the steak in batches (do not crowd the pan) and brown, about 3 minutes per batch. Remove the steak from the pan, place in a bowl, and set aside. Repeat with the remaining beef.

2 Using the same pot, reduce the heat to medium and cook the onion, celery, and carrots until just tender, about 7 minutes. Add the wine and beef broth.

3 Dissolve the cornstarch in the cold water. Slowly add the cornstarch mixture to the broth mixture and bring to a boil. Reduce the heat and stir until thickened, 4 to 5 minutes.

4 Stir in the browned beef with any accumulated juices, the peas, corn, green beans, pepper, and salt. Arrange the potato slices on top of the beef mixture. Cover and bake for 45 minutes. Remove the cover and bake for 45 minutes longer.

TIP: Ovenproof means that the cookware can be used on top of the stove as well as in the oven. If you don't have an ovenproof Dutch oven, pre-pare the recipe as directed using a large saucepan or Dutch oven but before baking, transfer the contents to a 3- to 4-quart casserole dish to bake.

PER SERVING: *Calories 285 (From Fat 151); Fat 17g (Saturated 5g); Cholesterol 47mg; Sodium 485mg; Carbohydrate 17g (Dietary Fiber 2g); Protein 17g.*

Goat Cheese and Tomato Tart

INGREDIENTS

210 grams (1½ cups) all-purpose flour

125 grams (4½ ounces) cold unsalted butter, cubed

1 teaspoon salt

1 egg

3 tablespoons ice-cold water

2 tablespoons mayonnaise

3 large ripe tomatoes, thinly sliced

1 tablespoon minced fresh thyme leaves

125 grams (½ cup) crumbled goat cheese (chevre)

½ teaspoon sea salt

½ teaspoon cracked pepper

28 grams (2 tablespoons) extra virgin olive oil

DIRECTIONS

1 Preheat the oven to 425 degrees with a baking sheet in the oven. Grease a 12-inch tart pan.

2 In a medium bowl, mix the flour, butter, and salt. Using a pastry blender or two knives, cut the butter into the flour until it resembles cornmeal. Stir in the egg and ice-cold water. Form into a ball. Place the ball onto a floured surface and gently roll into a 14-inch circle. Place the dough into the tart pan and work the dough into the grooves. This doesn't need to be perfect and can have a rustic appearance. Brush the dough with mayonnaise and set aside.

3 Place the sliced tomatoes onto a tea towel and gently pat the surface to remove the excessive moisture. Place the tomatoes in the tart pan, overlapping the tomatoes as needed. Top the tomatoes with thyme, goat cheese, salt, and pepper. Place the tart pan on the preheated baking sheet and bake the tart for 30 minutes.

4 Drizzle the top of the tart with olive oil and serve warm or at room temperature.

TIP: Use tomatoes when they're at peak season.

NOTE: Refer to the color insert for a photo of this recipe.

PER SERVING: *Calories 273 (From Fat 176); Fat 20g (Saturated 10g); Cholesterol 59mg; Sodium 405mg; Carbohydrate 19g (Dietary Fiber 1g); Protein 6g.*

Going Italian — Calzones and Pizzas

Pizzas and calzones are easy to make. You may find that they're perfect to serve if you're inviting a group of people over who all like a variety of different things. If you have the ingredients ready, it's so simple to let all your guests make their own pizzas or calzones. You'll save yourself a bunch of work, and everyone will love what they've created. Consider using some of the following:

>> Sautéed vegetables, such as mushrooms, bell peppers, onions, broccoli, zucchini, or eggplant

>> Black and green olives

>> Marinated artichoke hearts

>> Sun-dried tomatoes packed in oil

>> Steamed spinach

>> Gorgonzola or feta cheese

>> Fresh tomato slices

>> Diced cooked ham, sliced pepperoni, cooked ground beef, or shredded cooked chicken

Believe it or not, you can also freeze the pizza dough. Let it rise once, punch it down, and then wrap it in an airtight wrap. Then, when you want to make pizza, let the dough thaw in the refrigerator or at room temperature, and you'll have fresh pizza whenever you want it.

TIP

Defrost a 1-pound loaf of frozen bread dough if you don't want to make your own pizza dough. Or you can even purchase a ready-made crust and just add the toppings.

☙ Weeknight Pizza Dough

PREP TIME: 35 MIN	BAKING TIME: 7 TO 10 MIN	YIELD: 4 SERVINGS

INGREDIENTS

6 grams (one [2¼ teaspoons] packet) active dry yeast

14 grams (2 teaspoons) honey

300 grams (1¼ cups) warm water

28 grams (2 tablespoons) extra virgin olive oil, plus more for the bowl

381 grams (3 cups) Type 00 flour or all-purpose flour, plus more for rolling

1 teaspoon salt

DIRECTIONS

1 In a large bowl, stir together all the ingredients, knead by hand in the bowl for 4 minutes. The dough will still be sticky. Place extra olive oil onto your hands and form the dough into a ball. Cover the bowl with a warm, damp towel and let the dough rise for 30 minutes.

2 Place the dough onto a floured surface and divide into two or four pieces, depending on desired pizza sizes and topping preference. Preheat oven to 550 degrees with a baking sheet in the oven. Roll into desired shape. Quickly place onto a pre-heated baking sheet, and top with desired toppings. Note, you will not be able to move the pizza dough once it hits the hot baking sheet. This helps the pizza bake completely. Place pizza in the oven and reduce heat to 500 degrees. Bake for 7 to 10 minutes or until fully cooked and desired browning. Repeat with remaining pizza dough.

TIP: This is my go-to weeknight pizza dough recipe. My family each like different toppings, so we make four smaller pizzas. Have the toppings ready, so when you place it onto the hot baking sheet you can quickly top and return to the oven. This dough works great on grills, too.

NOTE: Type 00 flour, also called double zero flour, is a finely ground Italian wheat flour used for making pizza and pasta.

PER SERVING: *Calories 424 (From Fat 72); Fat 8g (Saturated 1g); Cholesterol 0mg; Sodium 584mg; Carbohydrate 76g (Dietary Fiber 3g); Protein 10g.*

☁ Calzones

INGREDIENTS

375 grams (1½ cups) ricotta cheese (or a mix of cottage cheese and ricotta cheese)

112 grams (1 cup) shredded mozzarella cheese

23 grams (¼ cup) grated Parmesan cheese

2 eggs

284 grams (one box [10 ounces]) frozen chopped broccoli, thawed (optional)

64 grams (¼ cup) pesto

1 clove garlic, diced

1 teaspoon black pepper

1 teaspoon salt

Weeknight Pizza Dough (see recipe earlier in this chapter) or 1-pound frozen bread dough, thawed

DIRECTIONS

1 Preheat the oven to 425 degrees. In a mixing bowl, combine all the ingredients except the pizza dough. Set aside.

2 Divide the pizza dough into six to eight pieces. Roll each piece out on a lightly floured surface to about ¼ inch thick.

3 Divide the filling evenly among the dough circles. Fold in half by stretching the dough across the top. Pinch the edges closed to seal.

4 Place the calzones on a baking sheet and bake for 20 to 30 minutes. Wait about 10 minutes before serving. The filling will be hot.

NOTE: Calzones are kind of like pizza pockets, without the sauce. They're pretty easy to make. This one, which is stuffed with cheese and broccoli, with a touch of pesto, is delicious.

VARY IT! Add these other fillings to the cheese mixture (you can omit the pesto, too): sautéed zucchini, mushrooms, garlic, and onions; steamed spinach; salami cut into thin strips; cooked Italian sausage; and shredded cooked chicken.

PER SERVING: *Calories 441 (From Fat 143); Fat 16g (Saturated 8g); Cholesterol 94mg; Sodium 677mg; Carbohydrate 54g (Dietary Fiber 3g); Protein 21g.*

Getting Creative with Quiches

Quiches are a delicious blend of eggs and cheese, with veggies and meat mixed in, that are usually baked in some type of crust. The following recipe uses a delicious potato crust, but you can substitute any crust, including a refrigerated or frozen one.

TIP

A great way to prevent a soggy crust is to put a layer of cheese between the dough and the egg mixture. It acts as a watertight barrier between the crust and egg custard.

Avoid watery quiches by baking them long enough that the center is set. You can vary the fillings or leave them out entirely. Remember: If you use mushrooms, cook them first to release some of the water. Otherwise, they may water down your custard too much, and then it won't set.

Broccoli and Cheese Quiche with Potato Crust

| PREP TIME: 25 MIN | BAKING TIME: 1 HR | YIELD: 8 TO 10 SERVINGS |

INGREDIENTS

3 medium-sized russet potatoes, peeled if desired, and cut into 1-inch cubes

2 tablespoons butter

1 large onion, chopped

182 grams (2 cups) chopped broccoli

114 grams (1 cup) shredded Cheddar cheese, firmly packed

4 eggs, beaten

61 grams (¼ cup) sour cream

61 grams (¼ cup) yogurt

120 grams (½ cup) milk or buttermilk

1½ tablespoons salt

1½ tablespoons pepper

DIRECTIONS

1   Preheat the oven to 350 degrees. Grease a deep-dish 9-inch pie plate. Place the potatoes in a large saucepan and cover with water. Bring to a boil over medium-high heat and cook until tender, about 15 minutes. Drain the potatoes and set aside to cool.

2   While the potatoes are cooking, melt 1 tablespoon of the butter in a medium-sized skillet over medium heat. Add the chopped onion and cook, stirring occasionally, until softened, 5 to 7 minutes. Remove half of the onions from the pan and set aside.

3   Add the broccoli to the remaining onions in the skillet, return to the heat, and continue cooking until the broccoli changes color to a bright green and is tender-crisp, about 5 minutes more (do not overcook the broccoli; it will continue to cook in the oven).

4   When the potatoes are cool enough to handle, add the remaining 1 tablespoon butter and the reserved onion and mash (you don't have to make the mixture perfectly smooth). Press the potato mixture evenly into the prepared pie plate.

5   Pat the cheese on top of the potatoes. Sprinkle the broccoli and onion mixture on top of the cheese.

6   In a mixing bowl, combine the eggs, sour cream, yogurt, milk, salt, and pepper, and beat well. Pour on top of the broccoli. Place the pie plate on a baking sheet and transfer to the oven. Bake the quiche for 1 hour, or until the quiche is set. Let the quiche cool for 10 minutes before serving.

(continued)

VARY IT! You can fill a quiche with just about anything you like: cooked ham, sautéed mushrooms and red onions, shredded zucchini, or bell peppers.

TIP: If you don't want a potato crust, substitute the Old-Fashioned Pie Dough (see Chapter 11 for the recipe) and bake the crust for 8 minutes before filling.

PER SERVING: *Calories 165 (From Fat 89); Fat 10g (Saturated 6g); Cholesterol 108mg; Sodium 464mg; Carbohydrate 12g (Dietary Fiber 2g); Protein 8g.*

Chapter **16**

Baking with Mixes and Premade Doughs

RECIPES IN THIS CHAPTER

☺ **Super Chocolate Cake**

☺ **Crazy-Good Pineapple Upside-Down Cake**

☺ **Super-Easy Veggie Party Pizza**

☺ **Cinnamon-Spiced Cheesecake Bars**

☺ **Apple Turnovers**

☺ **Cream Cheese and Cherry Danishes**

B aking mixes and refrigerated or frozen doughs can be a baker's best friend. Tasty and quick, they come already mixed with the right amounts of flour and leavener, and all you need to do is add the fat and liquid and — presto! — you have a perfect cake.

As the days seem to grow shorter and my to-do list longer, I've become a great fan of quick and easy recipes. Incorporating refrigerated doughs and box mixes into your baking life will allow you to still create a delicious baked good while reducing the need to have many ingredients on hand, not to mention the time it takes to make it.

Cakes and other homemade goodies are a source of comfort. Plus, they can be associated with celebrations and special times. Unfortunately, they're sometimes viewed as a challenge to make and a mess to clean up. Using mixes, however, can make preparation easier and the results more predictable. And a cake from a mix can be made on the spur of the moment.

Maybe you're one of those people who is too busy to bake everything from scratch or hasn't gained a tremendous amount of confidence in the kitchen. The best part about working with box mixes and frozen or refrigerated doughs is that they're sure-fire confidence builders.

You can find premade doughs in funny places throughout the supermarket. The following table gives a brief rundown of where I find my products. Even though your grocery may not shelve things identically, you have an idea of where to start looking.

What You're Looking For	Where to Find It
Cake mixes	In the baking aisle
Frozen bread dough	Frozen foods section, usually found with pretzels and near frozen pizzas and other frozen bread products; sold in multi-packs of 1-pound loaves
Refrigerated pie dough, refrigerated crescent rolls	In the refrigerated section, near the butter and eggs
Puff pastry/phyllo dough	In the frozen foods section, found with other desserts (frozen layer cakes and pies) and frozen fresh fruit

The more comfortable you become with baking cakes and breads by using these ingredients, the more likely you will be to venture a few steps farther and start baking completely from scratch. I love the collection of recipes that follow because they're easy and tasty and will surely become part of your everyday recipe group.

Baking with Mixes

You can use any brand of cake mixes, but you need to know about a couple differences between mixes and cakes from scratch:

>> The pudding-in-the-mix brands produce a heavier cake that has a lot of moisture. The plain mixes produce a slightly lighter cake and have what I consider a classic cake texture. They both are good, so you just need to choose which works best for the cake you want to make.

>> Size doesn't matter when it comes to box cakes. Cake mixes vary in weight from brand to brand. I tested all my cake recipes with a variety of brands, so you can choose the brand you like and be ensured good results.

If you're an experienced box-cake maker, you may realize that sometimes the cakes rise a lot in the middle but the sides aren't so high. You may also notice that your cake tunnels or has lots of air pockets. To avoid tunnels and puffy centers in your baked cake, either sharply tap the filled cake pan several times on the kitchen counter before you place it in the oven or run a knife through the batter in an *S* pattern to pop the bubbles. Also, spread the batter evenly in the pans after you pour it in.

One drawback to baking with mixes is that you aren't working with all-natural ingredients. Most cake mixes have artificial flavoring. You can combat the fake taste of cake mixes by using nice natural flavors or extracts. Orange juice, lemon zest, almond extract, or even chocolate chips or peanut butter chips can disguise artificial flavors when stirred into a mix. Mixes also contain *emulsifiers*, which bind together the fat and liquid and prevent them from separating. This can be helpful because box cakes stay fresh longer than those made from scratch, but it is another artificial ingredient you wouldn't have if you baked from scratch.

The following recipes use box mixes but taste just like you made them from scratch. Having cake mixes on hand can really simplify your life when you want to bake on the spur of the moment. Box mixes make baking easier because you don't have to worry whether you have all the little ingredients on hand. You may find yourself baking more often because baking with mixes is easy, fun, and really, really tasty.

BAKING OUTSIDE THE BOX

It may come as a big surprise to you, but you can tinker quite a bit with cakes and breads, and they still come out great. I encourage you to doctor up your own cake mixes. Here are some suggestions to go out of the box for delicious box cake results:

- Use whole eggs instead of just the whites. Your cake will benefit from the yolks, giving it a richer flavor and a tender texture.

- Instead of adding oil, substitute half the oil with melted butter for a better taste and texture.

- Instead of flouring cake pans with flour, use cocoa when making chocolate cakes.

- Try adding ½ cup toasted coconut to the batter of a yellow or angel food cake.

- Coffee and chocolate go hand in hand. Replace half of the liquid called for with brewed and cooled coffee or espresso.

Super Chocolate Cake

PREP TIME: 25 MIN | BAKING TIME: 30 MIN | YIELD: 12 SERVINGS

INGREDIENTS

525 grams (one [18½ ounce]) box chocolate cake mix

113 grams (½ cup/1 stick) butter, room temperature

6 eggs

126 grams (½ cup) whipping cream

120 grams (½ cup) water

1 tablespoon grated lemon peel

Chocolate Chip Frosting (see the following recipe)

DIRECTIONS

1 Preheat the oven to 350 degrees. Grease two 9-inch cake pans.

2 Prepare the cake: Combine the cake mix, butter, eggs, whipping cream, water, and lemon peel in a large mixing bowl. Beat with an electric mixer on low speed for 1 minute. Increase the speed to medium-high and beat an additional minute.

3 Divide the batter evenly into the pans. Bake for 30 minutes, or until a wooden tester inserted in the center comes out clean. Remove the cakes from the pans and allow to cool completely on a wire rack.

Chocolate Chip Frosting

INGREDIENTS

630 grams (2½ cups) chilled whipping cream

125 grams (10 tablespoons) sugar

38 grams (6 tablespoons) unsweetened cocoa powder

220 grams (1½ cups) miniature semisweet chocolate chips (about 8 ounces)

DIRECTIONS

1 Using an electric mixer, beat the whipping cream, sugar, and cocoa in large bowl until stiff peaks form, 3 to 5 minutes. Fold in the chocolate chips. Frost the cake with the frosting.

PER SERVING: *Calories 652 (From Fat 411); Fat 46g (Saturated 24g); Cholesterol 209mg; Sodium 416mg; Carbohydrate 60g (Dietary Fiber 2g); Protein 8g.*

Crazy-Good Pineapple Upside-Down Cake

PREP TIME: 10 MIN	BAKING TIME: 30 TO 35 MIN	YIELD: 16 SERVINGS

INGREDIENTS

525 grams (one [18½ ounce]) box yellow cake mix

180 grams (¾ cup) sour cream

2 eggs

28 grams (2 tablespoons) vegetable oil

1 teaspoon vanilla extract

1 teaspoon cinnamon

568 grams (one [20 ounce] can) pineapple slices in their own juice

213 grams (1 cup) light brown sugar, firmly packed

85 grams (6 tablespoons/ ¾ stick) butter, melted

10 maraschino cherries (optional)

DIRECTIONS

1 Preheat the oven to 375 degrees. In a mixing bowl, combine the cake mix, sour cream, eggs, oil, vanilla, cinnamon, and ½ cup pineapple juice from the slices. Mix well with a whisk. If the batter is too thick, add 1 tablespoon more of the pineapple juice.

2 Combine the brown sugar, melted butter, and the remaining pineapple juice (it should be 2 to 3 tablespoons) in the bottom of a 9-x-13-inch baking pan. Mix together well. The sugar should be pretty well dissolved.

3 Arrange the pineapple slices in the bottom of the pan on top of the sugar mixture. (You should have three rows: four slices in one row and three in the other two rows. You could even it out by eating one slice.) Dot the centers of the pineapples with cherries, if desired. Pour the batter evenly on top of the pineapple slices.

4 Bake for 30 to 35 minutes, until a toothpick inserted into the center comes out clean. Remove from the oven and let cool about 10 minutes.

TIP: When you preheat the oven, place the pan in the oven with the unmelted stick of butter in it. When the oven reaches the right temperature, remove the pan (the butter will be melted) and stir in the brown sugar and remaining pineapple juice. The sugar dissolves really easily, and you have one less bowl to wash. Just be careful! The pan will be hot.

VARY IT! Mix in ⅓ cup sweetened coconut and ¼ cup chopped pecans with the melted butter and sugar mixture. Don't limit yourself to canned pineapple. Try peaches, apricots, or even pears. It's heavenly!

NOTE: Low-fat sour cream is okay to use.

PER SERVING: *Calories 301 (From Fat 115); Fat 13g (Saturated 5g); Cholesterol 44mg; Sodium 235mg; Carbohydrate 45g (Dietary Fiber 1g); Protein 3g.*

Baking with Refrigerated and Frozen Dough

I must admit, I'm a huge fan of refrigerated pie dough. It makes putting a pie together as simple as . . . well, pie. Essentially, it eliminates the need to chill and roll the dough, which are the two most time-consuming tasks of making pie. Although I think the piecrust companies could stand to make the circles just an inch larger, I'm generally happy enough with the results of the pie dough that I highly recommend it to beginning bakers. You can even get creative with the pie dough — cut out small shapes or even cut it into 1-inch strips and make a lattice piecrust.

Frozen bread dough has many purposes:

>> You can roll the dough out into logs, shape it like a pretzel, dip it in butter, and bake it.

>> You can roll the dough out thin to use it as a pizza crust.

>> You can shape the dough into a loaf (round or square) or small balls for rolls and bake it for fresh bread for your table.

You can really doctor up bread doughs — with a few add-ins, you can make cinnamon-raisin bread or French bread. The ideas are endless. I highly recommend experimenting with a frozen loaf or two. The recipes in this section are designed to get you thinking about ways to use premade doughs. Then, when you have the time, you'll be better able to branch out and start making doughs from scratch.

☕ Super-Easy Veggie Party Pizza

PREP TIME: 10 TO 15 MIN	BAKING TIME: 30 MIN	YIELD: 8 SLICES

INGREDIENTS

227 grams (one [8-ounce] tube) refrigerated crescent roll dough

42 grams (3 tablespoons) olive oil

1 clove garlic, crushed

1 teaspoon dried basil

1 teaspoon dried oregano

½ teaspoon salt

½ teaspoon ground black pepper

2 cups sliced vegetables (choose from fresh mushrooms, green and red bell pepper, chopped red onion, fresh broccoli, sliced olives, zucchini or squash, or corn)

177 grams (1½ cups) shredded mozzarella cheese

113 grams (1 cup) shredded sharp Cheddar cheese

43 grams (½ cup) shredded Asiago cheese (optional)

43 grams (½ cup) shredded fresh Parmesan cheese

DIRECTIONS

1 Adjust a rack in the oven to the lowest shelf. Place the baking stone on a cookie sheet and place in the oven on the low rack (a baking sheet will work, too, if you don't have a stone). Preheat the oven to 475 degrees. Let the stone heat in the oven for at least 30 minutes or up to 45 minutes.

2 Fifteen minutes before the stone is preheated, start making the pizza. Spray the center area of a piece of aluminum foil that's at least 18 inches long with nonstick cooking spray or dust with cornmeal. In the center of the foil, arrange the triangles of dough into a circle, with the small points all meeting in the center (they will overlap slightly).

3 In a small cup, combine the oil, garlic, basil, oregano, salt, and pepper. Drizzle the mixture over the dough. In a mixing bowl, combine the vegetables, 1 cup of the mozzarella cheese, ½ cup of the cheddar cheese, plus the Asiago cheese, if desired, and the Parmesan cheese. Arrange the mixture evenly over the dough, leaving a ½-inch border around the edge. Sprinkle the remaining ½ cup mozzarella cheese and remaining ½ cup Cheddar cheese on top of the pizza. Roll the edges of the dough toward the center to create a crust.

4 Carefully remove the pizza stone from the oven and place near the pizza. Reduce the temperature to 400 degrees. Transfer the pizza to the pizza stone by lifting it with the aluminum foil and centering it onto the stone. Bake for 30 minutes, or until the vegetables are cooked and the crust is golden. Remove from the oven and, using the aluminum foil, carefully slide the pizza onto a large plate to serve.

PER SERVING: *Calories 305 (From Fat 202); Fat 23g (Saturated 10g); Cholesterol 39mg; Sodium 641mg; Carbohydrate 12g (Dietary Fiber 0g); Protein 13g.*

Cinnamon-Spiced Cheesecake Bars

PREP TIME: 15 MIN	BAKING TIME: 30 MIN TO 35 MIN	YIELD: 12 SERVINGS

INGREDIENTS

454 grams (two [8 ounce] tubes) cream cheese, at room temperature

250 grams (1¼ cup) granulated sugar, divided

1½ teaspoons vanilla extract

454 grams (two [8 ounce] cans) refrigerated crescent rolls

1½ teaspoons ground cinnamon

¼ teaspoon ground nutmeg

113 grams (½ cup) unsalted butter, at room temperature

DIRECTIONS

1 Preheat the oven to 350 degrees. Grease a 9-x-13-inch cake pan.

2 In a stand mixer or with a hand mixer, beat cream cheese, ¾ cup sugar, and vanilla extract until creamy and fluffy.

3 Unroll 1 can of crescent rolls and place on the bottom of the cake pan. Top with cream cheese mixture, and then top with second can of crescent rolls.

4 In a separate small bowl, mash cinnamon, nutmeg, remaining ½ cup sugar, and butter until combined. Dot the top of the crescent rolls with the cinnamon butter mixture. Bake for 30 to 35 minutes or until golden brown in color.

5 Cool on a wire rack for 30 minutes for best results in cutting or serve warm.

TIP: Consider buying crescent sheets, which makes this dish come together quicker if you can find it!

NOTE: Store covered and refrigerated for up to 3 days.

NOTE: Flip to the color insert for a photo of this recipe.

PER SERVING: Calories 383 (From Fat 200); Fat 22g (Saturated 13g); Cholesterol 62mg; Sodium 304mg; Carbohydrate 41g (Dietary Fiber 1g); Protein 6g.

🍎 Apple Turnovers

PREP TIME: 20 MIN | BAKING TIME: 35 TO 45 MIN | YIELD: 4 SERVINGS

INGREDIENTS

300 grams (3 cups) diced apples (about 4 medium apples)

½ cup plus 1 tablespoon sugar, divided

120 grams (½ cup) apple juice

¼ teaspoon ground cinnamon, nutmeg, or cardamom

1 tablespoon cornstarch dissolved in 1 tablespoon water

490 grams (one [17¼ ounces] package) frozen puff pastry (2 sheets), thawed

1 egg, beaten

DIRECTIONS

1 Preheat the oven to 375 degrees. Combine the apples, ½ cup sugar, apple juice, and cinnamon in a heavy medium saucepan. Bring to a boil, stirring. Reduce heat to medium; simmer until apples are soft, about 6 minutes. Add the cornstarch mixture and stir until the mixture thickens and boils, about 1 minute. Cool.

2 Cut the pastry into four even squares (6 x 6 inches). Place ¼ cup apple mixture on top of the center of each pastry square. Brush the pastry edges with the beaten egg. Fold the pastry over the filling, forming triangles and pressing the edges gently with a fork to seal.

3 Transfer to a baking sheet. Repeat with the remaining pastry and apple mixture. Brush the tops of the turnovers with the beaten egg and sprinkle with remaining sugar, if desired.

4 Bake for 35 to 45 minutes, or until golden brown. Remove and let cool slightly before serving, at least 15 minutes.

NOTE: I like to make my turnovers with two different types of apples, one a sweeter baking apple and the other a tart apple. It adds a depth of flavor that I really enjoy.

VARY IT: You can dice up any fruit to mix in with the apples, such as pears, peaches, or raspberries.

PER SERVING: *Calories 870 (From Fat 427); Fat 48g (Saturated 7g); Cholesterol 0mg; Sodium 311mg; Carbohydrate 104g (Dietary Fiber 4g); Protein 9g.*

Cream Cheese and Cherry Danishes

INGREDIENTS

490 grams (one [17¼ ounces] package) frozen puff pastry (2 sheets), thawed according to package instructions

227 grams (8 ounces) cream cheese

1 medium egg

¼ teaspoon almond extract

¼ teaspoon ground nutmeg

3 tablespoons granulated sugar

8 tablespoons cherry pie filling or preserves

1 egg yolk, whisked

DIRECTIONS

1   Preheat the oven to 375 degrees. Line two baking sheets with parchment paper.

2   In a mixing bowl or with a hand mixer, beat the cream cheese, egg, almond extract, nutmeg, and sugar until light and fluffy, about 3 minutes.

3   On a lightly floured surface, unfold the puff pastry sheets. Using a sharp knife or pizza cutter, cut each sheet into four squares. Place the four puff pastry squares spaced apart onto each baking pan. Cover one set of dough with a towel so they don't dry out. Using a paring knife or a small knife, place the tip of the knife ½ inch in from the top left corner of the pastry dough. Cut downward but stop ½ inch from the bottom. Return the knife to the top and repeat across the top. Place your knife tip at the bottom right corner and make the same cuts along the bottom and right side of the pastry dough. Lift each cut corner and take the bottom right and place it on the top left and the top left to the bottom right, creating a border to the pastry. Repeat with remaining squares.

4   Using a cookie scoop, place a heaping scoop of cream cheese mixture into the center of each puff pastry. Create an indent and fill with 1 tablespoon of cherry pie filling or preserves. Mix egg yolk with 1 tablespoon water and brush the edges of the pastry with the egg wash. Bake for 25 to 30 minutes or until puffed and golden brown in color.

5   Cool the baking sheets on a wire rack for 15 minutes. Serve warm or at room temperature.

TIP: If you have guests for breakfast, defrost puff pastry overnight so you can whip together this simple and elegant breakfast danish.

NOTE: An alternative shape is to fold in the corners, creating an octagon shape. There are many ways to serve these pastries.

NOTE: Refer to the color insert for a photo.

PER SERVING: *Calories 487 (From Fat 309); Fat 34g (Saturated 12g); Cholesterol 81mg; Sodium 261mg; Carbohydrate 38g (Dietary Fiber 1g); Protein 7g.*

4 Dealing with Other Important Stuff

Store your baking creations with tips on how to cool, wrap, and freeze.

Take your baked goods from ordinary to extraordinary, from how to slice and present with flair.

» **Knowing when you need to refrigerate**

» **Freezing frosted or unfrosted cakes**

» **Taking good care of your cookies**

Chapter **17**

Storing Your Creations

O kay, so you've baked your cakes, cookies, pies, and breads, and now you're wondering what to do with them. You want them to stay fresh and tasting good, but maybe you're not sure how long something will keep or what the best method for storage is.

There are many ways to store something. The most important thing to keep in mind is that you don't want your baked things to sit in the open. Baked goods will dry out if they're left out; foods such as slices of bread or cakes can get dry and stale in just a few hours. If you know that your baked goods will stick around for a few days, you may want to keep them refrigerated or even frozen. This chapter offers some advice on storage and the best ways to keep your treats fresh.

Wrapping Your Baked Goods

No kitchen is complete without a supply of plastic wrap, aluminum foil, and waxed paper. If you go to the trouble of baking something special, you need to be able to store it properly. Foils and wraps can keep air away from your creations, which will dry them out and make them stale. Home-baked items don't have preservatives, so it's up to you to store everything properly so that it will last until tomorrow. However, like many tasty treats, they may not last that long, but the following sections give you some tips for storing your creations.

Plastic wrap

Plastic wrap seals bowls, wraps cakes, and covers containers. I like plastic wrap because you can see through it and know what you've stored. Plastic wrap has a number of other advantages, too:

>> It's *nonreactive,* which means that it won't react with acidic or alkaline ingredients, making it good for storing just about anything.

>> It's microwave safe.

>> It creates airtight seals over bowls and other containers.

Find the brand of plastic wrap you like best. It should cling to itself, and you should be able to pull it tightly without ripping it.

WARNING

Under no circumstances should plastic wrap be put in the oven or over a hot item that just came out of the oven. It will melt immediately and isn't good for you to breathe or ingest.

Beeswax wraps

Beeswax wraps are a great way to avoid using plastic and a more ecofriendly way to wrap and store food. These wraps can last upward of a year if cared for properly; just make sure you follow the package instructions for care.

TIP

To revitalize your beeswax wraps, place the wax part of the wrap on parchment paper. On the highest setting of an iron, iron out the wrinkles to reset the beeswax. After the beeswax is worn thin, it will no longer adhere to a bowl's edge. You can either discard the fabric or melt more beeswax on it.

To make your own beeswax wraps, stick to these steps:

1. **After purchasing some beeswax pellets (Amazon has plenty of options), find a piece of 100 percent cotton and cut the fabric to fit over a desired bowl or pie pan.**

2. **Place foil down on an ironing board and then place the fabric (pretty side down) onto the foil.**

3. **Sprinkle a little bit of beeswax pellets onto the fabric to cover the area.**

4. **Cover the beeswax with parchment paper and using the highest setting on an iron, heat the beeswax pellets until they have spread and melted.**

   Let the wrap cool for 30 minutes before using it.

Aluminum foil

Aluminum foil is a great tool in the kitchen because it won't cling to items like plastic wrap can. Unlike plastic wrap, aluminum foil can be used in the oven for baking. Foil is also better for wrapping and stabilizing loose or irregularly shaped items like cookies on a paper plate or unfrosted cakes because you can mold it to whatever shape you need it to be. Because aluminum foil molds to itself, you can create an airtight seal with it. And it works well in the freezer. You can write directly on the foil so that you know what you've wrapped. The one drawback to aluminum foil is that it can't be used in the microwave.

Waxed paper

In the old days before plastic wrap and foil, there was waxed paper. Cooks used it for everything from storing leftovers to keeping cakes fresh in the ice box. Waxed paper is underutilized these days for storage in my opinion. The waxy paper offers a breathable seal for your baked goods, so they stay fresh but don't get soggy-moist. Waxed paper is very useful in the kitchen because you can use it to line baking sheets and pans and place it between layers for storage. It's also safe for the microwave and for wrapping items (as long as an airtight seal is not required).

TIP

A sheet of waxed paper can act as a movable part of your kitchen counter or a bowl you don't need to wash. Spread out a sheet on your counter and sift ingredients onto it or use it to hold breadcrumbs or other coating.

Glassware or plastic

I'm a big fan of glassware or plastic. I find it to be perfect for everything from packing lunches to holding leftovers to storing everything I've baked. Sealable containers make great storage items because the airtight seals keep your baked items fresher longer. Clear glass and plastic allows you to see what you've stored (which is a great memory aid), and they're generally spacious and can hold many items.

FOIL FOILS MESSY CLEANUP

If you're using a baking sheet to catch drips from a pie or overflowing cake pan, place a piece of aluminum foil on top of the baking sheet. All the burned-on mess will drip onto the foil, not the baking sheet, making cleanup a snap.

Know that sturdy plasticware will more than likely outlive you, so don't skimp on quality when you purchase it. Look for sturdy containers with good lids that offer airtight closure. Be sure that the lids fit well and you don't have to struggle every time you want to seal it. If you have a microwave, use the glassware instead of plastic.

Now, you can buy inexpensive reusable plastic containers that make me want to bake and share with everyone. They come in a variety of shapes and sizes and are perfect for storing large and small items and giving, without worrying about getting them back.

Tins

Decorative tins can serve as both holder and wrapping if you like to give baked goods as gifts. They're also great items to recycle, so you can use them many times and for many different purposes. Keep a few things in mind, though, when you choose decorative tins:

>> **Tins generally don't have airtight seals.** Baked items won't stay as fresh for as long in tins as they do when stored in plastic containers.

>> **Tins don't have as much holding capacity as plastic and glassware containers.** So you may want to pack two dozen cookies in a decorative tin but find that you can fit only one dozen! If you have many cookies to store, tins aren't the best choice.

Tins are great if you want to give a sampling of cookies or brownies to a friend; be sure to layer the baked goods with wax paper so they don't stick to one another. If you want to send a few dozen cookies as a care package, skip the tin and send them in a plastic container instead. That way, you can be sure they'll be fresh when they arrive.

TIP

A great way to keep baked goods fresh longer is to store the baked goods with a slice of bread in an airtight container. This particularly helps if you're mailing a care package. Just don't try eating the bread slice later.

Storing at Room Temperature

Chances are if you live with roommates or have a family, you won't have to worry too much about anything freshly baked hanging around too long. From the first sniff of anything baking, you'll have an audience in the kitchen, waiting for the treats to be cool enough to sink their teeth into. In those cases, as long as you want the items to be consumed right away, most freshly baked items are fine if you leave them on a plate for a while. But there may be times you bake in large batches and want the goodies to stay fresher, longer. In that case, earmark this section.

Cookies

Most cookies can sit on the counter for the better part of a day (about 12 hours) before they need to be stored. If they need to be stored in the refrigerator, the recipe will say so. Otherwise, most cookies can be stored in an airtight plastic container on the kitchen counter for up to three days.

Cookie jars are cute, but unfortunately, most of them don't have an airtight seal. If you have a high turnover for your cookies (meaning that they'll float out of the cookie jar within a few days), a cookie jar is fine to use. If you don't put them in an airtight container, you run the risk of the cookies turning stale faster. If you love the cookie jar but still want to keep your cookies fresh, store them in a sealable plastic bag in the jar. And don't forget the slice of bread!

Cakes

As long as your cake doesn't contain custard, raw egg, fresh whipped cream, or meringue topping — all of which require refrigeration — most cakes can be stored at room temperature for several days.

To store your cakes, you can purchase a *cake keeper*, which is a large plastic cake holder with an airtight lid that fits on top. I find cake keepers very useful because I can fit a cake on a serving plate on the base of the cake keeper, snap on the lid and, even if the plate slides around, it doesn't damage the frosted sides of the cake at all. You can also use a cake dome, usually a metal or plastic cover with a lid that you place over the cake itself. The dome doesn't provide an airtight seal, but if the cake will sit for just a few days, that shouldn't matter.

If you don't have either a cake keeper or a cake dome, you can invert a large mixing bowl over the cake. Just make sure the bowl is large enough that it won't smash down the top of the cake or touch the sides. A bowl is slightly more difficult to lift because it doesn't have a handle, but it does provide an adequate cover.

Another way to prevent the cut surface of a cake from becoming stale while it's being stored is to press a piece of waxed paper or aluminum foil against the cut surface.

If you'll be traveling with your cake and its appearance is important to you, pack some extra frosting and your frosting spatula (and pastry bag, if necessary) with you. That way, if you reach your destination and find that your cake has suffered some nicks and bruises, you can fix it up in a jiffy and people will be none the wiser.

Pies

Whole fresh fruit pies can be kept on the kitchen counter, covered, for about a day. Store any leftovers, covered, in the refrigerator. I have a large sealable plastic container that I use to store pies. My 9-inch pie plate fits perfectly in the container, and the lid is high enough that it doesn't damage my crust. It's a great container to use in the refrigerator because I can store items on top of the container (and maximize fridge space) without my pie picking up other flavors or getting bumped around in the fridge.

Bread

Bread can be stored at room temperature, sealed in a plastic or paper bag, for several days. Homemade bread tends to lose its freshness faster at room temperature, so you may want to keep it in the refrigerator even if you plan to use it up within a day or so.

If you don't eat a lot of bread, freezing is an excellent way to keep bread fresh. Then you can defrost what you need and warm it briefly in a toaster oven. Just be sure to wrap the bread tightly in freezer plastic (which is different from regular plastic wrap), foil, or freezer-plastic bags.

Keeping Things Cool

Many baked goods, such as cookies and breads, can be stored at room temperature. However, some items must be kept in the refrigerator to ensure that they won't melt or spoil. If you aren't sure whether you should refrigerate items, refrigeration won't harm them, so go ahead and wrap them up and keep them in the fridge. Note the time of year, too. In the winter and fall, items can stay at room temperature longer than in the summertime, when even pies should be stored in the refrigerator to ensure that they don't mold or go bad. These sections guide you about when to make space in the refrigerator.

If you're traveling with a cake or pie that needs to be refrigerated, keep it in the air-conditioned part of the car with you. Don't put it in the trunk. If you don't have air conditioning, keep it in a cooler (if it fits), or you can double-box the cake and surround it with ice packs (one box to hold the cake, and the other box to hold the ice packs around the boxed cake).

Baked goods that should be chilled

All cheesecakes must be stored in the refrigerator, as should cakes, cookies, and pies that contain custard, raw egg, fresh whipped cream, or meringue topping (although they'll weep a little from the cold). Any cake *can* be stored in the refrigerator, unless otherwise specified in the instructions, to extend its freshness. If you keep a cake in the refrigerator, be sure that it's well covered either in a cake saver or with a cake dome or bowl placed over it (see the section, "Storing at Room Temperature," earlier in this chapter).

If you place a cut cake uncovered and unwrapped in the refrigerator for more than a few hours, it will most likely pick up refrigerator flavors, the icing will harden, and the cake will dry up and become stale.

Cookies

You can store cookies in the refrigerator in an airtight plastic container for about two weeks. After the first week, they won't be as fresh as they once were, but you can always pop them in the oven for a few minutes or even zap them in the microwave for a few seconds if you want that fresh-from-the-oven feeling. If you don't want to be bothered, I find that a not-so-fresh cookie makes a perfect dunker in milk. It sops up lots of milk but doesn't fall apart. Yum.

Pies

Pies can be stored in the refrigerator for several days as long as they're well wrapped (with plastic or foil) and not made with custard, cream, or meringue. You can store pies in a cake saver or just cover with plastic wrap, beeswax wrap, or aluminum foil. After a day or two, the crust may become a bit soggy, but you can rewarm the pie in the oven if you want. If your house is quite hot in the summer, be sure to keep the pie in the refrigerator so that it doesn't mold quickly or get too runny.

Breads

Because homemade breads lack the preservatives that store-bought breads have to increase their shelf life, your breads won't keep for nearly as long. To extend the life of your bread, store it in the refrigerator. I've kept bread, wrapped in a plastic bag, for up to one week without a molding problem.

Bread, sliced or unsliced, also freezes well. You can always rewarm breads in the oven for 10 or 15 minutes to get the crust crispy and fresh again. Also, choose a recipe with some fat in it (butter, eggs, or oil). Fat acts as a preservative for breads and extends their life by several days.

Freezing Your Baked Goodies

The freezer is a huge help to bakers because it enables you to prepare foods when you have the time. Then you can remove them from the freezer and defrost them when you need them.

Even though most items freeze well, if you have the time to bake your items fresh, that's always the better choice. Frozen goods experience an inescapable loss of moisture and tend to dry out faster after they're brought back to room temperature for baking. Never freeze custards or cream pies.

REMEMBER

Always label and date items you put in the freezer. You may even want to keep a master list on the freezer door so you know what's inside. Frozen unbaked doughs have a relatively short freezer life, so you need to know what you have on hand so that you can use it up in time.

Cookies

Baked cookies are pretty easy to freeze. Just stack them in an airtight plastic container with waxed paper in between each layer and freeze. You also can store cookies in sealable plastic bags. Most every cookie freezes well, but you may find that filled cookies and some bar cookies with dried fruit are a bit softer after they're defrosted — but they're still just as good in flavor.

Cookie dough

Uncooked cookie dough will last about two months frozen. Before freezing, shape the cookie dough into long logs and wrap the logs in plastic wrap. After they're frozen, double-wrap the logs in aluminum foil or an airtight container. Be sure to label the dough. You can even slice the cookies before you freeze them to make preparing them later easier.

TIP

The best cookie doughs to freeze are those with a lot of fat in them. If you want to experiment with different doughs, start with chocolate chip, oatmeal, or peanut butter cookies. Roll the dough into 2-inches-round x 12-inches-long logs. Slice the logs (either still frozen or refrigerated) into 1-inch slices. Bake the slices on a cookie sheet in a 350- to 375-degree oven for 8 to 10 minutes (frozen dough may take a few minutes longer). It couldn't be any easier.

Instead of logs, you can scoop out the cookies, freeze them on a cookie sheet, and then transfer the frozen balls of dough into a freezer-plastic sealable bag. Then just drop them onto a cookie sheet and bake as directed in the preceding paragraph.

Bread dough

To freeze bread dough, prepare the dough as usual but add a teaspoon more yeast to the recipe. Allow the dough to rise once, punch down the dough, and then shape it into loaves. (You can freeze the loaves in the pans you'll bake them in; then remove the frozen dough from the pan and wrap it in freezer plastic until you're ready to bake it.) Don't keep frozen bread dough for more than ten days in the freezer. Defrost the loaves at room temperature or in the refrigerator overnight, let rise a second time, and then bake as instructed.

Rolls can be frozen in the same manner, but don't keep them in the freezer for more than a week. Freeze the individual rolls on a baking tray for 2 hours and then wrap them in freezer plastic and store them in an airtight container. When defrosting rolls, allow them to rise in a warm area, covered, until doubled in bulk (anywhere from 1½ to 4 hours) and bake as instructed.

Cakes

Most cakes can be frozen for up to two months. For unfrosted cake layers, cool the layers completely before wrapping them: first in freezer-plastic wrap and then in aluminum foil. You also can wrap the layers well and then seal them in a large freezer-plastic bag. The purpose is to create an airtight package for your cake layers. Label each item (you can write directly on the plastic bag or foil or label a piece of masking tape and stick it onto the bag or foil).

You also can freeze frosted layer cakes. Place the frosted cake in the freezer, unwrapped (you can place toothpicks in the cake to keep the plastic wrap from touching the cake if you like, but doing so is not necessary). When the cake has frozen through (the frosting should be frozen solid), wrap the cake in plastic and then wrap it in aluminum foil.

Cake layers, unfrosted, can be frozen for up to two months. A frosted layer cake will keep frozen for up to four months. Spice cakes should not be frozen for more than one month, to ensure that the flavor stays true. To defrost the cake, place it at room temperature, unwrapped but covered with a cake dome or cake saver lid, until you're ready to serve it.

WARNING

I don't recommend freezing cake batter. The leavening used to make cakes rise may react differently after being defrosted, and the flavor of the cake will change.

Pies

Assemble the pie in a pie plate you don't mind sacrificing to the freezer for a while. If that's a problem, you may want to purchase aluminum foil pie plates for freezing. The best pies to freeze are fresh fruit pies because the fruit filling and pie dough don't seem to sacrifice their quality in the freezer. You can't freeze pies made with pudding, custard, meringue, or other creamy fillings. Keep the following in mind when freezing pies:

>> **Uncooked pies:** To freeze an uncooked pie, prepare the pie as usual, except use 1½ times the amount of cornstarch, tapioca, or flour in the filling (for example, if the recipe calls for 1 tablespoon, increase it to 1½ tablespoons). Freeze the pie solid before wrapping it in plastic wrap and aluminum foil or an airtight container. Bake the unthawed pie for 15 minutes in a 425-degree oven, and then reduce the temperature to 375 degrees and continue baking for about 40 minutes more. If the pie has a top crust, be sure to poke air holes in that crust before baking.

>> **Baked pies:** Before freezing a baked pie, make sure that it's completely cool. When you're ready to serve it, thaw the pie for several hours at room temperature if you want to serve it cold. To serve the pie warm, place the frozen pie in a preheated 375-degree oven for about 30 minutes. Again, don't freeze baked pudding, custard, or meringue pies.

>> **Pie pastry:** Pie pastry made with shortening or butter freezes very well. You can freeze pie pastry in many different ways:

- You can just wrap the dough in an airtight container. Defrost the dough, roll it out, and use as instructed. Label whether it's dough for an 8- or 9-inch pie.

- You can roll out the dough and place it on a greased baking sheet to freeze. After the dough is frozen, just wrap and label. Defrost and use as normal.

- You can press the piecrust into a pie plate and freeze it like that. You may want to use a disposable foil pie plate unless you don't mind storing the pie plate in the freezer for a while. Freeze the crust on the pie plate until frozen solid, and then wrap tightly and seal in an airtight container or double-bag it in large sealable plastic bags. You can bake these shells without thawing them at 425 degrees for 10 to 15 minutes.

Avoiding freezer burn

Air left in containers dries out food during storage. That air can cause freezer burn and will draw additional moisture from the food, which forms those ice crystals that you find on the lids of many home–frozen items. Freezer burn also can happen if foods aren't wrapped tightly enough.

When wrapping food for freezing, remember the following:

» Choose wrappers that are moisture-proof to keep your foods from drying out and to prevent freezer odor from penetrating the foods. Heavy-duty aluminum foil is great for the freezer because you can mold it to shape the item being frozen.

» Press out all the air to get a good seal. Large, sealable freezer-plastic bags are a good choice for freezing irregularly shaped items.

» Consider double-wrapping or double-bagging items. Plastic wrap should be nonporous freezer plastic and can be used with heavy-duty aluminum foil for the best seal.

» Look for hard, plastic freezer containers to protect your baked goods from damage in the freezer.

COOKIES THAT CAN STAND THE TEST OF TIME

Some baked goods are perfect for longer storage. Some even taste better the longer they sit. The Lebkuchen cookies are often prepared weeks before Christmas in Germany, and they still taste just as delicious three weeks later. Shortbread, butter, and gingersnap cookies can also stand the test of time.

Living in a hot and humid climate affects the storage. Macarons, the classic French cookie, prefer a rest of three days before being consumed, making them a great bake-ahead cookie. Biscotti cookies are also great cookies for longer storage. Any cookie with lower moisture content will hold up longer than peanut butter or chocolate chip cookies. You can find all these recipes in Chapter 8.

Chapter **18**

Making the Ordinary Extraordinary

When you spend time baking, you want to be able to show off your finished products and enjoy all the oohs and ahhs when you put them on display. This chapter gives you some ideas for making everything you bake just a little more special.

Cutting Your Baked Goods Neatly and Evenly

Believe it or not, there is a correct way to cut cakes and pies. Well, it may not be "correct," but it does ensure that you get slices of equal sizes.

Most people cut out one slice and then work their way around, eyeballing each piece and ending up with irregularly sized slices. The problem reveals itself when you get to slice number eight and realize how tiny slices nine and ten will have to be. A simple technique for slicing cakes and pies makes it easy to know how many slices you'll get before you make the first cut. Plus, you've gone to all this trouble to bake from scratch; why just hack away at it? Neat slices add to the appeal of your creations, and my intention in these sections is to share how you can cut neat slices.

Pies and layer cakes can be cut the same way. You want to use a long, thin, sharp knife to cut. You also may want to use a cake server (a fancy triangular spatula) to transfer the slices to plates.

Cutting cakes and pies into even slices

When you serve a layer cake, follow these steps to ensure even slices (Figure 18-1 shows you what to do.):

1. **Slice the cake completely in half.**

2. **Depending on the richness of the cake and/or the number of people you have to serve, cut each cake half in half again, and then cut each quarter in half or in thirds.**

    This method of even division ensures that you make even cuts instead of going around the cake and eyeballing each cut.

FIGURE 18-1:
Cutting a cake into wedges.

If you want to measure out the wedges *before* you cut into the cake, do the following:

1. **Make a nick in the icing by gently letting the knife blade sink into the icing.**

2. **Mark the cake all the way around, using the method explained in the preceding steps to cut each section into halves, thirds, or quarters.**

   If you want to vary the sizes of the slices, divide one-quarter of the cake in thirds and the other in half.

3. **If you're satisfied with the sizes of the wedges, cut all the way through the cake according to the nicks you made.**

   If you need more wedges, "erase" the cut marks by smearing the icing and then re-mark the cake until you have the number of slices you need.

The same goes for pies. You can make a nick in the crust or a small cut in the top, or, if the pie doesn't have a top crust, you can mark the filling.

Cutting cheesecakes cleanly

Cheesecake can get messy when you cut it. The moist cake tends to stick to the knife, increasing the thickness of the knife with each slice. You can conquer this problem in a few ways.

If you're planning to cut the cheesecake before you present it:

>> Wet a nonserrated knife with hot water, shake off any excess water (but don't dry it), and then cut the cake. The heat and moisture from the knife enable you to get a clean slice each time. You'll have to rewet the knife every second slice or so.

>> Slice the cheesecake with clean dental floss. Get a piece of floss a few inches longer than the cake. Wrap the ends of the floss around your fingers and press the floss down and through the cake. Then release one side of the floss and pull it through the cake. Repeat this process until the whole cake is sliced. Doing so gives you neat, clean slices.

If you have to cut the cake at the table, you can always use two knives: one to slice and the other to scrape off the slicing knife between slices.

Cutting sheet cakes, bar cookies, and brownies

Sheet cakes, bar cookies, and brownies share the same cutting technique. It's easy, but you need to use a thin, sharp knife. You just have to cut the cake into equal-sized squares. If necessary, you can use the same technique you used on layer cakes to mark the icing before you slice to make sure that you'll get a high enough yield out of your cake or bars.

Cutting loaves and rolled cakes

Slice loaves and rolled cakes with a serrated knife. (A regular blade can compress the crumb of the cake and doesn't offer as nice a cut as a serrated knife does.) If you have an electric serrated knife, you can use that. It may be a little more horse-power than you need for cake or bread cutting, but it does the trick and enables you to cut thinner slices. Don't press straight down when you cut; use a gentle sawing motion. The thickness of each slice depends on the richness of the bread or cake.

Presenting with Flair

Decorated store-bought cakes tend to be ornamental and have that fussed-over appearance. That's all well and good for some people's taste, but I prefer the simple and basic. Not being a terribly artistic person myself, I think that less is definitely more. When I try to get too fancy, I usually have to explain my abstract art to the people looking at the cake: "Okay, this is the baby stroller, and this is Anne. . . ."

Food should look nice as well as taste good, so how you present your desserts really does make a difference. Although it doesn't have to be picture perfect, you can do some simple things to jazz up the presentation of your desserts.

Try piping a simple shell border or stars around the edge of the cake instead of going crazy with design. I recommend simple designs for beginner designers. See Chapter 10 for tips on decorating cakes. The following are suggestions for decorating cakes without having to apply to art school first:

>> **Anniversary:** A big heart, two interlocking rings, the number of years celebrated

>> **Birthday:** Balloons (if the name is short, you can put the letters of the person's name in the balloons), the person's age, a present with a bow

>> **Good luck/bon voyage:** A horseshoe, champagne glasses toasting with colored confetti (sprinkles or colored icings), a four-leaf clover, a hot-air balloon

>> **New baby:** A baby bottle, blocks with letters on them, a rattle

If you have a lot of people to serve, sheet cakes are a good solution. They're the easiest to frost, and their large, flat tops give you lots of decorating room.

TIP

If you don't have a platter or plate large enough to accommodate a sheet cake, you can make your own. Find a sturdy corrugated cardboard box and cut out a large enough piece of cardboard to accommodate your cake. (Use the cake pan to see how large your cake will be and leave at least a 2-inch border around the edge.) Wrap aluminum foil around the cardboard and — voilà! — you have a serving platter.

Remember, no one was born with the natural ability to decorate cakes and other baked goods, so go easy on yourself if you don't get it just right the first few times. Techniques take time to perfect.

Creating Quick, Spiffy Garnishes

Sometimes, frosting a cake just isn't enough — you want to dress it up a little more. Garnishing a cake lets you add your personal touch. The following sections give you some ideas for making simple, fun garnishes.

Garnishes for cakes

You don't have to limit cake garnishes to sugary flowers or fancy decorations. The following are a few suggestions for simple garnishes made of ingredients you probably have on hand:

>> Press sliced almonds, chopped nuts, shaved chocolate, or crushed candy (peppermint works great) onto the sides of a frosted cake. To do so, frost the sides of the cake (but not the top), hold the cake with one hand, and press the garnish onto the side with the palm of your other hand. Or sprinkle the garnish onto a piece of waxed paper and roll the cake sides into the garnish (see Figure 18-2). Set the cake back on the serving plate and then finish frosting the top.

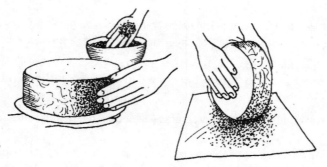

FIGURE 18-2:
Press the garnish onto the cake with the palm of your hand or roll the cake in the garnish to coat.

© John Wiley & Sons, Inc.

>> Lightly dust the top of an iced yellow, carrot, spice, or chocolate cake with ground spice — cinnamon, nutmeg, or allspice. Don't shake the spice onto the cake directly from the jar; you might add too much. Instead, take a pinch of spice and sprinkle it on top.

>> Melt some chocolate and dip a fork in it; then drizzle the chocolate over top of a frosted cake.

>> Make balloons with whole cookies (vanilla wafers or chocolate cream-filled cookies) and use licorice for strings.

>> Add a little color to your cakes with colored and chocolate sprinkles or beads.

>> Give a cake a polka-dotted top by sprinkling candy-covered chocolates on top of the frosting.

>> Forget the frosting and dust the top of the cake with confectioners' sugar or cocoa or a mixture of the two. You can cut out a message in a piece of paper, lay the paper on top of the cake, and then dust the top of the cake. When you remove the paper, your message will be written in sugar. You also can make a pretty pattern by using the same method — just use a paper doily instead of a paper cutout.

Also, check your local kitchen-supply store. There you'll find many garnishes, such as candy flowers, candy letters, and even edible glitter.

Fruit garnishes

Fresh fruit always makes a simple, elegant garnish. Cut up the fruit at the last minute to make sure that it stays fresh. You also can garnish with whole pieces of fruit dipped in chocolate — strawberries are just about everyone's favorite, or you can use raspberries, blackberries, blueberries, sliced mango, or even sliced peaches. Prevent discoloration by tossing the peaches in lemon juice before you use them for garnish. You can either garnish each slice of cake with fruit or top whole cakes or tarts with fruit.

Whipped cream and flavored creams

A dollop of whipped cream on top of cakes and pies is always a welcome treat. Although a variety of premade whipped toppings are available, making your own is easy. Just follow these steps to make 2 cups of whipped cream:

1. **Place 1 pint of heavy (whipping) cream into a chilled bowl.**

   Don't substitute light cream or half-and-half; it won't whip up.

2. **With an electric or hand mixer or a wire whisk, beat the cream until it begins to thicken and stiffen.**

   If you can, chill these tools, too; your cream will thicken faster.

3. **Add 2 tablespoons of sugar or 4 tablespoons of confectioners' sugar, plus 1 teaspoon of vanilla, and beat a little bit longer until soft peaks form.**

   See Chapter 5 for tips on whipping.

4. **Taste and add more sugar if desired.**

PUTTING TOGETHER FLAVORFUL COMBINATIONS

Maybe you're feeling creative in the kitchen. Or maybe you're looking to jazz up a recipe. If you're looking for that little extra something, try the following flavoring combinations. You can flavor whipped cream or plain frosting with a few drops of extract or 1 teaspoon of spice. You may be pleasantly surprised by the flavor boost it gives your desserts. If you aren't feeling particularly adventurous, try flavoring the cream you serve with the coffee or select a corresponding flavor of ice cream or sorbet to match your dessert.

If Your Dominant Flavor Will Be . . .	You Can Accent with These Flavors
Blueberry	Lemon
Chocolate	Almond, apricot, cinnamon, mint, orange, raspberry
Pumpkin	Cinnamon, maple, rum
Strawberry	Almond, lemon
Vanilla	Anise, cherry, hazelnut, lemon, mango, maple, strawberry

Try substituting different flavored extracts for the vanilla. Some of my favorites are almond, lemon, and maple. Almond cream is great in coffee, on cherry pies, and in fruit cobblers. Lemon cream is great paired with lemon tarts or anything minty, and maple cream is delightful on pancakes, pies, and baked apples.

Decorating plates

If you're serving a simple dessert that you don't want to bombard with creams or toppings, but you want to enhance its appearance, you can decorate the plates on which you serve it. Try a few of these tricks:

>> Grease the edge of the dessert plate with shortening (just a thin coating). Sprinkle the edge with spices (cinnamon has a nice color) or cocoa and then tap off the excess. Place your dessert in the center of the plate and let your guests ogle.

>> Get some squeeze bottles at a dime store and fill them with fruit sauce or chocolate sauce. Squeeze out a decoration (squiggles, lines, circles) onto each plate before serving. You can make your own fruit purees by peeling and slicing fresh fruits such as mango, peaches, nectarines, or raspberries and pureeing them in a food processor or blender. Press the fruit through a fine mesh strainer if it has lots of seeds (as raspberries do) and then transfer it to a squeeze bottle.

>> Use a simple slice of colorful fresh fruit to make a nice garnish for plates.

5

The Part of Tens

Give your baked goods a nutritious boost, from nuts to new grains.

Share the kitchen with your kids and discover culinary life lessons everyone can embrace.

Chapter **19**

Ten Ways to Boost Nutrition When Baking

Many people often believe to make a dessert healthy they need to rewrite the recipe and use low-fat or low-calorie ingredients. That's not what this chapter is about. In truth, you can simply add in extras to boost or ramp up the nutrition content without ever rewriting a recipe. After living in Europe, I realized how often American recipes get the good stuff stripped out without leaving much of what's healthy. Baking can be highly nutritious and nourishing. As a dietitian and an avid baker, here I share with you my simple additions or modifications to health-ify my baking recipes.

Adding in Seeds

Chia, flax, pumpkin, sunflower, sesame, and millet seeds are all packed with fiber, antioxidants, and vitamins and minerals. Consider adding them in when you're baking the following:

» **Cakes:** You can add chia and flax seeds to the flour mixture (¼ cup) or stir a couple tablespoons into the jam filling for a layered cake.

- **» Frostings:** You can also use seeds as part of the decoration. Black sesame seeds look stunning on a white frosting or toasted millet seeds look great on a chocolate frosting.

- **» Crisps:** Add seeds such as pumpkin, sesame, and sunflower seeds (add a ¼ cup to the crumble).

- **» Cookies:** Some bakers use seeds as an egg replacement for cookies (check out Chapter 6 for more information).

- **» Breads:** If you're baking bread, soak ¼ cup of seeds in warm water for 15 minutes, drain, and add to the dough.

Ramping Up the Nuts

Nuts once got a bad rap for being high in fat; however, nutrition experts have since learned that nuts boast antioxidants, vitamins, minerals, and phytochemicals that improve blood cholesterol levels, aid in cognition, and are heart healthy. In short, bring on the nuts! Peanuts, walnuts, hazelnuts, almonds, and pistachios are some of my favorites to bake with.

You can finely chop ½ cup to 1 cup nuts and stir them into your favorite quick bread, cake, or muffin batter. Try more recipes using nut flours, such as the Gluten-Free Chocolate Hazelnut Cake or the Lemon Rosemary Almond Cake, both in Chapter 9, or try the French Macarons, classically made with almond flour or German Lebkuchen cookies, both in Chapter 8. Nuts make for a great addition to crisps, cobblers, and cakes, whether they're stirred in or used as a topping.

WARNING

Nut flours can become rancid quickly. Be sure to store nut flours in the freezer or use within 3 months.

Exploring Whole Grains

Bleached flour isn't something you'll find in Europe, and I often wonder why bakers use it at all in the United States. Americans have grown accustomed to white wheat flour, but in other cultures around the globe, spelt, oat, and other whole grains are frequently used (or exclusively used) when baking.

Because recipes change when you use a different flour, start with whole wheat pastry flour (King Arthur Flours makes my favorite). Start with replacing half of your white flour with the whole wheat pastry flour as a 1:1 ratio in a recipe, such as cookies or quick breads. Try swapping in ½ cup rye or whole grain spelt flour in your favorite bread recipes. Rye has a distinct flavor, and spelt is old world wheat and doesn't have as strong of a flavor profile as rye.

Scaling Back the Sugar

Sugar has an important role in many baked goods, from tenderness to sweetness, so I prefer to keep sugar in my recipes. Some like it sweet, and some like it extremely sweet. Americans tend to ramp up the sugar content in all baked goods. So much so that when I moved to Europe for the first time I recall thinking, "Wow, their sweets aren't even sweet."

With time, I realized just how sweet many traditional cakes, cookies, and sweet breads are and perhaps that they don't need to be so sweet. I began slowly cutting back sugar in many of my baked goods. Even trimming back ¼ cup to ½ cup sugar in a recipe can lessen the sweet load. Quick breads, muffins, and cakes are a great starting point for slowly reducing sugar.

Stirring in Fruits

For many years the popular thing to do was replace oil with applesauce, but science has evolved and nutrition experts know that fats are beneficial to a person's health. Fruits are a great way to boost nutrition in baked goods because they add fiber, phytochemicals, antioxidants, and vitamins and minerals. They're also flavorful, colorful, and delicious. Adding dried fruits is a great way to increase nutrition in cookies and quick breads. You can also swirl pureed fruits, such as bananas, apples, pears, and berries into frostings or layered between cakes.

Grating in Greens

Vegetables, of all colors, add nutrition, and many people fall short eating enough veggies. So why not grate in more? Grated carrots and zucchini or pureed pumpkin are simple ways to stir in more veggies. Brownies and chocolate cakes are great starting places for grated zucchini or carrots; just start with ½ cup per batch. Mashed avocado is a great way to cut butter use. Mash ½ cup avocado and replace ½ cup of butter or oil in any baked good, from cakes to cookies.

Baking with Beans

If you have a picky eater, blending in beans is a great way to boost nutrition. Beans are packed with fiber, which can also help balance blood sugars. Here are a few beans you can use:

>> **Black beans:** Mash and add them to brownies.

>> **White beans:** Mash and add into muffins or quick breads.

For whichever bean you choose, start with ½ cup mashed beans and replace ½ cup of the fat.

Focusing On Quality over Quantity

Cheap ingredients often come with less desirable ingredients. Swapping out store bought piecrusts with a homemade crust instantly reduces the ingredient list. Using vegetable-based food colorings removes food dyes, which are banned in many countries. High quality chocolate has high cacao amounts and cuts out the fillers. High quality ingredients have more flavor, and a more robust flavor provides satisfaction when eating. When you can, choose to skip the imitation flavors and opt for the real deal.

Swapping in Fermented Foods

Using cottage cheese or Greek yogurt is an easy replacement for sour cream, buttermilk, and whipping cream. Whether making frosting, muffins, scones, or quick breads, adding cultured Greek yogurt is a great way to boost protein and nutrition. You can use a 1:1 ratio to replace sour cream and buttermilk. With whipping cream, start with replacing half with whole fat Greek yogurt.

Making Peace with Enjoying Desserts

The greatest health benefit you can gain from eating desserts is making peace with them. The amount of shame and guilt that is often rolled into each bite is worse on your health and mental well-being than anything in the bite.

Chapter **20**

Ten Ways to Get Kids Baking

B aking with kids of all ages has benefits, both physically and mentally. Baking is a life skill too many have lost. Empower the kids in your life to know about where foods come from and how to make their own. Who knows when another pandemic will strike and they'll need to bake a loaf of bread? As a chef, dietitian, and mom here are my ten reasons why I bake with kids, and I hope it encourages you to do the same.

Grocery Shopping

From young learners writing grocery lists to searching for ingredients and older kids helping you decide the better deal by calculating unit price, the grocery store holds a lot of life lessons for children. Even toddlers can help by placing the items into the grocery basket and picking out produce. Get them involved and help them learn how to navigate the grocery at an early age, and maybe one day they'll be doing the shopping for you.

Reading Recipes

For young readers, looking at recipes and telling you the amounts is a great starting point. Teach them the symbols of cups, tablespoons, and teaspoons and if you work with a scale, show them how to pour and read the numbers. All of this can be done with young children. For older kids, have them help you prepare the ingredients and read the instructions.

Working through the Math

Recipes are all tasty math problems. Teach kids to see the math without telling them it's math. Measure the ingredients with volumetric measurements (cups), then have them weigh it . . . does this match the amount anticipated? I love baking muffins with young children, letting them measure and tasting the rewards.

Crafting Science Experiments

Baking is also a science. Younger and older children both can experience the science of baking. An easy one to start with is to try baking muffins with different leavening agents, from baking soda, to baking powder, and then omit the leavening agent. Bake all of the muffins and talk about the results. Taste the results. These little life lessons can have a lasting impact on kids in the kitchen.

Encouraging Knife Skills

Knife skills are critical skills and withheld from children out of fear. Kids can slice, dice, and cut foods and children need to work on these skills in order to get better and be efficient in the kitchen. You can start little toddlers with a butter knife, from slicing soft bananas or cutting fat into flour. As kids become more skilled, they can be advanced to a silicon or plastic knife. With guidance and patience kids will gain more confidence in their skills and progress. Offer them opportunities and they'll eventually be chopping by your side.

Letting Kids Set the Pace

In today's fast-paced world it's important to breathe, pause, and let your children set the pace. Let them ask questions, feel the dough, taste (when safe), and experience the process. Perhaps only on weekends could this be possible, but it'll be important to find a day you can take time and make a single recipe with your kids. Do it so many times that they become experts at this recipe. The confidence this will build is priceless and so are the memories made.

Encouraging Explorations and Mistakes

Everyone makes mistakes in the kitchen, yes even experts. Sometimes they're tasty mistakes, and sometimes the mistake lands in the compost. Let children know that making mistakes is okay. Recipes fail, and every failure presents a discovery. My favorite baking experiment with kids is to give them the ingredients for bread — flour, water, yeast, and salt. Let them explore and mix as they'd like. Both of you may be surprised at the outcome. You can bake some of the bread, make rolls, and roll out and cook on a skillet for flatbread. Bread is such a versatile food to play with and explore.

Finding Kid-Friendly Kitchen Tools

Have tools just for your kids. A mixing bowl, a rubber spatula, a baking scale, a knife, and a cutting board. Place these tools on a shelf and let kids know what pantry staples they can experiment with should the urge strike. I don't recommend buying kids baking equipment because often these kits are full of cheap, plastic tools that can break and cause frustration. Buy things you would use, but just for them. Tovla (https://tovlajr.com/) makes kid-safe knives and cutting gloves. These are great tools for young chefs.

Expanding Vocabulary

Kitchen lingo has its own set of vocabulary words. A baking glossary is a great starting point for discovering, but having kids read recipes puts the words in action. Help them discover new descriptive terms to tell you about what they are tasting. I love challenging kids (and adults) to use words to describe foods and to go beyond "yucky" and "yummy." Talk about the taste, the texture, and see where that leads your little foodie or picky eater.

Experiencing with Recipes

A great place to kick off a baking experience with kids is to first start with recipes they like. Then consider a quick bread, muffins, brownies, scones, or biscuits. These recipes have room for success, are quick and easy, and are simple enough for little ones to help.

Appendix A

Glossary of Baking Terms

bain-marie: See *water bath.*

bake: To cook in a hot, dry environment in a closed area (your oven!). Foods are baked uncovered for dry, crisp surfaces and covered for moistness and to prevent excess browning.

batter: An uncooked semiliquid mixture containing flour and other ingredients used to make a cake or bread. Generally a batter contains more liquid, and sometimes more fat and/or sugar, than a dough does.

beat: A mixing method in which ingredients are vigorously agitated to incorporate air and develop *gluten,* a protein that is found in wheat and other varieties of flour and that, when beaten, becomes more elastic and gives a cohesiveness to doughs. Beating requires the use of a spoon, beaters, or a mixer with a paddle attachment.

bind: To add an ingredient that holds other ingredients together. Most commonly, binding occurs when an ingredient is added to a hot liquid (flour, eggs, cream, cheese), causing it to thicken.

blanch: A technique in which food is plunged into boiling water for a short time (about 30 seconds) and then sometimes plunged into ice water to stop the cooking, followed by draining well. This technique preserves the color, taste, and texture of the food. Blanching is also used to remove the skins of harder-to-peel fruits, vegetables, and nuts.

blend: A mixing method in which two or more ingredients are combined just until they're evenly distributed; a spoon, rubber spatula, whisk, beaters, or mixer with a paddle attachment is generally used.

boil: To heat a liquid until bubbles rise to the surface and break, and steam is given off. Water boils at 212 degrees. A *rolling boil* means the bubbles are forming rapidly and can't be stopped when stirred.

broil: To cook foods directly under a very hot heat source. Generally, this technique is used for quickly browning tops of dishes or cooking meats and fish with little or no added fat.

caramelize: To cook sugar over medium heat until it liquefies and turns a rich caramel brown.

chill: To place hot or room-temperature foods in the refrigerator or freezer. Gelatin and puddings change from liquids to solids when chilled. Creams also thicken upon chilling.

chop: To cut foods into coarse or fine pieces using a large chef's knife, food processor, or blender.

coat: To cover food evenly with flour, sugar, a crumb mixture, or a sauce.

come together: A term used in pastry making. When small amounts of water are added to the crumbled mixture, it "comes together" and forms a rough dough.

cool: To allow hot foods to come to room temperature. Putting food on a wire rack allows air to circulate around it; stirring hot liquids cools them faster because it allows the steam to escape. You can also cool liquids in the refrigerator.

core: To remove the center of fruits, usually apples, pears, and pineapples.

cream: A mixing method in which a softened fat and sugar are vigorously combined to incorporate air; used for quick breads, cookies, and some cakes. Creaming can be done with a wooden spoon or electric mixer, and the fat becomes lighter when you're finished.

crush: To press into very fine bits.

curdle: The separation of milk or egg mixtures into solid or liquid components; caused by overcooking, high heat, or acidic ingredients (such as lemon juice or vinegar). If you add lemon juice to milk, the milk thickens and curdles, which is fine if you're making sour milk or buttermilk.

cut-in: A mixing method in which solid fat is incorporated into dry ingredients, using a pastry blender, two knives, or a fork, resulting in a coarse texture, as when making piecrust, biscuits, crumb toppings, and so on.

dash: Less than $\frac{1}{8}$ teaspoon of an ingredient.

dough: A mixture of flour and other ingredients used in baking; it has a low moisture content and is often stiff enough to hold a shape.

drain: To remove excess liquid by placing the food in a colander or strainer that has been set over the sink, or over a bowl if you have to reserve the liquids you're draining.

drizzle: To pour a liquid (such as a sauce, frosting, or topping) in a thin stream over food. Usually, it's done quickly with a small amount of liquid.

dust: To sprinkle lightly with flour, confectioners' sugar, cocoa, and the like.

egg wash: A beaten egg (sometimes mixed with a little water or milk), brushed on top of pastry or dough before baking. It gives a sheen to bread, piecrusts, pastries, and so on, after they're baked.

finely chop (mince): To cut into very small pieces. Done with a knife or in a food processor or blender.

flute: To pinch pastry edges with your fingers to make a decorative edge and extend the height of the crust edge, helping to hold in juicy pie fillings.

fold: A mixing method used to gently incorporate light, airy products into heavier ingredients (for example, mixing beaten egg whites into a cake batter). Usually a rubber spatula is used. First, you cut down vertically through the mixture, and then you slide the spatula across the bottom of the bowl and up the other side, turning the mixture over. You continue this down-across-up-over motion while rotating the bowl a quarter turn each time. Continue this motion just until the ingredients are incorporated. Don't use a stirring motion.

garnish: Any food used as an attractive decoration. Popular garnishes for baked goods include chocolate curls, whole strawberries, edible or sugar flowers, chopped nuts, and orange halves.

glaze: A shiny coating applied to food or a thin, sometimes flavored, coating poured or dripped onto a cake or pastry.

grate: To shred food (such as cheese) by rubbing it against a serrated metal plate known as a grater.

grease: To rub the inside of a baking pan with a thin, even coating of butter, margarine, or shortening (or to spray with a nonstick cooking spray) to prevent foods from sticking to the pan while baking. Generally used for cakes. Use shortening, not butter, if baking sheets need to be greased for cookies.

grind: To pulverize or reduce food to very small particles by using a mechanical grinder, mortar and pestle, or food processor.

hull: To remove the caps from strawberries. This can be done with a small knife, an inexpensive tool called a strawberry huller (short, fat tweezers), or a straw. With the knife or huller, just pinch off the green cap. To use the straw, insert the straw in the narrow end of the strawberry and push it through to the top of the strawberry. The green cap should pop right off.

knead: To work dough to develop the gluten present in the flours. During kneading, the gluten strands stretch and expand throughout the dough, enabling the dough to hold in the gas bubbles released by the leavener (usually yeast). You can knead by hand by repeating a series of steps: pressing into the dough with the heel of your hand, folding the dough in half, and giving a turn. You can also use a large mixer with a dough hook or a food processor equipped with a plastic blade. Well-kneaded dough becomes smooth and elastic.

macaronage: The point in preparing French macarons in which the batter becomes smooth, shiny, and silky.

macerate: To soak foods in a liquid (often juice or liqueur) to soften them, absorb the flavor of the soaking liquid, and release its flavor. Both liquids and solids are used for the dish, as in a dessert fruit topping.

melt: A process where certain foods, especially those high in fat, gradually soften and then liquefy when heated.

mince: See *finely chop*.

mix: To combine ingredients by hand or with an electric appliance so they are evenly dispersed.

nonreactive: Used when talking about cooking equipment. Nonreactive equipment is made of a metal that doesn't react with acidic foods. Examples of nonreactive materials are stainless steel, Teflon, and glass. Reactive metals are aluminum and copper. When foods and metal equipment do react, generally the foods turn an undesirable brown color. Tomato sauces, red wine sauces, and lemon juice are examples of foods that will react with metals.

pare: To peel. A paring knife is a small, short knife.

pipe: To force a softened mixture (frosting or whipped cream) through a pastry bag in order to decorate a cake.

pit: To remove the hard seeds from the center of fruits.

preheat: To allow the oven to reach its proper baking temperature before food is placed in it. An oven takes between 10 and 20 minutes to properly preheat.

proof: A test given to yeast to determine whether it is alive. The yeast is dissolved in warm water (wrist temperature, not above 115 degrees) with a pinch of sugar and then set aside for about 5 minutes. If the mixture becomes foamy, it's alive.

pulse: Short on-and-off bursts of a food processor. Pulsing is generally used to chop or mince foods.

punch down: To firmly push your fist into risen dough with your fist to deflate it so it will become more tender and even-grained. It's not a physical punch, but more of a gentle pressure.

puree: To process food to achieve a smooth pulp. Usually done by using a food processor or blender or by pushing softened foods through a fine mesh strainer or food mill.

reduce: To cook a liquid until its quantity decreases due to evaporation. Typically this is done to intensify flavors and thicken the liquid.

rest: To allow dough to stand for a certain period of time before shaping it into a shape such as a roll or braid. The dough will relax and be easier to work with after a rest.

scald: To heat a liquid, usually milk, uncovered, to just below the boiling point.

score: To cut very shallow slits across food before cooking. Scoring can be decorative, as when making French bread. Scoring also can be functional: It helps loosen skin in preparation for peeling foods such as peaches or tomatoes, and it helps marinated foods absorb flavors.

seed: To remove the seeds from a fruit or vegetable.

set: To chill a custard or gelatin, transforming it from a liquid to a solid.

shave: To cut in very thin layers with a vegetable peeler (usually done with chocolate).

shell: To remove the hard outer casing of nuts.

shred: To cut into thin but irregular pieces. Often done with a grater or food processor with a shredding disk.

sift: To shake a dry ingredient (such as flour or sugar) through a sieve or sifter to remove lumps and incorporate air. Sifting also is used to combine dry ingredients.

simmer: To maintain the temperature of a liquid just below the boiling point. Small bubbles continually but gently break the surface of the cooking mixture.

slice: To cut an item into relatively broad, thin pieces.

soften: To allow food, usually butter, cream cheese, or margarine, to stand at room temperature until it is no longer hard. Perishable foods shouldn't stay at room temperature any longer than 30 minutes.

sprinkle: To scatter something, usually a garnish, lightly over the surface of food.

steep: To soak foods in a hot liquid in order to extract flavor or to soften the texture, such as when you make tea.

stir: A mixing method in which ingredients are gently combined until blended.

strain: To pour foods through a sieve, mesh strainer, or cheesecloth to separate or remove the liquid or smaller particles from larger particles.

toast: To brown food in an oven or broiler. Nuts and spices are toasted by cooking them in a dry skillet over very low heat for several minutes, stirring often, until they brown slightly and become aromatic.

unmold: To remove food — usually a cake, custard, or gelatin — from its container and place it on a serving plate.

water bath: Also called a *bain-marie*, a large baking dish filled with hot water in which food in individual cups is gently baked. Usually used for custards and baked puddings.

whip: A mixing method in which foods are vigorously beaten in order to incorporate air. A handheld whisk or an electric mixer with a whisk attachment is used.

whisk: A wire whip used to beat foods to incorporate air into them.

work in: A mixing method in which an ingredient is incorporated into other ingredients, resulting in a uniform mixture. For example, butter is worked into flour to create a delicate pastry.

yield: The total amount of a product made from a specific recipe or the number of servings a recipe will produce.

zest: The outer skin of citrus fruits that contains the fragrant oils. You want to avoid the white underneath (the pith), which tastes bitter.

Appendix B

Metric Conversion Guide

Note: The recipes in this cookbook were not developed or tested using metric measures. There may be some variation in quality when converting to metric units.

Common Abbreviations

Abbreviation(s)	What It Stands For
C, c	cup
g	gram
kg	kilogram
L, l	liter
lb	pound
mL, ml	milliliter
oz	ounce
pt	pint
t, tsp	teaspoon
T, TB, Tbl, Tbsp	tablespoon

Volume

U.S Units	Canadian Metric	Australian Metric
¼ teaspoon	1 mL	1 ml
½ teaspoon	2 mL	2 ml
1 teaspoon	5 mL	5 ml
1 tablespoon	15 mL	20 ml
¼ cup	50 mL	60 ml
⅓ cup	75 mL	80 ml
½ cup	125 mL	125 ml
⅔ cup	150 mL	170 ml
¾ cup	175 mL	190 ml
1 cup	250 mL	250 ml
1 quart	1 liter	1 liter
1½ quarts	1.5 liters	1.5 liters
2 quarts	2 liters	2 liters
2½ quarts	2.5 liters	2.5 liters
3 quarts	3 liters	3 liters
4 quarts	4 liters	4 liters

Weight

U.S. Units	Canadian Metric	Australian Metric
1 ounce	30 grams	30 grams
2 ounces	55 grams	60 grams
3 ounces	85 grams	90 grams
4 ounces (¼ pound)	115 grams	125 grams
8 ounces (½ pound)	225 grams	225 grams
16 ounces (1 pound)	455 grams	500 grams
1 pound	455 grams	½ kilogram

Measurements

Inches	Centimeters
½	1.5
1	2.5
2	5.0
3	7.5
4	10.0
5	12.5
6	15.0
7	17.5
8	20.5
9	23.0
10	25.5
11	28.0
12	30.5
13	33.0

Temperature (Degrees)

Fahrenheit	Celsius
32	0
212	100
250	120
275	140
300	150
325	160
350	180
375	190
400	200
425	220
450	230
475	240
500	260

Index

A

active dry yeast, 20–21, 270
air fryers, 46, 103
alcoholic beverages, 32
allergies
  dairy, 91–92
  eggs, 89–90
  gluten, 88–89
  nuts, 90
  overview, 87
  wheat, 88–89
all-purpose flour, 13, 272
almonds
  Lemon Rosemary Almond Cake, 173
  overview, 29–30
aluminum foil, 323
aluminum pie plate, 43
Angel Food Cake, 160, 166–168
Anisette Biscotti, 134
apple corer, 55–56
apples
  overview, 35
  peeling/pitting, 81
  recipes
    Apple Crisp, 239
    Apple Turnovers, 317
    Applesauce Cake, 156
    Cinnamon Apple Dumplings, 219
    Cran-Apple and Pear Pie, 230
    German Apple Kuchen with Streusel, 157
    You'll-Be-Glad-You-Tried-It Apple Pie, 218
apricots
  peeling/pitting, 81
  recipes
    Apricot-Date Half-Moons, 131
    Quick Apricot Glaze, 196
avocados, 35

B

Bacon Cheddar and Chives Scones, 268
baked goods
  freezing, 328–331
  refrigerating, 326–328
  storing at room temperature, 324–326
  wrapping, 321–324
baking
  with beans, 346
  choosing quality over quantity, 346
  cleaning and, 104–105
  cooking vs., 8
  defined, 351
  energy costs and, 102–103
  at high elevations, 101–102
  involving kids in, 347–350
  nutrition and, 343–346
  overview, 7–10
  preparation and, 9, 93–95
  recipes and
    considering skill level, 95
    overview, 95
    reading, 96–97
    servings, 97–98
    taking inventory, 98
    understanding instructions, 96
    using correct kitchen equipment, 98–100
  terminology, 351–355
  timing and, 101
baking pans, 40–44
baking powder, 19–20
baking soda, 19
bananas
  Banana Bread, 251
  Banana Cream Pie, 226
  Banana-Sour Cream Bundt Cake, 158
  overview, 35

bars
    Cinnamon-Spiced Cheesecake Bars, 316
    Crunchy Granola Bars, 146
    cutting, 336
    Lemon Bars, 146
    overview, 143
Basic Cookie Press Cookies, 136
Basic Hamburger Buns, 288–289
Basic White Buttermilk Bread, 282
batters, 351
beans
    baking with, 346
    as pie weights, 37
beating technique, 351
beef, 301
beeswax wraps, 322
berries
    buying tips, 35
    Sour Cherry-Berry Pie, 229
binding ingredients, 351
biscotti, 134
biscuits
    Bacon Cheddar and Chives Scones, 268
    Buttermilk Biscuits, 265
    Cheesy Cheese Biscuits, 266
    cutters, 50
    forming, 264
    Lemon Blueberry Scones, 267
    mixing dough, 263
    storing, 264
bittersweet chocolate, 28
black beans, 346
Black-and-White Brownies, 145
blanching, 351
blenders, 46
blending, 351
blueberries
    Blueberry Crunch, 240
    Blueberry Muffins, 261
    Blueberry Pie, 220
    Lemon Blueberry Scones, 267
boiling, 351
Boston Brown Bread, 257
bourbon, 245
box graters, 55–56

Braided Egg Bread, 283–284
bread
    adding seeds to, 344
    baking, 279–281
    biscuits
        Bacon Cheddar and Chives Scones, 268
        Buttermilk Biscuits, 265
        Cheesy Cheese Biscuits, 266
        forming, 264
        Lemon Blueberry Scones, 267
        mixing dough, 263
        storing, 264
    buns and rolls
        Basic Hamburger Buns, 288–289
        Crescent Rolls, 291
        Fluffy Dinner Rolls, 292
        Molly's Sweet Cardamom Rolls, 294
        No-Fail Rolls, 290
        Sesame-Topped Rolls, 293
    cutting, 336
    kneading, 276–277
    loaves
        Basic White Buttermilk Bread, 282
        Braided Egg Bread, 283–284
        Honey-Oatmeal Bread, 285
        Jeff's Potato Bread, 286
    mixing, 275–276
    muffins, 259–262
    rising dough, 278–279
    savory quick bread
        Boston Brown Bread, 257
        overview, 256
        Southern Corn Bread, 258
    shaping, 279–281
    storing
        freezing, 329
        refrigerating, 328
        at room temperature, 328
        wrapping, 326
    sweet quick bread
        Banana Bread, 251
        Chocolate Zucchini Bread, 252
        Cranberry-Orange Bread, 253
        Crumbcake, 254
        overview, 249

Pumpkin Bread, 250
Sweet Chocolate Chip Pull-Apart Bread, 255
yeast
  eggs, 275
  fat, 274
  flour, 272–273
  liquids, 275
  overview, 270–272
  salt, 274
  sweeteners, 274
bread flour, 13, 272
bread machine yeast, 270
Bread Pudding with Bourbon Caramel Sauce, 245
Broccoli and Cheese Quiche with Potato Crust, 307–308
broiling, 351
brown sugar, 15–16
brownies
  Black-and-White Brownies, 145
  cutting, 336
  Dense Chocolate Brownies, 144
  overview, 143–145
bulk foods, storing, 12
Bundt pans
  Banana-Sour Cream Bundt Cake, 158
  overview, 41–42
buns, 288–289
burning, preventing, 40–41
butter
  alternatives, 91
  overview, 22–24
  softening, 355
butter cakes
  Applesauce Cake, 156
  Banana-Sour Cream Bundt Cake, 158
  Carrot Cake, 155
  German Apple Kuchen with Streusel, 157
  Light and Fluffy Yellow Cake, 152
  Martha's Chocolate Cake, 153
  overview, 149–151
  Texas Chocolate Sheath Cake, 154
buttercream frosting, 188
buttermilk
  alternatives, 91
  Basic White Buttermilk Bread, 282

Buttermilk Biscuits, 265
overview, 26–27
Butterscotch Drops, 119

C

cake flour, 13
cake mixes
  Crazy-Good Pineapple Upside-Down Cake, 313
  overview, 309–311
  Super Chocolate Cake, 312
cake pans, 42
cake rounds, 196
cake tester, 56
cakes
  adding seeds to, 343
  butter cakes
    Applesauce Cake, 156
    Banana-Sour Cream Bundt Cake, 158
    Carrot Cake, 155
    German Apple Kuchen with Streusel, 157
    Light and Fluffy Yellow Cake, 152
    Martha's Chocolate Cake, 153
    overview, 149–151
    Texas Chocolate Sheath Cake, 154
  cheesecakes
    Classic Cheesecake, 178
    Lemon Curd Cheesecake, 180–181
    overview, 176–177
    Pumpkin Cheesecake, 179
  cooling, 159–160
  Crazy-Good Pineapple Upside-Down Cake, 313
  cupcakes
    Chocolate Cupcakes, 164
    Lemon Cupcakes, 165
    overview, 163–165
  cutting, 334–335
  frosting, 194–195
  garnishes for, 337–338
  pound cakes
    Chocolate Swirl Pound Cake, 162
    Classic Pound Cake, 161
    overview, 159–162
  sponge cakes

cakes *(continued)*
    Angel Food Cake, 166–168
    Gluten-Free Chocolate Hazelnut Cake, 174
    Jelly Roll, 169–170
    Lemon Rosemary Almond Cake, 173
    Molten Lava Cake, 175
    overview, 166–167
    Tres Leches with Mango, 171–172
  storing
    freezing, 329–330
    wrapping, 325–326
calzones, 303–305
caramel, 245
caramelizing, 351
cardamom, 294
carrots
  Carrot Cake, 155
  overview, 35
ceramic pie plates, 43
cheese
  alternatives, 91
  recipes
    Broccoli and Cheese Quiche with Potato Crust, 307–308
    Cheese Soufflé, 297–298
    Cheesy Cheese Biscuits, 266
    Cream Cheese Frosting, 186
    Goat Cheese and Tomato Tart, 302
cheesecakes
  cooling, 159
  cutting, 335
  overview, 176–177
  recipes
    Cinnamon-Spiced Cheesecake Bars, 316
    Classic Cheesecake, 178
    Lemon Curd Cheesecake, 180–181
    Pumpkin Cheesecake, 179
  storing, 327
chef's knives, 51
cherries
  peeling/pitting, 82
  recipes
    Cherry Crumb Pie, 221
    Cream Cheese and Cherry Danishes, 318
    Sour Cherry-Berry Pie, 229
  shopping for, 35

Chicken Potpie, 300
chilling, 352
chives, 268
chocolate and cocoa
  alternatives, 91
  melting, 84–85
  overview, 27–29
  recipes
    Black-and-White Brownies, 145
    Chocolate Chip Frosting, 312
    Chocolate Cream Pie, 225
    Chocolate Cupcakes, 164
    Chocolate Drop Cookies, 115
    Chocolate Frosting, 191
    Chocolate Swirl Pound Cake, 162
    Chocolate Zucchini Bread, 252
    Chocolate-Coconut Macaroons, 118
    Crispy Chocolate Chip Cookies, 114
    Dense Chocolate Brownies, 144
    Gluten-Free Chocolate Hazelnut Cake, 174
    Martha's Chocolate Cake, 153
    Rich Chocolate Pudding, 244
    Super Chocolate Cake, 312
    Sweet Chocolate Chip Pull-Apart Bread, 255
    Texas Chocolate Sheath Cake, 154
chopping, 352
cinnamon
  Cinnamon Apple Dumplings, 219
  Cinnamon-Spiced Cheesecake Bars, 316
citrus fruits
  reamer for, 56
  shopping for, 35
  zesting, 82–84, 355
Classic Cheesecake, 178
Classic Oatmeal-Raisin Cookies, 116
Classic Pound Cake, 161
Classic Sugar Glaze, 197
cleavers, 50
coating technique, 352
cobbler recipe, 241
coconuts
  overview, 32
  recipes
    Chocolate-Coconut Macaroons, 118
    Coconut Cream Pie, 227

coffee, 187

Colorado State University's Food Science and Human Nutrition Department, 101

come together, defined, 352

compressed cake yeast, 270–271

condensed milk, 27, 91

confectioners' sugar, 15

convection ovens, 68

conversion guide, 357–359

cookie cutters, 50

cookie sheets, 40–41

cookies

  adding seeds to, 344

  bars

    Crunchy Granola Bars, 146

    Lemon Bars, 146

    overview, 143

  Basic Cookie Press Cookies, 136

  brownies

    Black-and-White Brownies, 145

    Dense Chocolate Brownies, 144

    overview, 143–145

  cutting, 336

  drop

    Butterscotch Drops, 119

    Chocolate Drop Cookies, 115

    Chocolate-Coconut Macaroons, 118

    Classic Oatmeal-Raisin Cookies, 116

    Crispy Chocolate Chip Cookies, 114

    Everything Cookies, 117

    French Macarons, 121–122

    overview, 112–113

    Poppy Seed Cookies, 120

  effect of fats on, 110

  overview, 109–110

  pressed, 135–136

  preventing burning, 40–41

  rolled

    Gingerbread Cookies with Royal Icing, 140–141

    overview, 137–139

    Tender Sugar Cookies, 142

  shaped

    Anisette Biscotti, 134

    Apricot-Date Half-Moons, 131

    Crisp Sugar Cookies, 127

    Gingersnaps, 128

    Lebkuchen, 129

    Lemon Cookies, 130

    overview, 123

    Peanut Butter Cookies, 124

    Rolled Sugar Cookies, 126

    Rosemary Shortbread Cookies, 132

    Russian Tea Balls, 133

    Snickerdoodles, 125

  Spritz, 135

  storing

    freezing, 328–329

    refrigerating, 327

    at room temperature, 327

    wrapping, 325

  techniques

    choosing pan, 111

    measuring ingredients, 110

    mixing, 110

    spacing, 112

cooking, baking vs., 8

cooling, 352

cooling racks, 49

coring, 352

corn bread, 258

cornmeal/starch, 37

Corriher, Shirley O., 207

cranberries

  recipes

    Cran-Apple and Pear Pie, 230

    Cranberry-Orange Bread, 253

  shopping for, 36

Crazy-Good Pineapple Upside-Down Cake, 313

cream

  alternatives, 91

  garnishes, 339–340

  overview, 26–27

  whipping, 80–81

cream cheese

  alternatives, 91

  recipes

    Cream Cheese and Cherry Danishes, 318

    Cream Cheese Frosting, 186

cream of tartar, 20

cream pies

  Banana Cream Pie, 226

  Chocolate Cream Pie, 225

  Coconut Cream Pie, 227

creaming, 352

Crescent Rolls, 291

Crisp Sugar Cookies, 127

crisps

  adding seeds to, 344

  Apple Crisp, 239

Crispy Chocolate Chip Cookies, 114

Crumbcake, 254

Crunchy Granola Bars, 146

crushing, 352

cupcakes

  overview, 163–165

  recipes

    Chocolate Cupcakes, 164

    Lemon Cupcakes, 165

custards, 242–246

cut-in mixing, 352

cutout pastry edge, 215

cutout top crust, 214

cutting, 333–336, 348–349

cutting boards, 50, 105

D

dairy

  butter

    alternatives, 91

    overview, 22–24

    softening, 355

  buttermilk

    alternatives, 91

    Basic White Buttermilk Bread, 282

    Buttermilk Biscuits, 265

    overview, 26–27

  cream

    alternatives, 91

    garnishes, 339–340

    overview, 26–27

    whipping, 80–81

  food allergies and, 91–92

  milk

    alternatives, 91

    overview, 26–27

    scalding, 85, 354

    Tres Leches with Mango, 171–172

  yogurt

    alternatives, 91

    Ginger-Spiced Key Lime Yogurt Pie, 233

    overview, 38

danishes, 318

dark chocolate, 28

dash, defined, 352

dates

  Apricot-Date Half-Moons, 131

  Sticky Date and Toffee Pudding, 246

decorating

  with frosting, 198–203

  pies and tarts, 215

  serving plates, 340

  techniques, 336–337

demerara sugar, 15–16

Dense Chocolate Brownies, 144

Department of Agriculture Extension Service, 101

double boiler, 44–45

double-crust pies

  overview, 213–214

  recipes

    Cran-Apple and Pear Pie, 230

    Sour Cherry-Berry Pie, 229

dough

  avoiding common mistakes, 236

  cake mixes, 309–311

  chilling, 208

  come together term, 352

  cutting in fat, 207

  decorating, 215

  defined, 352

  flour and, 207

  freezing, 329

  frozen, 314–318

  mixing, 206, 263

  overview, 37

  prebaking, 212

  punch down, 354

  recipes

    Apple Turnovers, 317

    Cinnamon-Spiced Cheesecake Bars, 316

    Crazy-Good Pineapple Upside-Down Cake, 313

    Cream Cheese and Cherry Danishes, 318

    Old-fashioned, 211

Stir-and-roll, 212
Super Chocolate Cake, 312
Super-Easy Veggie Party Pizza, 315
Weeknight Pizza Dough, 304
resting, 354
rising, 278–279
rolling out, 208–209
storing, 328–329
transferring to pie plate, 209–210
draining, 352
dried fruits, 31
drizzling, 352
drop cookies
overview, 112–113
recipes
Butterscotch Drops, 119
Chocolate Drop Cookies, 115
Chocolate-Coconut Macaroons, 118
Classic Oatmeal-Raisin Cookies, 116
Crispy Chocolate Chip Cookies, 114
Everything Cookies, 117
French Macarons, 121–122
Poppy Seed Cookies, 120
drop flower tips, pastry bag, 200
dry ingredients, measuring, 73–74
dry yeast, 20–21
dumplings, 219
dusting, 352
dutch oven, 45

E

eggs
alternatives, 89–90
food allergies and, 89–90
as leavener, 22
overview, 17–18
recipes
Angel Food Cake, 166
Braided Egg Bread, 283–284
separating, 78–79
wash, 352
whipping whites, 79–80
yeast breads, 275
electric ovens, 67
electrical, 46–49, 62
emulsifiers, 311

equipment, kitchen. *See* kitchen equipment
evaporated milk, 27
Everything Cookies, 117
extracts, 34

F

fats
butter, 22–24, 91
in butter cakes, 150
cutting in dough, 207
effect on cookies, 110
lard, 24–25
measuring, 73–74
monosaturated, 26
nonstick cooking spray, 25–26
oil, 25
overview, 22
purchasing, 12
saturated, 25
shortening, 24
yeast breads, 274
fermented foods, boosting nutrition with, 346
flour
alternatives, 88–89
cornmeal/starch, 37
dough and, 207
gluten-free, 88–89
nutrition and, 344–345
overview, 12–15
sifter, 57
yeast breads, 272–273
Fluffy Dinner Rolls, 292
flute, 353
folding, 353
food allergies
dairy, 91–92
eggs, 89–90
gluten, 88–89
nuts, 90
overview, 87
wheat, 88–89
food coloring, 37
food processors, 46–47
food safety, 104–105
fork pastry edge, 215
freezing, 330–331

French Macarons, 121–122

fresh compressed yeast, 21

fresh fruits, 35–36

frostings

  adding seeds to, 344

  cakes, 194–195

  cooked, 189–192

  decorating with, 198–203

  determining amount, 185

  glazes, 195–197

  overview, 37

  quick, 185–188

  recipes

    Basic Vanilla Buttercream Frosting, 188

    Chocolate Chip Frosting, 312

    Chocolate Frosting, 191

    Classic Sugar Glaze, 197

    Cream Cheese Frosting, 186

    Martha's Sweet and Creamy Frosting, 192

    Mocha Frosting, 187

    Quick Apricot Glaze, 196

    Sweetened Whipped Cream Frosting, 190

  types of, 183–184

frozen dough

  Apple Turnovers, 317

  Cinnamon-Spiced Cheesecake Bars, 316

  Cream Cheese and Cherry Danishes, 318

  overview, 37, 314–318

  Super-Easy Veggie Party Pizza, 315

fruits

  boosting nutrition with, 345

  citrus, 35

  crisps and cobblers, 238–241

  dried, 31

  fresh, 35–36

  garnishes, 338

  peeling and pitting, 81–82

  zesting, 82–84

funnel, 57

G

galettes, 235

garnishes

  defined, 353

  overview, 337–340

  sprinkling, 355

gas ovens, 66–67

gear. *See* kitchen equipment

German Apple Kuchen with Streusel, 157

ginger

  Gingerbread Cookies with Royal Icing, 140–141

  Gingersnaps, 128

  Ginger-Spiced Key Lime Yogurt Pie, 233

glass measuring cups, 52

glass pie plates, 43

glassware, 323–324

glazes, 195–197, 353

gluten, 13, 88–89

Gluten-Free Chocolate Hazelnut Cake, 174

Goat Cheese and Tomato Tart, 302

graded measuring cups, 52

granola, 146

granulated sugar, 15

grating, 353

greasing, 353

grills, 103

grinding, 353

grocery shopping, 12, 35–36, 39, 347

H

half-and-half cream, 27

half-moon cookies, 131

handheld mixers, 47–48

hazelnuts

  Gluten-Free Chocolate Hazelnut Cake, 174

  overview, 30

heat, controlling oven, 70

heavy cream, 27

herbs, 34

high elevations, baking at, 101–102

Honey-Oatmeal Bread, 285

hot spots in oven, 68

hulling, 353

I

icing

  cakes, 194–195

  cooked, 189–192

  decorating with, 198–203

  determining amount, 185

  glazes, 195–197

quick, 185–188
recipes
  Basic Vanilla Buttercream Frosting, 188
  Chocolate Frosting, 191
  Classic Sugar Glaze, 197
  Cream Cheese Frosting, 186
  Gingerbread Cookies with Royal Icing, 140–141
  Martha's Sweet and Creamy Frosting, 192
  Mocha Frosting, 187
  Quick Apricot Glaze, 196
  Sweetened Whipped Cream Frosting, 190
types of, 183–184
ingredients
  binding, 351
  extracts, 34
  fresh fruit and vegetables, 35–36
  measuring
    dry ingredients, 73–74
    fats and solids, 73–74
    liquids, 74–75
    overview, 71–75
    premeasuring, 99
    recipes and, 96
    with scale, 72–73
    with teaspoons and tablespoons, 73
  overview, 11–12
  storing
    bulk foods, 12
    butter, 23–24
    chocolate and cocoa, 28
    flour, 15
    nuts and oats, 30–31
  using high quality, 346
Instant Pot, 48, 103, 181

J

Jeff's Potato Bread, 286
Jelly Roll, 169–170

K

King Arthur Flour, 101
kitchen equipment
  air fryers, 46, 103
  aluminum pie plates, 43
  apple corer, 55–56
  biscuit cutters, 50
  blenders, 46
  box graters, 55–56
  cake rounds, 196
  cake tester, 56
  ceramic pie plates, 43
  chef's knives, 51
  citrus juicer, 56
  cleavers, 50
  cookie cutters, 50
  cookie sheets, 40–41
  cooling racks, 49
  cutting boards, 50, 105
  double boiler, 44–45
  dutch oven, 45
  electrical, 46–49, 62
  flour sifters, 57
  food processors, 46–47
  funnel, 57
  glass measuring cups, 52
  glass pie plates, 43
  graded measuring cups, 52
  handheld mixers, 47–48
  Instant Pot, 48, 103, 181
  kid-friendly tools, 349
  knives, 50–51
  measuring
    cups, 52
    scales, 54, 72–73, 100
    spoons, 53, 73
  metal spoons, 55
  microplanes, 58
  mixing bowls, 53
  muffin tins, 41
  multicookers, 48, 103, 181
  nonreactive, 354
  oven
    controlling heat, 70
    convection, 68
    electric, 67
    gas, 66–67
    hot spots in, 68
    inspecting, 94
    preheating, 69–70, 354

kitchen equipment *(continued)*
    racks, 68–69
    types of, 65–68
  oven mitts, 53–54
  oven thermometers, 58
  pans
    baking, 40–44
    Bundt, 41–42
    cake, 42
    loaf, 42–43
    preparing, 75–77
    saucepans, 44
    springform, 43–44
    tube, 41–42, 77
  parchment paper, 111
  paring knives, 51
  pastry bags and tips
    choosing, 198–200
    drop flower tips, 200
    filling bag, 201
    how to use, 202–203
    leaf tips, 200
    overview, 58
    petal tips, 200
    star tips, 200
    writing tips, 200
  pastry blender, 59
  pastry brush, 59
  pie plates, 43, 206, 209–210
  pie weights, 60
  polyurethane cutting boards, 50
  potholders, 53–54
  pots, 44–45
  reamer, 56
  rolling pins/mats, 54
  scissors, 58
  shopping for, 39
  sieve/strainers, 60
  Silpat, 61
  spatulas, 61
  spoons, 55
  stand mixers, 48–49
  thermometers, 58
  thin plastic cutting boards, 50
  timers, 62
  tongs, 62
  trivets, 62
  using correctly, 98–100
  vegetable peeler, 62
  wire whisk, 62
  wooden cutting boards, 50
  wooden spoons, 55
kitchen scissors, 58
kneading, 353
knives, 50–51
kosher salt, 16

L

lard, 24–25
lattice crust, 213–214
leaf tips, pastry bag, 200
leaveners
  baking powder, 19–20
  baking soda, 19
  cream of tartar, 20
  egg yolks and whites, 22
  sourdough starter, 21–22
  yeast, 20–21, 270–271
Lebkuchen, 129
lemons
  Ginger-Spiced Key Lime Yogurt Pie, 233
  Lemon Bars, 146
  Lemon Blueberry Scones, 267
  Lemon Cookies, 130
  Lemon Cupcakes, 165
  Lemon Curd Cheesecake, 180–181
  Lemon Poppy Seed Muffins, 262
  Lemon Rosemary Almond Cake, 173
  Tart Lemon Tart, 232
Light and Fluffy Yellow Cake, 152
light cream, 27
liquids
  liquors, 32
  measuring, 74–75
  overview, 26–27
  reducing, 354
  yeast breads, 275

liquors, 32, 245
loaves
  cutting, 336
  pans for, 42–43
  recipes
    Basic White Buttermilk Bread, 282
    Braided Egg Bread, 283–284
    Honey-Oatmeal Bread, 285
    Jeff's Potato Bread, 286

M

macarons
  Chocolate-Coconut Macaroons, 118
  definition, 353
  French Macarons, 121–122
macerating, 353
mangoes
  shopping for, 36
  Tres Leches with Mango, 171–172
maple syrup, 33
Martha's Chocolate Cake, 153
Martha's Sweet and Creamy Frosting, 192
measuring ingredients
  cookies, 110
  with cups, 52
  dry ingredients, 73–74
  fats and solids, 73–74
  involving kids in, 348
  liquids, 74–75
  overview, 71–75
  premeasuring, 99
  recipes and, 96
  with scale, 72–73
  with spoons, 53, 73
melting, defined, 353
metal spoons, 55
metric conversion guide, 357–359
microplanes, 58
milk
  alternatives, 91
  overview, 26–27
  scalding, 85, 354
  Tres Leches with Mango, 171–172
milk chocolate, 28

mincing, 352
mixing bowls, 53
mixing methods
  beating, 351
  blending, 351
  cutting-in, 352
  defined, 354
  folding, 353
  stirring, 355
  whipping/whisking, 355
Mocha Frosting, 187
molasses, 33
Molly's Sweet Cardamom Rolls, 294
Molten Lava Cake, 175
monosaturated fats, 26
muffin tins, 41
muffins, 259–262
multicookers, 48, 103, 181

N

nectarines, 36, 81
No-Fail Rolls, 290
nonreactive kitchen equipment, 354
nonstick cooking spray, 25–26
nutrition, baking and, 343–346
nuts
  alternatives, 90
  boosting nutrition with, 344
  food allergies and, 90
  overview, 29–31
  peanut butter, 32
  toasting, 86

O

oats
  Classic Oatmeal-Raisin Cookies, 116
  Honey-Oatmeal Bread, 285
  overview, 32
oils, 25
Old-fashioned dough, 211
oranges, 253
oven mitts, 53–54
oven thermometers, 58

ovens
  controlling heat, 70
  convection, 68
  electric, 67
  gas, 66–67
  hot spots in, 68
  inspecting, 94
  preheating, 69–70, 354
  racks, 68–69
  types of, 65–68

P

pans
  baking, 40–44
  Bundt, 41–42, 158
  cake, 42
  choosing, 111
  lining, 76–77
  muffins, 259
  preparing, 75–77
  saucepans, 44
  springform, 43–44
  tube, 41–42, 77
parchment paper, 111
paring knives, 51, 354
pastry bags and tips, 58, 198–203
pastry blender, 59
pastry brush, 59
peaches
  overview, 36
  Peach Cobbler, 241
  peeling/pitting, 82
peanut butter
  overview, 32
  Peanut Butter Cookies, 124
pears
  Cran-Apple and Pear Pie, 230
  overview, 36
  peeling/pitting, 81
  Wonderful Pear Tart, 234
pecans
  overview, 30
  Pecan Pie, 223
peeling/pitting fruits, 81–82
petal tips, pastry bag, 200

pie plates, 43, 206, 209–210
pie weights, 60
pies and tarts
  choosing appropriate plate, 206
  cream filling
    Banana Cream Pie, 226
    Chocolate Cream Pie, 225
    Coconut Cream Pie, 227
  cutout top crust, 214
  cutting, 334–335
  decorating, 215
  double-crust
    Cran-Apple and Pear Pie, 230
    overview, 213–214
    Sour Cherry-Berry Pie, 229
  dough
    avoiding common mistakes, 236
    chilling, 208
    cutting in fat, 207
    flour, 207
    mixing, 206
    Old-fashioned, 211
    prebaking, 212
    rolling out, 208–209
    Stir-and-roll, 212
    transferring to, 209–210
  fruit and nut fillings
    Blueberry Pie, 220
    Cherry Crumb Pie, 221
    Cinnamon Apple Dumplings, 219
    overview, 215–216
    Pecan Pie, 223
    Pumpkin Pie, 217
    Rhubarb Pie, 222
    You'll-Be-Glad-You-Tried-It Apple Pie, 218
  Ginger-Spiced Key Lime Yogurt Pie, 233
  lattice crust, 213–214
  pastry edges, 215
  Plum Galette, 235
  solid top crust, 213
  storing
    freezing, 330–331
    refrigerating, 327
    at room temperature, 327
    wrapping, 326

Tart Lemon Tart, 232
  Wonderful Pear Tart, 234
pinch pastry edge, 215
pine nuts, 30
pineapple
  Crazy-Good Pineapple Upside-Down Cake, 313
  shopping for, 36
piping, 354
pizzas
  overview, 303–305
  Super-Easy Veggie Party Pizza, 315
  Weeknight Pizza Dough, 304
plastic containers, 323–324
plastic wrap, 322
Plum Galette, 235
polyurethane cutting boards, 50
poppy seeds
  Lemon Poppy Seed Muffins, 262
  Poppy Seed Cookies, 120
potatoes
  Broccoli and Cheese Quiche with Potato Crust, 307–308
  Jeff's Potato Bread, 286
  Potato-Beef Potpie, 301
potholders, 53–54
potpies, 299–302
pots, 44–45
pound cakes
  overview, 159–160
  recipes
    Chocolate Swirl Pound Cake, 162
    Classic Pound Cake, 161
powdered sugar, 15
preheating ovens, 69–70, 354
premeasuring ingredients, 99
pressed cookies, 135–136
proofing dough, 271, 354
puddings, 242–246
pulsing, 354
pumpkin
  recipes
    Pumpkin Bread, 250
    Pumpkin Cheesecake, 179
    Pumpkin Custard, 243
    Pumpkin Pie, 217
  shopping for, 36

punch down dough, 354
puréeing, 354

Q

quiches, 306–308
Quick Apricot Glaze, 196
quick bread
  overview, 247–248
  savory
    Boston Brown Bread, 257
    overview, 256
    Southern Corn Bread, 258
  sweet
    Banana Bread, 251
    Chocolate Zucchini Bread, 252
    Cranberry-Orange Bread, 253
    Crumbcake, 254
    overview, 249
    Pumpkin Bread, 250
    Sweet Chocolate Chip Pull-Apart Bread, 255

R

racks, ovens, 68–69
raisins
  Classic Oatmeal-Raisin Cookies, 116
  overview, 31
reamer, 56
recipes
  considering skill level, 95
  involving kids, 348, 350
  overview, 95
  reading, 96–97
  servings, 97–98
  taking inventory, 98
  understanding instructions, 96
  using correct kitchen equipment, 98–100
Rhubarb Pie, 222
Rich Chocolate Pudding, 244
rolled cookies
  Gingerbread Cookies with Royal Icing, 140–141
  overview, 137–139
  Tender Sugar Cookies, 142
rolling pins/mats, 54

rolls
  cutting, 336
  recipes
    Crescent Rolls, 291
    Fluffy Dinner Rolls, 292
    Jelly Roll, 169–170
    Molly's Sweet Cardamom Rolls, 294
    No-Fail Rolls, 290
    Sesame-Topped Rolls, 293
rosemary
  Lemon Rosemary Almond Cake, 173
  Rosemary Shortbread Cookies, 132
ruby chocolate, 28
Russian Tea Balls, 133
rye flour, 14

S

salt, 16–17, 274
saturated fats, 25
saucepans, 44
sauces
  Bread Pudding with Bourbon Caramel Sauce, 245
  Cinnamon Apple Dumplings, 219
  Sticky Date and Toffee Pudding, 246
savory quick bread
  Boston Brown Bread, 257
  overview, 256
  Southern Corn Bread, 258
scalding milk, 85
scales, 54, 72–73, 100
scones
  Bacon Cheddar and Chives Scones, 268
  Lemon Blueberry Scones, 267
scoring, 354
sea salt, 16
seeding, 354
seeds, boosting nutrition with, 343–344
self-rising flour, 272
semisweet chocolate, 28
serrated knives, 51
Sesame-Topped Rolls, 293
shaped cookies
  Anisette Biscotti, 134
  Apricot-Date Half-Moons, 131
  Crisp Sugar Cookies, 127

Gingersnaps, 128
Lebkuchen, 129
Lemon Cookies, 130
Peanut Butter Cookies, 124
Rolled Sugar Cookies, 126
Rosemary Shortbread Cookies, 132
Russian Tea Balls, 133
Snickerdoodles, 125
sheet cakes, 336
shelling, 355
shopping, 12, 35–36, 39, 347
shortbread, 132
shortening, 24, 75–76
shredding, 355
sieve/strainer, 60
sifting, 355
Silpat, 61
simmering, 355
slicing, 355
Snickerdoodles, 125
soft/stiff peaks, 80
solid top crust, 213
soufflés, 295–298
Sour Cherry-Berry Pie, 229
sour cream
  alternatives, 91
  Banana-Sour Cream Bundt Cake, 158
sourdough starter, 21–22
Southern Corn Bread, 258
spatulas, 61
spelt, 14
spices, 12, 33–34
sponge cakes
  cooling, 160
  overview, 166–167
  recipes
    Angel Food Cake, 166–168
    Gluten-Free Chocolate Hazelnut Cake, 174
    Jelly Roll, 169–170
    Lemon Rosemary Almond Cake, 173
    Molten Lava Cake, 175
    Tres Leches with Mango, 171–172
spoons, 55
springform pans, 43–44
Spritz cookies, 135
stand mixers, 48–49

star tips, pastry bag, 200
starters, sourdough, 21–22
steeping, 355
Sticky Date and Toffee Pudding, 246
Stir-and-roll dough, 212
stirring, 355
storing
  aluminum foil, 323
  baked goods
    in freezer, 328–331
    refrigerating, 326–328
    at room temperature, 324–326
    wrapping, 321–324
  beeswax wraps, 322
  biscuits, 264
  bread, 326, 328, 329
  cakes, 325–326, 329–330
  cookies, 141, 325, 327, 328–329
  glassware or plastic, 323–324
  ingredients
    bulk foods, 12
    butter, 23–24
    chocolate and cocoa, 28
    flour, 15
    nuts, 30
    oats, 31
  overview, 321
  pies, 326, 327, 330–331
  plastic wrap, 322
  tins, 324
  waxed paper, 323
straining, 355
streusel, 157
sugars
  maple syrup and molasses, 33
  overview, 15–16
  recipes
    Classic Sugar Glaze, 197
    Crisp Sugar Cookies, 127
    Tender Sugar Cookies, 142
  using less, 345
  yeast bread, 274
Super Chocolate Cake, 312
sweet chocolate, 28
Sweet Chocolate Chip Pull-Apart Bread, 255

sweet quick bread
  Banana Bread, 251
  Chocolate Zucchini Bread, 252
  Cranberry-Orange Bread, 253
  Crumbcake, 254
  Pumpkin Bread, 250
  Sweet Chocolate Chip Pull-Apart Bread, 255
Sweetened Whipped Cream Frosting, 190

T

table salt, 16
tapioca, 37
tarts. *See also* pies and tarts
  Goat Cheese and Tomato Tart, 302
  overview, 299–302
  Tart Lemon Tart, 232
  Wonderful Pear Tart, 234
tea, 133
teaspoons and tablespoons, 73
techniques
  beating, 351
  biscuits
    forming, 264
    mixing dough, 263
    storing, 264
  blending, 351
  coating, 352
  creaming, 352
  cut-in mixing, 352
  cutting, 333–336
  decorating, 336–337
  decorating plates, 340
  dough
    avoiding common mistakes, 236
    chilling, 208
    cutout top crust, 214
    cutting in fat, 207
    decorating, 215
    flour and, 207
    lattice crust, 213–214
    mixing, 206
    Old-fashioned, 211
    prebaking, 212
    rolling out, 208–209

techniques *(continued)*
    solid top crust, 213
    Stir-and-roll, 212
    transferring to pie plate, 209–210
  eggs, 78–80
  folding, 353
  frosting cakes, 194–195
  fruits, 81–84
  garnishes, 337–340
  glazing cakes, 195–197
  measuring ingredients
    cookies, 110
    with cups, 52
    dry ingredients, 73–74
    fats and solids, 73–74
    involving kids in, 348
    liquids, 74–75
    overview, 71–75
    premeasuring, 99
    recipes and, 96
    with scale, 72–73
    with spoons, 53, 73
  melting chocolate, 84–85
  mixing
    defined, 351–355
    overview, 110
  overview, 9–10
  preparing pans, 75–77
  scalding milk, 85
  toasting nuts, 86
  whipping cream, 80–81
  yeast bread
    baking, 279–281
    kneading, 276–277
    mixing, 275–276
    rising dough, 278–279
    shaping, 279–281
Tender Sugar Cookies, 142
Texas Chocolate Sheath Cake, 154
thermometer, 58
thin plastic cutting boards, 50
timer, 62
tins, 324
tips, pastry bag, 198–203
toasting, 86, 355

toffee, 246
tomatoes, 302
tongs, 62
Tovla, 349
Tres Leches with Mango, 171–172
trivets, 62
tube pans, 41–42, 77
turnovers, 317
twisted pastry edge, 215

U

unbleached white flour, 272
unmolding, 355
unsweetened chocolate, 28

V

vanilla, 188
vegetable peeler, 62
vegetables
  boosting nutrition with, 345
  shopping for, 35–36
vegetarian recipes
  Angel Food Cake, 166–168
  Anisette Biscotti, 134
  Apple Crisp, 239
  Apple Turnovers, 317
  Applesauce Cake, 156
  Apricot-Date Half-Moons, 131
  Banana Bread, 251
  Banana Cream Pie, 226
  Banana-Sour Cream Bundt Cake, 158
  Basic Hamburger Buns, 288–289
  Basic Vanilla Buttercream Frosting, 188
  Basic White Buttermilk Bread, 282
  Black-and-White Brownies, 145
  Blueberry Crunch, 240
  Blueberry Muffins, 261
  Blueberry Pie, 220
  Boston Brown Bread, 257
  Braided Egg Bread, 283–284
  Bread Pudding with Bourbon Caramel Sauce, 245
  Broccoli and Cheese Quiche with Potato Crust, 307–308
  Buttermilk Biscuits, 265
  Butterscotch Drops, 119

Carrot Cake, 155
Cheese Soufflé, 297–298
Cheesy Cheese Biscuits, 266
Cherry Crumb Pie, 221
Chocolate Chip Frosting, 312
Chocolate Cream Pie, 225
Chocolate Cupcakes, 164
Chocolate Drop Cookies, 115
Chocolate Frosting, 191
Chocolate Swirl Pound Cake, 162
Chocolate Zucchini Bread, 252
Chocolate-Coconut Macaroons, 118
Cinnamon Apple Dumplings, 219
Cinnamon-Spiced Cheesecake Bars, 316
Classic Cheesecake, 178
Classic Oatmeal-Raisin Cookies, 116
Classic Pound Cake, 161
Classic Sugar Glaze, 197
Coconut Cream Pie, 227
Cran-Apple and Pear Pie, 230
Cranberry-Orange Bread, 253
Crazy-Good Pineapple Upside-Down Cake, 313
Cream Cheese and Cherry Danishes, 318
Cream Cheese Frosting, 186
Crescent Rolls, 291
Crisp Sugar Cookies, 127
Crispy Chocolate Chip Cookies, 114
Crumbcake, 254
Crunchy Granola Bars, 146
Dense Chocolate Brownies, 144
Everything Cookies, 117
Fluffy Dinner Rolls, 292
French Macarons, 121–122
German Apple Kuchen with Streusel, 157
Gingerbread Cookies with Royal Icing, 140–141
Gingersnaps, 128
Ginger-Spiced Key Lime Yogurt Pie, 233
Gluten-Free Chocolate Hazelnut Cake, 174
Goat Cheese and Tomato Tart, 302
Honey-Oatmeal Bread, 285
Jeff's Potato Bread, 286
Jelly Roll, 169–170
Lebkuchen, 129
Lemon Bars, 146
Lemon Blueberry Scones, 267

Lemon Cookies, 130
Lemon Cupcakes, 165
Lemon Curd Cheesecake, 180–181
Lemon Poppy Seed Muffins, 262
Lemon Rosemary Almond Cake, 173
Light and Fluffy Yellow Cake, 152
Martha's Chocolate Cake, 153
Martha's Sweet and Creamy Frosting, 192
Mocha Frosting, 187
Molly's Sweet Cardamom Rolls, 294
Molten Lava Cake, 175
No-Fail Rolls, 290
Old-fashioned dough, 211
Peach Cobbler, 241
Peanut Butter Cookies, 124
Pecan Pie, 223
Plum Galette, 235
Poppy Seed Cookies, 120
Pumpkin Bread, 250
Pumpkin Cheesecake, 179
Pumpkin Custard, 243
Pumpkin Pie, 217
Quick Apricot Glaze, 196
Rhubarb Pie, 222
Rich Chocolate Pudding, 244
Rolled Sugar Cookies, 126
Rosemary Shortbread Cookies, 132
Russian Tea Balls, 133
Sesame-Topped Rolls, 293
Snickerdoodles, 125
Sour Cherry-Berry Pie, 229
Southern Corn Bread, 258
Sticky Date and Toffee Pudding, 246
Stir-and-roll dough, 212
Super Chocolate Cake, 312
Super-Easy Veggie Party Pizza, 315
Sweet Chocolate Chip Pull-Apart Bread, 255
Sweetened Whipped Cream Frosting, 190
Tart Lemon Tart, 232
Tender Sugar Cookies, 142
Texas Chocolate Sheath Cake, 154
Tres Leches with Mango, 171–172
Weeknight Pizza Dough, 304
Wonderful Pear Tart, 234
You'll-Be-Glad-You-Tried-It Apple Pie, 218

W

walnuts, 30
water bath, 355
waxed paper, 323
wheat, 88–89
Wheat-free Flour Blend, 89
whipped cream
    garnishes, 339–340
    Sweetened Whipped Cream Frosting, 190
whipping cream
    ingredient, 27
    technique, 80–81
whipping/whisking, 355
white beans, 346
white chocolate, 28
White Lily brand flour, 263
whole grains, boosting nutrition with, 344–345
wire whisk, 62
Wonderful Pear Tart, 234
wooden cutting boards, 50
wooden spoons, 55
writing tips, pastry bag, 200

Y

yeast, 20–21, 270–271
yeast bread
    baking, 279–281
    buns and rolls
        Basic Hamburger Buns, 288–289
        Crescent Rolls, 291
        Fluffy Dinner Rolls, 292
        Molly's Sweet Cardamom Rolls, 294
        No-Fail Rolls, 290
        Sesame-Topped Rolls, 293
    eggs, 275
    fat, 274
    flour, 272–273
    kneading, 276–277
    liquids, 275
    loaves
        Basic White Buttermilk Bread, 282
        Braided Egg Bread, 283–284
        Honey-Oatmeal Bread, 285
        Jeff's Potato Bread, 286
    mixing, 275–276
    overview, 270–272
    rising dough, 278–279
    salt, 274
    shaping, 279–281
    sweeteners, 274
yield, 355
yogurt
    alternatives, 91
    Ginger-Spiced Key Lime Yogurt Pie, 233
    overview, 38
You'll-Be-Glad-You-Tried-It Apple Pie, 218

Z

zesting, 82–84, 355
zucchini
    Chocolate Zucchini Bread, 252
    shopping for, 36

About the Author

Wendy Jo Peterson, MS, RDN, is an award-winning author, speaker, culinary nutritionist, proud military wife, and mom. Whether at work or at the table, Wendy Jo believes in savoring life. Check out her other titles: *Bread Making For Dummies, Mediterranean Diet Cookbook For Dummies, Air Fryer Cookbook For Dummies,* and *Instant Pot Cookbook For Dummies.* When she's not in her kitchen, you can find Wendy Jo strolling a SoCal beach or bouncing around Europe with her family and exploring the great outdoors in #OlafTheCampervan. You can catch her on social media at @just_wendyjo or check out her website, www.justwendyjo.com.

Dedication

To all those in search of the perfect cupcake or cookie, may you find them in these pages.

Author's Acknowledgments

Baking is something I do with my whole heart, and I share it with those I love. Thank you to my friends and family for sampling my recipes along the way.

No book is ever achieved without a great team, and I'm blessed to have worked with this team on many books. To my agent, Matt Wagner, for continually advocating for me as the writer. I'm forever grateful for Tracy Boggier, Senior Acquisitions Editor at Wiley, who believes in me and recipes. To Chad Sievers, my project and copy editor, for keeping me on track with deadlines and helping me better express my creative ideas. To Grace Geri Goodale for bouncing around the globe with me to capture just the right images for this book. I thoroughly enjoy the creative process working with each of you. Thank you for your collaboration!

Publisher's Acknowledgments

Senior Acquisitions Editor: Tracy Boggier

Project Manager and Editor: Chad R. Sievers

Senior Managing Editor: Kristie Pyles

Recipe Tester/Nutrition Analyst: Rachel Nix

Production Editor: Tamilmani Varadharaj

Cover and Insert Photos: © Steven/ Adobe Stock Photos, Wendy Jo Peterson and Grace Geri Goodale

Leverage the power

Dummies is the global leader in the reference category and one of the most trusted and highly regarded brands in the world. No longer just focused on books, customers now have access to the dummies content they need in the format they want. Together we'll craft a solution that engages your customers, stands out from the competition, and helps you meet your goals.

Advertising & Sponsorships

Connect with an engaged audience on a powerful multimedia site, and position your message alongside expert how-to content. Dummies.com is a one-stop shop for free, online information and know-how curated by a team of experts.

- Targeted ads
- Video
- Email Marketing

- Microsites
- Sweepstakes sponsorship

20 **MILLION**
PAGE VIEWS
EVERY SINGLE MONTH

15 MILLION **UNIQUE**
VISITORS PER MONTH

43%
OF ALL VISITORS
ACCESS THE SITE
VIA THEIR MOBILE DEVICES

700,000 NEWSLETTER SUBSCRIPTIONS
TO THE INBOXES OF
300,000 UNIQUE INDIVIDUALS EVERY WEEK

# of dummies

Custom Publishing

Reach a global audience in any language by creating a solution that will differentiate you from competitors, amplify your message, and encourage customers to make a buying decision.

- Apps
- Books
- eBooks
- Video
- Audio
- Webinars

Brand Licensing & Content

Leverage the strength of the world's most popular reference brand to reach new audiences and channels of distribution.

For more information, visit dummies.com/biz

PERSONAL ENRICHMENT

Staying Sharp
9781119187790
USA $26.00
CAN $31.99
UK £19.99

Facebook
9781119179030
USA $21.99
CAN $25.99
UK £16.99

Guitar
9781119293354
USA $24.99
CAN $29.99
UK £17.99

Investing
9781119293347
USA $22.99
CAN $27.99
UK £16.99

Beekeeping
9781119310068
USA $22.99
CAN $27.99
UK £16.99

Digital Photography
9781119235606
USA $24.99
CAN $29.99
UK £17.99

Meditation
9781119251163
USA $24.99
CAN $29.99
UK £17.99

Pregnancy
9781119235491
USA $26.99
CAN $31.99
UK £19.99

Samsung Galaxy S7
9781119279952
USA $24.99
CAN $29.99
UK £17.99

iPhone
9781119283133
USA $24.99
CAN $29.99
UK £17.99

Crocheting
9781119287117
USA $24.99
CAN $29.99
UK £16.99

Nutrition
9781119130246
USA $22.99
CAN $27.99
UK £16.99

PROFESSIONAL DEVELOPMENT

Windows 10
9781119311041
USA $24.99
CAN $29.99
UK £17.99

AutoCAD
9781119255796
USA $39.99
CAN $47.99
UK £27.99

Excel 2016
9781119293439
USA $26.99
CAN $31.99
UK £19.99

QuickBooks 2017
9781119281467
USA $26.99
CAN $31.99
UK £19.99

macOS Sierra
9781119280651
USA $29.99
CAN $35.99
UK £21.99

LinkedIn
9781119251132
USA $24.99
CAN $29.99
UK £17.99

Windows 10
9781119310563
USA $34.00
CAN $41.99
UK £24.99

SharePoint 2016
9781119181705
USA $29.99
CAN $35.99
UK £21.99

Fundamental Analysis
9781119263593
USA $26.99
CAN $31.99
UK £19.99

Networking
9781119257769
USA $29.99
CAN $35.99
UK £21.99

Office 2016
9781119293477
USA $26.99
CAN $31.99
UK £19.99

Office 365
9781119265313
USA $24.99
CAN $29.99
UK £17.99

Salesforce.com
9781119239314
USA $29.99
CAN $35.99
UK £21.99

Coding
9781119293323
USA $29.99
CAN $35.99
UK £21.99

dummies.com

dummies
A Wiley Brand